Ancestry of
Ewald Conrad Swanson (1900-1987)
of Vassar, Michigan

Compiled by Michael Conrad Swanson
2012

Ancestry of Ewald Conrad Swanson (1900 -1987) of Vassar, Michigan

Copyright © 2012 Michael Conrad Swanson

ISBN-13: 978-1475255768
ISBN-10: 1475255764

Printed by CreateSpace, Charleston, South Carolina.

Preface

More than a decade ago I began researching the ancestry of my grandfather, Ewald Conrad Swanson. My project was to separate fact from fiction in the oral history, and to use primary sources to verify and extend his ancestral record. I enlisted the help of family members and historical societies, and I pored over thousands of documents such as census books, ship manifests, and church records. The purpose of this book is to compile this research in an organized form.

This book is organized into nine chapters. The first chapter is about Ewald Swanson's parents and grandparents. The next eight chapters present the ancestry of his eight great-grandparents.

Each chapter contains a pedigree chart and an ancestral report. The key to reading an ancestral report is the "ahnentafel" numbering system. The first person in a report has the number 1, and numbers are assigned to ancestors according a simple rule: a child's number is some number X, the father's number is 2 times X, the mother's number is 2 times X add 1. Thus, if a person's number is 1 then the father's number is 2 and the mother's number is 3; and if a person's number is 10 then the father's number is 20 and the mother's number is 21.

In the last eight chapters, the generation numbers indicate the "great-grandparent" relationships. For example, an ancestor in the eighth generation is Ewald Swanson's eighth great-grandparent.

I am indebted to a number of people who have helped me compile this genealogy. My late father, Richard Swanson, kept in touch with cousins living in Sweden, saved genealogical information they sent him, and gathered immigration information on his visit to Sweden. My brother, Mark Swanson, was the first in our family to enter what we knew about Ewald Swanson's ancestry into a database which he shared with me several years ago. He has also worked hard to scan and preserve the old family photos.

Torbjörn Nikus, of Ylöjärvi, Finland, has helped me for many years. He provided me with extensive information about my Vörå ancestry and sent me many old photos. Torbjörn gave my family a tour of Vörå when we visited "the old country" in 2006. Torbjörn is an author, a Vörå Emigration Center board member, and a noted historian. According to church records, we are cousins in at least thirteen ways.

Mats-Olof Sander, of Göteborg, Sweden, introduced me to the ArkivDigita online database of Swedish parish records and helped me with translations. Mats-Olof is a webmaster of Släktdata, a Swedish database for genealogy research. We share Finnish ancestors in Vörå.

June Pelo, who lives in Florida, and several other members of the Swedish-Finn Historical Society, introduced me to the HiSki online database and provided emigration information. June and I share a common paternal-line ancestor (which we have not yet identified) according to our DNA tests.

The Noraskog Heritage Society provided old pictures of Nora parish, Sweden.

Maggie Keefe, who lives in D.C., sent me her research and photos of shared relatives in Newberry, Michigan.

Michael Conrad Swanson
Franklin, Tennessee
24 April 2012

Table of Contents

Table of Contents

Table of Contents

Table of Contents

Introduction

Ewald Conrad Swanson was born in a remote railroad section house in Upper Michigan on Lake Superior in 1900. His father, a railroad section foreman, was the youngest son of a farm-owner in Ostrobothnia, Finland. His mother, a midwife, was the daughter of a laborer from Örebro county, Sweden. Both of Ewald Swanson's parents had emigrated separately from Scandinavia in 1892, and their paths crossed in Michigan.

After medical school, Ewald moved to a small town in Lower Michigan called Vassar, where he was a family doctor. He became a civic leader in Vassar and eventually served as the executive officer of the Michigan State Medical Society. He died in Saginaw, Michigan in 1987.

Ewald Swanson's mother

Ewald Swanson's mother, Clara Fredrika Spångberg (1876-1946), was born in a forest cottage in Lämtjärnsfallet near Skärhyttan village, Nora mining parish, Örebro county, Sweden. Nora parish lies in the mountains of south-central Sweden about 110 miles west of Stockholm.

Clara was not the first of her family to come to America. Clara's uncle, Erik Spångberg, immigrated to America in 1889. Clara immigrated after her mother died in 1891, arriving in Boston in 1892 before making her way to Michigan. Her sisters and father arrived a few years later. In America, Clara Spångberg changed her name to Clara Carlson. She married Michael Swanson in 1897 and they resided in Newberry, Upper Michigan. Her work as a midwife inspired several of their children to enter the medical profession.

Clara's father, Carl Fredrik Spångberg, was a coal burner in Nora parish. When his work horse died, he was forced to move from his cottage to an apartment. He wife, Christina Barken, died at age 45, and this left Carl to raise a grandchild named August Spångberg and their youngest children alone. August Spångberg would become the youngest person ever elected to the Swedish parliament, and he played an important role in helping people escape the Nazis in World War II.

Ewald Swanson's father

Ewald Swanson's father, Mickel Mickelsson Svens (1874 -1961), was born on a farm in Leistus, Rejpelt village, Vörå parish, Ostrobothnia, Finland. Vörå, called the "Realm of Rye," is in an agricultural region of hills and plains near Finland's west coast, about 15 miles east of the port city of Vasa. An archaic dialect of Swedish is the majority language in Vörå.

As a teenager in Finland, Mickel Svens faced a future of poverty and probable conscription into the Russian army. In 1892 he left Finland for America and settled in Newberry. Mickel emigrated without permission, and was listed in a Finnish "wanted" pamphlet for not reporting to a draft lottery. His sister Lisa arrived in Newberry two years earlier in 1890, his brother Johan arrived in 1893, and his father Mickel immigrated in 1901. In America, he changed his name to Michael Swanson on the advice of his brother-in-law, Andrew Westin. He became a railroad section foreman in Upper Michigan.

Some say Mickel Svens was "Swedish." He was, in one sense: the Swedish-speaking Finns, called Swede-Finns, identify with the period before the Russian take-over in 1809 when Finland was in the Swedish empire and Swedish was the language used in government and universities. However, genealogically speaking, Swede-Finns do not descend predominately from Swedish immigrants, but have deep roots in Finland.

Naming traditions

Ewald Swanson's Finnish and Swedish ancestors used Swedish patronyms. A Swedish patronymic name is created by adding -son or -dotter to the father's first name. For example, the son of Mickel is named Mickelsson, and his daughter is named Mickelsdotter. Patronymic names were in constant use in rural Sweden and western Finland until the mid-1800s, after which some families started to replace them with heritable surnames. (Note: Old Swedish names had alternative spellings, e.g. Eriksson is the same as Ersson, Pettersson is the same as Persson, Olsson is the same as Olofsson, and Hendricksson is the same as Hindersson. I have not standardized the spellings in this book.)

The Spångberg surname was created by Clara's paternal grandfather about 1840 when he rose from peasant laborer to the position of foundry manager and employer. Spångberg means, roughly, "mountain walkway." Clara's father, Carl, used his patronym with his surname; however, his daughter Clara Spångberg was not given a patronym.

The Svens surname sprang from a different tradition. The rural Swede-Finns used "farm names" with their Swedish patronyms. Farm names were not heritable, and people always changed their farm names when they moved.

Introduction

Interestingly, Mickel Svens and his father Mickel Storkarhu were born on the same farm but had different farm names at birth. The explanation is simple: The Storkarhu farm was renamed "Svens farm." The old name, Storkarhu, is a compound Swedish-Finnish word meaning "big bear."

Ewald Swanson's Finnish great-grandparents

Here are some highlights from chapters 2 through 5. The numbers before the names are the ahnentafel numbers in the reports.

Chapter 2 starts with Ewald Swanson's great-grandfather, #1 Mårten Mårtensson Storkarhu (1788-1828), a farm owner at Storkarhu farm in Rejpelt, Vörå, Finland. His father, #2 Mårten Storkarhu, was a saltpeter (gunpowder) maker and his grandfather, #4 Mårten Storkarhu, was a boot maker. Disaster struck #2 Mårten's family in 1828 when he, and his son, Anders, died on the same day of typhoid fever. His son, #1 Mårten, and his grandson of the same name died a couple weeks later. Earlier in the male line, #16 Sigfred Bertilsson Storkarhu disappeared after the Russians invaded the area in 1714. He was probably a soldier who fought the Russian invaders and either retreated to the north or, more likely, was taken prisoner by the Russian army. The church records show he returned to his farm before 1727.

Chapter 3 starts with Ewald Swanson's great-grandmother, #1 Lisa Samuelsdotter Miemois (1792-1866), wife of Mårten Mårtensson Storkarhu from chapter 2. Her grandfather, #6 Sune Hansson, born in Småland, Sweden, was the son of a Swedish cavalry soldier. Sune Hansson was sent to Vörå, Finland and ordered to teach others how to make saltpeter (a component of gunpowder). Lisa's third great-grandfather, #30 Johan Andersson Israels, was killed in the disastrous 1714 Battle of Storkyro against the Russians. Subsequently, during the Greater Wrath, the Russians pillaged Vörå and made the Vörå parish church into a horse stable (ironically, saving it from destruction).

Chapter 4 starts with Ewald Swanson's great-grandfather, #1 Johan Eriksson Wäst (1799-1878), who was a farm owner at Svens and Klemets farms in Rejpelt, Vörå, Finland. His great-grandmother, #9 Lisa Esajasdotter Wäst, was born on a farm named Wäst in Oravais parish, which lies 25 miles north of Rejpelt. His fourth great-grandfather, #74 Bertel Bertilsson, moved from Lapua, Finland to a deserted farm in Rejpelt in 1723. Bertel's mother, #149 Lisa Sigfridsdotter, saw many of her relatives die in the plague and famine of 1697 and 1698, which killed a third of the Finnish population.

Chapter 5 starts with Ewald Swanson's great-grandmother, #1 Lisa Johansdotter Wäst (1789-1856), wife of Johan Eriksson Wäst of chapter 4. Her great-grandfather, #8 Johan Mattsson, was a Finnish speaker who, in 1723, moved to Rejpelt from Keuruu parish in Central Finland where he was known as Juho Matinpoika. Lisa's eighth great-grandfather was #1792 Henrik Olsson, a juryman (nämndeman) in Vörå parish. Henrik Olsson is the earliest ancestor found for Ewald Swanson.

Ewald Swanson's Swedish great-grandparents

Here are some highlights from chapters 6 through 9. Again, the numbers before the names are the ahnentafel numbers in the reports.

Chapter 6 starts with Ewald Swanson's great-grandfather, #1 Jan Ersson (1808-1857), who started as a poor blast furnace laborer in Grythyttan parish, Örebro county, Sweden. His fortunes changed when, in 1831, he took over the farm of his father-in law in Skärhyttan, Nora parish. He did not squander the opportunity. By 1836 he was a smelting master, had employees, and in 1838 he named his flourishing homestead "Spångberg." His father, #2 Erik Nilsson, had previously taken over a widow's homestead at Spångtorp and did well as a foundry master.

Chapter 7 starts with Ewald Swanson's great-grandmother, #1 Maria Helena Persdotter (1811-1887), wife of Jan Spångberg from chapter 6. Her fourth great-grandfather, #84 Anders Embjörnsson, was a respected miner in Glifsån, Ramsberg parish, Örebro county. He became embroiled in a court case in 1669 concerning a young lady whom he was assigned to protect on a voyage from Stockholm. Despite this precaution, the sailor of the ship sent to transport the woman was found in possession of some of her clothing while in Stockhom, and to avoid blaim he accused the woman of promiscuous behavior. The partially dressed woman found another ship home, but a court case ensued in which Anders Embjörnsson was asked to testify, and the court ruled that the sailor was to blame for the incident. Anders Embjörnsson's father, #168 Embjörn Persson, was one of the founders of Glifsån (established in 1629) and was involved in setting the boundaries to protect himself from settlers encroaching on his mine. Some of his family came from northern Sweden, near Umeå.

Chapter 8 starts with Ewald Swanson's great-grandfather, #1 Anders Jansson (1814-1851), who was born on the Barken homestead in Grythyttan parish. In 1849 he took the surname Barken. His father, #2 Jan Olsson, moved to

Introduction

Barken in 1812, and he appears to be its first resident. The homestead was then known as Ullnäs Barken because it was part of the Ullnäs estate of Rockesholm manor.

Chapter 9 starts with Ewald Swanson's great-grandmother, #1 Anna Helena Persdotter, (1816- 1887), wife of Anders Jansson Barken in chapter 8. Her third great-grandfather, #42 Per Larsson Körning, was an early post bonde (mail farmer) in Grythyttan parish. His duty was to keep a horse ready to carry mail to the next post at the sound of an approaching carrier's horn. He was required to carry a sword and a horn. The penalty in the law for interfering with the mail was death.

Visiting the old country

All that remains of the old Svens/Storkarhu farm houses at Leistus, and Carl Spångberg's forest cottage at Lämtjärnsfallet, are a few foundation stones. In Leistus the foundations were removed or were tilled under by farmers, and in Lämtjärnsfallet they were covered by the mountain forest's undergrowth. Fortunately, local historical societies have preserved old maps so that the places can be located.

In Nora parish, Sweden, the Noraskog Heritage Society has a museum at Göthlinska Gården in historic Trästaden Nora. Another place of interest is the Stadra Manor, a beautiful mansion from the 1700s where the powerful Carlssons lived, which was the family that employed Carl Spångberg and many of his relatives. The restored Stadra Manor hosts cultural, historical, and theatrical events. Carl Spångberg's father was born in nearby Grythyttan parish, and there you will find the Grythyttan Gästgivaregård established in 1640, a world-renowned hotel comprised of 22 buildings some of which were built in the 17th century.

In Vörå parish, Finland, the Vörå Emigration Center, run by the Vörå Genealogy and Heritage Society, is housed in Vörå Kulturhus, which is an old bank building. Vörå parish church, the oldest wooden church in Finland, was built in 1626. The Fädernegården Museum in Rejpelt and the Brage Open-Air Museum in Vasa have preserved old cottages, houses, and other structures -- even the interiors -- so that one can experience how ancestors lived.

Since Vörå and Nora parishes are in rural areas, always check before planning a trip, since some sites have limited hours or are open by appointment.

Photo: Three Generations in Newberry

Mickel (Svens) Swanson and Clara (Spångberg) Swanson and family in Newberry, Michigan

Back row: George Swanson, Albin Swanson, Jenny Spångberg, Ewald Swanson. Front row: Sigfrid Swanson, Michael Swanson, Karl Spångberg, Celia Swanson, Clara (Spångberg) Swanson. [Provided by Mark Swanson/Swanson Media. From family collection.]
(Cir 1910)

Maps: Michigan and Scandinavia

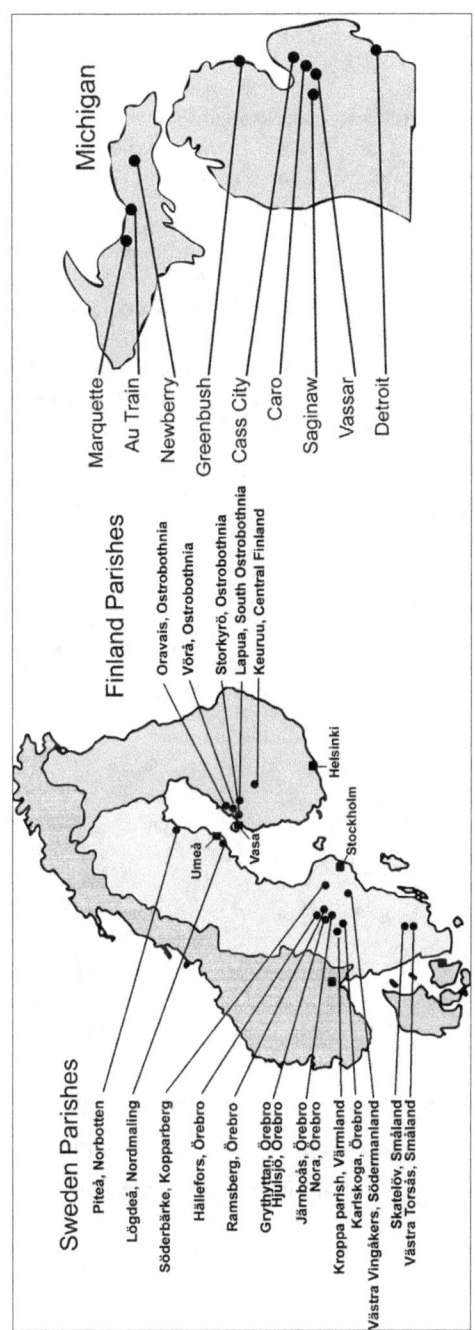

Ewald Swanson's ancestors lived and worked in listed the Michigan towns and Scandinavian parishes.

Chapter 1. Ancestor Report for Ewald Conrad Swanson M. D.

First Generation

1. Ewald Conrad Swanson M. D., son of **Mickel Mickelsson Svens** and **Clara Fredrika Spångberg,** was born on 3 Jan 1900 in Au Train, Alger, Michigan, [1] died on 26 Sep 1987 in Saginaw, Saginaw, Michigan, [1] and was buried in Woodlawn Cemetery, Detroit, Wayne, Michigan. Another name for Ewald was Dib Swanson.

Ewald Swanson

General Notes: Dr. Ewald C. Swanson graduated from Alma College in central Michigan in 1923 and worked as a woodworker for Ford Motor Co in Detroit. After working in the medical department at Ford he entered Wayne State University College of Medicine. He interned at Receiving Hospital, Detroit, and became house physician at Wyandotte General Hospital. In 1932 he moved to Vassar, Michigan, and took over the practice of Dr. W. A. Wellmeyer. He was executive secretary of the Michigan State Medical Society. He maintained a summer home in Greenbush, Michigan, on Lake Huron.

Noted events in his life were:
- Resided: 1900, Au Train, Alger, Michigan. [2]

- Resided: 1910, McMillan, Luce, Michigan. [3]

- Graduation: Newberry High School, 1918, Newberry, Luce, Michigan.

- Occupation: die repairman at auto factory, 1920, Detroit, Wayne, Michigan. [4]

- Occupation: medic in an automobile factory, 1924, Detroit, Wayne, Michigan.

- Graduation: Alma College, 1923, Alma, Gratiot, Michigan.

- Resided: 1930, Detroit, Wayne, Michigan. [4]

- Occupation: medical attendant at auto plant, 1930, Detroit, Wayne, Michigan. [4]

- Graduation: Wayne State University Medical School, 1931, Detroit, Wayne, Michigan. [5]

- Occupation: physician, 1932, Vassar, Tuscola, Michigan.

- Property: summer cottage, After 1940, Greenbush, Alcona, Michigan.

- Event: visited by August Spangberg, 1955, Newberry, Luce, Michigan. [6] August Spångberg, Swedish member of parliament, visited his relatives in Newberry. Ewald took time off from his medical practice to escort August on his trip. Ewald was August's first cousin.

- Organizations: Executive Secretary of the Michigan State Board of Registration, Between 1956 and 1967.

- Elected: president of the Federation of State Medical Boards of the United States, 1963.

- Fact: Y-DNA test. Ewald's Y-DNA (via a test of Michael Swanson) shows his patrilineal ancestors were in haplotype N1c1. Approximately 60% of all Finns are in this haplogroup, and its earliest ancestors originated in Southern Siberia circa 10,000 years ago and migrated to Finland circa 5000 years ago.

1. *"Michigan Deaths, 1971-1996" (ancestry.com). .... Social Security Death Index (ancestry.com).*
2. *1900 US Census.*
3. *1910 US Census.*
4. *1930 US Census.*
5. *Arch Ophthalmol. 1988; 106: 303-431. (http://archopht.ama-assn.org).*
6. *August Spångberg, Stream of Time (1966).*

Ancestor Report for Ewald Conrad Swanson M. D.

Ewald married **Alma Marie Weidemann,** daughter of **Oscar Christian Weidemann** and **Mary Monahan,** on 22 Jan 1928 in Detroit, Wayne, Michigan.

Alma Weidemann

General Notes: Alma Marie Weidemann was born in Erie, Pennsylvania. She was baptized in St Andrew's Catholic Church, Erie, Pennsylvania 23 July 1904 as the "child of Oscar Weidemann and Maria E. Monahan." She moved to Detroit with her parents at early age. Orphaned at age 15 as a result of a murder suicide, she then lived with aunts in Detroit (Carrie, Emma and Tillie). She graduated from Michigan Normal School (now Eastern Michigan University, Ypsilanti, Michigan). She taught Physical Education in the Detroit Public Schools. She married Ewald Swanson in 1928 and lived in Vassar, Michigan, until 2001. She worked for the state of Michigan in the 60's and 70's as a visual and hearing screener in the public schools. She resided with with her daughters after 2001 until her death in 2005.

Noted events in her life were:
- Baptism: 23 Jul 1904, Erie, Erie, Pennsylvania. [7] St. Andrew's Catholic Church

- Resided: 1910, Detroit, Wayne, Michigan. [8]

- Orphaned: 9 Feb 1920, Detroit, Wayne, Michigan. [9]

- Residence: with her aunt Alma Weidemann, 1920-1923, Detroit, Wayne, Michigan. [10]

- Graduation: Michigan State Normal School (Eastern Michigan University), Est 1926, Ypsilanti, Washtenaw, Michigan.

- Occupation: a physical education teacher at Webster School, 1928, Detroit, Wayne, Michigan. [11]

- Resided: 1930, Detroit City, Wayne, Michigan. [12]

- Resided: 1935-1993, Vassar, Tuscola, Michigan. [13]

- Obituary: Vassar Pioneer Times, Sep 2004, Vassar, Tuscola, Michigan. [14]
    Alma Swanson of Ann Arbor, and formerly of Vassar, died on Thursday, August 26, 2004, in Ann Arbor. She was 100 years of age. She was born in Erie, Pennsylvania, the daughter of Oscar and Mary (Moynihan) Weidemann. Her husband, Dr. E. C. Swanson, preceded her in death.
    Mrs. Swanson is survived by three children, Shirley Smith, of St. Charles, Illinois, Richard (Jo) Swanson of Newland, North Carolina, and Margery (Jay) Haite of Ann Arbor; nine grandchildren; and seven great grandchildren.
    A family burial will take place in Detroit at Woodlawn Cemetery.
    Those planning an expression of sympathy may wish to consider the Bullard Sanford Memorial Library of Vassar or a memorial of choice.

7. *St. Andrews Catholic Church, Erie, Pennsylvania, baptism book.*
8. *1910 US Census.*
9. *Margery Haite, Wolff Family (5 typewritten pages, circa 1978).*
10. *Richard Swanson notes (written in margins of Wolff Family genealogy from Haite).*
11. *Journal of proceedings of the Michigan Board of Education (1928).*
12. *1930 US Census.*
13. *U.S. Public Records Index, Volume 2 (Ancestry.com).*
14. *Vassar Pioneer Times, Obituary Date: 2 Sep 2004.*

- Obituary: Vassar Pioneer Times as a letter to the editor by Buck Service, Sep 2004.

Another era in Vassar history has just passed. Mrs. Alma Swanson at 100 years of age has gone to her heavenly reward.

For decades the Swanson family set a standard for the people of Vassar and Mrs. Swanson was quietly elegant. In all the years I have known her, she was always calm and unflappable.

She raised her three children, Shirley, Richard and Margie to remain quiet, studious, and ambitious. The only member of the family that was beyond her control was her husband, "Doc" E.C. Swanson. He was as outgoing as she was quiet.

Mrs. Swanson even bore a striking resemblance to the movie star Gloria Swanson, although there was never an actual connection between the two women.

In recent years she lived alone at her home on North Main Street in Vassar and only moved in with her daughter Shirley when she was no longer able to drive. More recently she moved in with her daughter, Margie, in Ann Arbor, and it was there she spent her last days.

Although gone, her memory still lives in the minds of all who knew her. She was perhaps the last of the old guard in Vassar. The changing of the century and the millennium signalled a time for the slow change of a new society. Will we have a new Alma Swanson to help us set our sights high? She was a grand lady the likes of which we will never see again.

Children from this marriage were:

i. **Shirley Jean Swanson** was born on 8 Sep 1928 in Detroit, Wayne, Michigan. Other names for Shirley are Shirley Jean Smith and Shirley Jean Zimmer. Shirley married **Alan Edward Zimmer** on 24 Jul 1948. Shirley next married **William Gibbs Smith** on 14 Jun 1968.

ii. **Richard Conrad Swanson D. D. S.** was born on 2 May 1933 in Caro, Tuscola, Michigan, [15] was christened in Newberry, Luce, Michigan, and died on 14 Dec 2009 in Fernandina Beach, Nassau, Florida. Richard married **Josephine Helen Osmun,** daughter of **Carroll Lee Osmun** and **Marian Catherine McHugh,** on 29 Nov 1958 in Pontiac, Oakland, Michigan.

iii. **Margery Marie Swanson** was born on 5 Dec 1935 in Saginaw, Saginaw, Michigan. Another name for Margery is Margery Marie Haite. Margery married **Jay Donald Haite** on 27 Sep 1964 in Vassar, Tuscola, Michigan.

---

15. Social Security Death Index (ancestry.com).

Ancestor Report for Ewald Conrad Swanson M. D.

Second Generation

2. Mickel Mickelsson Svens,[1] son of **Mickel Mårtensson Storkarhu** and **Lisa Johansdotter Wäst**, was born on 19 Jun 1874 in Leistus, Rejpelt, Vörå, Finland,[2] died on 12 Nov 1961 in Newberry, Luce, Michigan,[1] and was buried in Forest Home Cemetery, Newberry, Luce, Michigan.[3] Other names for Mickel were Karhu Mix Mickelsson,[4] Mickel Svens, and Michael Swanson.[5]

Michael (Svens) Swanson

General Notes: Mickel Svens grew up in Vörå, a Swedish-speaking municipality in the Ostrobothnia region of Finland. Vörå Lutheran Church records indicated he could read and write well, and at 16 he was confirmed. He worked as a dräng (laborer) on nearby Ehrs farm until he was 18. He drew Lot 0 in the Russian army draft, which exempted him from military service until the next draft. In the summer of 1892 he took a ship from Vasa to Hull, England, then went by train from Hull, England to Liverpool where he boarded, on 3 May 1892, the Cunard Line's steam ship Gallia to cross the Atlantic. He arrived on 12 May 1892 at Ellis Island, New York, and was processed the next day. The manifest indicated he had just one piece of luggage and slept in the hallway of the ship. His Ellis Island record said he could not speak English. According to Richard Swanson, "When Mike Svens came to Newberry [in the upper peninsula of Michigan] he reported to the Westin's General Store which was run by Andrew Westin who helped him change his name to Mike Swanson." He was a railroad construction gang foreman for the Duluth, South Shore, and Atlantic Railroad and traveled through Michigan overseeing track repair sometimes bringing his family.

Noted events in his life were:
• Ethnic Identity: Swede-Finn.

• Occupation: farm hand on Ehrs farm, 1892, Rejpelt, Vörå, Finland. [1]

• Military: drew lott 0 (exempt) in the Russian army draft, 1892, Vörå, Finland. [4] Mickel Svens was listed on a 1896 "wanted list"in Vörå indicating his whereabouts were unknown, probably indicating he left the country illegally. When the Russians looked for him in 1896 for the subsequent draft, he had already left the country.

• Immigration: on the ship Gallia from Liverpool, England, 12 May 1892, Ellis Island, New York, New York, New York.[6] He settled in Newberry, Luce, Michigan. There is a memorial brick at Ellis Island for Michael Swanson.

• Name change: to Swanson, 1892, Newberry, Luce, Michigan. Mickel Svens changed his name to Michael Swanson after consulting with the Eric Westin in Newberry, Michgan. Svens was the name of his birth farm in Finland, and most Swede-Finn farmers used thir farm names as their surnames. The farm name Svens(possessive of Sven) is probably the first name of a 16th century owner or the founder of the farm. The farmname was changed to Svens in the mid 18th century from Storkarhu (stor means "big" in Swedish and karhu means "bear" in Finnish), when all farms with Finnish-language were changed in the parish.

• Occupation: rail road section foreman, 1900, Au Train, Alger, Michigan. [7]

• Residence: 1910, McMillan, Luce, Michigan. [8]

• Military: WW1 draft registration, 12 Sep 1918, Newberry, Luce, Michigan. [9]

---

1. Torbjörn Nikus, Storkarhu (unpublish document, 2008).

2. New York Passenger Lists, 1820-1957 (Ancestry.com). .... Torbjörn Nikus, Storkarhu (unpublish document, 2008).

3. Torbjörn Nikus, Storkarhu (unpublish document, 2008). .... Duane & Jacquelyn Hargis, Headstones at Forest Home Cemetery, Newberry, Luce County, Michigan (http://files.usgwarchives.net/mi/luce/cemeteries/f62302.txt).

4. Email from Torbjörn Nikus.

5. Duane & Jacquelyn Hargis, Headstones at Forest Home Cemetery, Newberry, Luce County, Michigan (http://files.usgwarchives.net/mi/luce/cemeteries/f62302.txt).

6. Ellis Island Website (www.ellisisland.org). .... New York Passenger Lists, 1820-1957 (Ancestry.com). .... Torbjörn Nikus, Storkarhu (unpublish document, 2008).

7. 1900 US Census.

8. 1910 US Census.

9. World War I Draft Registration Cards, 1917-1918 (ancestry.com).

Ancestor Report for Ewald Conrad Swanson M. D.

- Resided: 1920, Newberry, Luce, Michigan.[10]

- Event: visited by August Spangberg, 1955, Newberry, Luce, Michigan.[11] August Spångberg, Swedish member of parliament, visited his relatives in Newberry. Mickel had married his aunt and had taken care of August's grandfather.

Mickel married **Clara Fredrika Spångberg** on 19 Jan 1897 in Marquette, Marquette, Michigan.[12]

Children from this marriage were:

i. **Col. George Ferdinand Swanson M.D.**[13] was born on 30 Mar 1897 in Newberry, Luce, Michigan,[14] died on 13 Mar 1967 in Armada, Macomb, Michigan,[15] and was buried on 17 Mar 1967 in Arlington National Cemetery, Arlington, Virgina. George married **Lucile Chenard,** daughter of **Peter Chenard** and **Emma Marie Beaudin,** in 1941. George next married **Marion McFaul,** daughter of **Hiram McFaul** and **Nellie Jeffers,**.

ii. **Albin Leonard Swanson D.D.S.** was born on 12 Sep 1898 in Newberry, Luce, Michigan[13] and died on 12 Jul 1969 in Menominee, Menominee, Michigan.[15] Another name for Albin was Nib Swanson. Albin married **Ora Wilhelmina Lewis R.N.,**[16] daughter of **William Lewis** and **Rose Ann Vanzant,** on 9 Aug 1929 in Newberry, Luce, Michigan.

1   iii. **Ewald Conrad Swanson M. D.** Ewald married **Alma Marie Weidemann,** daughter of **Oscar Christian Weidemann** and **Mary Monahan,** on 22 Jan 1928 in Detroit, Wayne, Michigan.

iv. **Clara Cecelia Swanson R.N.** was born on 20 Apr 1901 in Newberry, Luce, Michigan[15] and died on 1 Apr 1984 in Newberry, Luce, Michigan.[15] Clara married **Hayden Duncan Palmer M.D.,** son of **Louis Nathan Palmer** and **Sadie Daker,**.

v. **Ester F. Swanson** was born on 4 Aug 1901 in Newberry, Luce, Michigan[17] and died on 4 Aug 1902 in Newberry, Luce, Michigan.[17]

vi. **Sigrid Fredricka Swanson** was born on 18 Aug 1905 in Newberry, Luce, Michigan[18] and died on 15 Feb 1980 in Cass City, Tuscola, Michigan.[18] Sigrid married **Arthur Paul Holmberg,** son of **Sven Holmberg** and **Esther Clementson,** on 18 Oct 1930 in Toledo, Lucas, Ohio.

3. Clara Fredrika Spångberg, daughter of **Carl Fredrik Jansson Spångberg** and **Christina Elisabet Andersdotter,** was born on 18 Sep 1876 in Lämtjärnsfallet, Skärhyttan, Nora, Örebro, Sweden,[19] died on 7 Aug 1946 in Newberry, Luce, Michigan,[20] and was buried in Forest Home Cemetery, Newberry, Luce, Michigan.[21] Another name for Clara was Clara Fredrika Carlson.[22]

Clara (Spångberg) Swanson

10. *1920 US Census.*
11. *August Spångberg, Stream of Time (1966).*
12. *1900 US Census.*
13. *World War I Draft Registration Cards, 1917-1918 (ancestry.com).*
14. *Social Security Death Index (ancestry.com). .... World War I Draft Registration Cards, 1917-1918 (ancestry.com).*
15. *Social Security Death Index (ancestry.com).*
16. *Green Bay Press Gazette (12 Mar 202).*
17. *Duane & Jacquelyn Hargis, Headstones at Forest Home Cemetery, Newberry, Luce County, Michigan (http://files.usgwarchives.net/mi/luce/cemeteries/f62302.txt). .... Michigan Death Records, 1897-1920 (seekingmichigan.com).*
18. *"Michigan Deaths, 1971-1996" (ancestry.com).*
19. *August Spångberg, Stream of Time (1966). .... Margery Haite's handwritten notes to Richard Swanson. .... Nora bergsförsamling AI:17d (1872-1881) Image 322 / page 668 (AID: v52022.b322.s668, NAD: SE/ULA/11098) . .... Nora bergsförsamling AI:18d (1882-1891) Image 364 / page 762 (AID: v52026.b364.s762, NAD: SE/ULA/11098) . .... Nora bergsförsamling AI:19c (1892-1901) Image 440 / page 924 (AID: v52029.b440.s924, NAD: SE/ULA/11098) . .... Nora bergsförsamling C:13 (1875-1899) Image 42 (AID: v53631.b42, NAD: SE/ULA/11098) .*
20. *Margery Haite's handwritten notes to Richard Swanson.*
21. *Duane & Jacquelyn Hargis, Headstones at Forest Home Cemetery, Newberry, Luce County, Michigan*

Ancestor Report for Ewald Conrad Swanson M. D.

General Notes: Clara lived in the village of Skärhyttan in Örebro, Sweden. In Newberry, Michigan she worked as a midwife and inspired several of her children to enter the medical profession.

Research Notes: Her uncle Eric immigrated in 1889 to Newberry. Clara immigrated to Michigan in 1892. This might have been prompted by the death of her mother in 1891. Her sisters Alma and Tena immigrated in 1899 to Newberry. Her father Carl immigrated in 1906 with her sister Jenny.

Noted events in her life were:
- Residence: 1890, Skärhyttan, Nora, Örebro, Sweden. [23]

- Resided: 1876-1892, Lämtjärnsfallet, Skärhyttan, Nora, Örebro, Sweden. [24]

- Emigrated: left home, 16 May 1982, Göteborg, Västra Götaland, Sweden. [24]

- Emigration: on the Ariosto to Hull, England, with Alma Carlson, 8 Jul 1892, Göteborg, Västra Götaland, Sweden. [25]

- Immigration: via Liverpool aboard the Cephalonia, 23 Jul 1892, Boston, Suffolk, Massachusetts.

- Name change: to Carlson, 1892, Newberry, Luce, Michigan. She dropped her last name Spångberg and used Carlson -- the Americanized version of her Swedish patronym Carlsdotter.

- Residence: 1897, Newberry, Luce, Michigan. [26]

- Residence: 1900, Au Train, Alger, Michigan. [27]

- Residence: 1910, McMillan, Luce, Michigan. [28]

- Residence: 1920, Newberry, Luce, Michigan. [29]

- Cause of death: stomach cancer.

Clara married **Mickel Mickelsson Svens** [30] on 19 Jan 1897 in Marquette, Marquette, Michigan. [27]

(http://files.usgwarchives.net/mi/luce/cemeteries/f62302.txt).
22. *Michigan Death Records, 1897-1920 (seekingmichigan.com). .... Michigan Marriages, 1868-1925 (familysearch.org).*
23. *Arkion 1890.*
24. *Nora bergsförsamling AI:19c (1892-1901) Image 440 / page 924 (AID: v52029.b440.s924, NAD: SE/ULA/11098) .*
25. *Emigranten Populär, 1783-1951 (ancestry.com). .... Göteborg, Sverige, passagerarlistor, 1869 - 1951 (ancestry.com).*
26. *Michigan Marriages, 1868-1925 (familysearch.org).*
27. *1900 US Census.*
28. *1910 US Census.*
29. *1920 US Census.*
30. *Torbjörn Nikus, Storkarhu (unpublish document, 2008).*

Ancestor Report for Ewald Conrad Swanson M. D.

Third Generation

4. Mickel Mårtensson Storkarhu,[1] son of **Mårten Mårtensson Storkarhu** and **Lisa Samuelsdotter Miemois,** was born on 15 Sep 1828 in Rejpelt, Vörå, Finland[1] and died on 16 May 1903 in Newberry, Luce, Michigan.[1] Other names for Mickel were Mickel Mårtensson Svens, Mickel Svens, and Michael Swanson.

General Notes: A bonde (farm owner) at No. 3 Storkarhu. When he retired, he and his wife moved to a cottage in Leistus paid for by the village. After his wife died, he traveled to Newberry, Michigan to live with his son Mickel.[1]

Research Notes: The family story that he his son Johan accompanied him on his trip to America seems to be false.

Noted events in his life were:
- Ethnic Identity: Swede-Finn.

- Occupation: A bonde (farm owner) at Storkarhu, Rejpelt, Vörå, Finland.[2]

- Emmigration: from Finland, 17 Aug 1901.[3]

- Departure: aboard the Numidian, 22 Aug 1901, Liverpool, Lancashire, England.[4]

- Arrival: from Liverpool, England aboard the Numidian, 1 Sep 1901, Quebec, Quebec, Canada.[1] He lied about his age and occupation since immigration requried an employment prospect. He said he is was painter and 55 (he was 72), and is visiting children and expects to find employment with his son-in-law Eric Westin. He appears to be traveling alone. He had $55.

- Emigrated: aboard the Numidian, 1 Sep 1901, St Albans, Franklin, Vermont.[5] There is a second manefest for Numidian with passengers disembarking in the USA. St. Albans is about 60 miles via channel from the Port of Montreal/Quebec.

Mickel married **Lisa Johansdotter Wäst**[6] on 8 Jul 1852 in Rejpelt, Vörå, Finland.[1]

Children from this marriage were:
- i. **Mårten Mickelsson Svens**[7] was born on 16 Mar 1853 in Rejpelt, Vörå, Finland[7] and died on 5 May 1874 in Sweden.[7]
- ii. **Lisa Mickelsdotter Svens**[8] was born on 22 Mar 1855 in Rejpelt, Vörå, Finland[8] and died on 22 Mar 1855 in Rejpelt, Vörå, Finland.[8]
- iii. **Lisa Mickelsdotter Svens**[8] was born on 24 Feb 1858 in Rejpelt, Vörå, Finland[8] and died in 1929 in Newberry, Luce, Michigan.[10] Another name for Lisa was Lisa Swenson. Lisa married **Erik Andersson Kastus**.[10]
- iv. **Greta Mickelsdotter Svens**[1] was born on 12 Nov 1863 in Rejpelt, Vörå, Finland[1] and died in 1903 in Palo, Storkyrö, Finland.[1] Another name for Greta was Greta Mickelsdotter Bergman. Greta married **J. Bergman**.
- v. **Johan Mickelsson Svens**[7] was born on 13 Jan 1871 in Rejpelt, Vörå, Finland[7] and died on 1 Dec 1920 in Finland.[7] Another name for Johan was John Svensson. Johan married **Anna Ulrika Mårtensdotter Åkers**[10] on 23 Aug 1900.[10]
- 2 vi. **Mickel Mickelsson Svens**.[1] Mickel married **Clara Fredrika Spångberg**, daughter of **Carl Fredrik Jansson Spångberg** and **Christina Elisabet Andersdotter,** on 19 Jan 1897 in Marquette, Marquette, Michigan.[11]

---

1. Torbjörn Nikus, Storkarhu (unpublish document, 2008).
2. Hiski database (http://hiski.genealogia.fi).
3. Siirtolaisuusinstituutti - Institute of Migration (http://www.migrationinstitute.fi).
4. Canadian Passenger Lists, 1865-1935 (ancestry.com).
5. Email from Torbjörn Nikus. .... Border Crossings: From Canada to U.S., 1895-1956 (ancestry.com).
6. Torbjörn Nikus, Storkarhu (unpublish document, 2008). .... Hiski database (http://hiski.genealogia.fi).
7. Email from Torbjörn Nikus. .... Torbjörn Nikus, Storkarhu (unpublish document, 2008).
8. Email from Torbjörn Nikus. .... Anders Enders, Några sidor på nätet om släktforskning (http://www.enges.org/gene/).
9. Anders Enders, Några sidor på nätet om släktforskning (http://www.enges.org/gene/).
10. Email from Torbjörn Nikus.
11. 1900 US Census.

Ancestor Report for Ewald Conrad Swanson M. D.

5. Lisa Johansdotter Wäst,[12] daughter of **Johan Eriksson Wäst** and **Lisa Johansdotter Wäst,** was born on 28 Nov 1829 in Rejpelt, Vörå, Finland,[12] was christened on 29 Nov 1829,[13] and died on 14 Feb 1901 in Rejpelt, Vörå, Finland.[14] Another name for Lisa was Lisa Johansdotter Dala.

General Notes: a housewife.[14]

Lisa married **Mickel Mårtensson Storkarhu**[14] on 8 Jul 1852 in Rejpelt, Vörå, Finland.[14]

Carl Fredrick Spångberg

6. Carl Fredrik Jansson Spångberg,[15] son of **Jan Ersson** and **Maria Helena Persdotter,** was born on 19 Feb 1844 in Skärhyttan, Nora, Örebro, Sweden[16] and died on 31 Jul 1917 in Newberry, Luce, Michigan.[17] Another name for Carl was Carl Fredrik Spångberg.

General Notes: "Karl Fredrik [was a] charcoal-burner. When the only horse in the family died in an accident they had to leave their forestcottage and move to Skärhyttan. To avoid ending up at the poor-house Karl Fredrik moved together with his youngest daughter Jenny to relatives in America." (Email from Håkan Blomqvist)[18]

Noted events in his life were:
- Resided: 1852, Koppartorp, Skärhyttan, Nora, Örebro, Sweden.[19]

- Resided: 1852-1857, Björnbo, Skärhyttan, Nora, Örebro, Sweden.[20]

- Occupation: employee of Johan Jacobsson, mining inspector, at Stadra estate, 1857-1859, Hällefors, Örebro, Sweden.[21]

- Resided: 1860-1870, Björnbo, Skärhyttan, Nora, Örebro, Sweden.[22]

- Occupation: day laborer, 1862-1870, Grekskog, Nora, Örebro, Sweden.[23]

- Resided: 1870-1873, Grekslund, Stadra, Nora, Örebro, Sweden.[24]

- Resided: torpare (tenant farmer), 1873-1898, Lämtjärnsfallet, Skärhyttan, Nora, Örebro, Sweden.[25]

- Event: foster father, 1893-1906, Nora, Örebro, Sweden.[26] He was the foster father to a grandson, August Spångberg (1893-1987). August's father left the family, and Carl took over parenting his grandchild even though he was a widower. In 1922, August was the youngest person ever to be elected to the Swedish parliament.

12. *Torbjörn Nikus, Storkarhu (unpublish document, 2008). .... Hiski database (http://hiski.genealogia.fi).*
13. *Hiski database (http://hiski.genealogia.fi).*
14. *Torbjörn Nikus, Storkarhu (unpublish document, 2008).*
15. *Nora bergsförsamling AI:14bb (1841-1850) Image 49 / page 195 (AID: v52007.b49.s195, NAD: SE/ULA/11098) .*
16. *Arkion 1890. .... August Spångberg, Stream of Time (1966). .... Duane & Jacquelyn Hargis, Headstones at Forest Home Cemetery, Newberry, Luce County, Michigan (http://files.usgwarchives.net/mi/luce/cemeteries/f62302.txt). .... Nora bergsförsamling AI:14bb (1841-1850) Image 49 / page 195 (AID: v52007.b49.s195, NAD: SE/ULA/11098) . .... Nora bergsförsamling AI:15eb (1851-1861) Image 59 / page 213 (AID: v52013.b59.s213, NAD: SE/ULA/11098). .... Nora bergsförsamling AI:18d (1882-1891) Image 364 / page 762 (AID: v52026.b364.s762, NAD: SE/ULA/11098). .... Nora bergsförsamling C:9b (1843-1856) Image 19 (AID: v53626.b19, NAD: SE/ULA/11098) . .... Nora bergsförsamling C:8b (1842-1858) Image 17 (AID: v53624.b17, NAD: SE/ULA/11098) .*
17. *Duane & Jacquelyn Hargis, Headstones at Forest Home Cemetery, Newberry, Luce County, Michigan (http://files.usgwarchives.net/mi/luce/cemeteries/f62302.txt).*
18. *Storytelling Evening 2005: Recollections of Ingvar Lundqvist (www.stadranejden.se). .... 18 Oct 2005, Email from Håkan Blomqvist.*
19. *Nora bergsförsamling AI:15eb (1851-1861) Image 59 / page 213 (AID: v52013.b59.s213, NAD: SE/ULA/11098) .*
20. *Nora bergsförsamling AI:15eb (1851-1861) Image 69 / page 223 (AID: v52013.b69.s223, NAD: SE/ULA/11098) .*
21. *Nora bergsförsamling AI:15eb (1851-1861) Image 87 / page 240 (AID: v52013.b87.s240, NAD: SE/ULA/11098) .*
22. *Nora bergsförsamling AI:16e (1861-1871) Image 289 / page 282 (AID: v52018.b289.s282, NAD: SE/ULA/11098) . .... Nora bergsförsamling AI:15eb (1851-1861) Image 73 / page 227 (AID: v52013.b73.s227, NAD: SE/ULA/11098) .*
23. *Nora bergsförsamling AI:16e (1861-1871) Image 324 / page 317 (AID: v52018.b324.s317, NAD: SE/ULA/11098) .*
24. *Nora bergsförsamling AI:16e (1861-1871) Image 320 / page 313 (AID: v52018.b320.s313, NAD: SE/ULA/11098) . .... Nora bergsförsamling AI:17d (1872-1881) Image 303 / page 649 (AID: v52022.b303.s649, NAD: SE/ULA/11098) .*
25. *Arkion 1890. .... Nora bergsförsamling AI:18d (1882-1891) Image 364 / page 762 (AID: v52026.b364.s762, NAD: SE/ULA/11098) . .... Nora bergsförsamling AI:19c (1892-1901) Image 440 / page 924 (AID: v52029.b440.s924, NAD: SE/ULA/11098) . .... Nora bergsförsamling AI:17d (1872-1881) Image 322 / page 668 (AID: v52022.b322.s668, NAD: SE/ULA/11098) .*
26. *August Spångberg, Stream of Time (1966).*

Ancestor Report for Ewald Conrad Swanson M. D.

- Moved to: an apartment (enrumslägenhet), 1898, Skärhyttan, Nora, Örebro, Sweden. [27]

- Occupation: charcoal-burner, Bef 1904, Skärhyttan, Nora, Örebro, Sweden. [27]

- Moved from: 10 Mar 1906, Skärhyttan, Nora, Örebro, Sweden. [27]

- Emigration: 30 Mar 1906, Göteborg, Västra Götaland, Sweden. [28]

- Immigration: on the Ivernia sailing 3 Apr from Liverpool, England, 12 Apr 1906, Boston, Suffolk, Massachusetts. [29] Passenger list indicates that he is a widower, accompanied by his daughter Jenny, and is suffering from senility.

- Residence: 1910, McMillan, Luce, Michigan. [30]

Carl married **Christina Elisabet Andersdotter** on 21 Jun 1870 in Hällefors, Örebro, Sweden. [31]

Children from this marriage were:

    i.   **Anna Lovisa Spångberg** was born on 13 Aug 1870 in Grekslund, Stadra, Nora, Örebro, Sweden [32] and died on 8 Apr 1916 in Eda, Värmland, Sweden. [33] Anna had a relationship with **August Carlsson**. This couple did not marry. Anna next had a relationship with **Anders Gustav Olsson** Est 1900.

    ii.   **August Wilhelm Spångberg** [34] was born on 20 Jun 1872 in Grekslund, Grecksjöhöjden, Nora, Örebro, Sweden [35] and died on 12 Dec 1875 in Lämtjärnsfallet, Skärhyttan, Nora, Örebro, Sweden. [34]

    iii.   **Carl Wilhelm Spångberg** [34] was born on 12 Mar 1873 in Lämtjärnsfallet, Skärhyttan, Nora, Örebro, Sweden [34] and died on 26 Sep 1876 in Lämtjärnsfallet, Skärhyttan, Nora, Örebro, Sweden. [36]

3   iv.   **Clara Fredrika Spångberg**. Clara married **Mickel Mickelsson Svens**, [37] son of **Mickel Mårtensson Storkarhu** and **Lisa Johansdotter Wäst**, on 19 Jan 1897 in Marquette, Marquette, Michigan. [38]

    v.   **Oskar Fredrik Spångberg** was born on 18 Jun 1878 in Lämtjärnsfallet, Skärhyttan, Nora, Örebro, Sweden [39] and died in Sweden. [33] Oskar married **Alma**.

    vi.   **Alma Maria Spångberg** was born on 21 Oct 1882 in Lämtjärnsfallet, Skärhyttan, Nora, Örebro, Sweden [40] and died in USA. Another name for Alma was Alma Carlson. [30]

    vii.   **Hilma Leontine Spångberg** was born on 3 Sep 1884 in Lämtjärnsfallet, Skärhyttan, Nora, Örebro, Sweden [40] and died in 1935 in Newberry, Luce, Michigan. [42] Another name for Hilma was Tena

27. August Spångberg, Stream of Time (1966).
28. Emigranten Populär, 1783-1951 (ancestry.com).
29. Boston Passenger and Crew Lists, 1820-1943 (ancestry.com).
30. 1910 US Census.
31. Nora bergsförsamling AI:18d (1882-1891) Image 364 / page 762 (AID: v52026.b364.s762, NAD: SE/ULA/11098) .
32. Arkion 1890. .... August Spångberg, Stream of Time (1966). .... Margery Haite's handwritten notes to Richard Swanson. .... Nora bergsförsamling AI:17d (1872-1881) Image 322 / page 668 (AID: v52022.b322.s668, NAD: SE/ULA/11098) . .... Nora bergsförsamling AI:18d (1882-1891) Image 364 / page 762 (AID: v52026.b364.s762, NAD: SE/ULA/11098) . .... Nora bergsförsamling AI:19c (1892-1901) Image 440 / page 924 (AID: v52029.b440.s924, NAD: SE/ULA/11098) . .... Nora bergsförsamling AI:16e (1861-1871) Image 320 / page 313 (AID: v52018.b320.s313, NAD: SE/ULA/11098) . .... Nora bergsförsamling C:12 (1861-1888) Image 317 (AID: v53630.b317, NAD: SE/ULA/11098)

33. Margery Haite's handwritten notes to Richard Swanson.
34. Nora bergsförsamling AI:17d (1872-1881) Image 322 / page 668 (AID: v52022.b322.s668, NAD: SE/ULA/11098) .
35. Nora bergsförsamling AI:17d (1872-1881) Image 322 / page 668 (AID: v52022.b322.s668, NAD: SE/ULA/11098) . .... Nora bergsförsamling C:12 (1861-1888) Image 365 (AID: v53630.b365, NAD: SE/ULA/11098) .
36. Nora bergsförsamling F:10 (1861-1894) Image 171 (AID: v53653.b171, NAD: SE/ULA/11098) . .... Nora bergsförsamling AI:17d (1872-1881) Image 322 / page 668 (AID: v52022.b322.s668, NAD: SE/ULA/11098) .
37. Torbjörn Nikus, Storkarhu (unpublish document, 2008).
38. 1900 US Census.
39. Arkion 1890. .... August Spångberg, Stream of Time (1966). .... Nora bergsförsamling AI:17d (1872-1881) Image 322 / page 668 (AID: v52022.b322.s668, NAD: SE/ULA/11098) . .... Nora bergsförsamling AI:18d (1882-1891) Image 364 / page 762 (AID: v52026.b364.s762, NAD: SE/ULA/11098) . .... Nora bergsförsamling AI:19c (1892-1901) Image 440 / page 924 (AID: v52029.b440.s924, NAD: SE/ULA/11098).
40. Arkion 1890. .... August Spångberg, Stream of Time (1966). .... Nora bergsförsamling AI:18d (1882-1891) Image 364 / page 762 (AID: v52026.b364.s762, NAD: SE/ULA/11098) . .... Nora bergsförsamling AI:19c (1892-1901) Image 440 / page 924 (AID: v52029.b440.s924, NAD: SE/ULA/11098).
41. Nora parish household inventory 1841-1850 (email from Marie Esplund-Lynn).
42. Margery Haite's handwritten notes to Richard Swanson. .... Duane & Jacquelyn Hargis, Headstones at Forest Home Cemetery, Newberry, Luce County, Michigan (http://files.usgwarchives.net/mi/luce/cemeteries/f62302.txt).
43. Duane & Jacquelyn Hargis, Headstones at Forest Home Cemetery, Newberry, Luce County, Michigan (http://files.usgwarchives.net/mi/luce/cemeteries/f62302.txt).
44. Email from Torbjörn Nikus, 27 Jan 2011.
45. Michigan Marriages, 1868-1925 (familysearch.org).

Carlson.[43] Hilma married **Isak Johansson Nordman**,[44] son of **Johan Abrahamsson Nordman** and **Anna Lisa Simonsdotter Knöös,** on 5 Dec 1906 in Newberry, Luce, Michigan.[45]

viii. **Jenny Elisabet Spångberg** was born on 2 Oct 1886 in Lämtjärnsfallet, Skärhyttan, Nora, Örebro, Sweden [46] and died on 21 Jun 1960 in Newberry, Luce, Michigan. Another name for Jenny was Jenny Elizabet Carlson.[47] Jenny married **Erik Alfred Eriksson Rådman,** son of **Erik Eriksson Rådman** and **Breta Mårtensdotter Rådman,** on 26 Mar 1910 in Newberry, Luce, Michigan.[47]

7. Christina Elisabet Andersdotter, daughter of **Anders Jansson** and **Anna Helena Persdotter,** was born on 3 Jun 1845 in Sandsjöhöjden, Nora, Örebro, Sweden [48] and died on 16 Mar 1891 in Lämtjärnsfallet, Skärhyttan, Nora, Örebro, Sweden.[49] Other names for Christina were Christina Elisabet Andersdotter Barkén and Christina Elisabet Barkén.

Noted events in her life were:

- Resided: with foster parents Jan Jansson and Lisa Persdotter, 1852-1856, Ringshyttan, Nora, Örebro, Sweden. [50] Her father died when she was six years old, and she was placed with forster parents.

- Name change: to Barken, After 1849. Barken was the name of her grandfather's homestead. Her father was using the name Barken in 1849 when her younger brother Anders was born.

- Resided: 1858, Blanka, Sandsjöhöjden, Nora, Örebro, Sweden. [51]

- Occupation: maid, 1867, Grekskog, Nora, Örebro, Sweden. [52] living in the same homestead as her future husband, Jan Ersson, where he was a laborer. It is therefore possible he was the father of her daughter Matilda, born out of wedlock.

- Resided: 1870-1873, Grekslund, Stadra, Nora, Örebro, Sweden. [53]

- Resided: 1873-1891, Lämtjärnsfallet, Skärhyttan, Nora, Örebro, Sweden. [54]

Christina had a child

The child from this marriage was:

i. **Karolina Matilda Barkén** was born on 20 May 1867 in Grekskog, Nora, Örebro, Sweden [55] and died about 1935. Another name for Karolina was Karolina Matilda Spångberg. Karolina married **Ferdinand Rosengren** in Sweden.

Christina next married **Carl Fredrik Jansson Spångberg** [56] on 21 Jun 1870 in Hällefors, Örebro, Sweden. [49]

---

46. *Arkion 1890. .... August Spångberg, Stream of Time (1966). .... Nora bergsförsamling AI:18d (1882-1891) Image 364 / page 762 (AID: v52026.b364.s762, NAD: SE/ULA/11098). .... Nora bergsförsamling AI:19c (1892-1901) Image 440 / page 924 (AID: v52029.b440.s924, NAD: SE/ULA/11098). .... Nora bergsförsamling C:13 (1875-1899) Image 211 (AID: v53631.b211, NAD: SE/ULA/11098)*

47. *Michigan Marriages, 1868-1925 (familysearch.org).*

48. *Nora bergsförsamling AI:17d (1872-1881) Image 322 / page 668 (AID: v52022.b322.s668, NAD: SE/ULA/11098) . .... Nora bergsförsamling AI:18d (1882-1891) Image 364 / page 762 (AID: v52026.b364.s762, NAD: SE/ULA/11098) . .... Nora bergsförsamling AI:16e (1861-1871) Image 324 / page 317 (AID: v52018.b324.s317, NAD: SE/ULA/11098) . .... Nora bergsförsamling C:9b (1843-1856) Image 38 (AID: v53626.b38, NAD: SE/ULA/11098).*

49. *Nora bergsförsamling AI:18d (1882-1891) Image 364 / page 762 (AID: v52026.b364.s762, NAD: SE/ULA/11098) .*

50. *Nora bergsförsamling AI:15b (1851-1861) Image 83 / page 76 (AID: v52009.b83.s76, NAD: SE/ULA/11098) .*

51. *Nora bergsförsamling AI:15eb (1851-1861) Image 113 / page 266 (AID: v52013.b113.s266, NAD: SE/ULA/11098) .*

52. *Nora bergsförsamling AI:16e (1861-1871) Image 324 / page 317 (AID: v52018.b324.s317, NAD: SE/ULA/11098) .*

53. *Nora bergsförsamling AI:16e (1861-1871) Image 320 / page 313 (AID: v52018.b320.s313, NAD: SE/ULA/11098) . .... Nora bergsförsamling AI:17d (1872-1881) Image 303 / page 649 (AID: v52022.b303.s649, NAD: SE/ULA/11098) .*

54. *Nora bergsförsamling AI:18d (1882-1891) Image 364 / page 762 (AID: v52026.b364.s762, NAD: SE/ULA/11098) . .... Nora bergsförsamling AI:17d (1872-1881) Image 322 / page 668 (AID: v52022.b322.s668, NAD: SE/ULA/11098) .*

55. *Arkion 1890. .... Nora bergsförsamling AI:18d (1882-1891) Image 364 / page 762 (AID: v52026.b364.s762, NAD: SE/ULA/11098) . .... Nora bergsförsamling AI:17d (1872-1881) Image 303 / page 649 (AID: v52022.b303.s649, NAD: SE/ULA/11098) . .... Nora bergsförsamling C:12 (1861-1888) Image 235 (AID: v53630.b235, NAD: SE/ULA/11098) .*

56. *Nora bergsförsamling AI:14bb (1841-1850) Image 49 / page 195 (AID: v52007.b49.s195, NAD: SE/ULA/11098) .*

Pedigree Chart for Ewald Conrad Swanson M. D.

8 Mårten Mårtensson Storkarhu
b. 15 Mar 1788
p. Rejpelt, Vörå, Finland
m. 30 Nov 1810
p. Vörå, Finland
d. 13 Oct 1828
p. Rejpelt, Vörå, Finland

4 Mickel Mårtensson Storkarhu
b. 15 Sep 1828
p. Rejpelt, Vörå, Finland
m. 8 Jul 1852
p. Rejpelt, Vörå, Finland
d. 16 May 1903
p. Newberry, Luce, Michigan

9 Lisa Samuelsdotter Miemois
b. 10 Dec 1792
p. Miemoisby, Vörå, Finland
d. 19 Nov 1866
p. Leistus, Rejpelt, Vörå, Finland

2 Mickel Mickelsson Svens
b. 19 Jun 1874
p. Leistus, Rejpelt, Vörå, Finland
m. 19 Jan 1897
p. Marquette, Marquette, Michigan
d. 12 Nov 1961
p. Newberry, Luce, Michigan

10 Johan Eriksson Wäst
b. 10 Mar 1799
p. Rejpelt, Vörå, Finland
m. 28 Dec 1819
p. Rejpelt, Vörå, Finland
d. 9 Jun 1878
p. Rejpelt, Vörå, Finland

5 Lisa Johansdotter Wäst
b. 28 Nov 1829
p. Rejpelt, Vörå, Finland
d. 14 Feb 1901
p. Rejpelt, Vörå, Finland

11 Lisa Johansdotter Wäst
b. 19 Sep 1789
p. Rejpelt, Vörå, Finland
d. 1 Jan 1856
p. Rejpelt, Vörå, Finland

1 Ewald Conrad Swanson M. D.
b. 3 Jan 1900
p. Au Train, Alger, Michigan
m. 22 Jan 1928
p. Detroit, Wayne, Michigan
d. 26 Sep 1987
p. Saginaw, Saginaw, Michigan
sp. Alma Marie Weidemann

12 Jan Ersson
b. 14 Jan 1808
p. Finhyttan, Grythyttan, Örebro, Sweden
m. 26 Dec 1830
p. Hällefors, Örebro, Sweden
d. 31 May 1857
p. Skärhyttan, Nora, Örebro, Sweden

6 Carl Fredrik Jansson Spångberg
b. 19 Feb 1844
p. Skärhyttan, Nora, Örebro, Sweden
m. 21 Jun 1870
p. Hällefors, Örebro, Sweden
d. 31 Jul 1917
p. Newberry, Luce, Michigan

13 Maria Helena Persdotter
b. 5 Mar 1811
p. Skärhyttan, Nora, Örebro, Sweden
d. 18 Mar 1887
p. Skärhyttan, Nora, Örebro, Sweden

3 Clara Fredrika Spångberg
b. 18 Sep 1876
p. Lämtjärnsfallet, Skärhyttan, Nora, Örebro~
d. 7 Aug 1946
p. Newberry, Luce, Michigan

14 Anders Jansson
b. 23 Jun 1814
p. Barken, Grythyttan, Örebro, Sweden
m. 30 Sep 1843
p. Grythyttan, Örebro, Sweden
d. 7 Mar 1851
p. Blanka, Sandsjöhöjden, Nora, Örebro, ~

7 Christina Elisabet Andersdotter
b. 3 Jun 1845
p. Sandsjöhöjden, Nora, Örebro, Sweden
d. 16 Mar 1891
p. Lämtjärnsfallet, Skärhyttan, Nora, Örebro~

15 Anna Helena Persdotter
b. 27 Nov 1816
p. Ryttarbacken, Stadra, Nora, Örebro, Sw~
d. 16 Apr 1887
p. Skärhyttan, Nora, Örebro, Sweden

Photos: Ewald Conrad Swanson, M. D.

Ewald Swanson

[Provided by Mark Swanson/Swanson Media.]

Photos: Ewald Conrad Swanson, M. D.

Ewald Swanson family

[Provided by Mark Swanson/Swanson Media.]

Ewald Swanson at Newberry

Col. George Swanson is in front row. [Provided by Mark Swanson/Swanson Media.]

Photos: Ewald Conrad Swanson, M. D.

Ewald Swanson, Alma and children

[Provided by Mark Swanson/Swanson Media.]
(1982)

Photos: Ewald Conrad Swanson, M. D.

Ewald Swanson

[Provided by Mark Swanson/Swanson Media.]
(Cir 1916)

Photos: Ewald Conrad Swanson, M. D.

Ewald Swanson holding son and daughter

[Provided by Mark Swanson/Swanson Media.]
(1933)

Photos: Ewald Conrad Swanson, M. D.

Ewald Swanson's home and office, Vassar, Michigan

[Provided by Mark Swanson © Richard Swanson/Swanson Media.]
(1973)

Ewald Swanson cleaning snow from car in Vassar

[Provided by Mark Swanson © Richard Swanson/Swanson Media.]
(1973)

Photos: Vassar, Michigan

Downtown Vassar, Michigan

[Provided by Mark Swanson/Swanson Media. Public domain.]
(circa 1920)

Photos: Vassar, Michigan

Downtown, Vassar, Michigan

[Provided by Mark Swanson/Swanson Media. Public domain.]
(circa 1930)

Boats on the Cass River in Vassar, Michigan

A tributary of the Cass ran behind Ewald Swanson's backyard on N. Main St. [Provided by Mark Swanson/Swanson Media. Public domain.]
(circa 1900)

Photos: Newberry, Michigan

Downtown Newberry, Michigan

[Provided by Jim Dwyer. Public domain.]
(circa 1935)

Westin's Store, Newberry, Michigan

Hogs being delivered to the store. Andrew Westin is standing between the hog sled and horse on the right. [Provided by Jim Dwyer. Public domain.]
(1913)

Photos: Newberry, Michigan

Westin's Store, Newberry, Michigan

[Provided by Jim Dwyer. Public domain.]
(March 28, 1930)

Swanson stone marking family plot in Forest Home Cemetery, Newberry, Michigan

[Picture provided by Maggie Keefe.]
(2003)

Photos: Newberry, Michigan

Newberry railroad station

The Duluth, South Shore & Atlantic Railway depot and train at Newberry, Michigan [Alan Loftis Collection. Public domain.]

Photos: Mickel Mickelsson Svens

Michael (Svens) Swanson

[Provided by Mark Swanson/Swanson Media. From family collection.]

Photos: Mickel Mickelsson Svens

Michael (Svens) Swanson wearing his railroad uniform.

Michael Swanson was a section foreman, which meant he was in charge of a crew that repaired and maintained sections of the track. [Provided by Mark Swanson/Swanson Media. From family collection.]
(1946)

Photos: Mickel Mickelsson Svens

Michael (Svens) Swanson and Clara Swanson

[Provided by Mark Swanson/Swanson Media. From family collection.]

Michael (Svens) Swanson and great grandson Michael

[Provided by Mark Swanson/Swanson Media. From family collection.]
(1960)

Photos: Mickel Mickelsson Svens

Michael (Svens) Swanson marker in Forest Home Cemetery, Newberry, MI

[Photograph provided by Maggie Keefe.]

Photos: Vörå parish, Finland

Rejpelt in Vörå, Finland

Harvested sheaves of rye in the field. Vörå was called the "Realm of Rye." [Provided by T. Nikus.]
(Cir 1910)

Rejpelt in Vörå, Finland

[Provided by T. Nikus.]
(1935)

Photos: Vörå parish, Finland

Rejpelt in Vörå, Finland

Picture probably taken from roof of Svens home. Leistus is a farm cluster in the village of Rejpelt.
[Provided by T. Nikus.]
(Cir 1920)

Rejpelt in Vörå, Finland

Svens structure probably at end of road. [Provided by T. Nikus.]
(Cir 1930)

Photos: Vörå parish, Finland

Rejpelt in Vörå, Finland

[Provided by T. Nikus.]
(Cir 1930)

Photos: Vörå parish, Finland

Vörå church, the oldest wooden church in Finland

Oldest wooden church in Finland, built in 1626, enlarged 1777, bell tower built in 1702. There is a stone sanctuary built in 1519. Inside the church are medieval sculptures, including a crucifix from circa 1370. (There is a legend that the crucifix was carved by a murderer while imprisoned.) When the Russian Cossacks invaded about 1720, they used the Church as a stable. [Photo by Rebecca Swanson.]
(2006)

Photos: Vörå parish, Finland

Vörå parish folk costume (Vörådräkt)

The official dress of Vörå was worn at feasts, celebrations, church, parades, marriages, and other special occasions. The skirt pattern is mostly red with stripes of blue, white, and green.

Photos: Vörå parish, Finland

Puukko knives, traditional Finnish knife

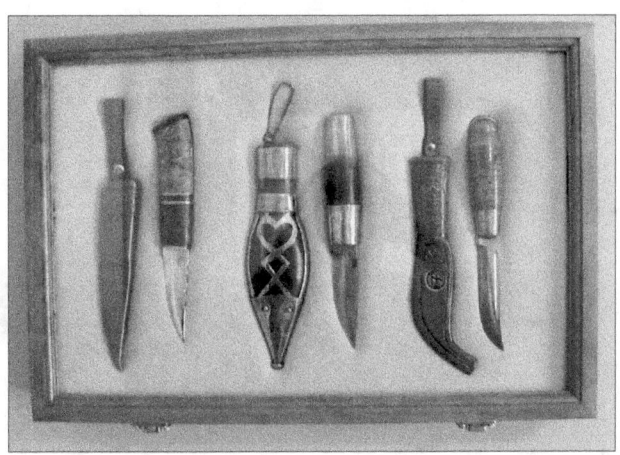

From left to right: Puukko made by Nils Härtull of Vörå, Finland; Masur birch handle. Vörå-kniv (unique to Vörå) made by Nils Härtull of Vörå, Finland; Nils is 7th cousin to Mickel Svens. Puukko made by Iisakki Järvenpää Oy, Kauhava, Finland; stacked birch bark handle, inscribed with "Mike Swansson" (owned by Mickel Svens). [Photo by Michael Swanson.]
(2010)

Photos: Vörå parish, Finland

Interior of an old farm house in Vörå, Finland

[Provided by T. Nikus.]
(1900)

Photos: Vörå parish, Finland

Arial view from Rejpelt of Bertby, Vörå

[Provided by T. Nikus.]
(Cir 1920)

Photos: Vörå parish, Finland

Owner´s marks (bomärken) used in Vörå, Finland

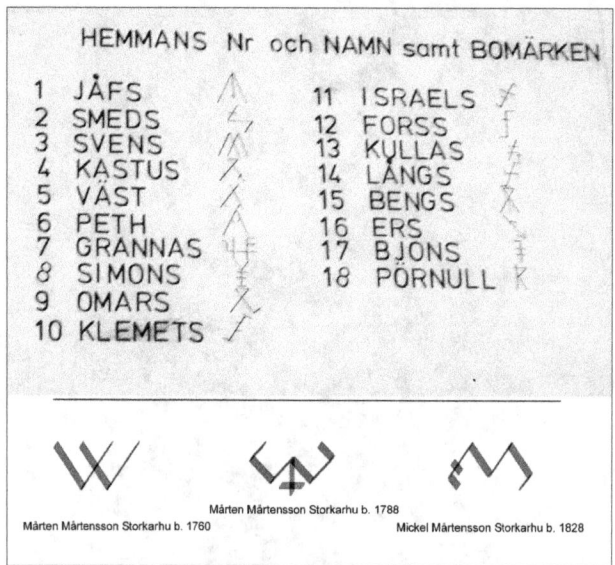

These are bomärken (owner's marks) used by farm owners in Vörå, Finland in the 1800s. The bottom row are marks used by three generations, starting with Ewald Swanson's grandfather's mark on the right. Owner's marks resemble the runes in the Viking Age alphabet. Each farm owner had a unique mark, and subsequent owners would make small changes to previous marks to distinguish them. A newmark had to be approved by the other villagers. [Photo by Michael Swanson.]
(2006)

Photos: Clara Fredrika Spångberg

Michael and Clara Swanson

Michael and Clara Swanson surrounded by son's family and Holmberg family. Front (the two girls): Margery (Swanson) Haite, Joan (Holmberg) Pollock. Middle: Alma (Weidemann) Swanson, Richard "Dick" Swanson, Michael Swanson (Mikel Svens), Clara Spångberg (Clara Swanson), Paul Holmberg (baby), Sigrid (Swanson) Holmberg. Back (standing): Ewald Conrad Swanson, Shirley (Swanson) Zimmer, Arthur Holmberg. [Provided by Mark Swanson/Swanson Media. From family collection.]
(1940s)

Michael and Clara (Spångberg) Swanson's children

George, Celia, Ewald, Albin Swanson [Provided by Mark Swanson/Swanson Media. From family collection.]
(1905)

Photos: Clara Fredrika Spångberg

Clara Swanson marker in Forest Home Cemetery, Newberry, MI

[Picture provided by Maggie Keefe.]

Photo: Carl Fredrik Jansson Spångberg

Carl Fredrick Spångberg

This picture was taken in Newberry, Michigan. [From book, Stream of Time. Presumed in the pulic domain.]
(after 1906)

Photos: Nora and Adjacent Parishes, Örebro, Sweden

Miners in Nora parish, Sweden

Miners dressed in bergsmanrockar (miners coats).   [Provided by the Noraskog Heritage Society.]
(Cir 1870)

Mining team in Nora parish

Elfstorp was a large estate in Nora with many homesteads. [Provided by the Noraskog Heritage
Society.]
(1901)

Photos: Nora and Adjacent Parishes, Örebro, Sweden

Typical miner's torp (rented homestead)

This torp, or rented homestead, was located in Nora parish, Örebro, and is typical of homes in the region. [Provided by the Noraskog Heritage Society.]
(1889)

Brötorp, Nora, Örebro, Sweden

Some ancestors lived at Brötorp/Bröstorp. [Provided by the Noraskog Heritage Society.]
(Cir 1900)

Photos: Nora and Adjacent Parishes, Örebro, Sweden

Rockesholm powerplant, Grythyttan, Örebro, Sweden

Rockesholm is very near Skärhyttan village where Clara Fredrika Spångberg was born. Several ancestors worked, and were buried, in Rockesholm. [Provided by the Noraskog Heritage Society.]
(1900)

Smelting furnace in Grythyttan parish

This furnace is possible one where ancestors in Grythyttan parish worked. [Public domain.]
(1906)

Photos: Nora and Adjacent Parishes, Örebro, Sweden

Grythyttan parish church

The Grythyttan parish church is a wooden church built in 1632. In that year the rector preached in both Swedish and Finnish. Two galleries were added in 1730 and the church tower was built in 1777. [Provided by the Noraskog Heritage Society.]

Chapel in Greksåsar, Nora, Örebro, Sweden,

This is a typical Nora parish chapel that served families who lived too far awar from the main parish church. This chapel is in Greksåsar where ancestor Nils Eriksson Körning lived. It is next to the villiage of Skärhyttan. [Provided by the Noraskog Heritage Society.]
(1960)

Photos: Nora and Adjacent Parishes, Örebro, Sweden

Järnboås parish, Örebro, Sweden

Carl Frederick Spangberg worked in Järnboås parish. [Provided by the Noraskog Heritage Society.]

Järnboås parish church, Örebro, Sweden

Järnboås church was built in 1659. The original church consisted only of a nave; they added the cross arm expansion in 1795. Some ancestors lived or worked in Järnboås parish. [Provided by the Noraskog Heritage Society.]

Photos: Nora and Adjacent Parishes, Örebro, Sweden

Nora folk costume (Nora-dräkt)

The Nora costume, worn at important events, has a striped pattern of earthen tones for the skirt with a red vest. [Post card, Noraskog Heritage Society.]

Photos: Nora and Adjacent Parishes, Örebro, Sweden

Stadra manor, Nora Parish

Several ancestors lived and worked on the old Stadra estate. It has been restored and is now a cultural center. [Provided by the Noraskog Heritage Society.]
(1930)

Nora city

Nora city was the largest city in Nora parish. Some of Clara Spångberg's ancestors were married there. [Provided by the Noraskog Heritage Society.]

Photos: Ships to America

Cunard Line steamship Gallia - Mickel Mickelsson Svens

Mickel Mickelsson Svens immigrated on the ship Gallia to Ellis Island from Liverpool, England, 12 May 1892. There is a memorial brick at Ellis Island for Michael Swanson. [Public domain.]

Cunard Line sail steamship Cephalonia - Clara Fredrika Spångberg

Clara Fredrika Spångberg traveled from Liverpool aboard the Cephalonia, 23 Jul 1892 to Boston, Suffolk, Massachusetts. Cunard Line steamship built 1882. [Public domain.]

Photos: Ships to America

Allan Line sail steamship Numidian - Mickel Mårtensson Storkarhu

Allan Line sail steamship built 1891. Mickel Mårtensson Storkarhu traveled from Liverpool,
England aboard the Numidian, arriving 1 Sep 1901 at St Albans, Franklin, Vermont via Quebec.
[Public domain.]

Cunard Line sail steamship Ivernia - Carl Fredrik Jansson Spångberg

Carl Fredrik Jansson Spångberg traveled on the Ivernia sailing 3 Apr 1906 from Liverpool,
England, 12 Apr 1906, to Boston, Suffolk, Massachusetts, accompanied by his daughter Jenny.
[Public domain.]

Narrative for Ewald Conrad Swanson M. D.: Medical Tribune, 1963

The following biographical sketch of Ewald Swanson appeared in the *Medical Tribune* on 16 Dec 1963.

LANSING, MICH. -- In the early part of this century, the Upper Peninsula, that part of the state of Michigan lying north of the straights of Mackinac, was inhabited mainly by lumber workers and miners.

Doctors were scarce, and many babies were delivered by midwives. One of these was Mrs. Clara Swanson of Newberry, whose husband, Mike Swanson, was a gang foreman for the Duluth, South Shore, and Atlantic Railroad.

When Mrs. Swanson answered appeals for help, she took along as assistants her small sons, George, Albin, and Ewald and daughter Celia.

"I remember going out on cases with Mother when I was eight years old," says Dr. Ewald C. Swanson, president of the Federation of State Medical Boards.

"Mother didn't expect to be paid for her services. They were poor homes that we visited, and we could see that the people appreciated her help. I think she inspired us with the desire to serve people, too. It certainly influenced our careers."

Thus, Dr. George Swanson retired recently as superintendent of the Philadelphia Veterans Hospital, Albin L. Swanson, D.D.S., practices dentistry in Newberry, Michigan, and their sister, Mrs. Celia Palmer, R.N., is the wife of Dr. Hayden Palmer of Pontiac, Mich.

Dr. Ewald C. Swanson is executive secretary of the Michigan State Board of Registration in Medicine, as well as a family doctor and civic leader.

In Vassar, Mich., where he practices medicine weekends while doing a full-time job in the state capitol, Dr. Swanson has served as township health officer, president and treasurer of the Rotary Club, president of the Board of Commerce, chairman of the Community Chest, Boy Scout and Y.M.C.A. executive council member, Tuscola County Defense Council chairman, and secretary and president of the Tuscola County Medical Society.

Born in Au Train, in Upper Peninsula, January 3, 1900, he worked as a water boy and timekeeper for the railroad and learned several languages, including Swedish, Danish, German, Polish, Italian, Norwegian, and "profanity," before he graduated from high school.

After graduating from Alma College in 1923, he went to Detroit and got a job in the woodworking shop of the Ford Motor Co. He soon obtained a transfer to the medical department and worked there three years. Then he was in a position to enter the Wayne State University College of Medicine.

During the next four years he worked in the medical department of the of the Dodge Brothers automobile plant while attending medical school. He got his M.D. in 1930 and interned at Receiving Hospital, Detroit, and then became house physician at Wyandotte (Mich.) General Hospital.

In April, 1932, Dr. Swanson moved to Vassar, in the Michigan Thumb District, to take over the practice of Dr. W. A. Wellmeyer, who was ill.

"The fields were green in that rich farm forming country, but there wasn't much green money around," says Dr. Swanson.

"I worked night and day, and during the first eight weeks my total cash income was $2. That was in the depth of the Great Depression, you know. Patients couldn't pay in money, but I did well in barter and was in no danger of starving."

"It was a community of wealthy farmers. Treat farmers right and they won"t let you down. Plenty of butter and quarters of beef came my way."

Tuscola County worked its way out of the Great Depression, and by 1940 Dr. Swanson was well enough off to go to New York for postgraduate education at Columbia University, New York Eye and Ear Hospital, and Mount Sinai Hospital.

"A physician," says Dr. Swanson, "has two main obligations to his community. He should serve not only as a physician but also accept his responsibility as a citizen."

So, in 1951, when the secretary of the Michigan State Medical Society telephoned to ask the Vassar family doctor to fill a vacancy for three months on the board, Dr. Swanson couldn't refuse.

As full-time executive secretary for the last seven years, Dr. Swanson has been zealous in his duties of law enforcement against quacks and charlatans but has been handicapped by lack of state financial support. His office is much more than self-supporting, but its goes into the State General Fund, and the work must depend on meager appropriations by the Legislature.

Officers and executive committee members of the federation meet with representatives of the American Medical Association, the Association of American Medical Colleges, and the Council on Medical Education and Hospitals to discuss licensure and educational problems.

Narrative for Ewald Conrad Swanson M. D.: Medical Tribune, 1963

Dr. Swanson's many professional affiliations include the A.M.A, the Michigan State Medical Society, Saginaw Academy of Ophthalmology and Otolaryngology, American Association of Railway Surgeons, Nu Sigma Nu Medical Fraternity, Saginaw Valley Mental Health Commission, and Wayne State University Library Commission.

Narrative for Ewald Conrad Swanson M. D.: Autobiography, 1985

The following autobiography was recorded by Ewald Swanson about 1985. The tape was digitally preserved by Mark Swanson and later transcribed by Michael Swanson.

I was born January 3rd, 1900 in a section house [railroad crew housing]. My father was a section foreman [person in charge of maintaining a 10 to 30 mile section of rail]. I was delivered by a midwife, Mrs. Zinker, who came to the house one month before I was born and she stayed one month after I was born. She performed the delivery. She charged $25 for the service.

I'll remember forever the first spanking I got from my mother. It was a very severe one. I was in the calling age and we had a large barrel out in the back with spring water in it. And the men put the fish in there when they would catch them from the streams. We had big speckled trout. I was ready to fall in the barrel [when] my mother caught me and give me a spanking and told me if I ever do that again she would give it twice as bad. I never went near that barrel again.

Three years later we moved to Newberry, Michigan, where my father was a section foreman in Newberry. When I was about ten years of age, my father accepted a position as extra gang foreman. We had our own engine and crew: an engineer, fireman, brakeman, and conductor. We traveled in boxcars in which the men slept in bunks. We also had a dining car and a dining van where tobacco and other utensils were sold. My brother, George, who was three years older than I was, was in charge of the van and sold tobacco, socks, shirts.-whatever men needed, we had in stock.

We were what they called the emergency crew. We had about ten men in the crew and we traveled from the Sault to Duluth. I remember once when we went Bitman [??], MN, when they had a washout and the men were fishing trout or sitting in the cars. The railroad was the Duluth, South Shore and Atlantic. And we had passes to go back to Newberry to school where we stayed with my father and mother. My father's nephew Andy Westin had come to America several years before he did and was running a large department store in Newberry where all the [campers? campus?] was supplied.

I went to school in Newberry - the Newberry Schools. We went home on weekends because we had passes and there were several trains running both ways on the Duluth South Shore in those days. Our family home consisted of a passenger car with four bedrooms, a toilet, a kitchen. The men slept in bunks over each other in the box car. My mother fed these crew members and took care of their bunks, but they washed their own cloths. During the summer months when we were out of school and attached to the train crew we made many friends in many towns up and down the road. We all loved the railroad; it was part of our life.

I remember one day when I was down at the depot down at Newberry, and the engine and the caboose alone were stationed in front of the depot getting some orders and I crawled up in the caboose, up in the cupola, and fell asleep. And my mother looked for me and they couldn't find me, and the caboose pulled out, and I went to home to where the boarding cars were. The brakeman finally found me up in the cupola sound asleep.

Before my father accepted the position of extra gang foreman we lived in a section house in Newberry which was located about two miles east of Newberry. We had a cow, a hay barn, chickens, and I had to take two quarts of milk in a pail on my way to school to Dr. Gibson's house. I remember that well. Dr. Gibson was a physician; his two sons are now practicing in Newberry, Michigan. When he left the extra gang, and came to Newberry, my folks bought a house at 309 John Street where we lived from then on.

While we were attending school, all three boys had jobs. My older brother worked in the Perry Engman [??] Pharmacy and became a pharmacist. My other brother, Albin, worked at Troy Litton [??] which was a clothing store on the corner. And I worked for John Vantell [??], a celery dealer. I used to get up in the morning at six o'clock and walk over to Vantell's farm which was about two miles from where we lived. And I had to take and haul this celery out of the pounds where it was kept for winter, take them over to the wash house, clean them, box them, and take them down to the depot where they were sent.

After I became older I worked for the Westin Store after school until eleven o'clock when the store would close. My job was to go around town, take grocery orders from homes, bring orders back before I went to school. I came back from school I would fill these grocery orders and deliver them.

I had an old black horse. I'll never forget him. We called him McGee. He was a very good horse.

We had a butcher in the store who was a very grouchy individual. And one day we got a phone call that I should deliver a twenty-five pound sack of sugar and a quart of oysters to the house. So I started out with me, the horse, we went to Fair's house. There I attempted to put the oysters on the table and the twenty-five pound sack of sugar. And the oysters slipped off, the sugar hit the pack of oysters, and the oysters flew all over the kitchen floor. I cleaned it up as best I could. I went back and bought another quart of oysters and brought it back to his house. Two

Narrative for Ewald Conrad Swanson M. D.: Autobiography, 1985

days later his wife says to me, "You left an oyster in the closet. You did a good job though." Art Fair, the husband, never knew what happened.

During the hunting season deers were very plentiful. One individual was allowed four deers per person per season. But my father used to go and get deer before season, and we hung them up in butcher shop at Westin's store. And those hunters who would come up from the Lower Peninsula and were unfortunate enough not to get any deer, my father sold his deer to them so they would have a deer to take home.

After graduating from high school, I went to Detroit, the war was on in 1918, and I worked at American Car and Foundry. They taught me how to run a lathe in two days. I did the finished turn on a ten-inch shell along with my friend Colbert Reisch [??] who recently died in Idaho. When he left home he and a barber named Bogart got a brand new Chevrolet and started out to see the world. He finally ended up in Las Vegas, Nevada, and he finally became postmaster in that town.

After being in Detroit for a few months, and had all kinds of money (I think they paid... I think it was six dollars an hour), help was scarce because everybody was in the service so I went home and I was going to join the United States Navy with my brother and some other boys. We had eighteen boys in the senior class; everyone was in the service. I had contracted influenza in Detroit when I came home. I was ill and unable to go with the boys to the Navy. I stayed in bed for about two weeks and then went up to the county clerk Parry Latonen [??] and told him I wanted to get in the service. So he swore me in (they could do that in those days). He put a band on my arm that said "USAF." I was taking a train and sitting in a seat when some woman came by and said "Isn't it a shame that that young boy has been drafted?" I was placed in the STU - the Student Naval Training Unit in Ann Arbor. Our company lived in the Chi Psi House, which is now taken over by the Law School [??]. And while I was there I contracted the flu again, and was in the university hospital for about four weeks. And next to me was Ernie Vick [??], from Toledo, who was an all-American center. They had no penicillin or sulfa in those days. All we got was aspirin and whiskey. [Inaudible] used to come and visit me almost every day and he brought a pint of whiskey strapped to his leg beneath his ballooning navy trousers never revealing what was beneath them. So I peddled the whiskey up and down the ward. There were thirteen in that room and none of us died. They were training us to be deck officers. At Michigan [??] Union they had a large swimming pool in the basement of the building and that is where the naval unit ate - that was their dining room. Ann Arbor was full of soldiers in training - soldiers and sailors and marines.

I had learned to roller skate in Newberry where we had a beautiful roller skating rink. So I went to Ann Arbor and the roller skating rink was the place for recreation for military personnel. So I spent many hours at the roller rink in Ann Arbor. The war ended November 11th, 1918, but we did not become released from the navy until late in December.

Albin and I went back to Newberry. He went to the University of Michigan; he graduated in dentistry. I went to Alma College, where a former superintendent of schools, Leslie Keflin [??], had arranged that all the Vassar [Newberry] boys - there were five of us -- would have jobs. My job was to work in the Tiffon Café first as a waiter, then I came to the Wright House, which was the hotel in Alma. My brother, George, who was a pharmacist, worked for Bruner Drug Store in Alma and made his money that way. I shoveled coal on at Alma College on Saturdays for my room, I got my meals by waiting tables at the Wright House. My oldest sister, Cecelia, went to Harper Hospital where she became a nurse. My youngest sister, Sigrid, went to Eastern Michigan University where she became a school teacher.

After graduating from the Detroit College of Medicine, I went to and had an internship at Detroit Receiving Hospital. I was the house physician at [inedible] General Hospital. I decided to open a practice. It was the start of the depression so I finally landed in Newberry with my sister and my brother. I remember distinctly coming out of the operating room into the waiting room and there was a drug salesman there. He said, "I've never seen you before. What can I sell you?" I said, "You can sell me a place to go to work." He said, "I think I can do it." He said, "There are two openings: one is in Muskogee and one is Vassar, Michigan." Well, when we went to college, we went home only twice: Christmas time and in the summer time. And I remembered Vassar being in a very fertile area, big farms, so I figured that if I would go to Vassar and get accepted, that is where I would go. So, my brother's wife and my wife left Newberry in the old Model A Ford we had, in 1929, which I bought for one hundred and seventy-five dollars in Detroit. We left for Vassar. We hit here on the first of April. Dr. Wellemeyer, who had a stroke, was in bed, was very gracious and wanted me to come there. His wife, Charlotte, acted as my nurse for several years. She had a beautiful alto voice. And she organized a quartet consisting of Dr. Renner [??], a German physician here who had a terrific bass voice, and she was an alto, and the banker's wife, Mrs. Dan Atkins, was the soprano, and I was the tenor because I had sung tenor in the Alma College choir and Alma College Glee Club for several years. We sang in most of the churches in Vassar on Sunday.

Narrative for Ewald Conrad Swanson M. D.: Autobiography, 1985

As I mentioned before, the Depression was in full swing. When I came here to Vassar, all banks were closed. Nobody had any money, nobody had a place to work, and I had to work night and day delivering babies because Dr. Wellemeyer was an obstetrician so I inherited that practice. I examined Dr. Wellemeyer and found that he had several bad [dead?] teeth so I called the local dentist, Dr. Ward Freelum [??], and he came down here and we took out all the bad teeth, and low and behold, in two weeks Dr. Wellemeyer was out of bed. He had no paralysis from his stroke. He must have had a cerebral hemorrhage of some kind without paralysis involvement.

When we first came here we left Shirley, our daughter, three years of age, at home with my father and mother in Newberry, and we lived in a small bedroom in the Wellemeyer home. One day I made a call to Mr. Rand Parks on East Street and he had a grapefruit grove in Texas and went away every winter. But this year he could not find anybody to take over his house. He told me, "I got this place for rent, all furnished for twenty-five dollars. Could you find a renter for me?" I said, "I think I could. You're looking at him right now." So we moved into Park's house on East Street where we lived for several years until Dr. Wellemeyer died, and then I bought his house -- an office-house combination.

Lewis Walton was sent here during the bank holidays. He had previously organized a Rotary Club in Ferndale and he thought Vassar should have one, and he organized one. It had about twenty members besides the four officers. In 1938, I was elected as president of the Rotary Club. During the year I was president of the Rotary Club we sponsored a club in Chesaning, Frankenmuth, and Pigeon. During my term in office we got the International President's Award for having a perfect attendance for every member of the club for one entire year. In December we had one of our members who broke a leg, and I took him to Saginaw General and fixed his leg, concerned about our attendance because we had had such a perfect attendance up to that time. Well, Mr. Perry Johnson, a local undertaker and ambulance driver said, "That's no question Doc, I'll take care of that." So he took his ambulance and went to Saginaw, brought Rudy Hiltener [??] back here and we wheeled him in the Rotary Club so he was present. After the meeting we took him back. We had a perfect attendance.

While I was president of the Rotary Club I wanted Rotary Club to sponsor Cub Scouts. After, I invited the secretary of the scout office in Saginaw to come down to the Rotary every Tuesday to meet in our club as my guest. And I introduced him every time and the third time the club finally decided they would sponsor Cub Scouts. We had sixty Cub Scouts which consisted of ten dens and Lloyd Miller, the local coach, was the scoutmaster and he was a dandy. Each of the scouts had fronted every parade including the band. So they led all parades for the last several years.

I served on the Saginaw Valley Trails Council because I was interested in Boy Scouts. And I picked out four of the scouts -- Paul Haines, Fred Atkins, Don Schmidt, and my son Richard - and I was determined to make four Eagles out of them. So I hauled the to Saginaw to get the swimming badges, I went to Camp Rotary which Saginaw Rotary Club sponsored for the scouts, I took them all over. All of them but Paul Haines became Eagles. He had other interests and he refused to come to the meetings. I contacted the Detroit Times, Detroit News, Detroit Free Press, and told them that we were going to have a grand opening [ceremony] for three Eagle Scouts. And they told me they never heard of three eagle scouts in a town this size, but all the reporters came. We got state publicity and everyone enjoyed it.

My mother died because of cancer of the stomach. I remember we all went down to Ann Arbor with her and Dr. Collard [??] did a total gastrectomy and that means removal of the entire stomach. But she died anyway after coming home for a while in Newberry. So she is buried in Newberry, Michigan.

I remember once we had a terrible flood in Vassar, water six feet deep on the main street, up into buildings. And how was I going to get across the river to take care of my patients? Finally the city established a rowboat with a man there so I could be transported to the other side of the river.

In 1949, which was the hundredth year anniversary for the city of Vassar we decided to have a centennial. Well, the centennial lasted for an entire week. We had farmers' day, children's day, peoples day, and the last day was church day. I was co-chairman with Mayor Priestly for this event and I had a lot of fun. A few days before our centennial, they had a centennial in Port Huron. I took the mayor with me and we went down to the Elks Club in Port Huron and I was told I could get information there. They told me they had four floats available for one hundred dollars apiece, and would take them up here with a Jeep and run them through the parade. I bought the four floats, including the queen's float, which was sixty feet long and it was beautiful. M15 was the way north in those days; there was no 75, so all the traffic came through Vassar going north from Detroit. So I placed a sign outside city limits that said "You are welcome to attend our centennial -- free." So we had so many people coming in here that it was difficult to control the traffic and the state police came down here and had to reroute them around.

My mother's sister Jenny and her father, Karl Spångberg, were coming to America. There were relatives she had

Narrative for Ewald Conrad Swanson M. D.: Autobiography, 1985

here who furnished money for her transportation. They landed in Montreal and from there they went to the Canadian Sault, and then across to the American Sault, and my father and George (my oldest brother) were supposed to meet them in Sault, but they refused to have anything to do with them when they saw them. They didn't believe that they were related [??] to his daughter and grandson. So after talking with him for a long time my father finally pulled a picture of his wife out - that solved the trick and they accepted them. So they brought them to Newberry, and they lived with us for many years.

After my brother George had attended college at Alma for two years, which was a requirement to enter medical school, he went to Detroit, and roomed with Carl Doggand [??], who also became a physician. After graduating from the Detroit College of Medicine, he went to Missoula, Montana, where he took his internship and surgical residency. While he attended Detroit College of Medicine, being a pharmacist, he was employed by St. Joseph Mercy Hospital, on Milwaukee Avenue. They did not have a pharmacist's license, because they were not big enough to afford one, so they used my brother's license as a pharmacist so the hospital could operate within the law. He spent four years here doing surgery before he even graduated from high school [medical school]. So he went to Missoula, and he went for the Northern Pacific Railroad, and he had terrific training in surgery with Dr. Bond [??] and [inaudible] had a small hospital over the drugstore where patients were taken in case of emergency. Surgical cases were no longer sent to the Sault and Marquette as my brother was able to do the surgery for the people in Newberry. The War Manpower Commission had refused to let him join the service in the First World War because he was a pharmacist and he was needed. There was just dearth of doctors so he filled in and did many things that a physician should do at that time. During World War II he went into the army, the reserves, and when the war broke out he was already on his way to New Caledonia in Australia. I remember him telling me that he and three other surgeons from the army were flown to Bougainville because the tremendous amount of casualties and he operated on Marines right on the beach. After the war he was no longer able to return to practice so he stayed n the army. He was in charge of the Marigold and other boats which transferred the wounded from Europe and the South Pacific to America and England. After leaving the army he joined the Veterans Association and became superintendent of several hospitals in Montana and West Virginia. His final assignment was in Philadelphia where he helped construct the hospital. I visited him several times in Philadelphia. When he left the service, he moved to Armada, Michigan, where he bought five acres of land outside of town and built a beautiful home there. The reason he went to Armada was that his wife's sister lived across the road. When he died the American Legion, the army, transferred his body to Washington, D.C. He is now buried in Arlington cemetery and is a full colonel.

My other brother, Albin, after practicing dentistry in Newberry for a long time, finally retired and went to Menomonee, Michigan, where his son lived who is also a dentist. His son is still practicing in Menomonee, Michigan. He's buried in a cemetery in Menomonee.

My sister, Cecelia, went to Harper Hospital to become a nurse, married Dr. Hayden Palmer of Pontiac - an ophthalmologist -- and they had three children, only one of which is living. Their son was a physician, he served in the Navy, and he was injured when in the navy and died. He was stationed at Bethesda, Maryland. [Inaudible] that time he'd been sent all over as a physician for the Navy in Europe and the South Pacific. Their youngest daughter, Sally, still alive, has two children. One is going to Albion College at the present time and the other one is going to college in Florida. She lives in Birmingham, Michigan. Her mother, Cecelia, also lives in Birmingham, Michigan. Sally married John Rogers, an attorney, in Pontiac. They are now divorced.

My younger sister Sigrid, after teaching school for many years, married Arthur Holmberg, the son of a Lutheran minister in Newberry. They had two children: Paul and Joanne. Paul is now the track coach at the high school in Lavonia. Joanne married Dr. Pollack who is a plastic surgeon. They lived in New Orleans, Louisiana, for several years and had three boys. The oldest son of theirs is at the present time, an exchange student in Germany; Elie is attending Michigan State University. Two other boys are still in high school, Brian and Blake. Joanne, Sigrid's daughter, after getting a divorce moved to Rochester, Michigan, and she is now employed by the Stanley Corporation and has an excellent job. Sigrid died a few years ago in Cass City and was buried in a cemetery there. She taught school in Cass city for several years. Her husband was the principal in high school for many years and is still living in Cass City.

Narrative for Ewald Conrad Swanson M. D.: Senate Resolution 39, 1967

Michigan State Senators Beadle and O'Brien offered the following concurrent resolution in 1967:

Michigan State Senate Concurrent Resolution No. 39 [1967]

A concurrent resolution of tribute to Ewald C. Swanson, M.D., of Vassar, Michigan.

Whereas, Dr. Ewald C. Swanson, Executive Secretary of the Michigan State Board of Registration in Medicine since 1956, retires March 17, 1967. As Vice President in 1954-55 and member in 1951-60, Dr. Swanson closes a distinguished career with the Board of sixteen years; and

Whereas, One Of his notable contributions was the program which he formulated and was implemented in Michigan in 1956-58 to determine the medical competence of graduates of foreign medical schools. The American Medical Association adopted his program in 1959, designated it The Educational Council for Foreign Medical Graduates, and gives examinations in twenty-one countries abroad and at thirty-three sites in the United States; and

Whereas, Born January 3, 1900 in Au Train, Michigan, Dr. Swanson was educated the Newberry public schools, at Alma College, and graduated in 1930 from the Wayne State University College of Medicine. He served at Wyondotte General Hospital, and in 1932 opened a general practice at Vassar. His postgraduate work was taken at Columbia University, 1940; New York Eye and Ear Hospital, 1941; and Mount Sinai Hospital, New York City, in 1942; and

Whereas, Dr. Swanson was president of the Federation of State Medical Boards of the United States in 1963-64 and a member of its Executive Committee for five years from 1958 to 1963. He served on the Ethics Committee of the Michigan State Medical Society; as president of the Tuscola County Medical Society; and was a member of the Wayne State University Study Commission, the Blue Cross-Blue Shield Commission and the Wayne State University Medical College Library Commission. He is a charter member of the Saginaw Valley Mental Health Commission and is affiliated with several associations of surgeons of the major railways and of numerous medical societies of the Nation, State and other areas; and

Whereas, Dr. Swanson's civic service includes membership on the Executive Councils of the Saginaw Valley Trails Boy Scents and of the Bay City YMCA Camp Iroquois; chairmanship of the Community Chest and presidency of the Board of Commerce-both at Vassar; now therefore be it

Resolved by the Senate (the House of Representatives concurring) that by these presents a tribute of esteem is accorded to Ewald C. Swanson, M.D., whose more than thirty-five years' professional, civic and State services firmly advanced the reputation of Michigan medicine, for his lifetime of devotion in fostering the careers of young medical aspirants; and for his abiding humanitarian influence in Michigan society; and be it further

Resolved, That copies of this resolution be presented to Dr. Swanson and to the Michigan State Board of Registration in Medicine, that there may be suitable record of the esteem of The Michigan Legislature.

Narrative for Carl Fredrik Spangberg: Excepts from Stream of Time

Ewald Swanson and August Spångberg shared a grandfather, Carl Fredrik Spangberg. The following two chapters of August Spångberg's autobiography, *The Stream of Time* (1966), describes Carl Fredrik Spangberg's life in Sweden and his emigration.

"Childhood"

Deep in the forest, a considerable distance from the highway, between the Rockesholm and Stadra estates, lay the little tenant farm of Lämtjärnsfallet, with its tiny patches of plowed ground.

My grandfather, Karl Fredrik Spangberg, had lived on this tenant farm for many years when, in 1898, he moved to a one room apartment in the neighboring village of Skärhyttan. His wife, Kristina Elisabet, had died in the year 1891.

On the little farm at Lämtjärnsfallet he had labored, cultivated and improved the soil, just as did all the tenant farmers in order to gain a bigger and better crop for his family's livelihood.

Huge piles of stone, raised up like giant monuments, lay near one another in the fields, as mute evidence of the diligence and labor that had been required to wrest each inch of tillable soil from the stone bound earth.

A short distance from the little farm lay the lake Lämtjämen, its shores covered with moss and mire. It was a poor playground for children. My cousin Harold -- he was a year older than I -- was thoroughly afraid of the lake, as was I. We had been told that it was the home of ghosts, and we believed it.

According to the folk tales, there dwelt an evil spirit near the lake. It was, so we were told, the spirit of a child, born, dead and buried in secret. Its soul, the story held, cried out for burial in consecrated soil.

Nor was it safe in the forest. It was best not to wander beyond sight of the cottage, especially when alone. Stories were told of mysterious bobbing lights, cows milked by strange hands, and children who had vanished without a trace. It was indeed fascinating to hear the older people tell tales about strange lights, trolls, and spooks, but it was also a frightening experience, which stayed with one through the years.

The forest was rich in wildlife; there were many kinds of birds, even elk and rabbits. One learned early in life to know the names of the birds. Late in March the lark came and each year the swallows made their nests under the eaves of the cottage. When they arrived, one knew that summer had at last come.

It was a hard life the tenant farmer led, with the combined work for the landlord and on his own little soil. Farm implements were poor. After a long day's work for the landlord, there was a great distance back to the cottage and one was tired indeed.

Wages were small and one was almost always in debt to the landlord. Food was given to the tenants one day a week and charged to their account.

The owner decided pretty well what the tenant was to do. Work went on, summer and winter. Holidays were few. Actually, the only free time was on Sunday.

Grandfather's job was to cut logs to supply 5 or 6 charcoal kilns, which was in itself a real task. Later, the kilns had to be prepared and fired. During the winter, the charcoal was hauled a mile or more to the iron furnace, It was necessary to get up real early in order to get back in time to re-load the supply of logs for the next day's trip. The children helped both at home and in the woods, and worked for the landlord too, when they were a bit older. The working day was a long one, usually twelve hours. Sometimes, if the landlord agreed, it might be cut an hour or two. In the woods, pay was by the amount of work done rather than by the hour, so that one worked a longer day to increase the wages.

When the children grew up, they usually left home and went out on their own. While this helped by decreasing the number of mouths to feed, it also cut the labor force which negated the small financial gain.

Our entire region, with its villages and tenant farms, its cottages and mines, belonged to the Stadra company, a family organization owned by the Carlssons, and was considered one of the area's little absolute monarchies. At the turn of the century, Stadra was ruled over by the elder Carlsson and his young nephew, whose name was Eberhard. The older Carlsson was always referred to as "Lord Carlsson" while the younger's title was "Mr. Carlsson." I can't remember how old I was before I learned that either had a first name.

The landlords decided arbitrarily all matters of wages, working hours, rents, and even what the future of the tenant's children should be. Occasionally, some of the children were offered an opportunity to go to school or learn a trade. Thus, my aunt Karin, who had shown herself to be talented and ambitious in grade school, was trained as a teacher.

The landlords owned also a slate quarry near Grythyttan, which employed some men. In addition to work at the quarry, some were sent out to various parts of the country to lay slate roofs. These workers received rather good wages, and had a chance to get out and see more of the country. It was a job worth striving for and provided a trade

Narrative for Carl Fredrik Spangberg: Excepts from Stream of Time

that was always in demand.

My mother, Anna Lovisa, born 1870, followed her husband, Anders Gustav Olsson, my stepfather, as he went from place to place in his work.

My mother had earlier been betrothed to a miller's son, August Carlsson, who was my father.

Mother related to me now they both awaited my arrival. On the 28th of March, the year 1893, there was a severe storm, with a heavy snowfall. Mother had to visit a neighboring farm and the walk through the deep snow was cold and strenuous. The drifts had piled more than a meter in height.

The next day, I was born, tiny and weak, fully a month premature.

My father sought more dependable pay and moved to America. He was a powerful man, regarded as the strongest along his fellow workers.

In America, he failed to find the luck he sought. He was injured on the job by heavy lifting and suffered from the results the rest of his life. I know nothing further about him, since my parents lost communication with each other and I went to live with my grandfather. My grandmother, as previously related, had died some years before my birth.

Hereafter, my stepfather became my father. For years, it was strange to accept him as my father but in later life we were united as a family, as I shall tell later on.

I can remember when grandfather sold his old horse and bought a new one. A horse was no doubt the tenant farmer's most important possession. The trade of horses of course increased grandfather's debt to the landlord. But the new horse was fast and strong. He pulled larger loads, both in the woods and on the roads. He was, however, easily frightened and shied away at a fluttering paper, a gun shot or a clap of thunder. One had to treat him carefully and handle him firmly lest he become a runaway horse. Nevertheless, he was a fine animal and worked hard for us.

Sundays were intended to be days of rest. The stables and yards could be cleared and the chores done in an hour or two. Then the day was to be free from labor. "Remember the Sabbath Day to keep it holy," was a good rule, especially for those who worked so hard the other six days. Only the most urgent work was to be done on Sunday.

The Sabbath was always kept in one way or another. The nearest church, in Rockesholm, was more than a half mile and we did not go there too often. Instead, the day's text was read from Martin Luther's meditation.

At home, grandfather read the lesson; he had a pleasant voice and read well. Sometimes, a younger member of the family was asked to read a part, an honor that was usually not welcomed by the children. During the reading, everyone must be quiet for the reading which was in place of service at the church. Grandfather was particular about such things and Sunday worship, whether at home or at church, was not to be neglected. I have a vivid memory of the reading of the Sunday meditation both by grandfather and by my uncle at Björnbo.

Sundays were also times for visiting among neighbors and relatives. These were times for special treats, such as white bread with our coffee. They were holiday hours which left deep impressions in one's memory of a life which otherwise held so much of labor and of care.

One pleasant summer Sunday stands out among the others. The work at home had been done. The cows had been pastured and the horse, Gralle, had been tethered near the little rise that lay beside the path leading to our neighboring farm, Björnbo. Just then, two boys came down the path. Mother's younger sisters watched at the window with interest. Surely the boys were not coming over to a join in the reading of the morning text!

But then everyone looked at the horse. Grandfather rushed from the house for Gralle had been frightened and began to run at full speed. What if he tripped on the tether rope and fell? Could grandfather reach him in time? We all kept hoping for the best but it was not to be. Down he went! Perhaps he was still unhurt. He lay motionless and in a moment we were all beside him. Grandfather looked carefully into his eyes but there were no signs of life. In falling, he had struck his forehead against a large stone. A few gray hairs on the rock showed where he had fallen. Now we no longer had a horse.

A great loss it was. Horsemeat one could not eat. The hide and a bit of oil were all that could be reclaimed.

Just how the loss was to be made up, we did not know. All we knew was that he was gone and there was no money to buy another. Grandfather had lost his work partner and helper.

Perhaps there was a way out. Grandfather would talk to the landlord. Perhaps something could be arranged.

Little boys often dwell in a world of their own. And so it was that I grieved alone for my friend, Gralle, and often went to the stone to gaze at the spot where his forehead had struck. To my childish way of thinking, it was all so unbelievable and difficult to comprehend. I began to realize how much even an animal friend could mean to my life.

Grandfather did talk to the landlord. He thought perhaps a horse could be loaned temporarily from the big stable. Then, grandfather was still not so old but that he might manage to buy another.

But grandfather thought differently. The farm was so small and his chances of paying for a new horse so slim that he decided as a result of his loss to move to the nearby village of Skärhyttan.

Narrative for Carl Fredrik Spangberg: Excepts from Stream of Time

Moving seemed to me an adventure, especially when it meant going from the tiny cottage in the woods to the village.

Skärhyttan consisted of four buildings with accommodations for six families. The largest house was called "Östergården" and was planned for three families. Therefore, one half the village's inhabitants lived there. Into the "west room" of this building we then moved.

Now, our life changed considerably. Imagine leaving the loneliness of the wood's cottage to share a home with two other families! To be able to see and talk daily with others than your own family! This was like coming into a new world!

We found our new surroundings pleasant. We got along well with our neighbors and life took on a new meaning.

The village had, as the name indicated, once had an iron furnace. It had been in operation as early as 1671. Ore was taken from nearby mines. But in 1786 the operation had been combined with furnaces at Greksåsar and the furnace at Skärhyttan was demolished. The remains of it were still visible and the area is well supplied with mines.

One of these, the Blanka mine, was still being worked in 1905. From this old mine, with its discarded shards from previous work, ore was being taken during my childhood and paid for at the rate of 50 cents a measure -- a large square box -- which was to be filled with prime ore.

I had a try at the ore workings for a while. My best output was only one measure a week. The work was slow, hard on clothing and shoes, and I soon had enough of it.

It was better working in the woods. During school vacations, even ten year old boys could begin work in the woods and for us it was almost like fun,

Even a young child could find many things with which to help in the woods and it was a pleasant job. Cutting the brush, felling the trees, was a job that showed some progress for one's effort. Work and pleasure were combined.

A pile of wood a meter high brought 7 cents. A strong and ambitious cutter could clear twenty or thirty piles a day. This brought between 1.5 and 2 kronor in pay. It was not easy work and often one had to walk a half mile or more each way to the job.   The children didn't earn a lot but every little bit helped. A few days' wages added a bit to the flour or other supplies that one might get when the day came to get monthly supplies. A little cash helped the family. Sometimes it even brought a bit of spending money for us. Besides, it taught us the importance of working for our support.

Everyone was supposed to earn something toward his keep. I was supposed to cut 3 piles of wood a week. Whatever I managed above that, I was given 5 cents per pile. The extra money served as a challenge to greater effort and provided a bit of money in my pocket.

I remember once having earned a total of 25 cents of my own. For some time I had wished for a cap pistol. It would be fun to have one but there were other things, too. School would soon begin and a pencil-box might be better, or a pocket knife. These also cost 25 cents. It was a difficult choice. Perhaps best of all would be to keep the money and let the other children know that I could buy whatever I chose.

Just what I finally bought, I do not remember, but I know I kept the money a long time before I decided.

Toys and playthings were almost unknown in our stores. Most such things were home made. Skis were fashioned from barrel staves or from birch wood. Sleds were made by the older men and both were commonly used by the children. I remember that young people from the area would gather at the lake during the winter for these pastimes. During the summer, fishing was a favorite pastime. This brought not only fun but also added food. Perch and other fish were welcome additions to a simple diet.

In grandfather's home grace was said before and after meals. We were careless about this at times, but not in his presence.

The children brought in water, cut and hauled in the wood, and ran errands to the store, as early as they were able.

Our nearest store, at Rockesholm, was a half mile distant. To go there shopping was a real treat. There was so much to see. Sometimes there remained a few cents to spend. The storekeeper might even throw in a candy or two. I would usually use my money to buy ginger cookies, which were large and filling. Sometimes a little contest was waged to see who could eat the most cookies. The loser paid for all of them. Usually, however, this was too costly a game for children to play.

The grown-ups, of course, could afford other pleasures. Some smoked a pipe and used snuff. Others got drunk at times. I always disliked liquor but thought tobacco might be fun.

One day I used my money to buy some snuff. Taking it to the woods, I sat down in a clearing to try it. It did not take long before the results were evident. Everything began to go in circles. Both my head and my stomach objected.

Narrative for Carl Fredrik Spangberg: Excepts from Stream of Time

It was an experience I was not soon to forget. For a long time thereafter, I determined to let the grown-ups enjoy their own pleasures.

Usually, I find it difficult to discard things but it did not take me long to throw away the snuff and I kept my little adventure a secret for a long time.

Children in the forest homes learned early in life to handle fire. An open fire was always a necessity when one stopped for a meal while working in the woods. Waste piles of wood were also burned in the spring. In school, too, we took turns keeping a fire in the stove. Making a fire and using matches were, therefore, not strange to us.

One Sunday, when three of us boys were about 9 to10 years of age, someone had the idea to start a fire in the woods. But this time, luck was not with us. The fire spread in the brush. Beating it with sticks failed to put it out and soon the blaze spread to the trees. What would happen? Where should we go? To avoid suspicion, we ran to the other side of the village and returned. We kept hoping the fire would burn itself out.

But the fire spread to the woods. Smoke and flame rose to the sky. People came running from all directions. No one blamed us. The fire was put out by older men who came from the village.

The next day it became known who had set the fire. An older brother of one of us had been on the lake and had seen it all. No longer need we try to keep it a secret. But we were not punished. But some time later, while I was working in the woods, Mr. Carlsson drove by in a horse and buggy. He stopped beside me. I became very frightened. "Well," he said, "So you are one of those who started the fire." I said nothing. "We'll let it go this time," he said, "but it better not happen again or you may land in the reform school."

The fire was not really my idea, nor had I started it. But I felt equally to blame and none of us sought to blame the other.

Naturally, we got into a bit of mischief occasionally. However, it was only in fun and never intentionally to cause anyone harm.

Writing on the windows, carving our names on a tree along the way to school, or perhaps taking an apple or two from an orchard -- these little pranks were fairly common and regarded generally as rather harmless little adventures.

"Grandpa travels to America"

It was no fun getting old at the time. My grandfather [Karl Spångberg] turned sixty on 19 Feb. 1904.

Soon his energy was not sufficient for the hard forest work. How would he decide where to live out his old age? Relatives did not want him to go to the poorhouse when he could not work anymore. The children living in Sweden could not easily arrange for him in their homes. Then came the idea of America. Many relatives had emigrated earlier. There he had a brother, Eric, and there were three children -- Clara, Alma and Leontin -- who had moved. Alma had died of typhoid fever and Leontin was sickly. But Klara, his eldest daughter, had a good home. Her husband Mick Swanson was a foreman at Milwaukbanan and lives in Newberry, Michigan. Klara was obviously a talented woman with will and power. She wrote back to Sweden regularly. She had sent tickets to two siblings and helped them to America. Many dollars were also sent and she really wanted to take her old father in his old age.

Grandpa was thinking about how it would happen. Soon, Jenny, the youngest girl, left home. His savings were exhausted and that could mean the poorhouse. Surely it was obvious to think of leaving Sweden for security, to escape poverty in his old age in another continent. But in a few years it could well be different. You have to think twice. You could not decide something like that at once.

Finally it was decided that my grandfather and Jenny were to leave. I might come later. But first I have to finish school and have a reading test with the priest. I was only 12 years old. It was too early for me to travel and leaving was not appropriate.

My home would be turned inside out. I would often sit and watch my grandfather so that I could remember him. Often I cried by myself. No one saw it. "Oh no, everything would go well." They said, "All would be well. It is probably good for you, too, you'll see. You will be kind and obedient and working and doing the best you can, so it is enough. Life has been good for others, why should it not go well for you?"

When on Sundays the family came to visit, as usual, they talked mostly about America and family there. Everyone in the region had close relatives out there.

I remember when we planed shingles at a plant in Greksåsar. It lay close to a mile from home. Here, the company had a house with a worker's room. In the same house lived an old mill man, who sometimes used to come to us and talked in the evenings. These chats would end when my grandfather leaves for America.

"We meet no more while we live. We will probably meet in heaven someday. You will see that we will probably

Narrative for Carl Fredrik Spangberg: Excepts from Stream of Time

recognize each other." So reasoned the two old friends.

The time before the trip to America was difficult for me, too. Where would I get to go? The foster father, who, because of his profession, moved and changed his residence often, was not appropriate for me before the last school term was over. Also, it would be one term into middle school.

It was agreed to give me away to a croft, Smällfallet, which was run by three siblings and become like "kids in the house."

My mother thought that we could agree to this but -- what was said in confidence between us -- as soon as the opportunity arose, that I would leave Smällfallet and come home so we could be together.

The trip to America was planned. Karl Andersson, one of our neighbors, made a chest, painted it brown and wrote with large white letters on the cover: "Karl Fredrik Spångberg Po Newberry Luce Co Mich. Nordamerika".

When my wife and I in the summer of 1955 visited America I saw the chest which was left with my cousin Albin Swanson, a dentist in the town of Newberry.

The furniture and household utensils -- there was not much -- were sold by private contract. Someone bought the cow and two sheep. I seem to remember that the debt to the company dropped to 20 kronor.

Then tickets to a boat on the Cunard Line arrived. And one day in early March, we waved goodbye to Grandpa and Jenny at the railway station in Rockesholm.

I do not know how poverty-assistance chairman Ekestubbe in Nora was informed of my being given away. And it was thought that he oversaw such matters. Perhaps it was his intervention that made it right. Children could go to the poorhouse, but there was never any possibility of this for me, as the poverty-assistance chairman was considered as some kind of guardian.

My father thought that now I should choose myself. There would be some poverty-assistance or guardianship from that quarter.

So, no more worries. I came home and lived with my two siblings, Sten, five, and Linnea, two years.

We moved to Järnboås, where my father received an order for a few tombstones. I got help with the work, blasting, drilling, chiseling and grinding, and all that belonged to the work of gravestone cutters.

Chapter 2. Ancestor Report for Mårten Mårtensson Storkarhu

First Generation

1. Mårten Mårtensson Storkarhu,[1] son of **Mårten Mårtensson Storkarhu** and **Margareta Carlsdotter Finnas,** was born on 15 Mar 1788 in Rejpelt, Vörå, Finland,[1] was christened on 16 Mar 1788,[2] died on 13 Oct 1828 in Rejpelt, Vörå, Finland[1] at age 40, and was buried on 19 Oct 1828.[2] Another name for Mårten was Mårten Mårtensson Nykarhu d.yngre.[2]

General Notes: a bonde (farm owner) and later a crofter (farm renter) on No. 3 Storkarhu. [1]

Research Notes: The Storkarhu farm was given the name Svens in the mid-1800s. The farm was briefly referred to as Nykarhu and Björns in church records. [1]

Noted events in his life were:
• Occupation: bonde (farm owner) at Storkarhu, 1811-1825, Rejpelt, Vörå, Finland. [2]

Mårten married **Lisa Samuelsdotter Miemois,**[3] daughter of **Samuel Mattsson Keskis** and **Lisa Sunedotter Israels,** on 30 Nov 1810 in Vörå, Finland. [1]

Children from this marriage were:

    i.   **Mårten Mårtensson Storkarhu**[3] was born on 3 Feb 1811 in Rejpelt, Vörå, Finland,[3] was christened on 5 Feb 1811,[2] died on 13 Nov 1828 in Rejpelt, Vörå, Finland[3] at age 17, and was buried on 16 Nov 1828.[2]

    ii.   **Greta Mårtensdotter Storkarhu**[2] was born on 7 Mar 1813 in Rejpelt, Vörå, Finland,[2] was christened on 9 Mar 1813,[2] died on 4 Jul 1813,[2] and was buried on 11 Jul 1813.[2]

    iii.   **Johan Mårtensson Storkarhu**[3] was born on 16 Jun 1815 in Rejpelt, Vörå, Finland,[3] was christened on 18 Jun 1815,[2] and died on 1 Dec 1888 in Finland[1] at age 73. Another name for Johan was Johan Mårtensson Nyberg. Johan married **Maria Mattsdotter Kjerp**[1] on 12 Jul 1835.

    iv.   **Lisa Mårtensdotter Storkarhu**[2] was born on 9 Aug 1817 in Rejpelt, Vörå, Finland,[2] was christened on 10 Aug 1817,[2] and died after 1850.[2] Another name for Lisa was Lisa Mårtensdotter Svens.[2] Lisa married **Jakob Mattsson Höijer**[2] on 21 Dec 1836.[2]

    v.   **Anna Beata Mårtensdotter Storkarhu**[3] was born on 25 Aug 1818 in Rejpelt, Vörå, Finland[3] and was christened on 30 Aug 1818.[2] Anna married **Mårten Mårtensson Klemets**[2] on 10 Jul 1835.[2]

    vi.   **Lisa Mårtensdotter Storkarhu**[2] was born on 23 Sep 1821 in Rejpelt, Vörå, Finland[2] and was christened on 24 Sep 1821.[2] Lisa married **Erik Eriksson Kaurajärvi**[2] on 16 Jan 1848.[2]

    vii.   **Greta Lisa Mårtensdotter Storkarhu**[3] was born on 2 Mar 1823 in Rejpelt, Vörå, Finland,[3] was christened on 3 Mar 1823,[2] and died on 12 Dec 1887 in Andiala, Vörå, Finland[1] at age 64. Another name for Greta was Greta Lisa Mårtensdotter Svens. Greta married **Erik Johansson Nyby**[1] on 28 Jun 1845.

    viii.   **Maria Mårtensdotter Storkarhu**[1] was born on 9 Apr 1824 in Rejpelt, Vörå, Finland,[3] was christened on 11 Apr 1824,[2] and died on 1 Aug 1855 in Finland[1] at age 31. Maria married someone.

    ix.   **Mickel Mårtensson Storkarhu**[2] was born on 30 Sep 1825 in Rejpelt, Vörå, Finland,[2] was christened on 2 Oct 1825,[2] died on 21 Apr 1826,[2] and was buried on 30 Apr 1826.[2]

    x.   **Brita Mårtensdotter Storkarhu**[3] was born on 26 Jul 1827 in Rejpelt, Vörå, Finland,[3] was christened on 29 Jul 1827,[2] and died on 26 Feb 1902 in Rejpelt, Vörå, Finland[1] at age 74. Brita married **Simon Mattsson Wäst**.[1]

    xi.   **Mickel Mårtensson Storkarhu**[1] was born on 15 Sep 1828 in Rejpelt, Vörå, Finland[1] and died on 16 May 1903 in Newberry, Luce, Michigan[1] at age 74. Other names for Mickel were Mickel Mårtensson Svens, Mickel Svens, and Michael Swanson. Mickel married **Lisa Johansdotter Wäst,**[3] daughter of **Johan Eriksson Wäst** and **Lisa Johansdotter Wäst,** on 8 Jul 1852 in Rejpelt, Vörå, Finland. [1]

1. Torbjörn Nikus, Storkarhu (unpublish document, 2008).
2. Hiski database (http://hiski.genealogia.fi).
3. Torbjörn Nikus, Storkarhu (unpublish document, 2008). .... Hiski database (http://hiski.genealogia.fi).

Ancestor Report for Mårten Mårtensson Storkarhu

Second Generation

2. Mårten Mårtensson Storkarhu,[1] son of **Mårten Thomasson Storkarhu** and **Karin Carlsdotter Jänt,** was born on 22 Nov 1760 in Rejpelt, Vörå, Finland,[1] was christened on 23 Nov 1760,[2] died on 27 Sep 1828 in Rejpelt, Vörå, Finland[1] at age 67, and was buried on 5 Oct 1828.[2] Other names for Mårten were Mårten Mårtensson Den Yngre, Mårten Mårtensson Nykarhu, and Mårten Mårtensson d. Ädre.

General Notes: A saltpeter maker and a bonde on Storkarhu (farm no. 3). After farming at Heikius farm, he returned to Storkarhu around 1787. He and his son, Anders, died the same day of nervfeber (typhoid fever). His son Mårten and his grandson of the same name died a few weeks later.[3]

Noted events in his life were:
- Occupation: gunpowder maker, 1783, Rejpelt, Vörå, Finland.[2]

- Occupation: bonde (farm owner) at Storkarhu/Nykarhu.[2]

Mårten married **Margareta Carlsdotter Finnas**[1] on 13 Dec 1782 in Vörå, Finland.[3]

Children from this marriage were:

i. **Margeta Mårtensdotter Storkaru**[1] was born on 20 Oct 1783 in Rejpelt, Vörå, Finland[1] and was christened on 2 Nov 1783.[2] Margeta married **Mickel Mårtensson Storkarhu**[2] on 20 Jan 1809 in Vörå, Finland.[2]

ii. **Maria Mårtensdotter Heikius**[1] was born on 1 Sep 1785 in Kaitsor, Vörå, Finland,[1] was christened on 4 Sep 1785,[2] and died on 3 May 1858 in Karleby, Finland[3] at age 72. Another name for Maria was Maria Mårtensdotter Keldo. Maria married **Matts Mickelsson Källström**[3] on 29 Oct 1809 in Karleby, Finland.[3]

1   iii. **Mårten Mårtensson Storkarhu**.[3] Mårten married **Lisa Samuelsdotter Miemois**,[1] daughter of **Samuel Mattsson Keskis** and **Lisa Sunedotter Israels,** on 30 Nov 1810 in Vörå, Finland.[3]

iv. **Karl Mårtensson Storkarhu**[3] was born on 24 Dec 1789 in Rejpelt, Vörå, Finland[3] and was christened on 24 Dec 1789.[2] Another name for Karl was Karl Mårtensson Lillkarhu. Karl married **Beata Eriksdotter Kulp**[3] on 20 Jun 1816.[3]

v. **Erik Mårtensson Storkarhu**[2] was born on 4 Oct 1792 in Rejpelt, Vörå, Finland[2] and was christened on 7 Oct 1792.[2] Erik married **Beata Johansdotter Ehrs**[3] on 24 Jun 1814 in Vörå, Finland.[1]

vi. **Anna Mårtensdotter Storkarhu**[2] was born on 6 Jan 1795 in Rejpelt, Vörå, Finland[2] and was christened on 6 Jan 1795.[2]

vii. **Anders Mårtensson Storkarhu**[1] was born on 5 Nov 1797 in Rejpelt, Vörå, Finland,[1] was christened on 7 Nov 1797,[2] died on 27 Sep 1828 in Rejpelt, Vörå, Finland[1] at age 30, and was buried on 5 Oct 1828.[2] Anders married **Anna Eriksdotter Knuts** on 1 Jul 1823.[3]

viii. **Johan Mårtensson Storkarhu**[2] was born on 2 Sep 1799 in Rejpelt, Vörå, Finland,[2] was christened on 9 Sep 1799,[2] died on 11 May 1808[2] at age 8, and was buried on 15 May 1808.[2]

ix. **Beata Mårtensson Nykarhu**[2] was born on 27 Jun 1802 in Rejpelt, Vörå, Finland,[2] was christened on 27 Jun 1802,[2] died on 24 Aug 1802,[2] and was buried on 29 Aug 1802.[2]

x. **Mickel Mårtensson Nykarhu**[1] was born on 24 Mar 1804 in Rejpelt, Vörå, Finland,[1] was christened on 25 Mar 1804,[2] died on 8 Nov 1828 in Rökiö, Vörå, Finland[1] at age 24, and was buried on 16 Nov 1828.[2] Another name for Mickel was Mickel Mårtensson Smårus. Mickel married **Lisa Larsdotter Turja**[3] on 6 Jul 1827.[3]

xi. **Simon Mårtensson Nykarhu**[2] was born on 6 Mar 1805 in Rejpelt, Vörå, Finland,[2] was christened on 7 Mar 1805,[2] died on 17 Jun 1805,[2] and was buried on 30 Jun 1805.[2]

xii. **Mårtensson Nykarhu**[2] was born on 6 Mar 1805 in Rejpelt, Vörå, Finland[2] and died on 6 Mar 1805.[2]

xiii. **Johan Mårtensson Nykarhu**[2] was born on 6 Dec 1808 in Rejpelt, Vörå, Finland,[2] died on 12 Dec 1808,[2] and was buried on 26 Dec 1808.[2]

xiv. **Johan Mårtensson Nykarhu**[2] was born on 18 Dec 1808 in Rejpelt, Vörå, Finland,[2] was christened on 19 Dec 1808,[2] died on 28 Mar 1809,[2] and was buried on 3 Apr 1809.[2]

---

1. Torbjörn Nikus, Storkarhu (unpublish document, 2008). .... Hiski database (http://hiski.genealogia.fi).
2. Hiski database (http://hiski.genealogia.fi).
3. Torbjörn Nikus, Storkarhu (unpublish document, 2008).

Ancestor Report for Mårten Mårtensson Storkarhu

3. Margareta Carlsdotter Finnas,[4] daughter of **Karl Johansson Finnas** and **Margareta Mickelsdotter Månsus,** was born on 15 Apr 1762 in Kaitsor, Vörå, Finland.[5]

General Notes: Margeta moved as a widow to Gamlakarleby, possibly joining her daughter Maria.

Margareta married **Mårten Mårtensson Storkarhu**[4] on 13 Dec 1782 in Vörå, Finland.[6]

---

4. Torbjörn Nikus, Storkarhu (unpublish document, 2008). .... Hiski database (http://hiski.genealogia.fi).
5. Torbjörn Nikus, Storkarhu (unpublish document, 2008). .... Vörå Kommunionbok 1819-1825 (http://digi.narc.fi/).
6. Torbjörn Nikus, Storkarhu (unpublish document, 2008).

Third Generation

4. Mårten Thomasson Storkarhu,[1] son of **Thomas Sigfridsson Storkarhu** and **Brita Johansdotter Ingå,** was born on 20 Nov 1733 in Rejpelt, Vörå, Finland,[2] was christened on 25 Nov 1733,[3] and died on 8 Sep 1809 in Rejpelt, Vörå, Finland[1] at age 75.

General Notes: In 1750 he was a dräng (farmhand) on Storkarhu and a bootmaker. He moved away from the farm in 1751. He lived once more on Storkarhu about 1758 perhaps with his uncle Mårten Sigfridsson, bonde at Storkarhu. He moved away with his wife Karin about 1762.[1]

Noted events in his life were:
- Occupation: shoemaker.[3]

- Resided: 1754, Tuckor, Vörå, Finland.[3]

- Moved to: Storkahu farm, Abt 1757, Rejpelt, Vörå, Finland.[3]

Mårten married **Karin Carlsdotter Jänt**[2] on 22 Dec 1754 in Vörå, Finland.[3]

Children from this marriage were:

	i.	**Brita Mårtensdotter Jänt**[3] was born on 26 Aug 1755 in Tuckor, Vörå, Finland,[3] was christened on 31 Aug 1755,[3] died on 11 Jan 1756 in Tuckor, Vörå, Finland,[3] and was buried on 18 Jan 1756.[3]
	ii.	**Thomas Mårtensson Jänt**[3] was born on 15 Sep 1756 in Tuckor, Vörå, Finland,[3] was christened on 19 Sep 1756,[3] died on 7 Nov 1757 in Tuckor, Vörå, Finland[3] at age 1, and was buried on 13 Nov 1757.[3]
	iii.	**Anna Mårtensdotter Storkarhu**[3] was born on 9 Mar 1758 in Rejpelt, Vörå, Finland,[3] was christened on 12 Mar 1758,[3] died on 11 Jun 1758 in Rejpelt, Vörå, Finland,[3] and was buried on 18 Jun 1758.[3]
	iv.	**Carl Mårtensson Storkarhu**[3] was born on 13 Aug 1759 in Rejpelt, Vörå, Finland,[3] was christened on 19 Aug 1759,[3] died on 16 Feb 1760 in Rejpelt, Vörå, Finland,[3] and was buried on 24 Feb 1760.[3]
2	v.	**Mårten Mårtensson Storkarhu.**[2] Mårten married **Margareta Carlsdotter Finnas,**[2] daughter of **Karl Johansson Finnas** and **Margareta Mickelsdotter Månsus,** on 13 Dec 1782 in Vörå, Finland.[1]
	vi.	**Johan Mårtensson Storkarhu**[3] was born on 16 Oct 1763 in Rejpelt, Vörå, Finland,[3] was christened on 23 Oct 1763,[3] died on 26 Jul 1764 in Rejpelt, Vörå, Finland,[3] and was buried on 29 Jul 1764.[3]
	vii.	**Margeta Mårtensdotter Storkarhu**[3] was born on 4 May 1765 in Rejpelt, Vörå, Finland,[3] was christened on 5 May 1765,[3] died on 8 Aug 1765 in Rejpelt, Vörå, Finland,[3] and was buried on 11 Aug 1765.[3]
	viii.	**Erich Mårtensson Storkarhu**[2] was born on 10 Jul 1766 in Rejpelt, Vörå, Finland,[2] was christened on 13 Jul 1766,[3] died on 20 Oct 1829 in Rejpelt, Vörå, Finland[3] at age 63, and was buried on 1 Nov 1829.[3] Erich married **Beata Mattsdotter Månsus** on 26 Jun 1787.
	ix.	**Maria Mårtensdotter Storkarhu**[2] was born on 11 Apr 1769 in Rejpelt, Vörå, Finland,[2] was christened on 14 Apr 1769,[3] died on 28 Aug 1837 in Lotlax, Vörå, Finland[3] at age 68, and was buried on 30 Aug 1837.[3] Maria married **Daniel Mattsson Rex**.
	x.	**Anna Mårtensdotter Storkarhu**[2] was born on 11 Sep 1772 in Rejpelt, Vörå, Finland,[2] was christened on 10 Nov 1772,[3] and died on 5 Mar 1859 in Lålax, Vörå, Finland[2] at age 86. Another name for Anna was Anna Mårtensdotter Skott. Anna married **Johan Mårtensson Skott** on 17 Dec 1802.

5. Karin Carlsdotter Jänt,[2] daughter of **Carl Andersson Jånt** and **Anna Mattsdotter,** was born on 28 Jul 1732 in Tuckor, Vörå, Finland,[2] was christened on 30 Jul 1732,[3] and died on 15 Apr 1805 in Rejpelt, Vörå, Finland[1] at age 72.

Karin married **Mårten Thomasson Storkarhu**[1] on 22 Dec 1754 in Vörå, Finland.[3]

6. Karl Johansson Finnas,[2] son of **Johan Johansson Finnas** and **Brita Andersdotter,** was born on 6 Jul 1737 in Kaitsor, Vörå, Finland,[2] was christened on 10 Jul 1737,[3] died on 5 Dec 1811 in Kaitsor, Vörå, Finland[2] at age 74, and was buried on 15 Dec 1811.[3] Another name for Karl was Karl Johansson Heikius.

---

1. Torbjörn Nikus, Storkarhu (unpublish document, 2008).

2. Torbjörn Nikus, Storkarhu (unpublish document, 2008). .... Hiski database (http://hiski.genealogia.fi).

3. Hiski database (http://hiski.genealogia.fi).

Ancestor Report for Mårten Mårtensson Storkarhu

Noted events in his life were:
• Occupation: bonde (farm owner) at Heikius. [4]

Karl married **Margareta Mickelsdotter Månsus** [5] on 12 Mar 1758 in Vörå, Finland.

Children from this marriage were:

    i.   **Brita Carlsdotter Finnas** [6] was born on 6 Jan 1759 in Kaitsor, Vörå, Finland, [7] was christened on 4 Jun 1759 in Oravais, Oravais, Finland, [4] died on 22 Sep 1844 in Bertby, Vörå, Finland [6] at age 85, and was buried on 29 Sep 1844. [4] Another name for Brita was Brita Carlsdotter Heikius. Brita married **Soldat Abraham Jacobsson** on 19 Dec 1780. [4] Brita next married **Johan Enroth** on 17 Jun 1798 in Vörå, Finland. [4]

    ii.   **Maria Carlsdotter Finnas** [4] was born on 3 May 1761 in Kaitsor, Vörå, Finland, [4] was christened on 11 May 1761, [4] died on 9 Oct 1761, [4] and was buried on 18 Oct 1761. [4]

3   iii.   **Margareta Carlsdotter Finnas**. [5] Margareta married **Mårten Mårtensson Storkarhu**, [5] son of **Mårten Thomasson Storkarhu** and **Karin Carlsdotter Jänt,** on 13 Dec 1782 in Vörå, Finland. [8]

    iv.   **Michel Carlsson Finnas** [4] was born on 15 Apr 1762 in Kaitsor, Vörå, Finland, [4] died on 7 Oct 1763 [4] at age 1, and was buried on 16 Oct 1763. [4]

    v.   **Carl Carlsson Heikius** [4] was born on 2 Apr 1767 in Kaitsor, Vörå, Finland, [4] was christened on 3 Apr 1767, [4] and died on 5 Sep 1785 [6] at age 18.

    vi.   **Simon Carlsson Heikius** [4] was born on 26 May 1768 in Kaitsor, Vörå, Finland, [4] was christened on 29 May 1768, [4] and died on 16 Mar 1840 in Kaitsor, Vörå, Finland [6] at age 71.

    vii.   **Anna Carlsdotter Heikius** [4] was born on 10 Oct 1771 in Kaitsor, Vörå, Finland, [4] was christened on 13 Oct 1771, [4] died on 25 Dec 1842 in Rejpelt, Vörå, Finland [4] at age 71, and was buried on 30 Dec 1842. [4] Anna married **Simon Johansson Smeds** [4] on 4 Jun 1793 in Rejpelt, Vörå, Finland. [4]

    viii.   **Johan Carlsson Heikius** [4] was born on 18 Oct 1775 in Kaitsor, Vörå, Finland, [4] was christened on 22 Oct 1775, [4] died on 9 Aug 1776, [4] and was buried on 11 Aug 1776. [4]

    ix.   **Lisa Carlsdotter Häikius** [4] was born on 18 Oct 1775 in Kaitsor, Vörå, Finland, [4] was christened on 22 Oct 1775, [4] died on 2 Apr 1776, [4] and was buried on 8 Apr 1776. [4]

7. Margareta Mickelsdotter Månsus, [5] daughter of **Mickel Mårtensson Månsus** and **Brita Larsdotter Knuts,** was born on 10 Sep 1736 in Kåfjoki, Vörå, Finland, [9] was christened on 12 Sep 1736, [4] died on 4 Dec 1796 in Kaitsor, Vörå, Finland [5] at age 60, and was buried on 11 Dec 1796. [4]

General Notes: At least five children died, a pair of twins in 1776. [8]

Margareta married **Karl Johansson Finnas** [5] on 12 Mar 1758 in Vörå, Finland.

---

4. Hiski database (http://hiski.genealogia.fi).
5. Torbjörn Nikus, Storkarhu (unpublish document, 2008). .... Hiski database (http://hiski.genealogia.fi).
6. Email from Torbjörn Nikus.
7. Email from Torbjörn Nikus. .... Hiski database (http://hiski.genealogia.fi).
8. Torbjörn Nikus, Storkarhu (unpublish document, 2008).
9. Torbjörn Nikus, Storkarhu (unpublish document, 2008). .... Hiski database (http://hiski.genealogia.fi). .... Vörå Kommunionsboken 1750-56 (http://www.enges.org).

Ancestor Report for Mårten Mårtensson Storkarhu

Fourth Generation

8. Thomas Sigfridsson Storkarhu,[1] son of **Sigfred Bertilsson Storkarhu** and **Margareta Åkesdotter Gråbbils,** was born about 1709 in Rejpelt, Vörå, Finland, [1] died on 8 Dec 1739 in Rejpelt, Vörå, Finland [1] about age 30, and was buried on 16 Dec 1739.[2]

Noted events in his life were:
• Occupation: bonde (farm owner) at Starkarhu, Rejpelt, Vörå, Finland. [3]

Thomas married **Brita Johansdotter Ingå**[1] on 21 Dec 1731 in Vörå, Finland. [1]

Children from this marriage were:
  - i. **Johan Thomasson Storkarhu**[4] was born on 10 Sep 1732 in Rejpelt, Vörå, Finland[4] and was christened on 10 Sep 1732.[2]
  - 4 ii. **Mårten Thomasson Storkarhu**.[1] Mårten married **Karin Carlsdotter Jänt,**[4] daughter of **Carl Andersson Jånt** and **Anna Mattsdotter,** on 22 Dec 1754 in Vörå, Finland.[2]
  - iii. **Margeta Thomasdotter Storkarhu**[1] was born on 6 Sep 1736 in Rejpelt, Vörå, Finland, [1] was christened on 12 Sep 1736,[2] and died on 4 Jul 1802 in Tuckor, Vörå, Finland[1] at age 65. Another name for Margeta was Margeta Thomasdotter Grind. Margeta married **Simon Mattsson Grind**[2] on 17 Dec 1758 in Vörå, Finland.[2]
  - iv. **Thomas Thomasson Storkarhu**[4] was born on 6 Sep 1739 in Rejpelt, Vörå, Finland[4] and was christened on 9 Sep 1739.[2]

9. Brita Johansdotter Ingå,[1] daughter of **Johan Mårtensson** and **Brita Mårtensdotter,** was born on 31 Aug 1700 in Lomby, Vörå, Finland,[4] was christened on 8 Sep 1700,[2] died on 22 Jun 1780 in Rejpelt, Vörå, Finland[4] at age 79, and was buried on 25 Jun 1780.[2]

Brita married **Thomas Sigfridsson Storkarhu**[1] on 21 Dec 1731 in Vörå, Finland.[1]

Brita next married **Jacob Jacobsson** on 16 Nov 1746 in Vörå, Finland.

10. Carl Andersson Jånt,[4] son of **Anders Andersson Jånt** and **Maria Thomasdotter,** was born on 26 Jan 1700 in Tuckor, Vörå, Finland,[2] died on 27 Oct 1774 in Tuckor, Vörå, Finland[2] at age 74, and was buried on 30 Oct 1774.[2]

Research Notes: According to his death record, he was born about 1706 but the Kommunionsboken 1750-56 comfirms his 1700 birth date.

Noted events in his life were:
• Occupation: bonde (farm owner) at Jänt.[5]

Carl married **Anna Mattsdotter**[4] on 24 Jun 1725 in Vörå, Finland.[2]

Children from this marriage were:
  - i. **Maria Carlsdotter Jänt**[2] was born on 31 Dec 1726 in Tuckor, Vörå, Finland,[2] was christened on 1 Jan 1727,[2] died on 23 Jan 1762 in Rejpelt, Vörå, Finland[2] at age 35, and was buried on 2 Feb 1762.[2] Maria married **Matts Hansson** on 29 Nov 1752.
  - ii. **Anders Carlsson Jänt**[2] was born on 3 Aug 1728 in Tuckor, Vörå, Finland,[2] was christened on 4 Aug 1728,[2] died on 21 Oct 1728 in Tuckor, Vörå, Finland,[2] and was buried on 28 Oct 1728.[2]
  - iii. **Anna Carlsdotter Jänt**[2] was born on 9 Jul 1729 in Tuckor, Vörå, Finland,[2] was christened on 14 Sep 1729,[2] died on 4 Oct 1729 in Tuckor, Vörå, Finland,[2] and was buried on 12 Oct 1729.[2]

---

1. Torbjörn Nikus, Storkarhu (unpublish document, 2008).
2. Hiski database (http://hiski.genealogia.fi).
3. Vörå Mantalslängden 1731 (http://www.enges.org). .... Vörå Mantalslängden 1730 (http://www.enges.org). .... Vörå Mantalslängden 1729 (http://www.enges.org).
4. Torbjörn Nikus, Storkarhu (unpublish document, 2008). .... Hiski database (http://hiski.genealogia.fi).
5. Vörå Kommunionsboken 1750-56 (http://www.enges.org).

iv. **Margeta Carlsdotter Jänt**[2] was born on 6 Aug 1730 in Tuckor, Vörå, Finland,[2] was christened on 9 Aug 1730,[2] died on 3 Jul 1736 in Tuckor, Vörå, Finland[2] at age 5, and was buried on 11 Jul 1736.[2]

v. **Mattz Carlsson Jänt**[6] was born in Aug 1731 in Tuckor, Vörå, Finland,[6] was christened on 5 Sep 1731,[6] died on 27 Jul 1732 in Tuckor, Vörå, Finland,[6] and was buried on 30 Jul 1732.[6]

5 vi. **Karin Carlsdotter Jänt.**[7] Karin married **Mårten Thomasson Storkarhu**,[8] son of **Thomas Sigfridsson Storkarhu** and **Brita Johansdotter Ingå**, on 22 Dec 1754 in Vörå, Finland.[6]

vii. **Carl Carlsson Jänt**[6] was born on 24 Dec 1733 in Tuckor, Vörå, Finland,[6] was christened on 26 Dec 1733,[6] died on 9 Oct 1795 in Tuckor, Vörå, Finland[6] at age 61, and was buried on 18 Oct 1795.[6] Carl married **Lisa Michelsdotter**[6] on 23 Nov 1755.

viii. **Anna Carlsdotter Jänt**[6] was born on 5 Apr 1735 in Tuckor, Vörå, Finland,[6] was christened on 9 Apr 1735,[6] died on 29 May 1735 in Tuckor, Vörå, Finland,[6] and was buried on 1 Jun 1735.[6]

ix. **Brita Carlsdotter Jänt**[6] was born on 28 Mar 1737 in Tuckor, Vörå, Finland,[6] was christened on 3 Apr 1737,[6] died on 11 Jun 1737 in Tuckor, Vörå, Finland,[6] and was buried on 12 Jun 1737.[6]

x. **Abraham Carlsson Jänt**[6] was born on 22 Apr 1738 in Tuckor, Vörå, Finland,[6] was christened on 30 Apr 1738,[6] died on 6 Jun 1789 in Tuckor, Vörå, Finland[6] at age 51, and was buried on 14 Jun 1789.[6]

xi. **Carlsson Jänt**[6] was born on 22 Apr 1738 in Tuckor, Vörå, Finland,[6] was christened on 30 Apr 1738,[6] and died on 22 Apr 1738.[6]

xii. **Jacob Carlsson Jänt**[6] was born on 10 Jan 1740 in Tuckor, Vörå, Finland,[6] was christened on 13 Jan 1740,[6] died on 17 Jan 1740 in Tuckor, Vörå, Finland,[6] and was buried on 20 Jan 1740.[6]

xiii. **Anders Carlsson Jänt**[6] was born on 13 Mar 1741 in Tuckor, Vörå, Finland,[6] was christened on 13 Mar 1741,[6] died on 14 Jan 1805 in Tuckor, Vörå, Finland[6] at age 63, and was buried on 27 Jan 1805.[6]

xiv. **Anna Carlsdotter Jänt**[6] was born on 18 Apr 1744 in Tuckor, Vörå, Finland,[6] was christened on 18 Apr 1744,[6] died on 15 Jun 1772 in Tuckor, Vörå, Finland[6] at age 28, and was buried on 21 Jun 1772.[6]

11. Anna Mattsdotter[7] was born in 1698 in Tuckor, Vörå, Finland,[9] died on 3 Nov 1778 in Tuckor, Vörå, Finland[6] at age 80, and was buried on 8 Nov 1778.[6] Another name for Anna was Anna Mattsdotter Jänt.

Death Notes: Listed as 63 at her death, which is either incorrect or refers to another person of the same nme.

Research Notes: Her surname Qvist was listed only with the birth record of her last child.

Anna married **Carl Andersson Jånt**[7] on 24 Jun 1725 in Vörå, Finland.[6]

12. Johan Johansson Finnas[10] was born in Sep 1706 in Kaitsor, Vörå, Finland,[10] died on 1 Mar 1775 in Kaitsor, Vörå, Finland[10] at age 68, and was buried on 5 Mar 1775.[6]

Research Notes: Parents are probably Johan Johansson and Walborg Michelsdr at Finnas in Kaitsor.

Johan married **Brita Andersdotter**[10] on 8 Jun 1729 in Vörå, Finland.[11]

Children from this marriage were:

i. **Brita Johansdotter Finnas**[11] was born on 13 May 1731 in Kaitsor, Vörå, Finland,[11] was christened on 16 May 1731,[6] and died before 1734.[6]

ii. **Anders Johansson Finnas**[10] was born on 15 Dec 1734 in Kaitsor, Vörå, Finland[10] and was christened on 20 Dec 1734.[6]

iii. **Brita Johansdotter Finnas**[10] was born on 15 Dec 1734 in Kaitsor, Vörå, Finland[10] and was christened on 20 Dec 1734.[11]

iv. **Lisa Johansson Finnas** was born in 1735 in Kaitsor, Vörå, Finland.[12]

6 v. **Karl Johansson Finnas.**[7] Karl married **Margareta Mickelsdotter Månsus**,[7] daughter of **Mickel Mårtensson Månsus** and **Brita Larsdotter Knuts**, on 12 Mar 1758 in Vörå, Finland.

---

6. *Hiski database (http://hiski.genealogia.fi).*
7. *Torbjörn Nikus, Storkarhu (unpublish document, 2008). .... Hiski database (http://hiski.genealogia.fi).*
8. *Torbjörn Nikus, Storkarhu (unpublish document, 2008).*
9. *Vörå Kommunionsboken 1750-56 (http://www.enges.org). .... Anders Enders, Några sidor på nätet om släktforskning (http://www.enges.org/gene/).*
10. *Anders Enders, Några sidor på nätet om släktforskning (http://www.enges.org/gene/).*
11. *Anders Enders, Några sidor på nätet om släktforskning (http://www.enges.org/gene/). .... Hiski database (http://hiski.genealogia.fi).*
12. *Vörå Kommunionsboken 1750-56 (http://www.enges.org).*

   vi.   **Michel Johansson Finnas**[6] was born in Apr 1739 in Kaitsor, Vörå, Finland, [13] died on 20 Sep 1803[6] at age 64, and was buried on 2 Oct 1803.[6] Michel married **Anna Mårtensdotter**[6] on 13 Dec 1761.[6]

   vii.   **Anna Johansdotter Finnas**[14] was born on 13 Nov 1741 in Kaitsor, Vörå, Finland[14] and was christened on 15 Nov 1741.[15]

   viii.   **Brita Johansdotter Finnas**[16] was born on 26 Dec 1743 in Kaitsor, Vörå, Finland, [17] died on 18 Mar 1818 in Andiala, Vörå, Finland[16] at age 74, and was buried on 30 Mar 1818.[16] Brita married **Anders Gustafsson Tarkkanen**[18] on 2 Dec 1764.[16]

   ix.   **Johan Johansson Finnas**[19] was born in 1746 in Kaitsor, Vörå, Finland, [19] died on 4 Jun 1824 in Kaitsor, Vörå, Finland[15] at age 78, and was buried on 13 Jun 1824.[15] Johan married **Margeta Mårtensdotter Jåfs**[15] on 10 Dec 1769 in Vörå, Finland.[15]

13. **Brita Andersdotter**[16] was born in Sep 1698 in Tuckor, Vörå, Finland[17] and died in 1779[16] at age 81. Another name for Brita was Brita Johansson.

   Research Notes: Parents are probably Anders Andersson and Maria Thomasdr at Jånt in Tuckur.

Brita married **Johan Johansson Finnas**[16] on 8 Jun 1729 in Vörå, Finland.[14]

14. **Mickel Mårtensson Månsus**,[16] son of **Mårten Månsson Månsus** and **Karin Hindersdotter,** was born on 22 Jul 1694 in Kåfjoki, Vörå, Finland[14] and died in 1770[16] at age 76.

Mickel married **Brita Larsdotter Knuts**.[15]

Children from this marriage were:

   i.   **Mårten Mickelsson Månsus**[16] was born on 26 Nov 1723 in Kåfjoki, Vörå, Finland, [16] was christened on 19 May 1725,[15] died on 16 May 1725[15] at age 1, and was buried on 19 May 1725.[15]

   ii.   **Anna Mickelsdotter Månsus**[16] was born on 13 Apr 1726 in Kåfjoki, Vörå, Finland, [16] was christened on 17 Apr 1726,[15] died on 13 Jul 1727 in Kåfjoki, Vörå, Finland[15] at age 1, and was buried on 16 Jul 1727.[15]

   iii.   **Beata Mickelsdotter Månsus**[16] was born on 25 Aug 1727 in Kåfjoki, Vörå, Finland, [17] was christened on 27 Aug 1727,[15] died on 7 Aug 1761 in Kåfjoki, Vörå, Finland at age 33, and was buried on 13 Aug 1761.[15] Beata married someone **Per Persson Enges**[16] on 18 Nov 1750.[16]

   iv.   **Michel Mickelsson Månsus**[16] was born on 24 Aug 1728 in Kåfjoki, Vörå, Finland, [16] was christened on 1 Sep 1728,[15] died on 19 Dec 1818 in Kåskeby, Vörå, Finland[15] at age 90, and was buried on 27 Dec 1818.[15] Michel married **Anna Erichsdotter**[15] on 9 Dec 1753.[15]

   v.   **Anna Mickelsdotter Månsus**[16] was born on 22 Sep 1729 in Kåfjoki, Vörå, Finland[16] and was christened on 28 Sep 1729.[15]

   vi.   **Brita Mickelsdotter Månsus**[16] was born on 2 Dec 1730 in Kåfjoki, Vörå, Finland, [16] was christened on 6 Dec 1730,[15] died on 17 Jun 1809 in Kåfjoki, Vörå, Finland[16] at age 78, and was buried on 24 Jun 1809.[15] Brita married **Matts Mattsson**[15] on 28 Oct 1753.[16]

   vii.   **Lisa Mickelsdotter Månsus**[16] was born on 22 Aug 1732 in Kåfjoki, Vörå, Finland, [16] was christened on 24 Aug 1732,[15] and died on 19 Dec 1804 in Tuckor, Vörå, Finland[16] at age 72. Lisa married **Carl Carlsson Jåntt**.[16]

7   viii.   **Margareta Mickelsdotter Månsus**.[20] Margareta married **Karl Johansson Finnas**,[20] son of **Johan Johansson Finnas** and **Brita Andersdotter,** on 12 Mar 1758 in Vörå, Finland.

   ix.   **Anna Mickelsdotter Månsus**[16] was born on 6 Aug 1741 in Kåfjoki, Vörå, Finland[16] and was christened on 9 Aug 1741.[15]

   14. Anders Enders, Några sidor på nätet om släktforskning (http://www.enges.org/gene/). .... Hiski database (http://hiski.genealogia.fi).

   15. Hiski database (http://hiski.genealogia.fi).

   16. Anders Enders, Några sidor på nätet om släktforskning (http://www.enges.org/gene/).

   17. Anders Enders, Några sidor på nätet om släktforskning (http://www.enges.org/gene/). .... Vörå Kommunionsboken 1750-56 (http://www.enges.org).

   18. Hiski database (http://hiski.genealogia.fi). .... Anders Enders, Några sidor på nätet om släktforskning (http://www.enges.org/gene/).

   19. Vörå Kommunionsboken 1750-56 (http://www.enges.org). .... Hiski database (http://hiski.genealogia.fi).

   20. Torbjörn Nikus, Storkarhu (unpublish document, 2008). .... Hiski database (http://hiski.genealogia.fi).

15. Brita Larsdotter Knuts,[21] daughter of **Lars Mattsson** and **Gertrud Mårtensdotter,** was born on 17 Aug 1695 in Palfvis, Vörå, Finland,[22] died on 16 Aug 1776 in Kåfjoki, Vörå, Finland[21] at age 80, and was buried on 18 Aug 1776.[21]

Brita married **Mickel Mårtensson Månsus**.[23]

---

21. *Hiski database (http://hiski.genealogia.fi).*
22. *Hiski database (http://hiski.genealogia.fi). .... Vörå Kommunionsboken 1750-56 (http://www.enges.org). .... Vörå Kommunionbok 1757-1763 (http://digi.narc.fi/digi).*
23. *Anders Enders, Några sidor på nätet om släktforskning (http://www.enges.org/gene/).*

Ancestor Report for Mårten Mårtensson Storkarhu

Fifth Generation

16. Sigfred Bertilsson Storkarhu,[1] son of **Bertel Eriksson Storkarhu** and **Unknown,** was born about 1658 in Rejpelt, Vörå, Finland,[2] died on 4 Sep 1732 in Rejpelt, Vörå, Finland [2] about age 74, and was buried on 10 Sep 1732.[3]

General Notes: Farmer and juror. He was absent from his farm during the Great Northern War (1700 - 1721). In 1719, he was not listed in the Russian tax records, and his wife was listed as the owner and unable to pay taxes, so he was presumed killed. According to church records, he was back at the farm in 1727, so he returned sometime after the war. During his absence, he may have retreated with the troops to northern Finland or he may have been taken prisoner by the Russians.[4]

Noted events in his life were:
- Occupation: bonde (farm owner) at Storkarhu, Rejpelt, Vörå, Finland.[5]
- Office: Nämndeman (juryman), 1697-1729.[6]

Sigfred married **Anna Hansdotter**.[7]

Children from this marriage were:
    i.   **Erik Sigfridsson Storkarhu**[7] was born in 1680 in Rejpelt, Vörå, Finland,[7] died on 21 Aug 1696 in Rejpelt, Vörå, Finland[7] at age 16, and was buried on 21 Aug 1696.[3]
    ii.   **Mårten Sigfridsson Storkarhu**[8] died after 1708.[9] Mårten married **Lijsa Olufsdotter**.[8]
    iii.   **Johan Sigfridsson Storkarhu**[7] was born in 1686 in Rejpelt, Vörå, Finland,[7] died on 28 Mar 1745 in Rejpelt, Vörå, Finland[7] at age 59, and was buried on 31 Mar 1745.[3] Johan married **Maria Mattsdotter**.[7] Johan next married **Maria Olofsdotter**[7] on 20 Jan 1745.[3]
    iv.   **Brita Sigfridsdotter Storkarhu**[10] was born before 1690.[10]
    v.   **Beata Sigfridsdotter Storkarhu**[10] was born before 1690.[10]

Sigfred next married **Margareta Åkesdotter Gråbbils**[2] about 1703.

Children from this marriage were:
    i.   **Erich Sigfredsson Storkarhu**[7] was born on 27 Apr 1704 in Rejpelt, Vörå, Finland [7] and died on 16 May 1704 in Rejpelt, Vörå, Finland.[7]
    ii.   **Anna Sigfridsdotter Storkarhu**[4] was born on 22 Jan 1705 in Rejpelt, Vörå, Finland.[4]
8   iii.   **Thomas Sigfridsson Storkarhu**.[4] Thomas married **Brita Johansdotter Ingå**,[4] daughter of **Johan Mårtensson** and **Brita Mårtensdotter,** on 21 Dec 1731 in Vörå, Finland.[4]
    iv.   **Mårten Sigfredsson Storkarhu**[11] was born in Feb 1710 in Rejpelt, Vörå, Finland,[12] died on 5 Dec 1806 in Rökiö, Vörå, Finland[7] at age 96, and was buried on 14 Dec 1806.[3] Another name for Mårten was Klärk Mårten Sigfredsson. Mårten married **Maria Henriksdotter**[4] on 14 Jun 1747.[4] Mårten next married **Anna Abramsdotter Måsa**.[4]
    v.   **Maria Sigfridsdotter Storkarhu**[4] was born about 1712 in Rejpelt, Vörå, Finland,[7] died on 26 May 1779 in Miemoisby, Vörå, Finland[7] about age 67, and was buried on 30 May 1779.[3] Maria married **Jakob Gustafsson** on 26 Dec 1740.[4]

---

1. Torbjörn Nikus, Storkarhu (unpublish document, 2008). .... Anders Enders, Några sidor på nätet om släktforskning (http://www.enges.org/gene/).
2. Torbjörn Nikus, Storkarhu (unpublish document, 2008). .... Anders Enders, Några sidor på nätet om släktforskning (http://www.enges.org/gene/). .... Hiski database (http://hiski.genealogia.fi).
3. Hiski database (http://hiski.genealogia.fi).
4. Torbjörn Nikus, Storkarhu (unpublish document, 2008).
5. Hiski database (http://hiski.genealogia.fi). .... Vörå Jordeboken 1709-10 (http://www.enges.org).
6. Henrik Mang, Katarina Udd's anor (www.netikka.net).
7. Torbjörn Nikus, Storkarhu (unpublish document, 2008). .... Hiski database (http://hiski.genealogia.fi).
8. Hiski database (http://hiski.genealogia.fi). .... Vörå Mantalslängden 1708 (http://www.enges.org/).
9. Vörå Mantalslängden 1708 (http://www.enges.org/).
10. Vörå Mantalslängden 1690-91 (http://www.enges.org).
11. Hiski database (http://hiski.genealogia.fi). .... Torbjörn Nikus, Storkarhu (unpublish document, 2008).
12. Torbjörn Nikus, Storkarhu (unpublish document, 2008). .... Vörå Kommunionsboken 1750-56 (http://www.enges.org). .... Hiski database (http://hiski.genealogia.fi).

17. Margareta Åkesdotter Gråbbils,[13] daughter of **Åke Johansson Gråbbil** and **Brita Erichsdotter Heinull,** was born on 15 Aug 1673 in Kåskeby, Vörå, Finland,[14] died on 5 Nov 1756 in Rejpelt, Vörå, Finland[13] at age 83, and was buried on 24 Nov 1756.[15]

General Notes: She ran an inn with her father. According to the Russia tax records in 1723, she ran the Storkarhu farm in her husband's absence during the Russian invasion. She died of "krefwtan" perhaps bowel cancer.[16]

Margareta married **Sigfred Bertilsson Storkarhu**[17] about 1703.

18. Johan Mårtensson.[18]

Johan married **Brita Mårtensdotter**.[15]

Children from this marriage were:

 i. **Johan Johansson Ingå**[15] was born on 19 Feb 1691 in Lomby, Vörå, Finland[15] and was christened on 22 Feb 1691.[15]

 ii. **Mårten Johansson Ingå**[15] was born on 20 Mar 1692 in Lomby, Vörå, Finland,[15] died on 1 Oct 1764 in Rejpelt, Vörå, Finland[15] at age 72, and was buried on 7 Oct 1764.[15] Another name for Mårten was Mårten Johansson Korfwolain. Mårten married **Anna Johansdotter Korfwolain**.

 iii. **Per Johansson Ingå**[15] was born on 18 Aug 1693 in Lomby, Vörå, Finland.[15]

 iv. **Anna Johansdotter Ingå**[15] was born on 17 Apr 1696 in Lomby, Vörå, Finland[15] and died in 1696.[15]

 v. **Maria Johansdotter Ingå**[15] was born on 16 Mar 1699 in Lomby, Vörå, Finland[15] and died in 1715[15] at age 16.

9 vi. **Brita Johansdotter Ingå**.[19] Brita married **Thomas Sigfridsson Storkarhu**,[19] son of **Sigfred Bertilsson Storkarhu** and **Margareta Åkesdotter Gråbbils,** on 21 Dec 1731 in Vörå, Finland.[19] Brita next married **Jacob Jacobsson** on 16 Nov 1746 in Vörå, Finland.

 vii. **Anna Johansdotter Ingå**[15] was born on 27 Feb 1702 in Lomby, Vörå, Finland.[15]

19. Brita Mårtensdotter[15] was born about 1663,[20] died on 8 Jan 1740 in Lomby, Vörå, Finland[15] about age 77, and was buried on 13 Jan 1740.[15]

Brita married **Johan Mårtensson**.[18]

20. Anders Andersson Jånt,[15] son of **Anders Carlsson** and **Unknown,**.

Anders married **Maria Thomasdotter**.[15]

Children from this marriage were:

 i. **Margeta Andersdotter Jånt**[15] was born on 10 Mar 1693 in Tuckor, Vörå, Finland,[15] died on 9 Dec 1771 in Karvsor, Vörå, Finland[15] at age 78, and was buried on 15 Dec 1771.[15]

 ii. **Mårten Andersson Jånt**[15] was born on 8 Apr 1694 in Tuckor, Vörå, Finland,[15] died on 29 Dec 1775 in Tuckor, Vörå, Finland[15] at age 81, and was buried on 7 Jan 1776.[15]

 iii. **Simon Andersson Jånt**[15] was born on 29 Sep 1696 in Tuckor, Vörå, Finland.[15]

---

 13. Torbjörn Nikus, Storkarhu (unpublish document, 2008). .... Anders Enders, Några sidor på nätet om släktforskning (http://www.enges.org/gene/). .... Hiski database (http://hiski.genealogia.fi).

 14. Torbjörn Nikus, Storkarhu (unpublish document, 2008). .... Anders Enders, Några sidor på nätet om släktforskning (http://www.enges.org/gene/). .... Hiski database (http://hiski.genealogia.fi). .... Vörå Kommunionsboken 1750-56 (http://www.enges.org).

 15. Hiski database (http://hiski.genealogia.fi).

 16. Torbjörn Nikus, Storkarhu (unpublish document, 2008). .... Anders Enders, Några sidor på nätet om släktforskning (http://www.enges.org/gene/). .... Vörå Mantalslängden 1723 (http://www.enges.org).

 17. Torbjörn Nikus, Storkarhu (unpublish document, 2008). .... Anders Enders, Några sidor på nätet om släktforskning (http://www.enges.org/gene/).

 18. Hiski database (http://hiski.genealogia.fi). .... Vörå Mantalslängden 1690-91 (http://www.enges.org). .... Vörå Mantalslängden 1695-96 (http://www.enges.org). .... Vörå Mantalslängden 1708 (http://www.enges.org/).

 19. Torbjörn Nikus, Storkarhu (unpublish document, 2008).

 20. Hiski database (http://hiski.genealogia.fi). .... Vörå Mantalslängden 1708 (http://www.enges.org/). .... Vörå Mantalslängden 1695-96 (http://www.enges.org). .... Vörå Mantalslängden 1690-91 (http://www.enges.org).

10   iv.   **Carl Andersson Jånt**.[21] Carl married **Anna Mattsdotter**[21] on 24 Jun 1725 in Vörå, Finland. [15]

21. Maria Thomasdotter.[22]

Maria married **Anders Andersson Jånt**.[22]

28. Mårten Månsson Månsus,[23] son of **Måns Mattsson** and **Unknown,** was born about 1648 in Kåfjoki, Vörå, Finland,[23] died on 15 Nov 1728 in Kåfjoki, Vörå, Finland [23] about age 80, and was buried on 24 Nov 1728. [22]

Noted events in his life were:
• Occupation: bonde (farm owner) of Månsus, 1677-1678, Kåfjoki, Vörå, Finland. [24]

Mårten married someone **Karin Hindersdotter**.[25]

Children from this marriage were:
  i.   **Marja Mårtensdotter Månsus** [26] was born in Kåfjoki, Vörå, Finland.
  ii.   **Mårten Mårtensson Månsus** was born in Kåfjoki, Vörå, Finland.[27] Mårten married **Barbru**.[28]
  iii. **Anders Mårtensson Månsus** [22] was born on 10 Dec 1689 in Kåfjoki, Vörå, Finland [22] and died in 1690[22] at age 1.
  iv.   **Mattz Mårtensson Månsus** [23] was born on 20 Aug 1691 in Kåfjoki, Vörå, Finland, [23] died on 5 Sep 1762[22] at age 71, and was buried on 12 Sep 1762. [22]
14 v.   **Mickel Mårtensson Månsus**.[23] Mickel married **Brita Larsdotter Knuts**,[22] daughter of **Lars Mattsson** and **Gertrud Mårtensdotter,**.

Mårten next married **Karin Hindersdotter**,[29] daughter of **Hendrich Mattsson** and **Anna Simonssdotter,**.

29. Karin Hindersdotter.[25]

Research Notes: She might be a second wife and not the mother to earlier children. More research is needed.

Karin married someone **Mårten Månsson Månsus**.[23]

30. Lars Mattsson died before 1708.[30]

Research Notes: His parents may have been Mattz Larsson Knuts and Helga Larsdotter.

Noted events in his life were:
• Occupation: bonde (farm owener) on Knuts, 1695-1696, Palfvis, Vörå, Finland. [31]

Lars married **Gertrud Mårtensdotter**.[22]

Children from this marriage were:
15 i.   **Brita Larsdotter Knuts**.[22] Brita married **Mickel Mårtensson Månsus**,[23] son of **Mårten Månsson Månsus** and **Karin Hindersdotter,**.
  ii.   **Matts Larsson Knuts** [22] was born on 17 Dec 1701 in Palfvis, Vörå, Finland. [22]
  iii. **Mårten Larsson Knuts** [22] was born on 25 Oct 1703 in Palfvis, Vörå, Finland [22] and died in 1703.[22]

---

22. Hiski database (http://hiski.genealogia.fi).
23. Anders Enders, Några sidor på nätet om släktforskning (http://www.enges.org/gene/).
24. Vörå Mantalslängden 1677-78.
25. Vörå Mantalslängden 1690-91 (http://www.enges.org). .... Vörå Mantalslängden 1677-78.
26. Vörå Mantalslängden 1723 (http://www.enges.org).
27. Vörå Mantalslängden 1695-96 (http://www.enges.org).
28. Vörå Mantalslängden 1690-91 (http://www.enges.org).
29. Vörå Mantalslängden 1677-78. .... Anders Enders, Några sidor på nätet om släktforskning (http://www.enges.org/gene/).
30. Vörå Mantalslängden 1708 (http://www.enges.org/).
31. Hiski database (http://hiski.genealogia.fi). .... Vörå Mantalslängden 1695-96 (http://www.enges.org).

31. Gertrud Mårtensdotter.[32]

Noted events in her life were:
• Resided: widow at Knuts farm, 1708, Palfvis, Vörå, Finland. [33]

Gertrud married **Lars Mattsson**.

---

32. Hiski database (http://hiski.genealogia.fi).
33. Vörå Mantalslängden 1708 (http://www.enges.org/).

Ancestor Report for Mårten Mårtensson Storkarhu

Sixth Generation

32. Bertel Eriksson Storkarhu,[1] son of **Unknown** and **Unknown**, died about 1676 in Rejpelt, Vörå, Finland. [2]

General Notes: His tract was on the Storkarhu farm.   He was a bonde (farm owner).

Research Notes: Bertel Eriksson's parents are not known because the Vörå church records were destroyed by the Russians after the Great Northern War during the occupation between 1714 and 1721. His son Erik took over the farm after 1675.[3]

Noted events in his life were:
* Residence: 1653, Rejpelt, Vörå, Finland. [4]

* Note: From T. Nikus.[4] I tried to find your family in old tax records. I found this: 1659 the farmer was Bertil Eriksson, 2 adult persons. 1653 Bertil payed tax for 4 barrels of rye, 4½ barrels of barley. / Bertil´s father must be some Erik. The farmers are mostly listed in the same order year after year. In 1644, according to the order, the farmer was Erik Klemetsson (not 100%, there were also Erik Larsson, Erik Jakobsson). In 1641 still Erik Klemetsson. / 1630s the only farmer with a surname was Jöns Karhu. Where did he come from? It seems to me that Karhu farm was then divided into Storkarhu, Lillkarhu, and Jåsskarhu.

* Note: on the farm name Storkarhu.[5] According to the "Vörå Sockens Historia" a Jöns Jönsson (Johan Johansson) Karhu was a juryman from 1543-1548. This may indicate that the larger farm (pre-subdivided) called Karhu existed from the early 1500s.

* Note: on renaming the farm to Svens. There was a Svensson listed among the early taxpayers in Rejpelt, and this could be the son of the farm's founder.

Bertel married someone.

Children from this marriage were:

	i.	**Erik Bertilsson Storkarhu**.[6] Erik married **Maria Andersdotter**.[7]
16	ii.	**Sigfred Bertilsson Storkarhu**.[8] Sigfred married **Anna Hansdotter**.[9] Sigfred next married **Margareta Åkesdotter Gråbbils**,[10] daughter of **Åke Johansson Gråbbil** and **Brita Erichsdotter Heinull**, about 1703.
	iii.	**Gertru Bertilsdotter Storkarhu**[11] was born about Nov 1659 in Rejpelt, Vörå, Finland[11] and died on 29 May 1723 in Rejpelt, Vörå, Finland[11] about age 63. Gertru married **Mårten Hendersson**.[11]
	iv.	**Brita Bertilsdotter Storkarhu**[12]

34. Åke Johansson Gråbbil,[2] son of **Johan Grelsson Gråbbil** and **Unknown,** died in 1708.[2]

General Notes: He was a bonde, postbonde, and gästgivare (peasant, postman, and inn keeper). [8]

  1. Torbjörn Nikus email to Michael Swanson (17 Jun 2010). .... Torbjörn Nikus, Storkarhu (unpublish document, 2008).
  2. Anders Enders, Några sidor på nätet om släktforskning (http://www.enges.org/gene/).
  3. Vörå Avkortningslängden 1675 (http://www.enges.org). .... Email from Torbjörn Nikus.
  4. Torbjörn Nikus email to Michael Swanson (17 Jun 2010).
  5. Henrik Mang's website (http://www.netikka.net/henrik.mangs/).
  6. Anders Enders, Några sidor på nätet om släktforskning (http://www.enges.org/gene/). .... Vörå Mantalslängden 1675-76 (http://www.enges.org).
  7. Anders Enders, Några sidor på nätet om släktforskning (http://www.enges.org/gene/). .... Vörå Mantalslängden 1677-78.
  8. Torbjörn Nikus, Storkarhu (unpublish document, 2008). .... Anders Enders, Några sidor på nätet om släktforskning (http://www.enges.org/gene/).
  9. Torbjörn Nikus, Storkarhu (unpublish document, 2008). .... Hiski database (http://hiski.genealogia.fi).
  10. Torbjörn Nikus, Storkarhu (unpublish document, 2008). .... Anders Enders, Några sidor på nätet om släktforskning (http://www.enges.org/gene/). .... Hiski database (http://hiski.genealogia.fi).
  11. Hiski database (http://hiski.genealogia.fi).
  12. Vörå Mantalslängden 1675-76 (http://www.enges.org).

Ancestor Report for Mårten Mårtensson Storkarhu

Noted events in his life were:
• Resided: Gråbbil farm, 1660-1705, Kåskeby, Vörå, Finland. [13]

Åke married **Brita Erichsdotter Heinull**.[14]

Children from this marriage were:
- i. **Erik Åkesson Gråbbil**[15] was born in Kåskeby, Vörå, Finland[16] and died in 1715 in Piteå, Norrbotten, Sweden.[16] Erik married **Anna Andersdotter**.
- ii. **Johan Åkesson Gråbbils**[16] was born about 1667 in Kåskeby, Vörå, Finland, [16] died on 18 Oct 1735 in Kåskeby, Vörå, Finland[16] about age 68, and was buried on 2 Nov 1735. [17] Johan married **Maria Thomasdotter**.[18]
- iii. **Sophia Åkesdotter Gråbbils**[17] was born in Jun 1670 in Kåskeby, Vörå, Finland, [17] died on 26 Dec 1751 in Bertby, Vörå, Finland[17] at age 81, and was buried on 12 Jan 1752. [17] Sophia married **Simon Mårtensson Tåppar**.
- 17 iv. **Margareta Åkesdotter Gråbbils**.[19] Margareta married **Sigfred Bertilsson Storkarhu**,[14] son of **Bertel Eriksson Storkarhu** and **Unknown,** about 1703.
- v. **Karin Åkesdotter Gråbbils**[16] was born in Jan 1675 in Kåskeby, Vörå, Finland, [16] died on 16 Jul 1735 in Lomby, Vörå, Finland[16] at age 60, and was buried on 20 Jul 1735. [17] Karin married **Markus Johansson Kylkis**.[20]

Åke next married **Maria Mårtensdotter**.[16]

35. Brita Erichsdotter Heinull[14] was born in Sep 1639 in Jörala, Vörå, Finland [14] and died on 18 May 1704 in Kåskeby, Vörå, Finland[19] at age 64. Another name for Brita was Brita Erichsdotter Gråbbil.

General Notes: Her father was probably Erik Andersson. [21]

Noted events in her life were:
• Resided: Jörala, Vörå, Finland. [16]

Brita married **Åke Johansson Gråbbil**.[16]

40. Anders Carlsson[18] was born in 1643[17] and died on 29 Feb 1704 in Tuckor, Vörå, Finland [17] at age 61.

Research Notes: Dates need additional research. Possibly two wives: Brita Mårtenssdåter and Lisa. In 1634, before his birth, the homestead is abandoned.

Noted events in his life were:
• Occupation: bonde (farm owner) of Jånt, 1695-1696, Tuckor, Vörå, Finland. [22]

Anders married someone.

Children from this marriage were:
- 20 i. **Anders Andersson Jånt**.[17] Anders married **Maria Thomasdotter**.[17]
- ii. **Mårten Andersson Jånt**[23]

---

13. *Torbjörn Nikus, Storkarhu (unpublish document, 2008).*
14. *Torbjörn Nikus, Storkarhu (unpublish document, 2008). .... Anders Enders, Några sidor på nätet om släktforskning (http://www.enges.org/gene/).*
15. *Anders Enders, Några sidor på nätet om släktforskning (http://www.enges.org/gene/). .... Vörå Mantalslängden 1695-96 (http://www.enges.org).*
16. *Anders Enders, Några sidor på nätet om släktforskning (http://www.enges.org/gene/).*
17. *Hiski database (http://hiski.genealogia.fi).*
18. *Vörå Mantalslängden 1695-96 (http://www.enges.org). .... Hiski database (http://hiski.genealogia.fi).*
19. *Torbjörn Nikus, Storkarhu (unpublish document, 2008). .... Anders Enders, Några sidor på nätet om släktforskning (http://www.enges.org/gene/). .... Hiski database (http://hiski.genealogia.fi).*
20. *Anders Enders, Några sidor på nätet om släktforskning (http://www.enges.org/gene/). .... Hiski database (http://hiski.genealogia.fi).*
21. *Vörå Jordeboken 1634 (http://www.enges.org).*
22. *Vörå Kommunionsboken 1750-56 (http://www.enges.org).*
23. *Vörå Mantalslängden 1690-91 (http://www.enges.org).*

Ancestor Report for Mårten Mårtensson Storkarhu

56. Måns Mattsson[24] was born about 1614 in Kåfjoki, Vörå, Finland,[24] died on 2 Apr 1698 in Kåfjoki, Vörå, Finland[24] about age 84, and was buried on 9 Apr 1698.[25]

Research Notes: Probably the source of the farmname Månsus.

Måns married someone.

Children from this marriage were:

28   i.   **Mårten Månsson Månsus**.[26] Mårten married someone **Karin Hindersdotter**.[27] Mårten married **Karin Hindersdotter**,[28] daughter of **Hendrich Mattsson** and **Anna Simonssdotter**,.

      ii.   **Gertru Månsdotter Månsus**[29]

     iii.   **Barbru Månsdotter Månsus**[29]

     iv.   **Anna Månsdotter Månsus**[29]

24. *Anders Enders, Några sidor på nätet om släktforskning (http://www.enges.org/gene/). .... Hiski database (http://hiski.genealogia.fi).*

25. *Hiski database (http://hiski.genealogia.fi).*

26. *Anders Enders, Några sidor på nätet om släktforskning (http://www.enges.org/gene/).*

27. *Vörå Mantalslängden 1690-91 (http://www.enges.org). .... Vörå Mantalslängden 1677-78.*

28. *Vörå Mantalslängden 1677-78. .... Anders Enders, Några sidor på nätet om släktforskning (http://www.enges.org/gene/).*

29. *Vörå Mantalslängden 1675-76 (http://www.enges.org).*

Seventh Generation

68. Johan Grelsson Gråbbil.

General Notes: Johan Grelsson accused in autumn 1643 that Lars Josefsson owed him a debt recorded in a book, "Nyie Testament." Johan claimed without proof that the father paid the debt. [1]

Johan married someone.

The child from this marriage was:
34   i.   **Åke Johansson Gråbbil.**[1] Åke married **Brita Erichsdotter Heinull**.[2] Åke next married **Maria Mårtensdotter**.[1]

1. Anders Enders, Några sidor på nätet om släktforskning (http://www.enges.org/gene/).
2. Torbjörn Nikus, Storkarhu (unpublish document, 2008). .... Anders Enders, Några sidor på nätet om släktforskning (http://www.enges.org/gene/).

Pedigree Chart for Mårten Mårtensson Storkarhu

No. 1 on this chart is the same as no. 8 on chart no. 1

8 Thomas Sigfridsson Storkarhu
b. Abt 1709   cont. __3__
p. Rejpelt, Vörå, Finland
m. 21 Dec 1731
p. Vörå, Finland
d. 8 Dec 1739
p. Rejpelt, Vörå, Finland

4 Mårten Thomasson Storkarhu
b. 20 Nov 1733
p. Rejpelt, Vörå, Finland
m. 22 Dec 1754
p. Vörå, Finland
d. 8 Sep 1809
p. Rejpelt, Vörå, Finland

9 Brita Johansdotter Ingå
b. 31 Aug 1700   cont. __4__
p. Lomby, Vörå, Finland
d. 22 Jun 1780
p. Rejpelt, Vörå, Finland

2 Mårten Mårtensson Storkarhu
b. 22 Nov 1760
p. Rejpelt, Vörå, Finland
m. 13 Dec 1782
p. Vörå, Finland
d. 27 Sep 1828
p. Rejpelt, Vörå, Finland

10 Carl Andersson Jånt
b. 26 Jan 1700   cont. __5__
p. Tuckor, Vörå, Finland
m. 24 Jun 1725
p. Vörå, Finland
d. 27 Oct 1774
p. Tuckor, Vörå, Finland

5 Karin Carlsdotter Jänt
b. 28 Jul 1732
p. Tuckor, Vörå, Finland
d. 15 Apr 1805
p. Rejpelt, Vörå, Finland

11 Anna Mattsdotter
b. 1698
p. Tuckor, Vörå, Finland
d. 3 Nov 1778
p. Tuckor, Vörå, Finland

1 Mårten Mårtensson Storkarhu
b. 15 Mar 1788
p. Rejpelt, Vörå, Finland
m. 30 Nov 1810
p. Vörå, Finland
d. 13 Oct 1828
p. Rejpelt, Vörå, Finland
sp. Lisa Samuelsdotter Miemois

12 Johan Johansson Finnas
b. Sep 1706
p. Kaitsor, Vörå, Finland
m. 8 Jun 1729
p. Vörå, Finland
d. 1 Mar 1775
p. Kaitsor, Vörå, Finland

6 Karl Johansson Finnas
b. 6 Jul 1737
p. Kaitsor, Vörå, Finland
m. 12 Mar 1758
p. Vörå, Finland
d. 5 Dec 1811
p. Kaitsor, Vörå, Finland

13 Brita Andersdotter
b. Sep 1698
p. Tuckor, Vörå, Finland
d. 1779
p.

3 Margareta Carlsdotter Finnas
b. 15 Apr 1762
p. Kaitsor, Vörå, Finland
d.
p.

14 Mickel Mårtensson Månsus
b. 22 Jul 1694   cont. __6__
p. Kåfjoki, Vörå, Finland
m.
p.
d. 1770
p.

7 Margareta Mickelsdotter Månsus
b. 10 Sep 1736
p. Kåfjoki, Vörå, Finland
d. 4 Dec 1796
p. Kaitsor, Vörå, Finland

15 Brita Larsdotter Knuts
b. 17 Aug 1695   cont. __7__
p. Palfvis, Vörå, Finland
d. 16 Aug 1776
p. Kåfjoki, Vörå, Finland

Pedigree Chart for Thomas Sigfridsson Storkarhu

No. 1 on this chart is the same as no. 8 on chart no. 2

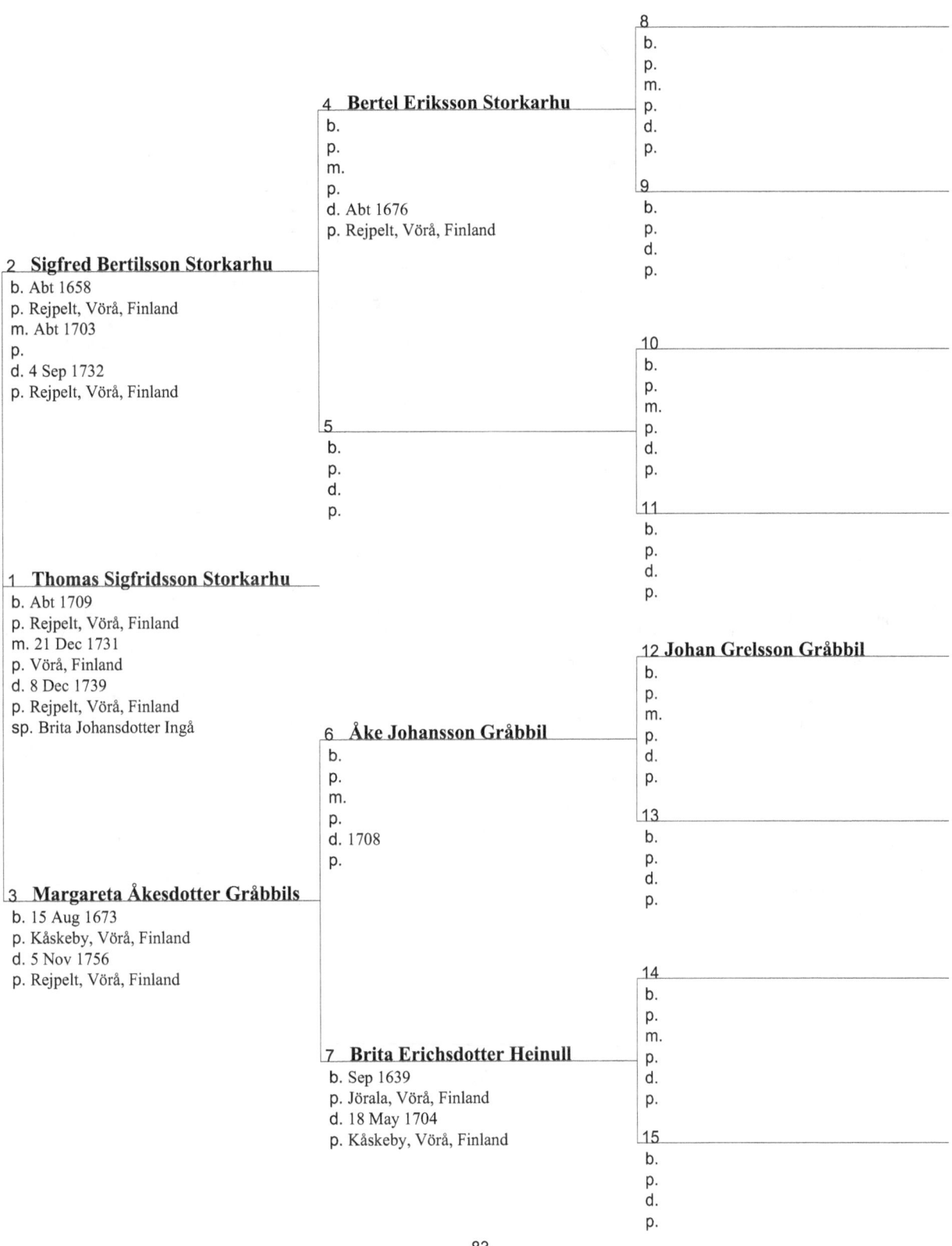

8 _____
b.
p.
m.
p.
d.
p.

4 Bertel Eriksson Storkarhu
b.
p.
m.
p.
d. Abt 1676
p. Rejpelt, Vörå, Finland

9 _____
b.
p.
d.
p.

2 Sigfred Bertilsson Storkarhu
b. Abt 1658
p. Rejpelt, Vörå, Finland
m. Abt 1703
p.
d. 4 Sep 1732
p. Rejpelt, Vörå, Finland

10 _____
b.
p.
m.
p.
d.
p.

5 _____
b.
p.
d.
p.

11 _____
b.
p.
d.
p.

1 Thomas Sigfridsson Storkarhu
b. Abt 1709
p. Rejpelt, Vörå, Finland
m. 21 Dec 1731
p. Vörå, Finland
d. 8 Dec 1739
p. Rejpelt, Vörå, Finland
sp. Brita Johansdotter Ingå

12 Johan Grelsson Gråbbil
b.
p.
m.
p.
d.
p.

6 Åke Johansson Gråbbil
b.
p.
m.
p.
d. 1708
p.

13 _____
b.
p.
d.
p.

3 Margareta Åkesdotter Gråbbils
b. 15 Aug 1673
p. Kåskeby, Vörå, Finland
d. 5 Nov 1756
p. Rejpelt, Vörå, Finland

14 _____
b.
p.
m.
p.
d.
p.

7 Brita Erichsdotter Heinull
b. Sep 1639
p. Jörala, Vörå, Finland
d. 18 May 1704
p. Kåskeby, Vörå, Finland

15 _____
b.
p.
d.
p.

Pedigree Chart for Brita Johansdotter Ingå

No. 1 on this chart is the same as no. 9 on chart no. 2

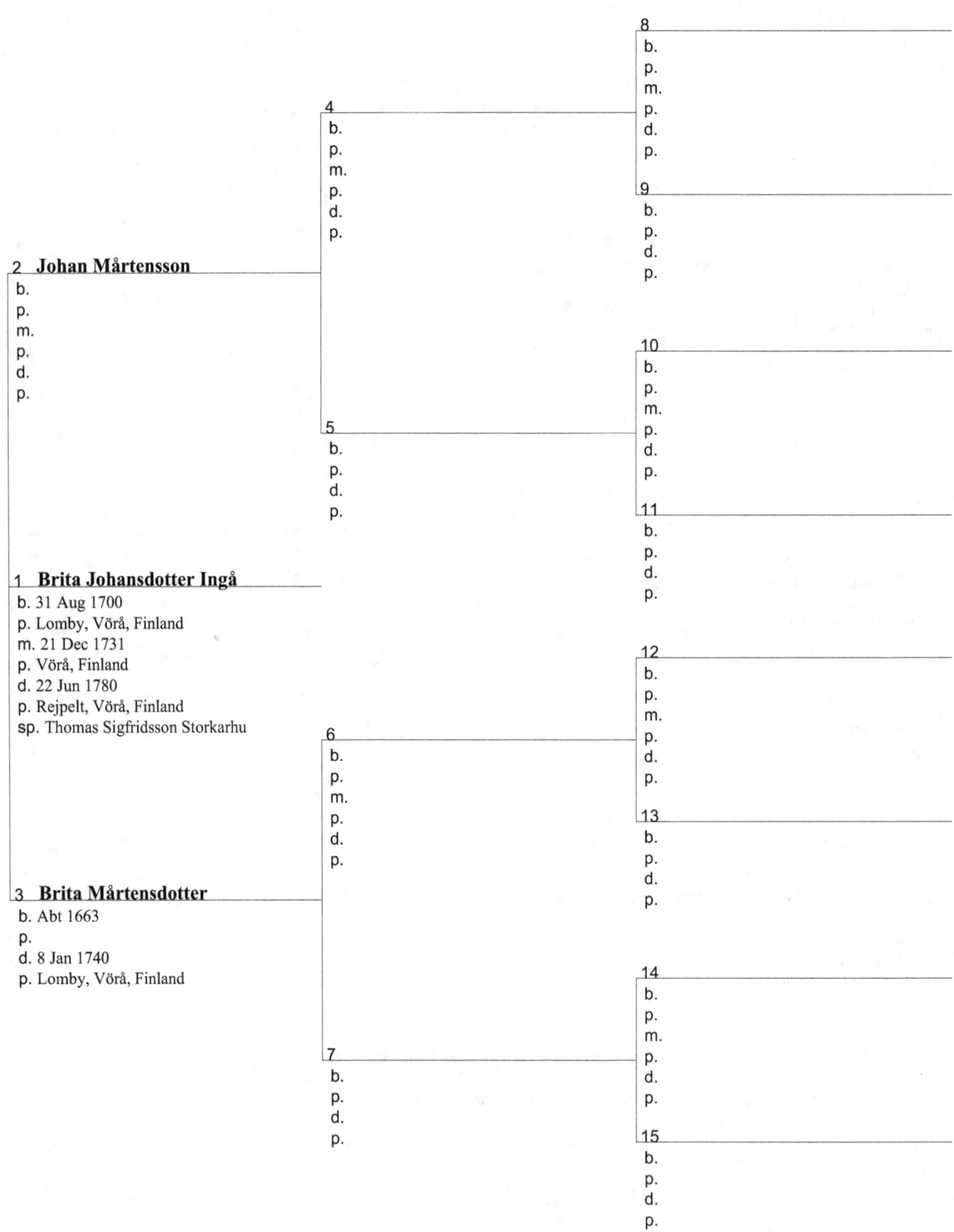

8 _____
b.
p.
m.
p.
d.
p.

4 _____
b.
p.
m.
p.
d.
p.

9 _____
b.
p.
d.
p.

2 **Johan Mårtensson**
b.
p.
m.
p.
d.
p.

10 _____
b.
p.
m.
p.
d.
p.

5 _____
b.
p.
d.
p.

11 _____
b.
p.
d.
p.

1 **Brita Johansdotter Ingå**
b. 31 Aug 1700
p. Lomby, Vörå, Finland
m. 21 Dec 1731
p. Vörå, Finland
d. 22 Jun 1780
p. Rejpelt, Vörå, Finland
sp. Thomas Sigfridsson Storkarhu

12 _____
b.
p.
m.
p.
d.
p.

6 _____
b.
p.
m.
p.
d.
p.

13 _____
b.
p.
d.
p.

3 **Brita Mårtensdotter**
b. Abt 1663
p.
d. 8 Jan 1740
p. Lomby, Vörå, Finland

14 _____
b.
p.
m.
p.
d.
p.

7 _____
b.
p.
d.
p.

15 _____
b.
p.
d.
p.

Pedigree Chart for Carl Andersson Jånt

No. 1 on this chart is the same as no. 10 on chart no. 2

4 Anders Carlsson
b. 1643
p.
m.
p.
d. 29 Feb 1704
p. Tuckor, Vörå, Finland

2 Anders Andersson Jånt
b.
p.
m.
p.
d.
p.

5
b.
p.
d.
p.

1 Carl Andersson Jånt
b. 26 Jan 1700
p. Tuckor, Vörå, Finland
m. 24 Jun 1725
p. Vörå, Finland
d. 27 Oct 1774
p. Tuckor, Vörå, Finland
sp. Anna Mattsdotter

6
b.
p.
m.
p.
d.
p.

3 Maria Thomasdotter
b.
p.
d.
p.

7
b.
p.
d.
p.

8
b.
p.
m.
p.
d.
p.

9
b.
p.
d.
p.

10
b.
p.
m.
p.
d.
p.

11
b.
p.
d.
p.

12
b.
p.
m.
p.
d.
p.

13
b.
p.
d.
p.

14
b.
p.
m.
p.
d.
p.

15
b.
p.
d.
p.

Pedigree Chart for Mickel Mårtensson Månsus

No. 1 on this chart is the same as no. 14 on chart no. 2

4 Måns Mattsson
b. Abt 1614
p. Kåfjoki, Vörå, Finland
m.
p.
d. 2 Apr 1698
p. Kåfjoki, Vörå, Finland

2 Mårten Månsson Månsus
b. Abt 1648
p. Kåfjoki, Vörå, Finland
m.
p.
d. 15 Nov 1728
p. Kåfjoki, Vörå, Finland

1 Mickel Mårtensson Månsus
b. 22 Jul 1694
p. Kåfjoki, Vörå, Finland
m.
p.
d. 1770
p.
sp. Brita Larsdotter Knuts

3 Karin Hindersdotter
b.
p.
d.
p.

5
b.
p.
d.
p.

6
b.
p.
m.
p.
d.
p.

7
b.
p.
d.
p.

8
b.
p.
m.
p.
d.
p.

9
b.
p.
d.
p.

10
b.
p.
m.
p.
d.
p.

11
b.
p.
d.
p.

12
b.
p.
m.
p.
d.
p.

13
b.
p.
d.
p.

14
b.
p.
m.
p.
d.
p.

15
b.
p.
d.
p.

Pedigree Chart for Brita Larsdotter Knuts

No. 1 on this chart is the same as no. 15 on chart no. 2

2 Lars Mattsson
b.
p.
m.
p.
d. Bef 1708
p.

1 Brita Larsdotter Knuts
b. 17 Aug 1695
p. Palfvis, Vörå, Finland
m.
p.
d. 16 Aug 1776
p. Kåfjoki, Vörå, Finland
sp. Mickel Mårtensson Månsus

3 Gertrud Mårtensdotter
b.
p.
d.
p.

4
b.
p.
m.
p.
d.
p.

5
b.
p.
d.
p.

6
b.
p.
m.
p.
d.
p.

7
b.
p.
d.
p.

8
b.
p.
m.
p.
d.
p.

9
b.
p.
d.
p.

10
b.
p.
m.
p.
d.
p.

11
b.
p.
d.
p.

12
b.
p.
m.
p.
d.
p.

13
b.
p.
d.
p.

14
b.
p.
m.
p.
d.
p.

15
b.
p.
d.
p.

Chapter 3. Ancestor Report for Lisa Samuelsdotter Miemois

First Generation

1. Lisa Samuelsdotter Miemois,[1] daughter of **Samuel Mattsson Keskis** and **Lisa Sunedotter Israels,** was born on 10 Dec 1792 in Miemoisby, Vörå, Finland,[1] was christened on 12 Dec 1792,[2] and died on 19 Nov 1866 in Leistus, Rejpelt, Vörå, Finland[3] at age 73.

Lisa married **Mårten Mårtensson Storkarhu**,[3] son of **Mårten Mårtensson Storkarhu** and **Margareta Carlsdotter Finnas,** on 30 Nov 1810 in Vörå, Finland.[3]

General Notes: a bonde (farm owner) and later a crofter (farm renter) on No. 3 Storkarhu.[3]

Research Notes: The Storkarhu farm was given the name Svens in the mid-1800s. The farm was briefly referred to as Nykarhu and Björns in church records.[3]

Noted events in his life were:
• Occupation: bonde (farm owner) at Storkarhu, 1811-1825, Rejpelt, Vörå, Finland. [2]

Children from this marriage were:
  i. **Mårten Mårtensson Storkarhu**[1] was born on 3 Feb 1811 in Rejpelt, Vörå, Finland, [1] was christened on 5 Feb 1811,[2] died on 13 Nov 1828 in Rejpelt, Vörå, Finland[1] at age 17, and was buried on 16 Nov 1828.[2]
  ii. **Greta Mårtensdotter Storkarhu**[2] was born on 7 Mar 1813 in Rejpelt, Vörå, Finland,[2] was christened on 9 Mar 1813,[2] died on 4 Jul 1813,[2] and was buried on 11 Jul 1813. [2]
  iii. **Johan Mårtensson Storkarhu**[1] was born on 16 Jun 1815 in Rejpelt, Vörå, Finland, [1] was christened on 18 Jun 1815,[2] and died on 1 Dec 1888 in Finland[3] at age 73. Another name for Johan was Johan Mårtensson Nyberg. Johan married **Maria Mattsdotter Kjerp**[3] on 12 Jul 1835.
  iv. **Lisa Mårtensdotter Storkarhu**[2] was born on 9 Aug 1817 in Rejpelt, Vörå, Finland,[2] was christened on 10 Aug 1817,[2] and died after 1850.[2] Another name for Lisa was Lisa Mårtensdotter Svens.[2] Lisa married **Jakob Mattsson Höijer**[2] on 21 Dec 1836.[2]
  v. **Anna Beata Mårtensdotter Storkarhu**[1] was born on 25 Aug 1818 in Rejpelt, Vörå, Finland[1] and was christened on 30 Aug 1818.[2] Anna married **Mårten Mårtensson Klemets**[2] on 10 Jul 1835.[2]
  vi. **Lisa Mårtensdotter Storkarhu**[2] was born on 23 Sep 1821 in Rejpelt, Vörå, Finland[2] and was christened on 24 Sep 1821.[2] Lisa married **Erik Eriksson Kaurajärvi**[2] on 16 Jan 1848.[2]
  vii. **Greta Lisa Mårtensdotter Storkarhu**[1] was born on 2 Mar 1823 in Rejpelt, Vörå, Finland, [1] was christened on 3 Mar 1823,[2] and died on 12 Dec 1887 in Andiala, Vörå, Finland[3] at age 64. Another name for Greta was Greta Lisa Mårtensdotter Svens. Greta married **Erik Johansson Nyby**[3] on 28 Jun 1845.
  viii. **Maria Mårtensdotter Storkarhu**[3] was born on 9 Apr 1824 in Rejpelt, Vörå, Finland, [1] was christened on 11 Apr 1824,[2] and died on 1 Aug 1855 in Finland[3] at age 31. Maria married someone.
  ix. **Mickel Mårtensson Storkarhu**[2] was born on 30 Sep 1825 in Rejpelt, Vörå, Finland, [2] was christened on 2 Oct 1825,[2] died on 21 Apr 1826,[2] and was buried on 30 Apr 1826. [2]
  x. **Brita Mårtensdotter Storkarhu**[1] was born on 26 Jul 1827 in Rejpelt, Vörå, Finland, [1] was christened on 29 Jul 1827,[2] and died on 26 Feb 1902 in Rejpelt, Vörå, Finland[3] at age 74. Brita married **Simon Mattsson Wäst**.[3]
  xi. **Mickel Mårtensson Storkarhu**[3] was born on 15 Sep 1828 in Rejpelt, Vörå, Finland[3] and died on 16 May 1903 in Newberry, Luce, Michigan[3] at age 74. Other names for Mickel were Mickel Mårtensson Svens, Mickel Svens, and Michael Swanson. Mickel married **Lisa Johansdotter Wäst**,[1] daughter of **Johan Eriksson Wäst** and **Lisa Johansdotter Wäst,** on 8 Jul 1852 in Rejpelt, Vörå, Finland. [3]

1. Torbjörn Nikus, Storkarhu (unpublish document, 2008). .... Hiski database (http://hiski.genealogia.fi).
2. Hiski database (http://hiski.genealogia.fi).
3. Torbjörn Nikus, Storkarhu (unpublish document, 2008).

Ancestor Report for Lisa Samuelsdotter Miemois

Second Generation

2. Samuel Mattsson Keskis,[1] son of **Matts Samuelsson Storkeskis** and **Anna Jakobsdotter,** was born on 4 Oct 1754 in Kieskis, Vörå, Finland,[1] was christened on 6 Oct 1754,[2] and died before 1810.[1]

General Notes: Only three 3 children did not reach adulthood.[1]

Samuel married **Lisa Sunedotter Israels**[3] on 28 Jun 1774 in Vörå, Finland.[2]

Children from this marriage were:

i. **Matts Samuelsson Miemois**[2] was born on 19 Apr 1775 in Miemoisby, Vörå, Finland,[2] was christened on 20 Apr 1775,[2] and died before 1781.[2]

ii. **Anna Samuelsdotter Miemois**[2] was born on 10 Jul 1776 in Miemoisby, Vörå, Finland,[2] was christened on 11 Jul 1776,[2] died on 2 Aug 1776,[2] and was buried on 4 Aug 1776.[2]

iii. **Johan Samuelsson Miemois**[2] was born on 27 Sep 1777 in Miemoisby, Vörå, Finland,[2] was christened on 28 Sep 1777,[2] died on 8 Oct 1777,[2] and was buried on 12 Oct 1777.[2]

iv. **Jacob Samuelsson Miemois**[2] was born on 18 Feb 1779 in Miemoisby, Vörå, Finland,[2] was christened on 21 Feb 1779,[2] died on 30 Jul 1780[2] at age 1, and was buried on 6 Aug 1780.[2]

v. **Matts Samuelsson Miemois**[2] was born on 29 Sep 1781 in Miemoisby, Vörå, Finland,[2] was christened on 30 Sep 1781,[2] and died on 31 Mar 1841 in Miemoisby, Vörå, Finland[2] at age 59. Matts married **Clara Simonsdotter Kåll**[2] on 28 Nov 1802.[2]

vi. **Lisa Samuelsdotter Miemois**[2] was born on 1 Oct 1782 in Miemoisby, Vörå, Finland,[2] was christened on 2 Oct 1782,[2] and died before 1792.

vii. **Anders Samuelsdotter Miemos**[2] was born on 15 Jan 1784 in Miemoisby, Vörå, Finland,[2] was christened on 18 Jan 1784,[2] died on 2 Feb 1784,[2] and was buried on 8 Feb 1784.[2]

viii. **Margeta Samuelsdotter Miemois**[2] was born on 24 Jun 1786 in Miemoisby, Vörå, Finland,[2] was christened on 25 Jun 1786,[2] died on 14 Jul 1786,[2] and was buried on 21 Jul 1786.[2]

ix. **Johan Samuelsson Miemos**[2] was born on 10 Nov 1787 in Miemoisby, Vörå, Finland,[2] was christened on 11 Nov 1787,[2] died on 7 Jul 1788,[2] and was buried on 13 Jul 1788.[2]

x. **Maria Caisa Samuelsdotter Miemois**[2] was born on 30 Jun 1789 in Miemoisby, Vörå, Finland[2] and was christened on 1 Jul 1789.[2]

xi. **Anna Beata Samuelsdotter Miemois**[2] was born on 1 Sep 1790 in Miemoisby, Vörå, Finland[2] and was christened on 4 Sep 1790.[2]

xii. **Brita Samuelsdotter Miemois**[2] was born on 23 Sep 1791 in Miemoisby, Vörå, Finland,[2] was christened on 25 Sep 1791,[2] died on 12 Oct 1791,[2] and was buried on 16 Oct 1791.[2]

1 xiii. **Lisa Samuelsdotter Miemois**.[3] Lisa married **Mårten Mårtensson Storkarhu**,[1] son of **Mårten Mårtensson Storkarhu** and **Margareta Carlsdotter Finnas,** on 30 Nov 1810 in Vörå, Finland.[1]

xiv. **Maria Samuelsdotter Miemois**[2] was born on 28 Dec 1793 in Miemoisby, Vörå, Finland,[2] was christened on 29 Dec 1793,[2] died on 23 May 1794,[2] and was buried on 1 Jun 1794.[2]

xv. **Gretha Samuelsdotter Miemois**[2] was born on 2 Mar 1795 in Miemoisby, Vörå, Finland,[2] was christened on 8 Mar 1795,[2] died on 5 Sep 1799[2] at age 4, and was buried on 8 Sep 1799.[2]

3. Lisa Sunedotter Israels,[3] daughter of **Sune Hansson** and **Anna Hansdotter Israels,** was born on 2 Sep 1754 in Rejpelt, Vörå, Finland,[3] was christened on 8 Sep 1754,[2] died on 26 Dec 1835 in Miemoisby, Vörå, Finland[3] at age 81, and was buried on 3 Jan 1836.[2] Another name for Lisa was Elisabet Sunderland.

Lisa married **Samuel Mattsson Keskis**[1] on 28 Jun 1774 in Vörå, Finland.[2]

1. Torbjörn Nikus, Storkarhu (unpublish document, 2008).
2. Hiski database (http://hiski.genealogia.fi).
3. Torbjörn Nikus, Storkarhu (unpublish document, 2008). .... Hiski database (http://hiski.genealogia.fi).

Ancestor Report for Lisa Samuelsdotter Miemois

Third Generation

4. Matts Samuelsson Storkeskis,[1] son of **Samuel Simonsson** and **Karin Hendriksdotter,** was born on 30 Aug 1726 in Kieskis, Vörå, Finland,[1] was christened on 4 Sep 1726,[1] died on 21 Sep 1789 in Miemoisby, Vörå, Finland[1] at age 63, and was buried on 27 Sep 1789.[1]

Noted events in his life were:
• Occupation: bonde (farm owner) of Storkeskis and later Miemos.[2]

Matts married **Anna Jakobsdotter**[1] on 28 Dec 1748.[1]

Children from this marriage were:
- i. **Carin Mattsdotter Kieskis**[1] was born on 16 Dec 1749 in Kieskis, Vörå, Finland[1] and was christened on 17 Dec 1749.[1]
- ii. **Margeta Mattsdotter Kieskis**[1] was born on 31 Mar 1751 in Kieskis, Vörå, Finland[1] and was christened on 1 Apr 1751.[1]
- iii. **Johan Mattsson Kieskis**[1] was born on 16 Jun 1752 in Kieskis, Vörå, Finland,[1] was christened on 19 Jun 1752,[1] and died on 26 Jun 1752.[1]
- iv. **Anna Mattsdotter Kieskis**[1] was born on 4 Jul 1753 in Kieskis, Vörå, Finland[1] and was christened on 8 Jul 1753.[1]
- 2 v. **Samuel Mattsson Keskis**.[3] Samuel married **Lisa Sunedotter Israels**,[4] daughter of **Sune Hansson** and **Anna Hansdotter Israels,** on 28 Jun 1774 in Vörå, Finland.[1]
- vi. **Marja Mattsdotter Kieskis**[1] was born on 27 Sep 1756 in Kieskis, Vörå, Finland[1] and was christened on 29 Sep 1756.[1]
- vii. **Lisa Mattsdotter Kieskis**[1] was born on 7 Aug 1758 in Kieskis, Vörå, Finland[1] and was christened on 13 Aug 1758.[1]
- viii. **Anna Mattsdotter Kieskis**[1] was born on 3 Dec 1759 in Kieskis, Vörå, Finland,[1] was christened on 9 Dec 1759,[1] and died on 15 May 1760.[1]
- ix. **Matts Mattsson Miemos**[1] was born on 25 Feb 1762 in Miemoisby, Vörå, Finland[1] and was christened on 28 Feb 1762.[1]
- x. **Jacob Mattsson Miemos**[1] was born on 8 Aug 1764 in Miemoisby, Vörå, Finland[1] and was christened on 12 Aug 1764.[1]

5. Anna Jakobsdotter[1] was born in Aug 1721,[1] died on 15 Apr 1801 in Miemoisby, Vörå, Finland[1] at age 79, and was buried on 19 Apr 1801.[1]

Anna married **Matts Samuelsson Storkeskis**[1] on 28 Dec 1748.[1]

6. Sune Hansson,[1] son of **Hans Georg Sommar** and **Elin Svensdotter,** was born on 13 Jan 1726 in Vrankunge, Skatelöv, Småland, Sweden,[5] died on 2 Oct 1798 in Rejpelt, Vörå, Finland[1] at age 72, and was buried on 7 Oct 1798.[1]

General Notes: He was a salpetersjudare, or nitre boiler, which means he made potassium nitrate which is used in gunpowder. He was born in Vrankunge, Skatelövs parish, Sweden, about 3 mil south of Växjö. From Torbjörn Nikus: "After the conclusion of peace, the crown began to send 'refiners' of saltpeter from Sweden to Swedish Ostrobothnia (Finland), to teach farmers how to 'boil' saltpeter. For some reason, the best refiners came from Småland (a province in southern Sweden). Among others who came to Vörå the 19-year old saltpeter refiner Sune Hansson arrived in 1745. He was stationed in the southern communities of Vörå. Sune the man from Småland fell in love with Anna Hansdotter at Israels (farm). She was two years older than he. Anna's mother Brita had survived the raids by cossacks. At the time of the battle at Nevo, Brita was 13 years old. Brita's father Anders never returned from the battle. Sune taught the secrets of refining saltpeter to the young men of the community and at the same

1. Hiski database (http://hiski.genealogia.fi).
2. Vörå Kommunionsboken 1750-56 (http://www.enges.org).
3. Torbjörn Nikus, Storkarhu (unpublish document, 2008).
4. Torbjörn Nikus, Storkarhu (unpublish document, 2008). .... Hiski database (http://hiski.genealogia.fi).
5. Hiski database (http://hiski.genealogia.fi). .... Plym Arnäs, Plym Arnäs's family research website (http://www.plymarnas.se). .... Skatelöv CI:2 (1720-1746) Image 24 / page 39 (AID: v30280.b24.s39, NAD: SE/VALA/00329) .

time ran the Israels farm. His brother-in-law Matts Hansson became one of the apprentices. About 1760, the farm/homestead was divided between Matts and Sune. Matts sold his share to Erik Mårtensson, also an apprentice. The Israels estate inventory taken in 1814. It is stated that a one-sixth share in a boiler [large kettle] was worth 19 rubels, while the farm's assets, including animals, land, and personal property was worth 196 rubels. A vodka/aquavit/spirits boiler was valued at 7 rubels." Sune died of "dropsy." Sunes parents are possibly Hans Georg Sommer and wife Elin Svensdotter in Wrankunge."[6]

Noted events in his life were:

• Arrived: from Småland, Sweden, 1745, Rejpelt, Vörå, Finland. [6]

• Occupation: salpetersjudare (gunpowder maker), Rejpelt, Vörå, Finland. [7]

Sune married **Anna Hansdotter Israels**[7] on 14 Sep 1746 in Rejpelt, Vörå, Finland. [7]

Children from this marriage were:

    i.   **Brita Sunedotter Israels**[7] was born on 8 Oct 1747 in Rejpelt, Vörå, Finland, [7] was christened on 11 Oct 1747,[7] died on 16 May 1809 in Rejpelt, Vörå, Finland[7] at age 61, and was buried on 22 May 1809.[7] Another name for Brita was Brita Ekman. Brita married **Corporal Adolph Ekman**[7] on 12 Nov 1771.[7]

    ii.   **Hans Sunesson Israels**[7] was born on 9 Mar 1749 in Rejpelt, Vörå, Finland, [7] was christened on 13 Mar 1749,[7] died on 7 May 1809 in Rejpelt, Vörå, Finland[7] at age 60, and was buried on 11 May 1809.[7] Hans married **Lisa Mattsdotter Kieskis**[7] on 3 Jun 1777.[7]

    iii.   **Johan Sunesson Israels**[7] was born on 1 Mar 1752 in Rejpelt, Vörå, Finland, [7] was christened on 8 Mar 1752,[7] and died on 9 Aug 1752.[7]

    iv.   **Erich Sunesson Israels**[7] was born on 10 Apr 1753 in Rejpelt, Vörå, Finland, [7] was christened on 15 Apr 1753,[7] and died on 19 Aug 1754[7] at age 1.

3   v.   **Lisa Sunedotter Israels**.[8] Lisa married **Samuel Mattsson Keskis**,[9] son of **Matts Samuelsson Storkeskis** and **Anna Jakobsdotter,** on 28 Jun 1774 in Vörå, Finland. [7]

    vi.   **Maria Sunedotter Israels**[7] was born on 14 Jan 1758 in Rejpelt, Vörå, Finland, [7] was christened on 15 Jan 1758,[7] and died on 26 Nov 1830 in Rejpelt, Vörå, Finland[7] at age 72. Another name for Maria was Maria Sunedotter Nordman. Maria married **Matts Bagge**[7] on 16 May 1775 in Mäkipää, Vörå, Finland. [7]

    vii.   **Anna Sunedotter Israels**[7] was born on 6 Dec 1760 in Rejpelt, Vörå, Finland, [7] was christened on 7 Dec 1760,[7] died on 6 Jan 1761,[7] and was buried on 11 Jan 1761. [7]

    viii.   **Beata Sunedotter Israels**[7] was born on 1 Mar 1762 in Rejpelt, Vörå, Finland, [7] was christened on 7 Mar 1762,[7] died on 10 Jan 1763,[7] and was buried on 16 Jan 1763. [7] Another name for Beata was Beata Sunedotter Murkais.

    ix.   **Margareta Sunedotter Israels**[7] was born on 29 Oct 1763 in Rejpelt, Vörå, Finland, [7] was christened on 30 Oct 1763,[7] died on 30 Jul 1764,[7] and was buried on 5 Aug 1764.[7]

    x.   **Anna Sunedotter Israels**[7] was born on 18 May 1765 in Rejpelt, Vörå, Finland[7] and was christened on 19 May 1765.[7] Anna married **Anders Andersson Carlspets**[7] before 1787.[7]

    xi.   **Beata Sunedotter Israels**[7] was born on 15 Nov 1766 in Rejpelt, Vörå, Finland, [7] was christened on 16 Nov 1766,[7] died on 13 Jun 1767,[7] and was buried on 21 Jun 1767.[7]

7. Anna Hansdotter Israels,[7] daughter of **Hans Mattsson** and **Brita Johansdotter Israels,** was born on 19 Sep 1724 in Rejpelt, Vörå, Finland, [7] was christened on 20 Sep 1724, [7] died on 25 Jan 1805 in Rejpelt, Vörå, Finland[7] at age 80, and was buried on 3 Feb 1805. [7] Another name for Anna was Anna Hansdotter Hansson.

Research Notes: According to Bror V. Åkerblom in Vörå parish history (1937), Anna Hansdotter Israels was a childless widow when she married Sune Hansson. [6]

Anna married **Sune Hansson**[7] on 14 Sep 1746 in Rejpelt, Vörå, Finland. [7]

---

6. *Email from Torbjörn Nikus.*
7. *Hiski database (http://hiski.genealogia.fi).*
8. *Torbjörn Nikus, Storkarhu (unpublish document, 2008). .... Hiski database (http://hiski.genealogia.fi).*
9. *Torbjörn Nikus, Storkarhu (unpublish document, 2008).*

Ancestor Report for Lisa Samuelsdotter Miemois

Fourth Generation

8. Samuel Simonsson[1] was born in 1687,[1] died on 24 Apr 1737 in Kieskis, Vörå, Finland[1] at age 50, and was buried on 1 May 1737.[1]

Research Notes: Father might be Simon Dahlkarl.

Samuel married **Karin Hendriksdotter**.[1]

Children from this marriage were:
  - i. **Hendrich Samuelsson**[1] was born on 25 Feb 1723 in Kåskeby, Vörå, Finland[1] and was christened on 1 Mar 1723.[1]
  - ii. **Simon Samuelsson Storkeskis**[1] was born on 29 Jan 1725 in Kieskis, Vörå, Finland[1] and was christened on 2 Feb 1725.[1]
4 iii. **Matts Samuelsson Storkeskis**.[1] Matts married **Anna Jakobsdotter**[1] on 28 Dec 1748.[1]
  - iv. **Samuel Samuelsson Storkeskis**[1] was born on 20 Oct 1728 in Kieskis, Vörå, Finland,[1] was christened on 28 Oct 1728,[1] died on 20 Nov 1807 in Miemoisby, Vörå, Finland[1] at age 79, and was buried on 29 Nov 1807.[1]
  - v. **Maria Samuelsdotter Storkeskis**[1] was born on 12 Mar 1732 in Kieskis, Vörå, Finland[1] and was christened on 19 Mar 1732.[1]

9. Karin Hendriksdotter[1] was born in Jul 1690,[1] died on 10 Feb 1771 in Miemoisby, Vörå, Finland[1] at age 80, and was buried on 17 Feb 1771.[1] Another name for Karin was Karin Simonsson.

Karin married **Samuel Simonsson**.[1]

12. Hans Georg Sommar[2] was born about 1688[3] and died on 2 Oct 1758 in Vrankunge, Skatelöv, Småland, Sweden[3] about age 70.

General Notes: Hans Georg was accepted as a rider for the root number 25 (Vrankunge) under Sunnerbo Company, and Småland Cavalry Regiment in about 1718. He served as the deputy sheriff for Johan Nyman and as Måns Persson's bachelor servant in Wrankunge. [4]

Noted events in his life were:
• Occupation: owner of farm Ryttartorpet (possibly equestrian farm), Vrankunge, Skatelöv, Småland, Sweden. [4]

• Occupation: soldier in cavalry, 1688-1718, Vrankunge, Skatelöv, Småland, Sweden. [5]

Hans married **Elin Svensdotter**[6] on 18 Jan 1721 in Västra Torsås, Småland, Sweden. [7]

Children from this marriage were:
  - i. **Ingegärd Hansdotter**[4] was born on 15 Nov 1720 in Vrankunge, Skatelöv, Småland, Sweden. [8]
  - ii. **Jöran Hansson**[4] was born on 10 Nov 1722 in Vrankunge, Skatelöv, Småland, Sweden. [9]

---

1. Hiski database (http://hiski.genealogia.fi).

2. Anders Enders, Några sidor på nätet om släktforskning (http://www.enges.org/gene/). …. Plym Arnäs, Plym Arnäs's family research website (http://www.plymarnas.se).

3. Plym Arnäs, Plym Arnäs's family research website (http://www.plymarnas.se). …. Skatelöv CI:3 (1747-1806) Image 296 / page 581 (AID: v30281.b296.s581, NAD: SE/VALA/00329).

4. Plym Arnäs, Plym Arnäs's family research website (http://www.plymarnas.se).

5. Plym Arnäs, Plym Arnäs's family research website (http://www.plymarnas.se). …. Skatelöv CI:2 (1720-1746) Image 24 / page 39 (AID: v30280.b24.s39, NAD: SE/VALA/00329).

6. Anders Enders, Några sidor på nätet om släktforskning (http://www.enges.org/gene/). …. Plym Arnäs, Plym Arnäs's family research website (http://www.plymarnas.se). …. Skatelöv CI:2 (1720-1746) Image 24 / page 39 (AID: v30280.b24.s39, NAD: SE/VALA/00329).

7. Plym Arnäs, Plym Arnäs's family research website (http://www.plymarnas.se). …. Västra Torsås C:2 (1720-1746) Image 148 / page 287 (AID: v29902.b148.s287, NAD: SE/VALA/00453).

8. Plym Arnäs, Plym Arnäs's family research website (http://www.plymarnas.se). …. Skatelöv CI:2 (1720-1746) Image 5 / page 3 (AID: v30280.b5.s3, NAD: SE/VALA/00329).

9. Plym Arnäs, Plym Arnäs's family research website (http://www.plymarnas.se). …. Skatelöv CI:2 (1720-1746) Image 10 / page 11 (AID: v30280.b10.s11, NAD: SE/VALA/00329).

Ancestor Report for Lisa Samuelsdotter Miemois

6   iii.   **Sune Hansson**.[1] Sune married **Anna Hansdotter Israels**,[1] daughter of **Hans Mattsson** and **Brita Johansdotter Israels,** on 14 Sep 1746 in Rejpelt, Vörå, Finland.[1]

    iv.   **Christian Hansson**[10] was born on 28 Dec 1728 in Vrankunge, Skatelöv, Småland, Sweden[11] and died on 4 Nov 1808 in Toftåsa Norreg, Almundsryd, Småland, Sweden[12] at age 79. Christian married **Elin Jönsdotter**[13] on 13 Oct 1751 in Almundsryd, Småland, Sweden.[14]

    v.   **Jöns Hansson**[10] was born on 11 Oct 1731 in Vrankunge, Skatelöv, Småland, Sweden.[15]

    vi.   **Anna Hansdotter**[10] was born on 15 Sep 1736 in Vrankunge, Skatelöv, Småland, Sweden.[16]

    vii.   **Kirstin Hansdotter**[10] was born on 15 Sep 1736 in Vrankunge, Skatelöv, Småland, Sweden.[16] Kirstin married **Anders Hallberg**[10] on 10 Jul 1791 in Skatelöv, Småland, Sweden.[17]

    viii.   **Sven Hansson Sommar**[10] was born on 18 Jan 1739 in Vrankunge, Skatelöv, Småland, Sweden.[18] Sven married **Swenborg Nilsdotter**.[19]

    ix.   **Maria Hansdotter**[10] was born on 21 Oct 1743 in Vrankunge, Skatelöv, Småland, Sweden.[20]

13. Elin Svensdotter,[21] daughter of **Sven Jakobsson** and **Svenborg Nilsdotter,** was born in Oct 1690 in Olofshult, Västra Torsås, Småland, Sweden,[22] was christened on 20 Oct 1690 in Västra Torsås, Småland, Sweden,[23] and died on 7 Jan 1754 in Vrankunge, Skatelöv, Småland, Sweden[22] at age 63.

Christening Notes: Trint. XVIII. Christening record does not list parents, only birthplace.

Noted events in her life were:
• Occupation: maid, 1721, Vrankunge, Skatelöv, Småland, Sweden.

Elin married **Hans Georg Sommar**[24] on 18 Jan 1721 in Västra Torsås, Småland, Sweden.[25]

14. Hans Mattsson[26] was born in Dec 1689,[27] died on 28 May 1766 in Rejpelt, Vörå, Finland[26] at age 76, and was buried on 1 Jun 1766.[26]

Birth Notes: The age in the death record and the Communion Book dates disagree.

---

10. *Plym Arnäs, Plym Arnäs's family research website (http://www.plymarnas.se).*

11. *Plym Arnäs, Plym Arnäs's family research website (http://www.plymarnas.se). .... Skatelöv CI:2 (1720-1746) Image 38 / page 67 (AID: v30280.b38.s67, NAD: SE/VALA/00329).*

12. *Plym Arnäs, Plym Arnäs's family research website (http://www.plymarnas.se). .... Almundsryd CI:2 (1762-1832) Image 291 / page 575 (AID: v29625.b291.s575, NAD: SE/VALA/00008).*

13. *Almundsryd CI:1 (1721-1762) Image 21 / page 35 (AID: v29624.b21.s35, NAD: SE/VALA/00008).*

14. *Plym Arnäs, Plym Arnäs's family research website (http://www.plymarnas.se). .... Almundsryd CI:1 (1721-1762) Image 21 / page 35 (AID: v29624.b21.s35, NAD: SE/VALA/00008).*

15. *Plym Arnäs, Plym Arnäs's family research website (http://www.plymarnas.se). .... Skatelöv CI:2 (1720-1746) Image 55 / page 101 (AID: v30280.b55.s101, NAD: SE/VALA/00329).*

16. *Plym Arnäs, Plym Arnäs's family research website (http://www.plymarnas.se). .... Skatelöv CI:2 (1720-1746) Image 83 / page 157 (AID: v30280.b83.s157, NAD: SE/VALA/00329).*

17. *Plym Arnäs, Plym Arnäs's family research website (http://www.plymarnas.se). .... Skatelöv CI:3 (1747-1806) Image 439 / page 865 (AID: v30281.b439.s865, NAD: SE/VALA/00329).*

18. *Plym Arnäs, Plym Arnäs's family research website (http://www.plymarnas.se). .... Skatelöv CI:2 (1720-1746) Image 98 / page 187 (AID: v30280.b98.s187, NAD: SE/VALA/00329).*

19. *Skatelöv AI:1 (1760-1769) Image 40 / page 33 (AID: v19267.b40.s33, NAD: SE/VALA/00329).*

20. *Plym Arnäs, Plym Arnäs's family research website (http://www.plymarnas.se). .... Skatelöv CI:2 (1720-1746) Image 122 / page 235 (AID: v30280.b122.s235, NAD: SE/VALA/00329).*

21. *Anders Enders, Några sidor på nätet om släktforskning (http://www.enges.org/gene/). .... Plym Arnäs, Plym Arnäs's family research website (http://www.plymarnas.se). .... Skatelöv CI:2 (1720-1746) Image 24 / page 39 (AID: v30280.b24.s39, NAD: SE/VALA/00329).*

22. *Plym Arnäs, Plym Arnäs's family research website (http://www.plymarnas.se). .... Skatelöv CI:3 (1747-1806) Image 288 / page 565 (AID: v30281.b288.s565, NAD: SE/VALA/00329). .... Västra Torsås C:1 (1681-1693) Image 17 / page 27 (AID: v29901.b17.s27, NAD: SE/VALA/00453).*

23. *Plym Arnäs, Plym Arnäs's family research website (http://www.plymarnas.se). .... Västra Torsås C:1 (1681-1693) Image 17 / page 27 (AID: v29901.b17.s27, NAD: SE/VALA/00453).*

24. *Anders Enders, Några sidor på nätet om släktforskning (http://www.enges.org/gene/). .... Plym Arnäs, Plym Arnäs's family research website (http://www.plymarnas.se).*

25. *Plym Arnäs, Plym Arnäs's family research website (http://www.plymarnas.se). .... Västra Torsås C:2 (1720-1746) Image 148 / page 287 (AID: v29902.b148.s287, NAD: SE/VALA/00453).*

26. *Hiski database (http://hiski.genealogia.fi).*

27. *Hiski database (http://hiski.genealogia.fi). .... Vörå Kommunionsboken 1750-56 (http://www.enges.org).*

Ancestor Report for Lisa Samuelsdotter Miemois

Hans married **Brita Johansdotter Israels** [28] Est 1723.

Children from this marriage were:

7   i.   **Anna Hansdotter Israels**.[28] Anna married **Sune Hansson**,[28] son of **Hans Georg Sommar** and **Elin Svensdotter,** on 14 Sep 1746 in Rejpelt, Vörå, Finland. [28]

ii.   **Lisa Hansdotter Israels**[28] was born on 6 Aug 1726 in Rejpelt, Vörå, Finland [28] and was christened on 7 Aug 1726.[28] Lisa married **Matths Danielsson Räx**[28] on 11 Jan 1747.[28]

iii.   **Maria Hansdotter Israels**[28] was born on 29 Oct 1728 in Rejpelt, Vörå, Finland, [28] was christened on 1 Nov 1728,[28] and died after 1768. Maria married **Soldat Simon Krigsbuss**[28] on 13 Jun 1756. [28] Maria next married **Anders Häisius**[28] on 25 Jan 1766.[28]

iv.   **Matts Hansson Israels**[29] was born about 1730 in Rejpelt, Vörå, Finland, [29] died on 12 Aug 1807[28] about age 77, and was buried on 16 Aug 1807. [28] Another name for Matts was Matts Hansson Antus. Matts married **Maria Carlsdotter** on 29 Nov 1752. Matts next married **Anna Johansdotter**[28] on 10 Jan 1763.[28] Matts next married **Lisa Mattsdotter**[28] on 17 Dec 1796.

v.   **Israel Hansson Israels**[28] was born on 9 Dec 1732 in Rejpelt, Vörå, Finland, [28] was christened on 10 Dec 1732,[28] died on 1 Nov 1733,[28] and was buried on 4 Nov 1733. [28]

vi.   **Margeta Hansdotter Israels**[28] was born on 23 Aug 1734 in Rejpelt, Vörå, Finland, [28] was christened on 25 Aug 1734,[28] and died before 1747.

vii.   **Johan Hansson Israels**[28] was born on 21 Jan 1737 in Rejpelt, Vörå, Finland [28] and was christened on 26 Jan 1737.[28]

viii.   **Brita Hansdotter Israels**[28] was born on 11 Mar 1738 in Rejpelt, Vörå, Finland, [28] was christened on 12 Mar 1738,[28] died 14.2.1740 [28] at age 1, and was buried on 25 Feb 1740. [28]

ix.   **Beata Hansdotter Israels**[28] was born on 13 Mar 1747 in Rejpelt, Vörå, Finland, [28] was christened on 15 Mar 1747,[28] died on 15 Aug 1748[28] at age 1, and was buried on 21 Aug 1748. [28]

x.   **Margeta Hansdotter Israels**[28] was born on 25 Nov 1748 in Rejpelt, Vörå, Finland [28] and was christened on 27 Nov 1748. [28]

15. Brita Johansdotter Israels,[28] daughter of **Johan Andersson Israels** and **Lisa Persdotter,** was born on 29 Aug 1702 in Rejpelt, Vörå, Finland, [30] died on 15 Feb 1782 in Rejpelt, Vörå, Finland [28] at age 79, and was buried on 24 Feb 1782.[28] Another name for Brita was Brita Johansdotter Mattsson.

Birth Notes: Her age given at her death in Hiski implies a birth year of 1697.

Brita married **Hans Mattsson**[28] Est 1723.

---

28. *Hiski database (http://hiski.genealogia.fi).*
29. *Email from Torbjörn Nikus. .... Hiski database (http://hiski.genealogia.fi).*
30. *Hiski database (http://hiski.genealogia.fi). .... Vörå Kommunionsboken 1750-56 (http://www.enges.org).*

Ancestor Report for Lisa Samuelsdotter Miemois

Fifth Generation

26. Sven Jakobsson[1] was born about 1654[2] and died on 15 Mar 1724 in Olofshult, Västra Torsås, Småland, Sweden[2] about age 70.

Sven married **Svenborg Nilsdotter**.[1]

The child from this marriage was:

13   i.   **Elin Svensdotter**.[3] Elin married **Hans Georg Sommar**[4] on 18 Jan 1721 in Västra Torsås, Småland, Sweden.[5]

27. Svenborg Nilsdotter[1] was born about 1663[6] and died on 6 Nov 1743 in Olofshult, Västra Torsås, Småland, Sweden[6] about age 80.

Svenborg married **Sven Jakobsson**.[1]

30. Johan Andersson Israels,[7] son of **Anders Mickelsson Israels** and **Brita Mårtensdotter,** was born in 1670[7] and died on 19 Feb 1714 in Napue, Storkyro, Finland[7] at age 44.

General Notes: He was a Swedish soldier in the Great Northern War at the Battle of Storkyro against the Russians and was killed.[7]

Noted events in his life were:
- Occupation: bonde (farm owner) at Israels, 1696, Rejpelt, Vörå, Finland. [8]

- Occupation: soldier. [7]

Johan married **Lisa Persdotter**.[9]

Children from this marriage were:

15   i.   **Brita Johansdotter Israels**.[9] Brita married **Hans Mattsson**[9] Est 1723.

      ii.   **Erik Johansson Israels**[9] was born on 19 Dec 1704 in Rejpelt, Vörå, Finland[9] and died in 1704.[9]

31. Lisa Persdotter[9] was born in Nov 1671,[10] died on 17 Apr 1751 in Rejpelt, Vörå, Finland[9] at age 79, and was buried on 28 Apr 1751.[9]

Lisa married **Johan Andersson Israels**.[7]

---

1. Plym Arnäs, Plym Arnäs's family research website (http://www.plymarnas.se).

2. Plym Arnäs, Plym Arnäs's family research website (http://www.plymarnas.se). .... Västra Torsås C:2 (1720-1746) Image 120 / page 231 (AID: v29902.b120.s231, NAD: SE/VALA/00453).

3. Anders Enders, Några sidor på nätet om släktforskning (http://www.enges.org/gene/). .... Plym Arnäs, Plym Arnäs's family research website (http://www.plymarnas.se). .... Skatelöv CI:2 (1720-1746) Image 24 / page 39 (AID: v30280.b24.s39, NAD: SE/VALA/00329) .

4. Anders Enders, Några sidor på nätet om släktforskning (http://www.enges.org/gene/). .... Plym Arnäs, Plym Arnäs's family research website (http://www.plymarnas.se).

5. Plym Arnäs, Plym Arnäs's family research website (http://www.plymarnas.se). .... Västra Torsås C:2 (1720-1746) Image 148 / page 287 (AID: v29902.b148.s287, NAD: SE/VALA/00453).

6. Plym Arnäs, Plym Arnäs's family research website (http://www.plymarnas.se). .... Västra Torsås C:2 (1720-1746) Image 144 / page 279 (AID: v29902.b144.s279, NAD: SE/VALA/00453).

7. Anders Enders, Några sidor på nätet om släktforskning (http://www.enges.org/gene/).

8. Vörå Jordeboken 1709-10 (http://www.enges.org).

9. Hiski database (http://hiski.genealogia.fi).

10. Vörå Kommunionsboken 1750-56 (http://www.enges.org).

Ancestor Report for Lisa Samuelsdotter Miemois

Sixth Generation

60. Anders Mickelsson Israels,[1] son of **Mickel Israelsson** and **Unknown,** was born in 1651 in Rejpelt, Vörå, Finland[1] and died on 2 Jun 1703 in Rejpelt, Vörå, Finland [1] at age 52.

Noted events in his life were:
• Occupation: bonde (farm owner) of Israels, 1675-1695, Rejpelt, Vörå, Finland. [2]

Anders married **Brita Mårtensdotter**.[3]

Children from this marriage were:
      i.   **Mickel Andersson Israels**
30   ii. **Johan Andersson Israels**.[4] Johan married **Lisa Persdotter**.[1]

61. Brita Mårtensdotter.[3]

Brita married **Anders Mickelsson Israels**.[1]

1. Hiski database (http://hiski.genealogia.fi).
2. Vörå Jordeboken 1695-96 (http://www.enges.org). .... Vörå Mantalslängden 1675-76 (http://www.enges.org).
3. Anders Enders, Några sidor på nätet om släktforskning (http://www.enges.org/gene/). .... Vörå Mantalslängden 1675-76 (http://www.enges.org).
4. Anders Enders, Några sidor på nätet om släktforskning (http://www.enges.org/gene/).

Ancestor Report for Lisa Samuelsdotter Miemois

Seventh Generation

120. Mickel Israelsson,[1] son of **Israel Larsson** and **Unknown,** was born in 1619,[2] died on 26 Jul 1691 in Rejpelt, Vörå, Finland[2] at age 72, and was buried on 26 Jul 1691.[2]

Noted events in his life were:
- Occupation: bonde (farm owner) of Israels, 1675, Rejpelt, Vörå, Finland. [3]

Mickel married someone.

Children from this marriage were:

  60   i.   **Anders Mickelsson Israels**.[2] Anders married **Brita Mårtensdotter**.[4]

         ii.   **Walborg Mickelsdotter Israels**[2] was born in 1652[2] and died on 1 Jan 1704 in Rökiö, Vörå, Finland[2] at age 52. Walborg married **Simon Simonsson**.[2]

---

1. *Vörå Avkortningslängden 1675 (http://www.enges.org). .... Hiski database (http://hiski.genealogia.fi).*

2. *Hiski database (http://hiski.genealogia.fi).*

3. *Vörå Avkortningslängden 1675 (http://www.enges.org).*

4. *Anders Enders, Några sidor på nätet om släktforskning (http://www.enges.org/gene/). .... Vörå Mantalslängden 1675-76 (http://www.enges.org).*

Ancestor Report for Lisa Samuelsdotter Miemois

Eighth Generation

240. Israel Larsson[1] died in 1654 in Rejpelt, Vörå, Finland.[2]

General Notes: According to Torbjörn Nikus, record of him in the record books in 1635, 1641 and 1653. His mother may have been 1615 Änka Elin (who possibly died at Israels farm). The farm name Israel probably come from this person. Former owners were 1565 Bengt Pedersson and 1575-1604 Lasse Bengtson.[3]

Israel married someone.

His child was:

120   i.   **Mickel Israelsson**.[4] Mickel married someone.

1. *Vörå Jordeboken 1634 (http://www.enges.org).*
2. *Anders Enders, Några sidor på nätet om släktforskning (http://www.enges.org/gene/).*
3. *Email from Torbjörn Nikus. .... Anders Enders, Några sidor på nätet om släktforskning (http://www.enges.org/gene/).*
4. *Vörå Avkortningslängden 1675 (http://www.enges.org). .... Hiski database (http://hiski.genealogia.fi).*

Pedigree Chart for Lisa Samuelsdotter Miemois

No. 1 on this chart is the same as no. 9 on chart no. 1

8 Samuel Simonsson
b. 1687
p.
m.
p.
d. 24 Apr 1737
p. Kieskis, Vörå, Finland

4 Matts Samuelsson Storkeskis
b. 30 Aug 1726
p. Kieskis, Vörå, Finland
m. 28 Dec 1748
p.
d. 21 Sep 1789
p. Miemoisby, Vörå, Finland

9 Karin Hendriksdotter
b. Jul 1690
p.
d. 10 Feb 1771
p. Miemoisby, Vörå, Finland

2 Samuel Mattsson Keskis
b. 4 Oct 1754
p. Kieskis, Vörå, Finland
m. 28 Jun 1774
p. Vörå, Finland
d. Bef 1810
p.

10
b.
p.
m.
p.
d.
p.

5 Anna Jakobsdotter
b. Aug 1721
p.
d. 15 Apr 1801
p. Miemoisby, Vörå, Finland

11
b.
p.
d.
p.

1 Lisa Samuelsdotter Miemois
b. 10 Dec 1792
p. Miemoisby, Vörå, Finland
m. 30 Nov 1810
p. Vörå, Finland
d. 19 Nov 1866
p. Leistus, Rejpelt, Vörå, Finland
sp. Mårten Mårtensson Storkarhu

12 Hans Georg Sommar
b. Abt 1688
p.
m. 18 Jan 1721
p. Västra Torsås, Småland, Sweden
d. 2 Oct 1758
p. Vrankunge, Skatelöv, Småland, Sweden

6 Sune Hansson
b. 13 Jan 1726
p. Vrankunge, Skatelöv, Småland, Sweden
m. 14 Sep 1746
p. Rejpelt, Vörå, Finland
d. 2 Oct 1798
p. Rejpelt, Vörå, Finland

13 Elin Svensdotter
b. Oct 1690   cont. 9
p. Olofshult, Västra Torsås, Småland, Swe~
d. 7 Jan 1754
p. Vrankunge, Skatelöv, Småland, Sweden

3 Lisa Sunedotter Israels
b. 2 Sep 1754
p. Rejpelt, Vörå, Finland
d. 26 Dec 1835
p. Miemoisby, Vörå, Finland

14 Hans Mattsson
b. Dec 1689
p.
m. Est 1723
p.
d. 28 May 1766
p. Rejpelt, Vörå, Finland

7 Anna Hansdotter Israels
b. 19 Sep 1724
p. Rejpelt, Vörå, Finland
d. 25 Jan 1805
p. Rejpelt, Vörå, Finland

15 Brita Johansdotter Israels
b. 29 Aug 1702   cont. 10
p. Rejpelt, Vörå, Finland
d. 15 Feb 1782
p. Rejpelt, Vörå, Finland

Pedigree Chart for Elin Svensdotter

No. 1 on this chart is the same as no. 13 on chart no. 8

8
b.
p.
m.
p.
d.
p.

4
b.
p.
m.
p.
d.
p.

9
b.
p.
d.
p.

2 **Sven Jakobsson**
b. Abt 1654
p.
m.
p.
d. 15 Mar 1724
p. Olofshult, Västra Torsås, Småland, Swe~

10
b.
p.
m.
p.
d.
p.

5
b.
p.
d.
p.

11
b.
p.
d.
p.

1 **Elin Svensdotter**
b. Oct 1690
p. Olofshult, Västra Torsås, Småland, Sweden
m. 18 Jan 1721
p. Västra Torsås, Småland, Sweden
d. 7 Jan 1754
p. Vrankunge, Skatelöv, Småland, Sweden
sp. Hans Georg Sommar

12
b.
p.
m.
p.
d.
p.

6
b.
p.
m.
p.
d.
p.

13
b.
p.
d.
p.

3 **Svenborg Nilsdotter**
b. Abt 1663
p.
d. 6 Nov 1743
p. Olofshult, Västra Torsås, Småland, Swe~

14
b.
p.
m.
p.
d.
p.

7
b.
p.
d.
p.

15
b.
p.
d.
p.

Pedigree Chart for Brita Johansdotter Israels

No. 1 on this chart is the same as no. 15 on chart no. 8

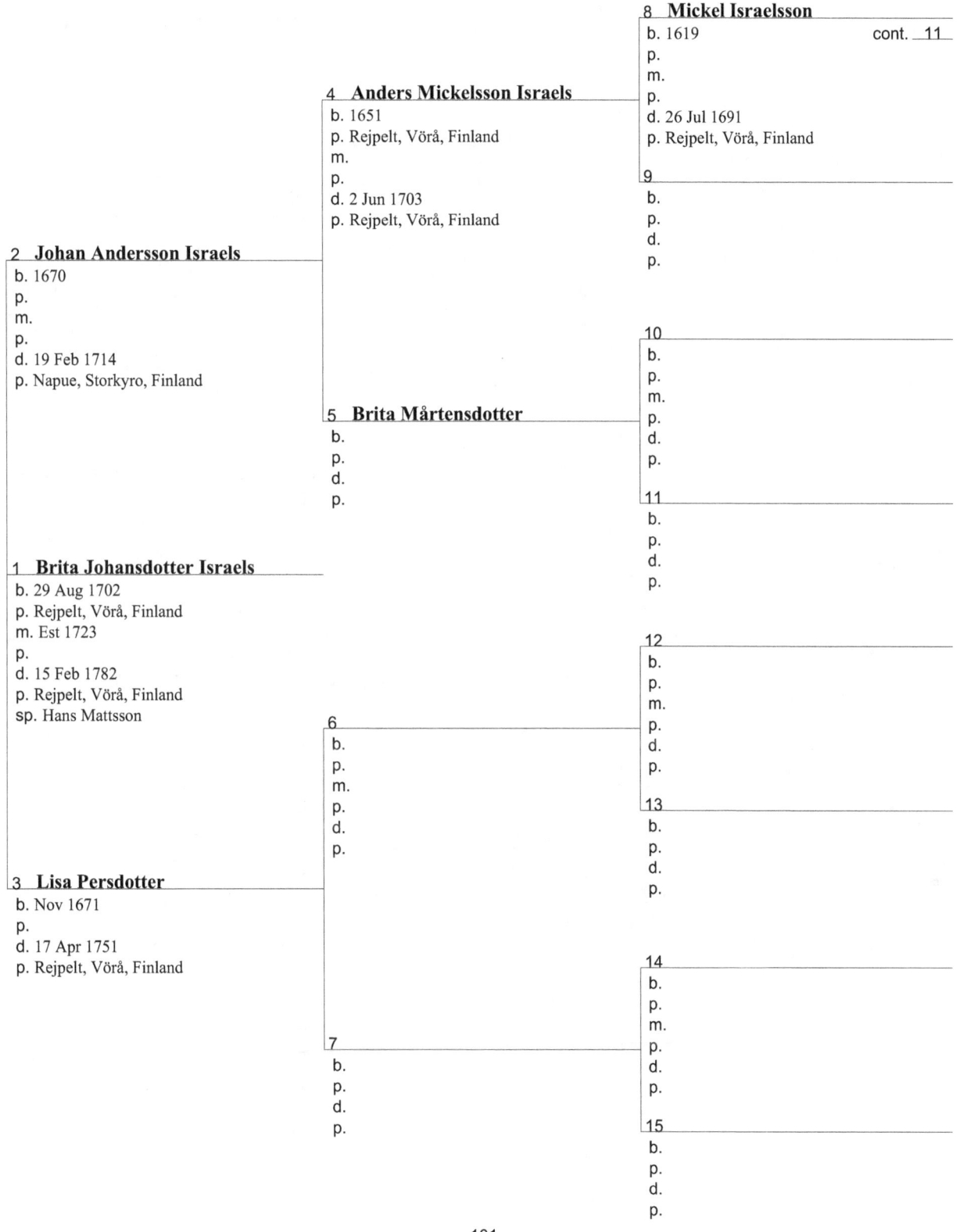

8 Mickel Israelsson
b. 1619   cont. __11__
p.
m.
p.
d. 26 Jul 1691
p. Rejpelt, Vörå, Finland

4 Anders Mickelsson Israels
b. 1651
p. Rejpelt, Vörå, Finland
m.
p.
d. 2 Jun 1703
p. Rejpelt, Vörå, Finland

9
b.
p.
d.
p.

2 Johan Andersson Israels
b. 1670
p.
m.
p.
d. 19 Feb 1714
p. Napue, Storkyro, Finland

10
b.
p.
m.
p.
d.
p.

5 Brita Mårtensdotter
b.
p.
d.
p.

11
b.
p.
d.
p.

1 Brita Johansdotter Israels
b. 29 Aug 1702
p. Rejpelt, Vörå, Finland
m. Est 1723
p.
d. 15 Feb 1782
p. Rejpelt, Vörå, Finland
sp. Hans Mattsson

12
b.
p.
m.
p.
d.
p.

6
b.
p.
m.
p.
d.
p.

13
b.
p.
d.
p.

3 Lisa Persdotter
b. Nov 1671
p.
d. 17 Apr 1751
p. Rejpelt, Vörå, Finland

14
b.
p.
m.
p.
d.
p.

7
b.
p.
d.
p.

15
b.
p.
d.
p.

101

Pedigree Chart for Mickel Israelsson

No. 1 on this chart is the same as no. 8 on chart no. 10

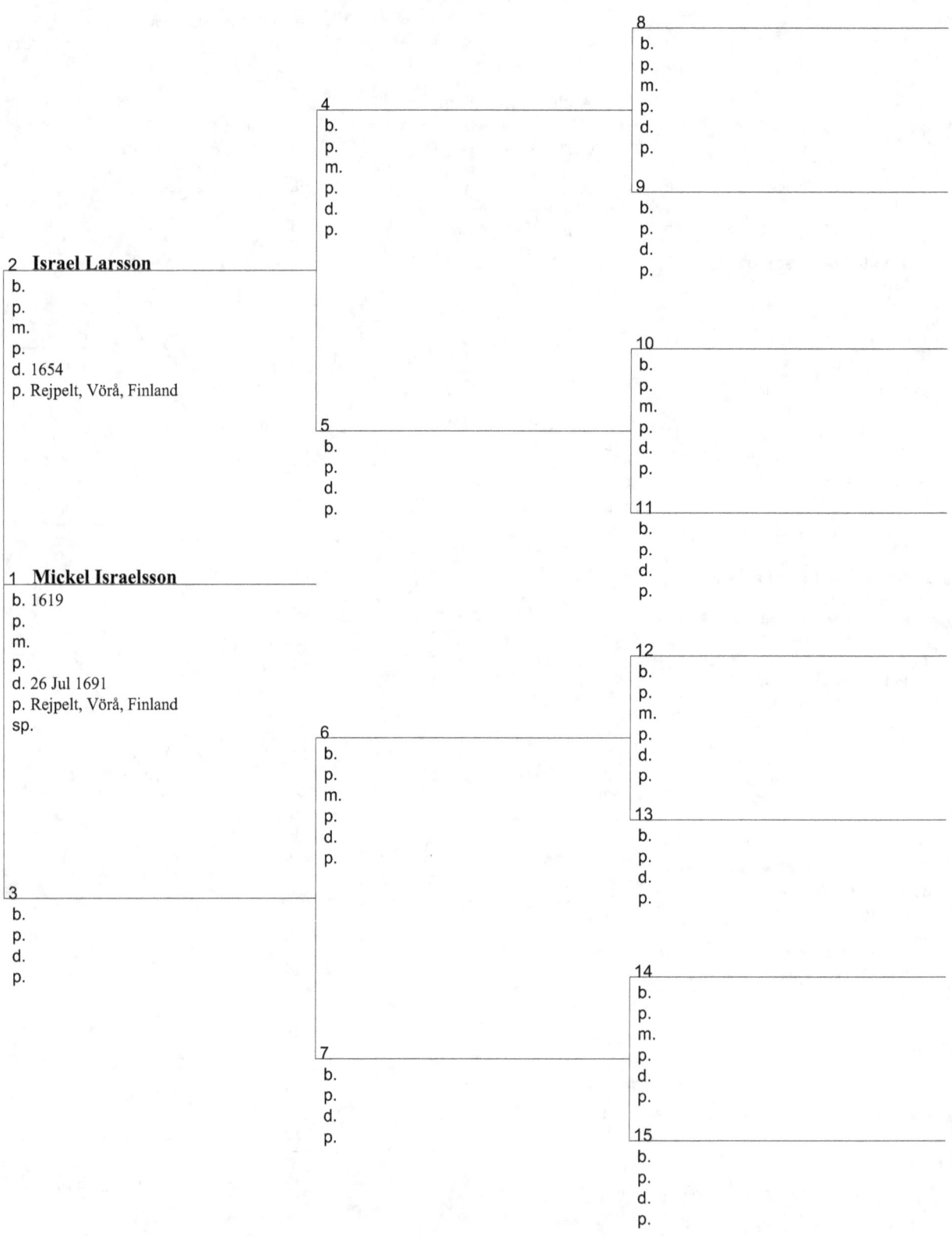

8 _____
b.
p.
m.
p.
d.
p.

4 _____
b.
p.
m.
p.
d.
p.

9 _____
b.
p.
d.
p.

2 **Israel Larsson**
b.
p.
m.
p.
d. 1654
p. Rejpelt, Vörå, Finland

10 _____
b.
p.
m.
p.
d.
p.

5 _____
b.
p.
d.
p.

11 _____
b.
p.
d.
p.

1 **Mickel Israelsson**
b. 1619
p.
m.
p.
d. 26 Jul 1691
p. Rejpelt, Vörå, Finland
sp.

12 _____
b.
p.
m.
p.
d.
p.

6 _____
b.
p.
m.
p.
d.
p.

13 _____
b.
p.
d.
p.

3 _____
b.
p.
d.
p.

14 _____
b.
p.
m.
p.
d.
p.

7 _____
b.
p.
d.
p.

15 _____
b.
p.
d.
p.

Chapter 4. Ancestor Report for Johan Eriksson Wäst

First Generation

1. Johan Eriksson Wäst,[1] son of **Erik Johansson Knuts** and **Margeta Johansdotter Kårvolain,** was born on 10 Mar 1799 in Rejpelt, Vörå, Finland,[1] was christened on 11 Mar 1799,[2] and died on 9 Jun 1878 in Rejpelt, Vörå, Finland[1] at age 79. Other names for Johan were Johan Eriksson Svens, Johan Eriksson Dala, and Johan Eriksson Klemets.

General Notes: Born on the Wäst farm and was later bonde at Svens and Klemets farm. [1]

Johan married **Lisa Johansdotter Wäst,**[3] daughter of **Johan Mårtensson Wäst** and **Margaretha Johansdotter Kattil,** on 28 Dec 1819 in Rejpelt, Vörå, Finland. [3]

General Notes: daughter of a farm owner (bonde) [1]

Children from this marriage were:

    i.   **Brita Stina Johansdotter Wäst**[2] was born on 30 Nov 1822 in Rejpelt, Vörå, Finland, [2] was christened on 1 Dec 1822,[2] died on 13 May 1847 in Rejpelt, Vörå, Finland[2] at age 24, and was buried on 16 May 1847.[4] Another name for Brita was Brita Johansdotter Klemets. Brita married **Mårten Mårtensson Långs**[2] on 1 Jul 1845. [2]

    ii.   **Erik Johansson Wäst**[2] was born on 13 Aug 1825 in Rejpelt, Vörå, Finland[2] and was christened on 14 Aug 1825.[2] Another name for Erik was Erik Johansson Svens.[2] Erik married someone **Brita Mickelsdotter Klafvus**[2] on 6 Feb 1846.[2]

    iii.   **Johan Johansson Wäst**[2] was born on 14 Jan 1828 in Rejpelt, Vörå, Finland[2] and was christened on 16 Jan 1828.[2]

    iv.   **Lisa Johansdotter Wäst**[3] was born on 28 Nov 1829 in Rejpelt, Vörå, Finland, [3] was christened on 29 Nov 1829,[2] and died on 14 Feb 1901 in Rejpelt, Vörå, Finland [1] at age 71. Another name for Lisa was Lisa Johansdotter Dala. Lisa married **Mickel Mårtensson Storkarhu,**[1] son of **Mårten Mårtensson Storkarhu** and **Lisa Samuelsdotter Miemois,** on 8 Jul 1852 in Rejpelt, Vörå, Finland. [1]

1. Torbjörn Nikus, Storkarhu (unpublish document, 2008).
2. Hiski database (http://hiski.genealogia.fi).
3. Torbjörn Nikus, Storkarhu (unpublish document, 2008). .... Hiski database (http://hiski.genealogia.fi).
4. Anders Enders, Några sidor på nätet om släktforskning (http://www.enges.org/gene/).

Ancestor Report for Johan Eriksson Wäst

Second Generation

2. Erik Johansson Knuts,[1] son of **Johan Isaksson Knuts** and **Lisa Mårtensdotter,** was born on 10 Feb 1774 in Rökiö, Vörå, Finland and was christened on 13 Feb 1774. Another name for Erik was Erik Johansson Wäst.

General Notes: Born on Knuts farm. Torpare (renter) at Wäst farm.

Erik married **Margeta Johansdotter Kårvolain**[1] on 10 Nov 1805 in Rejpelt, Vörå, Finland.[1]

Children from this marriage were:

1   i.   **Johan Eriksson Wäst**.[2] Johan married **Lisa Johansdotter Wäst**,[3] daughter of **Johan Mårtensson Wäst** and **Margaretha Johansdotter Kattil,** on 28 Dec 1819 in Rejpelt, Vörå, Finland.[3]

     ii.   **Anna Eriksdotter Wäst**[1] was born on 24 Nov 1803 in Rejpelt, Vörå, Finland[1] and was christened on 27 Nov 1803.[1]

     iii.   **Brita Eriksdotter Wäst**[1] was born on 11 Nov 1805 in Rejpelt, Vörå, Finland[1] and was christened on 12 Nov 1805.[1]

     iv.   **Erik Eriksson Wäst**[1] was born on 11 May 1807 in Rejpelt, Vörå, Finland[1] and was christened on 12 May 1807.[1]

     v.   **Lisa Eriksdotter Wäst**[1] was born on 28 Sep 1808 in Rejpelt, Vörå, Finland[1] and was christened on 3 Oct 1808.[1]

     vi.   **Erik Eriksson Wäst**[1] was born on 17 May 1811 in Rejpelt, Vörå, Finland[1] and was christened on 19 May 1811.[1]

     vii.   **Greta Eriksdotter Wäst**[1] was born on 5 Aug 1813 in Jörala, Vörå, Finland[1] and was christened on 8 Aug 1813.[1]

     viii.   **Matts Eriksson Wäst**[1] was born on 18 Apr 1816 in Rejpelt, Vörå, Finland[1] and was christened on 21 Apr 1816.[1]

     ix.   **Erik Eriksson Wäst**[1] was born on 5 Dec 1817 in Rejpelt, Vörå, Finland[1] and was christened on 7 Dec 1817.[1]

3. Margeta Johansdotter Kårvolain,[1] daughter of **Johan Mårtensson** and **Brita Eriksdotter,** was born on 2 Dec 1776 in Rejpelt, Vörå, Finland,[1] was christened on 4 Dec 1776,[1] died on 6 Jun 1850 in Rejpelt, Vörå, Finland[1] at age 73, and was buried on 9 Jun 1850.[1] Other names for Margeta were Greta Johansdotter Kattil and Greta Johansdotter Wäst.

Margeta married **Erik Johansson Knuts**[1] on 10 Nov 1805 in Rejpelt, Vörå, Finland.[1]

---

1. *Hiski database (http://hiski.genealogia.fi).*
2. *Torbjörn Nikus, Storkarhu (unpublish document, 2008).*
3. *Torbjörn Nikus, Storkarhu (unpublish document, 2008). .... Hiski database (http://hiski.genealogia.fi).*

Ancestor Report for Johan Eriksson Wäst

Third Generation

4. Johan Isaksson Knuts,[1] son of **Isak Isaksson Knus** and **Lisa Esajasdotter Wäst,** was born on 22 Jun 1833 in Rökiö, Vörå, Finland[1] and was christened on 24 Jun 1833.[1]

Johan married **Lisa Mårtensdotter**[1] on 18 Dec 1757 in Rökiö, Vörå, Finland.[1]

Children from this marriage were:

	i.	**Maria Johansdotter Knuts**[1] was born on 2 Jan 1759 in Rökiö, Vörå, Finland[1] and was christened on 6 Jan 1759.[1]
	ii.	**Isac Johansson Knuts**[1] was born on 25 Jan 1760 in Rökiö, Vörå, Finland[1] and was christened on 27 Jan 1760.[1]
	iii.	**Mårten Johansson Knuts**[1] was born on 10 Apr 1761 in Rökiö, Vörå, Finland[1] and was christened on 12 Apr 1761.[1]
	iv.	**Johan Johansson Knuts**[1] was born on 24 Aug 1762 in Rökiö, Vörå, Finland[1] and was christened on 29 Aug 1762.[1]
	v.	**Michel Johansson Knuts**[1] was born on 4 Jan 1765 in Rökiö, Vörå, Finland[1] and was christened on 6 Jan 1765.[1]
	vi.	**Matts Johansson Knuts**[1] was born on 13 Jan 1767 in Rökiö, Vörå, Finland[1] and was christened on 18 Jan 1767.[1]
	vii.	**Anna Johansdotter Knuts**[1] was born on 10 May 1770 in Rökiö, Vörå, Finland[1] and was christened on 13 May 1770.[1]
	viii.	**Simon Johansson Knuts**[1] was born on 12 Oct 1771 in Rökiö, Vörå, Finland[1] and was christened on 13 Oct 1771.[1]
	ix.	**Brita Johansdotter Knuts**[1] was born on 29 Jan 1773 in Rökiö, Vörå, Finland[1] and was christened on 31 Jan 1773.[1]
2	x.	**Erik Johansson Knuts.**[1] Erik married **Margeta Johansdotter Kårvolain,**[1] daughter of **Johan Mårtensson** and **Brita Eriksdotter,** on 10 Nov 1805 in Rejpelt, Vörå, Finland.[1]
	xi.	**Magdalena Johansdotter Knuts**[1] was born on 20 May 1779 in Rökiö, Vörå, Finland[1] and was christened on 24 May 1779.[1]

5. Lisa Mårtensdotter,[1] daughter of **Mårten Isaksson** and **Maria Mattsdotter,** was born on 25 Mar 1732 in Kåskeby, Vörå, Finland[1] and was christened on 26 Mar 1732.[1] Another name for Lisa was Lisa Mårtensdotter Nyberg.

Noted events in her life were:
• Resided: 1757, Kåskeby, Vörå, Finland.[1]

Lisa married **Johan Isaksson Knuts**[1] on 18 Dec 1757 in Rökiö, Vörå, Finland.[1]

6. Johan Mårtensson,[1] son of **Mårten Johansson** and **Anna Johansdotter,** was born on 3 Jan 1731 in Rejpelt, Vörå, Finland,[1] was christened on 6 Jan 1731,[1] died on 1 Jun 1803 in Rejpelt, Vörå, Finland[1] at age 72, and was buried on 5 Jun 1803.[1]

Noted events in his life were:
• Resided: 5 Dec 1756, Rejpelt, Vörå, Finland.[1]

Johan married **Brita Eriksdotter**[1] on 5 Dec 1756.[1]

Children from this marriage were:

	i.	**Johan Johansson Kårvolain**[1] was born on 13 Sep 1757 in Rejpelt, Vörå, Finland[1] and was christened on 18 Sep 1757.[1]
	ii.	**Anna Johansdotter Kårvolain**[1] was born on 19 Nov 1759 in Rejpelt, Vörå, Finland[1] and was christened on 21 Nov 1759.[1]
	iii.	**Brita Johansdotter Kårvolain**[1] was born on 3 Apr 1762 in Rejpelt, Vörå, Finland[1] and was christened

---

1. Hiski database (http://hiski.genealogia.fi).

on 4 Apr 1762.[1]

    iv.   **Brita Johansdotter Kårvolain**[2] was born on 14 Oct 1764 in Rejpelt, Vörå, Finland[2] and was christened on 21 Oct 1764.[2]

    v.   **Margeta Johansdotter Kårvolain**[2] was born on 8 Jun 1767 in Rejpelt, Vörå, Finland[2] and was christened on 10 Jun 1767.[2]

    vi.   **Maria Johansdotter Kårvolain**[2] was born on 2 Sep 1768 in Rejpelt, Vörå, Finland,[2] was christened on 4 Sep 1768,[2] died on 13 May 1809 in Mäkipää, Vörå, Finland[2] at age 40, and was buried on 16 May 1809.[2] Maria married **Anders Andersson Grägg** on 14 Jun 1793 in Mäkipää, Vörå, Finland.[2]

    vii.   **Beata Johansdotter Kårvolain**[2] was born on 17 Dec 1774 in Rejpelt, Vörå, Finland,[2] was christened on 26 Dec 1774,[2] died on 31 Jan 1825 in Bergby, Vörå, Finland[2] at age 50, and was buried on 6 Feb 1825.[2] Beata married **Simon Johansson Smeds**[2] on 9 Dec 1800 in Bergby, Vörå, Finland.

3   viii.   **Margeta Johansdotter Kårvolain**.[2] Margeta married **Erik Johansson Knuts**,[2] son of **Johan Isaksson Knuts** and **Lisa Mårtensdotter,** on 10 Nov 1805 in Rejpelt, Vörå, Finland.[2]

7. Brita Eriksdotter,[2] daughter of **Erich Åkesson** and **Brita Simonsdotter,** was born on 12 Feb 1734 in Mäkipää, Vörå, Finland,[2] was christened on 17 Feb 1734, died on 28 Aug 1791 in Rejpelt, Vörå, Finland[2] at age 57, and was buried on 4 Sep 1791.[2] Another name for Brita was Brita Mårtensson.

Noted events in her life were:
• Resided: 5 Dec 1756, Mäkipää, Vörå, Finland.[2]

Brita married **Johan Mårtensson**[2] on 5 Dec 1756.[2]

---

2. Hiski database (http://hiski.genealogia.fi).

Ancestor Report for Johan Eriksson Wäst

Fourth Generation

8. Isak Isaksson Knus,[1] son of **Isak Johansson Knus** and **Maria Johansdotter Skått,** was born on 20 Jul 1792 in Rökiö, Vörå, Finland[1] and was christened on 23 Jul 1792.[1]

Noted events in his life were:
• Resided: Knuts farm, 1821.[1]

Isak married **Lisa Esajasdotter Wäst**[1] on 23 Apr 1821 in Oravais, Finland.[1]

Children from this marriage were:
  i.   **Isaac Isaksson Knuts**[1] was born on 29 Jun 1823 in Rökiö, Vörå, Finland[1] and was christened on 3 Jul 1823.[1] Isaac married **Maja Lisa Eriksdotter Markus**[1] in 1849.[1]
  ii. **Matts Isaksson Knuts**[1] was born on 19 Feb 1826 in Rökiö, Vörå, Finland[1] and was christened on 23 Feb 1826.[1] Matts married **Beata Nordberg**[1] on 29 Apr 1849.[1]
  iii. **Elisabeth Isaksdotter Knuts**[1] was born on 29 Nov 1828 in Rökiö, Vörå, Finland[1] and was christened on 4 Dec 1828.[1]
  iv. **Anna Isaksdotter Knuts**[1] was born on 12 May 1832 in Rökiö, Vörå, Finland[1] and was christened on 13 May 1832.[1]
4 v.   **Johan Isaksson Knuts.**[1] Johan married **Lisa Mårtensdotter,**[1] daughter of **Mårten Isaksson** and **Maria Mattsdotter,** on 18 Dec 1757 in Rökiö, Vörå, Finland.[1]

9. Lisa Esajasdotter Wäst,[1] daughter of **Esajas Esajasson Bengs** and **Anna Mårtensdotter Wäst,** was born on 1 Oct 1798 in Oravais, Oravais, Finland[1] and was christened on 3 Oct 1798.[1]

Noted events in her life were:
• Resided: Wäst farm, 1821, Oravais, Oravais, Finland.[1]

Lisa married **Isak Isaksson Knus**[1] on 23 Apr 1821 in Oravais, Finland.[1]

10. Mårten Isaksson.[1]

Mårten married **Maria Mattsdotter.**[1]

The child from this marriage was:
5 i.   **Lisa Mårtensdotter.**[1] Lisa married **Johan Isaksson Knuts,**[1] son of **Isak Isaksson Knus** and **Lisa Esajasdotter Wäst,** on 18 Dec 1757 in Rökiö, Vörå, Finland.[1]

11. Maria Mattsdotter.[1]

Maria married **Mårten Isaksson.**[1]

12. Mårten Johansson,[1] son of **Johan Mårtensson** and **Brita Mårtensdotter,** was born on 20 Mar 1692 in Lomby, Vörå, Finland,[1] died on 1 Oct 1764 in Rejpelt, Vörå, Finland[1] at age 72, and was buried on 7 Oct 1764.[1]

Mårten married **Anna Johansdotter.**[1]

Children from this marriage were:
  i.   **Maria Mårtensdotter**[1] was born on 7 Sep 1723 in Rejpelt, Vörå, Finland[1] and was christened on 8 Sep 1723.[1]
  ii. **Anna Mårtensdotter**[1] was born on 20 Nov 1724 in Rejpelt, Vörå, Finland,[1] was christened on 22 Nov 1724,[1] died on 6 Jan 1798 in Lomby, Vörå, Finland[1] at age 73, and was buried on 14 Jan 1798.[1] Anna married **Soldat Mårten Rabbs**[1] on 17 Nov 1754.[1]
  iii. **Brita Mårtensdotter**[1] was born on 10 Jun 1728 in Rejpelt, Vörå, Finland[1] and was christened on 12 Jun

1. Hiski database (http://hiski.genealogia.fi).

1728.[1]

6   iv.   **Johan Mårtensson**.[2] Johan married **Brita Eriksdotter**,[2] daughter of **Erich Åkesson** and **Brita Simonsdotter,** on 5 Dec 1756.[2]

      v.   **Margeta Mårtensdotter**[2] was born on 5 Oct 1733 in Rejpelt, Vörå, Finland, [2] was christened on 7 Oct 1733,[2] died on 4 Nov 1766 in Mäkipää, Vörå, Finland[2] at age 33, and was buried on 9 Nov 1766.[2] Margeta married **Isak Abramsson** on 24 Jun 1760 in Mäkipää, Vörå, Finland.

     vi.   **Mattz Mårtensson**[2] was born on 14 Sep 1737 in Rejpelt, Vörå, Finland, [2] was christened on 19 Sep 1737,[2] died on 20 May 1813 in Rejpelt, Vörå, Finland[2] at age 75, and was buried on 23 May 1813.[2] Another name for Mattz was Mattz Mårtensson Clemets. Mattz married someone **Margeta Hansdotter**[2] on 8 Jun 1761.

    vii.   **Mårten Mårtensson**[2] was born on 8 Aug 1743 in Rejpelt, Vörå, Finland, [2] was christened on 9 Aug 1743,[2] died on 27 Dec 1812 in Rejpelt, Vörå, Finland[2] at age 69, and was buried on 3 Jan 1813. [2] Mårten married **Maria Mattsdotter**[2] on 7 Dec 1766.

13. Anna Johansdotter[2] was born about 1705,[2] died on 8 Jun 1766 in Rejpelt, Vörå, Finland[2] about age 61, and was buried on 22 Jun 1766.[2]

Anna married **Mårten Johansson**.[2]

14. Erich Åkesson,[2] son of **Åke Sigfersson** and **Maria Andersdotter,** was born about 1697 in Kaitsor, Vörå, Finland,[2] died on 15 Dec 1772 in Mäkipää, Vörå, Finland[2] about age 75, and was buried on 20 Dec 1772. [2]

Erich married **Brita Simonsdotter**.[2]

Children from this marriage were:

      i.   **Simon Eriksson**[2] was born on 2 Aug 1723 in Mäkipää, Vörå, Finland[2] and was christened on 4 Aug 1723.[2]

     ii.   **Erich Eriksson**[2] was born on 18 Sep 1724 in Mäkipää, Vörå, Finland[2] and was christened on 21 Sep 1724.[2]

    iii.   **Lisa Eriksdotter**[2] was born on 3 Oct 1727 in Mäkipää, Vörå, Finland[2] and was christened on 8 Oct 1727.[2]

     iv.   **Thomas Eriksson**[2] was born on 17 Dec 1728 in Mäkipää, Vörå, Finland[2] and was christened on 22 Dec 1728.[2]

      v.   **Erich Eriksson**[2] was born on 24 Sep 1730 in Mäkipää, Vörå, Finland[2] and was christened on 27 Sep 1730.[2]

     vi.   **Anders Eriksson**[2] was born on 26 Nov 1731 in Mäkipää, Vörå, Finland, [2] was christened on 28 Nov 1731,[2] died on 6 Mar 1805 in Mäkipää, Vörå, Finland[2] at age 73, and was buried on 17 Mar 1805. [2]

    vii.   **Margeta Eriksdotter**[2] was born on 25 Jan 1733 in Mäkipää, Vörå, Finland[2] and was christened on 28 Jan 1733.[2]

7   viii.   **Brita Eriksdotter**.[2] Brita married **Johan Mårtensson**,[2] son of **Mårten Johansson** and **Anna Johansdotter,** on 5 Dec 1756.[2]

15. Brita Simonsdotter[2] was born about 1684,[2] died on 9 Nov 1736 in Mäkipää, Vörå, Finland[2] about age 52, and was buried on 14 Nov 1736.[2]

Brita married **Erich Åkesson**.[2]

---

2. Hiski database (http://hiski.genealogia.fi).

Fifth Generation

16. Isak Johansson Knus,[1] son of **Johan Isaksson Knus** and **Lisa Mårtensdotter Jåfs**, was born on 25 Jan 1760 in Rökiö, Vörå, Finland,[1] died on 15 May 1809 in Rökiö, Vörå, Finland[1] at age 49, and was buried on 22 May 1809.[1]

Isak married **Maria Johansdotter Skått**[1] on 18 May 1783 in Rökiö, Vörå, Finland.[1]

Children from this marriage were:

    i.   **Lisa Isaksdotter Knus**[1] was born on 23 Feb 1784 in Rökiö, Vörå, Finland[1] and was christened on 24 Feb 1784.[1] Lisa married **Carl Jacobsson Präst**[1] on 21 May 1804 in Kaitsor, Vörå, Finland.[1]

    ii.   **Maria Isaksdotter Knus**[1] was born on 25 Dec 1785 in Rökiö, Vörå, Finland[1] and was christened on 26 Dec 1785.[1] Maria married **Erik Eriksson Lillknäck**[1] on 15 Jun 1817 in Kåskeby, Vörå, Finland.[1]

    iii.   **Anna Isaksdotter Knus**[1] was born on 16 Apr 1787 in Rökiö, Vörå, Finland[1] and was christened on 16 Apr 1787.[1] Anna married **Johan Mårtensson Brännars**[1] on 4 Dec 1814.[1]

    iv.   **Margeta Isaksdotter Knus**[1] was born on 13 Aug 1788 in Rökiö, Vörå, Finland[1] and was christened on 13 Aug 1788.[1]

    v.   **Johan Isaksson Knus**[1] was born on 7 Jan 1791 in Rökiö, Vörå, Finland[1] and was christened on 7 Jan 1791.[1] Johan married **Brita Mattsdotter Bagg**[1] on 18 Dec 1818. Johan next married **Maria Simonsdotter Nygård**[1] on 18 Dec 1823.[1]

8   vi.   **Isak Isaksson Knus**.[1] Isak married **Lisa Esajasdotter Wäst**,[1] daughter of **Esajas Esajasson Bengs** and **Anna Mårtensdotter Wäst**, on 23 Apr 1821 in Oravais, Finland.[1]

    vii.   **Matts Isaksson Knus**[1] was born on 12 Feb 1796 in Rökiö, Vörå, Finland[1] and was christened on 14 Feb 1796.[1]

    viii.   **Johan Isaksson Knus**[1] was born on 9 May 1798 in Rökiö, Vörå, Finland[1] and was christened on 11 May 1798.[1] Johan married **Brita Mattsdotter Bagg**[1] on 18 Dec 1818 in Rökiö, Vörå, Finland.[1] Johan next married **Maria Simonsdotter Nygård**[1] 18.12.1823 in Rökiö, Vörå, Finland.

    ix.   **Brita Isaksdotter Knus**[1] was born on 23 Dec 1805 in Rökiö, Vörå, Finland[1] and was christened on 23 Dec 1805.[1]

17. Maria Johansdotter Skått,[1] daughter of **Johan Mårtensson** and **Lisa Mattsdotter,** was born on 9 May 1759 in Tuckor, Vörå, Finland,[1] was christened on 13 May 1759,[1] died on 22 Feb 1843 in Rökiö, Vörå, Finland[1] at age 83, and was buried on 26 Feb 1843.[1]

Research Notes: Birth date and parentage is uncertain.

Noted events in her life were:
• Resided: 1783, Mäkipää, Vörå, Finland.[1]

Maria married **Isak Johansson Knus**[1] on 18 May 1783 in Rökiö, Vörå, Finland.[1]

18. Esajas Esajasson Bengs,[1] son of **Esajas Isaksson Bengs** and **Maria Bertilsdotter Pörnull,** was born on 10 Sep 1768 in Kåskeby, Vörå, Finland,[1] was christened on 11 Sep 1768,[1] died on 18 Mar 1853 in Kåskeby, Vörå, Finland[1] at age 84, and was buried on 28 Mar 1853.[1] Another name for Esajas was Esaias Esajasson Wäst.

Noted events in his life were:
• Occupation: farmhand, 1796.[1]

Esajas married **Anna Mårtensdotter Wäst**[1] on 17 Jul 1796 in Oravais, Finland.[1]

Children from this marriage were:

    i.   **Anna Esajasdotter Wäst**[1] was born on 11 Aug 1797 in Oravais, Oravais, Finland,[1] was christened on 13 Aug 1797,[1] and died on 26 Aug 1797 in Oravais, Oravais, Finland.[1]

9   ii.   **Lisa Esajasdotter Wäst**.[1] Lisa married **Isak Isaksson Knus**,[1] son of **Isak Johansson Knus** and **Maria Johansdotter Skått,** on 23 Apr 1821 in Oravais, Finland.[1]

---

1. Hiski database (http://hiski.genealogia.fi).

iii.   **Esajas Esajasson Wäst**[1] was born on 1 Aug 1800 in Oravais, Oravais, Finland[1] and was christened on 3 Aug 1800.[1]

iv.   **Maria Esajasdotter Wäst**[2] was born on 20 Jul 1804 in Oravais, Oravais, Finland[2] and was christened on 20 Jul 1804.[2]

v.   **Anna Esajasdotter Wäst**[2] was born on 28 Mar 1813 in Oravais, Oravais, Finland,[2] was christened on 30 Mar 1813,[2] and died on 7 Jan 1849 in Oravais, Oravais, Finland[2] at age 35.

vi.   **Mårten Esajasson Wäst**[2] was born on 1 Mar 1816 in Oravais, Oravais, Finland,[2] was christened on 3 Mar 1816,[2] died on 8 Nov 1861 in Oravais, Oravais, Finland at age 45, and was buried on 17 Nov 1861. Mårten married **Brita Isaksdotter Wäst** on 21 Dec 1838 in Oravais, Finland.[2] Mårten next married **Kaisa Pehrsdotter Wäst** on 21 Jul 1850.[2]

19. Anna Mårtensdotter Wäst,[2] daughter of **Mårten Carlsson** and **Lisa Hansdotter,** was born on 9 Aug 1770 in Oravais, Oravais, Finland,[2] was christened on 11 Aug 1770,[2] and died on 19 Apr 1846 in Oravais, Finland[2] at age 75.

Anna married **Esajas Esajasson Bengs**[2] on 17 Jul 1796 in Oravais, Finland.[2]

24. Johan Mårtensson.

Johan married **Brita Mårtensdotter**.[2]

Children from this marriage were:

i.   **Johan Johansson**[2] was born on 19 Feb 1691 in Lomby, Vörå, Finland[2] and was christened on 22 Feb 1691.[2]

12   ii.   **Mårten Johansson**.[2] Mårten married **Anna Johansdotter**.[2]

iii.   **Maria Johansdotter**[2] was born on 16 Mar 1699 in Lomby, Vörå, Finland[2] and died in 1715[2] at age 16.

iv.   **Anna Johansdotter**[2] was born on 27 Feb 1702 in Lomby, Vörå, Finland.[2]

25. Brita Mårtensdotter.[2]

Brita married **Johan Mårtensson**.

28. Åke Sigfersson.[2]

Åke married **Maria Andersdotter**.[2]

Children from this marriage were:

i.   **Beata Åkesdotter**[2] was born on 4 Mar 1692 in Kaitsor, Vörå, Finland[2] and died in 1705 in Kaitsor, Vörå, Finland[2] at age 13.

ii.   **Margeta Åkesdotter**[2] was born on 20 Apr 1693 in Kaitsor, Vörå, Finland[2] and died in 1693 in Kaitsor, Vörå, Finland.[2]

iii.   **Mårten Åkesson**[2] was born on 8 Jul 1694 in Kaitsor, Vörå, Finland.[2]

iv.   **Johan Åkesson**[2] was born on 14 Aug 1695 in Kaitsor, Vörå, Finland[2] and died in 1696 in Kaitsor, Vörå, Finland[2] at age 1.

v.   **Mattz Åkesson**[2] was born on 9 Dec 1696 in Kaitsor, Vörå, Finland[2] and died in 1696 in Kaitsor, Vörå, Finland.[2]

vi.   **Maria Åkesdotter**[2] was born on 9 Dec 1696 in Kaitsor, Vörå, Finland[2] and died in 1696 in Kaitsor, Vörå, Finland.[2]

14   vii.   **Erich Åkesson**.[2] Erich married **Brita Simonsdotter**.[2]

viii.   **Anders Åkesson**[2] was born on 29 Sep 1699 in Kaitsor, Vörå, Finland.[2]

ix.   **Margeta Åkesdotter**[2] was born on 26 Oct 1701 in Kaitsor, Vörå, Finland[2] and died in 1702 in Kaitsor, Vörå, Finland[2] at age 1.

---

2. Hiski database (http://hiski.genealogia.fi).

29. Maria Andersdotter.[3]

Maria married **Åke Sigfersson**.[3]

---

3. Hiski database (http://hiski.genealogia.fi).

Sixth Generation

32. Johan Isaksson Knus,[1] son of **Isack Isaksson** and **Maria Johansdotter,** was born on 3 Nov 1735 in Rökiö, Vörå, Finland,[2] was christened on 9 Nov 1735,[3] and died on 16 Jan 1809 in Rökiö, Vörå, Finland[2] at age 73.

Johan married **Lisa Mårtensdotter Jåfs**[4] on 18 Dec 1757.[3]

Children from this marriage were:

      i.   **Maria Johansdotter Knus**[3] was born on 2 Jan 1759 in Rökiö, Vörå, Finland[3] and was christened on 6 Jan 1759.[3]

16   ii.   **Isak Johansson Knus**.[3] Isak married **Maria Johansdotter Skått**,[3] daughter of **Johan Mårtensson** and **Lisa Mattsdotter,** on 18 May 1783 in Rökiö, Vörå, Finland.[3]

     iii.   **Mårten Johansson Knus**[3] was born on 10 Apr 1761 in Rökiö, Vörå, Finland[3] and was christened on 12 Apr 1761.[3]

     iv.   **Johan Johansson Knus**[3] was born on 24 Aug 1762 in Rökiö, Vörå, Finland[3] and was christened on 29 Aug 1762.[3]

     v.   **Johan Johansson Knuts**[3] was born on 22 Sep 1763 in Rökiö, Vörå, Finland[3] and was christened on 29 Sep 1763.[3]

     vi.   **Michel Johansson Knuts**[3] was born on 4 Jan 1765 in Rökiö, Vörå, Finland[3] and was christened on 6 Jan 1765.[3]

     vii.   **Matts Johansson Knus**[2] was born on 13 Jan 1767 in Rökiö, Vörå, Finland[2] and died on 28 Dec 1809 in Rökiö, Vörå, Finland[2] at age 42.

     viii.   **Anna Johansdotter Knuts**[3] was born on 10 May 1770 in Rökiö, Vörå, Finland[3] and was christened on 13 May 1770.[3]

     ix.   **Simon Johansson Knuts**[3] was born on 12 Oct 1771 in Rökiö, Vörå, Finland[3] and was christened on 13 Oct 1771.[3]

     x.   **Brita Johansdotter Knuts**[3] was born on 29 Jan 1773 in Rökiö, Vörå, Finland[3] and was christened on 31 Jan 1773.[3]

     xi.   **Erich Johansson Knuts**[3] was born on 10 Feb 1774 in Rökiö, Vörå, Finland[3] and was christened on 13 Feb 1774.[3]

     xii.   **Magdalena Johansdotter Knuts**[3] was born on 20 May 1779 in Rökiö, Vörå, Finland[3] and was christened on 24 May 1779.[3]

33. Lisa Mårtensdotter Jåfs,[4] daughter of **Mårten Michelsson Jåfs** and **Anna Johansdotter,** was born on 3 May 1738 in Jörala, Vörå, Finland,[2] was christened on 5 May 1738,[3] and died on 11 Apr 1788[2] at age 49.

Noted events in her life were:
• Resided: 1757, Kåskeby, Vörå, Finland.[3]

Lisa married **Johan Isaksson Knus**[1] on 18 Dec 1757.[3]

34. Johan Mårtensson.[3]

Noted events in his life were:
• Resided: 1746, Tuckor, Vörå, Finland.[3]

Johan married someone **Lisa Mattsdotter**[3] on 7 Dec 1746.[3]

1. Anders Enders, Några sidor på nätet om släktforskning (http://www.enges.org/gene/). .... Hiski database (http://hiski.genealogia.fi).
2. Anders Enders, Några sidor på nätet om släktforskning (http://www.enges.org/gene/).
3. Hiski database (http://hiski.genealogia.fi).
4. Hiski database (http://hiski.genealogia.fi). .... Anders Enders, Några sidor på nätet om släktforskning (http://www.enges.org/gene/).

Children from this marriage were:

i. **Mårten Johansson Skått**[5] was born on 27 Aug 1747 in Tuckor, Vörå, Finland,[5] was christened on 30 Aug 1747,[6] and died on 12 Oct 1823 in Tuckor, Vörå, Finland[7] at age 76. Mårten married **Anna Abrahamsdotter Jussil.**[7]

ii. **Anna Johansdotter Skått**[5] was born on 2 Feb 1750 in Tuckor, Vörå, Finland[5] and was christened on 4 Feb 1750.[6]

iii. **Maria Johansdotter Skått**[5] was born on 2 Feb 1750 in Tuckor, Vörå, Finland[5] and was christened on 4 Feb 1750.[6]

iv. **Johan Johansson Skått**[5] was born on 2 Mar 1751 in Tuckor, Vörå, Finland,[5] was christened on 3 Mar 1751,[6] and died on 18 Sep 1751 in Tuckor, Vörå, Finland.[5]

v. **Margeta Johansdotter Skått**[5] was born on 24 Apr 1752 in Tuckor, Vörå, Finland,[5] was christened on 26 Apr 1752,[6] and died on 29 Jun 1752 in Tuckor, Vörå, Finland.[7]

vi. **Simon Johansson Skått**[7] was born on 27 May 1753 in Tuckor, Vörå, Finland[7] and died on 2 Jun 1753 in Tuckor, Vörå, Finland.[7]

vii. **Brita Johansdotter Skått**[5] was born on 3 Sep 1754 in Tuckor, Vörå, Finland,[5] was christened on 8 Sep 1754,[6] and died on 11 Sep 1754 in Tuckor, Vörå, Finland.[7]

viii. **Lisa Johansdotter Skått**[5] was born on 19 Jan 1756 in Tuckor, Vörå, Finland,[5] was christened on 21 Jan 1756,[6] and died on 7 Feb 1756 in Tuckor, Vörå, Finland.[5]

ix. **Erich Johansson Skått**[5] was born on 7 Apr 1757 in Tuckor, Vörå, Finland[5] and was christened on 10 Apr 1757.[6]

17 x. **Maria Johansdotter Skått**.[6] Maria married **Isak Johansson Knus**,[6] son of **Johan Isaksson Knus** and **Lisa Mårtensdotter Jåfs**, on 18 May 1783 in Rökiö, Vörå, Finland.[6]

xi. **Anna Johansdotter Skått**[5] was born on 2 Apr 1761 in Tuckor, Vörå, Finland[5] and was christened on 5 Apr 1761.[6]

xii. **Brita Johansdotter Skått**[5] was born on 20 Aug 1762 in Tuckor, Vörå, Finland[5] and was christened on 22 Aug 1762.[6]

35. Lisa Mattsdotter,[6] daughter of **Matts Påhlsson** and **Lisa Johansdotter,** was born on 17 Jan 1723 in Lomby, Vörå, Finland,[6] was christened on 25 Jan 1723,[6] died on 28 Jul 1766 in Tuckor, Vörå, Finland[6] at age 43, and was buried on 1 Aug 1766.[6]

Noted events in her life were:
• Resided: 1746, Rökiö, Vörå, Finland.[6]

Lisa married someone **Johan Mårtensson**[6] on 7 Dec 1746.[6]

36. Esajas Isaksson Bengs,[8] son of **Isack Sigfersson** and **Brita Esajasdotter Trött,** was born on 31 Dec 1733 in Kåskeby, Vörå, Finland,[7] died on 11 Mar 1809 in Kåskeby, Vörå, Finland[7] at age 75, and was buried on 26 Mar 1809.[6]

Noted events in his life were:
• Resided: 1764, Kåskeby, Vörå, Finland.[8]

Esajas married someone **Maria Bertilsdotter Pörnull**[8] on 3 Jun 1764 in Kåskeby, Vörå, Finland.[6]

Children from this marriage were:

i. **Isac Esajasson Bengs**[6] was born on 28 Feb 1765 in Kåskeby, Vörå, Finland[6] and was christened on 3 Mar 1765.[6]

ii. **Matts Esajasson Bengs**[6] was born on 9 Mar 1766 in Kåskeby, Vörå, Finland[6] and was christened on 16 Mar 1766.[6]

iii. **Brita Esajasdotter Bengs**[6] was born on 15 Apr 1767 in Kåskeby, Vörå, Finland,[6] was christened on 17 Apr 1767,[6] and died on 2 Nov 1839 in Kåskeby, Vörå, Finland[6] at age 72.

---

5. *Anders Enders, Några sidor på nätet om släktforskning (http://www.enges.org/gene/). .... Hiski database (http://hiski.genealogia.fi).*

6. *Hiski database (http://hiski.genealogia.fi).*

7. *Anders Enders, Några sidor på nätet om släktforskning (http://www.enges.org/gene/).*

8. *Hiski database (http://hiski.genealogia.fi). .... Anders Enders, Några sidor på nätet om släktforskning (http://www.enges.org/gene/).*

18 iv. **Esajas Esajasson Bengs**.[6] Esajas married **Anna Mårtensdotter Wäst**,[6] daughter of **Mårten Carlsson** and **Lisa Hansdotter,** on 17 Jul 1796 in Oravais, Finland. [6]

  v. **Johan Esajasson Bengs**[9] was born on 24 Oct 1769 in Kåskeby, Vörå, Finland[9] and was christened on 29 Oct 1769.[9]

  vi. **Erich Esajasson Bengs**[9] was born on 13 Mar 1772 in Kåskeby, Vörå, Finland[9] and was christened on 15 Mar 1772.[9]

  vii. **Margeta Esajasdotter Bengs**[9] was born on 26 Mar 1773 in Kåskeby, Vörå, Finland[9] and was christened on 28 Mar 1773.[9]

  viii. **Michel Esajasson Bengs**[9] was born on 27 Mar 1774 in Kåskeby, Vörå, Finland[9] and was christened on 1 Apr 1774.[9]

  ix. **Maria Esajasdotter Bengs**[9] was born on 13 Jan 1776 in Kåskeby, Vörå, Finland[9] and was christened on 18 Jan 1776.[9]

  x. **Lisa Esajasdotter Bengs**[9] was born on 22 Jan 1777 in Kåskeby, Vörå, Finland,[9] was christened on 26 Jan 1777,[9] and died on 8 Jan 1818 in Kåskeby, Vörå, Finland[9] at age 40.

  xi. **Maria Esajasdotter Bengs**[9] was born on 6 Dec 1778 in Kåskeby, Vörå, Finland[9] and was christened on 13 Dec 1778.[9]

  xii. **Esajasson Bengs**[9] was born on 13 Sep 1781 in Kåskeby, Vörå, Finland[9] and died on 27 Sep 1781 in Kåskeby, Vörå, Finland.[9]

  xiii. **Anders Esajasson Bengs**[9] was born on 10 Oct 1783 in Kåskeby, Vörå, Finland,[9] was christened on 10 Oct 1783,[9] died on 18 Oct 1783 in Kåskeby, Vörå, Finland,[9] and was buried on 26 Oct 1783. [9]

37. Maria Bertilsdotter Pörnull,[10] daughter of **Bertel Bertilsson** and **Margareta Hendersdotter,** was born on 28 Nov 1739 in Rejpelt, Vörå, Finland[11] and was christened on 30 Nov 1739.[9]

Noted events in her life were:
- Resided: 1764, Kåskeby, Vörå, Finland.[9]

Maria married someone **Esajas Isaksson Bengs**[10] on 3 Jun 1764 in Kåskeby, Vörå, Finland.[9]

38. Mårten Carlsson,[9] son of **Carl Johansson** and **Maria Andersdotter,** was born on 21 Nov 1740 in Oravais, Oravais, Finland,[9] was christened on 21 Nov 1740,[9] died on 15 Apr 1804[9] at age 63, and was buried on 22 Apr 1804 in Oravais, Oravais, Finland.[9] Another name for Mårten was Mårten Carlsson Wäst.

Research Notes: Son of a bonde. Died of flussfeber (cold that had turned into pleuresy). [9]

Noted events in his life were:
- Occupation: Wäst farm (formerly bonde), 1804, Oravais, Oravais, Finland. [9]

Mårten married **Lisa Hansdotter**[9] on 10 Nov 1765 in Oravais, Finland.[9]

Children from this marriage were:

  i. **Maria Mårtensdotter Wäst**[9] was born on 18 Aug 1766 in Oravais, Oravais, Finland[9] and was christened on 19 Aug 1766.[9]

  ii. **Catharina Mårtensdotter Wäst**[9] was born on 27 Aug 1767 in Oravais, Oravais, Finland[9] and was christened on 30 Aug 1767.[9]

  iii. **Carl Mårtensson Wäst**[9] was born on 3 Apr 1769 in Oravais, Oravais, Finland,[9] was christened on 4 Apr 1769,[9] died on 26 Nov 1850 in Oravais, Oravais, Finland[9] at age 81, and was buried on 8 Dec 1850.[9] Carl married **Brita Samuelsdotter**[9] on 27 Nov 1792 in Oravais, Finland.[9] Carl next married **Caisa Johansdotter Lolander**[9] on 25 Sep 1836.

19 iv. **Anna Mårtensdotter Wäst**.[9] Anna married **Esajas Esajasson Bengs**,[9] son of **Esajas Isaksson Bengs** and **Maria Bertilsdotter Pörnull,** on 17 Jul 1796 in Oravais, Finland. [9]

  v. **Mårten Mårtensson Wäst**[9] was born on 8 Oct 1771 in Oravais, Oravais, Finland[9] and was christened on 8 Oct 1771.[9]

---

9. Hiski database (http://hiski.genealogia.fi).

10. Hiski database (http://hiski.genealogia.fi). .... Anders Enders, Några sidor på nätet om släktforskning (http://www.enges.org/gene/).

11. Anders Enders, Några sidor på nätet om släktforskning (http://www.enges.org/gene/). .... Hiski database (http://hiski.genealogia.fi).

vi. **Mickel Mårtensson Wäst** [9] was born on 4 Sep 1773 in Oravais, Oravais, Finland [9] and was christened on 5 Sep 1773. [9] Mickel married **Margareta Johansdotter** [9] on 4 Oct 1761 in Oravais, Finland. [9]

vii. **Johan Mårtensson Wäst** [12] was born on 7 Jun 1775 in Oravais, Oravais, Finland [12] and was christened on 7 Jun 1775. [12]

viii. **Maria Mårtensdotter Wäst** [12] was born on 19 Oct 1777 in Oravais, Oravais, Finland [12] and was christened on 21 Oct 1777. [12]

ix. **Hans Mårtensson Wäst** [12] was born on 23 Feb 1779 in Oravais, Oravais, Finland [12] and was christened on 23 Feb 1779. [12]

x. **Johan Mårtensson Wäst** [12] was born on 15 Jan 1781 in Oravais, Oravais, Finland [12] and was christened on 16 Jan 1781. [12]

xi. **Mårten Mårtensson Wäst** [12] was born on 10 Aug 1784 in Oravais, Oravais, Finland [12] and was christened on 11 Aug 1784. [12]

xii. **Lisa Mårtensdotter Wäst** [12] was born on 10 Aug 1787 in Oravais, Oravais, Finland, [12] was christened on 12 Aug 1787, [12] and died on 10 Dec 1819 in Oravais, Oravais, Finland [12] at age 32. Lisa married **Anders Andersson Friman** [12] on 2 Nov 1806. [12]

39. Lisa Hansdotter [12] was born about 1743, [12] died on 13 Jul 1814 [12] about age 71, and was buried on 17 Jul 1814 in Oravais, Oravais, Finland. [12]

Research Notes: Daughter of a bonde. Died of old age. [12]

Lisa married **Mårten Carlsson** [12] on 10 Nov 1765 in Oravais, Finland. [12]

---

12. Hiski database (http://hiski.genealogia.fi).

Ancestor Report for Johan Eriksson Wäst

Seventh Generation

64. Isack Isaksson,[1] son of **Isak Isaksson** and **Maria Mattsdotter,** was born about 1708 in Kåskeby, Vörå, Finland,[1] died on 24 Sep 1754 in Rökiö, Vörå, Finland[1] about age 46, and was buried on 29 Sep 1754.[1]

Research Notes: Isack b. 1708 is attributed to parents Isacsson and Maria Mattzdotter based on possible sibling births in records.

Isack married **Maria Johansdotter**[1] on 14 Jan 1733 in Kåskeby, Vörå, Finland.[1]

Children from this marriage were:

	i.	**Isak Isaksson**[1] was born on 5 Oct 1733 in Kåskeby, Vörå, Finland[1] and was christened on 7 Oct 1733.[1]
	ii.	**Maria Isaksdotter Knus**[1] was born on 14 Dec 1734 in Rökiö, Vörå, Finland.[1]
32	iii.	**Johan Isaksson Knus.**[2] Johan married **Lisa Mårtensdotter Jåfs,**[3] daughter of **Mårten Michelsson Jåfs** and **Anna Johansdotter,** on 18 Dec 1757.[1]
	iv.	**Lisa Isaksdotter Knus**[1] was born on 5 Jan 1737 in Rökiö, Vörå, Finland.[1]
	v.	**Maria Isaksdotter Knus**[1] was born on 20 Mar 1738 in Rökiö, Vörå, Finland.[1]
	vi.	**Margeta Isaksdotter Knus**[1] was born on 29 Jan 1740 in Rökiö, Vörå, Finland.[1]
	vii.	**Brita Isaksdotter Knus**[1] was born on 11 Jun 1743 in Rökiö, Vörå, Finland,[1] was christened on 12 Jun 1743,[1] and died on 11 May 1822 in Rökiö, Vörå, Finland[1] at age 78.
	viii.	**Anna Isaksdotter Knus**[1] was born on 13 Sep 1744 in Rökiö, Vörå, Finland,[1] was christened on 14 Sep 1744,[1] and died on 30 Aug 1813 in Rökiö, Vörå, Finland[1] at age 68.
	ix.	**Isaksson Knus**[1] was born in 1748 in Rökiö, Vörå, Finland[1] and was christened on 16 Sep 1748.[1]
	x.	**Isac Isaksson Knus**[1] was born on 14 Jan 1750 in Rökiö, Vörå, Finland[1] and was christened on 14 Jan 1750.[1]
	xi.	**Mårten Isaksson Knus**[1] was born on 18 Mar 1751 in Rökiö, Vörå, Finland[1] and was christened on 23 Mar 1751.[1]
	xii.	**Erich Isaksson Knus**[1] was born on 21 Apr 1752 in Rökiö, Vörå, Finland[1] and was christened on 26 Apr 1752.[1]

65. Maria Johansdotter[1] was born about 1712 in Rejpelt, Vörå, Finland,[1] died on 9 Mar 1758 in Rökiö, Vörå, Finland[1] about age 46, and was buried on 19 Mar 1758.[1]

Research Notes: There is a gap in birth records which makes it diffucult to determine parents.

Maria married **Isack Isaksson**[1] on 14 Jan 1733 in Kåskeby, Vörå, Finland.[1]

66. Mårten Michelsson Jåfs,[4] son of **Mickel Michelsson** and **Kirstin Larsdotter Jåfs,** was born on 17 Oct 1702 in Jörala, Vörå, Finland,[5] died on 27 Feb 1788 in Jörala, Vörå, Finland[6] at age 85, and was buried on 27 Feb 1788.[1]

1. *Hiski database (http://hiski.genealogia.fi).*
2. *Anders Enders, Några sidor på nätet om släktforskning (http://www.enges.org/gene/). .... Hiski database (http://hiski.genealogia.fi).*
3. *Hiski database (http://hiski.genealogia.fi). .... Anders Enders, Några sidor på nätet om släktforskning (http://www.enges.org/gene/).*
4. *Anders Enders, Några sidor på nätet om släktforskning (http://www.enges.org/gene/). .... Hiski database (http://hiski.genealogia.fi). .... Email from Torbjörn Nikus.*
5. *Hiski database (http://hiski.genealogia.fi). .... Anders Enders, Några sidor på nätet om släktforskning (http://www.enges.org/gene/). .... Vörå Kommunionsboken 1750-56 (http://www.enges.org). .... Email from Torbjörn Nikus.*
6. *Anders Enders, Några sidor på nätet om släktforskning (http://www.enges.org/gene/). .... Email from Torbjörn Nikus. .... Hiski database (http://hiski.genealogia.fi).*
7. *Vörå Kommunionsboken 1750-56 (http://www.enges.org). .... Email from Torbjörn Nikus. .... Hiski database (http://hiski.genealogia.fi).*

Ancestor Report for Johan Eriksson Wäst

Noted events in his life were:
* Occupation: owner of Jåfs farm, 1750, Jörala, Vörå, Finland. [7]

Mårten married **Anna Johansdotter** [8] on 5 Dec 1725. [9]

Marriage Notes: Possibly received permission to marry outside Vörå. [9]

Children from this marriage were:

- i. **Lars Mårtensson Jåfs** [10] was born on 20 Dec 1726 in Jörala, Vörå, Finland, [10] was christened on 21 Dec 1726, [10] died on 29 Jul 1808 in Jörala, Vörå, Finland [11] at age 81, and was buried on 31 Jul 1808. [9]
- ii. **Maria Mårtensdotter Jåfs** [10] was born on 26 Dec 1727 in Jörala, Vörå, Finland, [10] was christened on 27 Dec 1727, [9] and died on 16 Dec 1808 in Rejpelt, Vörå, Finland [11] at age 80.
- iii. **Michel Mårtensson Jåfs** [9] was born on 7 Mar 1729 in Jörala, Vörå, Finland, [9] was christened on 9 Mar 1729, [9] died on 16 Mar 1729, [9] and was buried on 23 Mar 1729. [9]
- iv. **Johan Mårtensson Jåfs** [9] was born on 8 Apr 1730 in Jörala, Vörå, Finland, [9] was christened on 12 Apr 1730, [9] died on 21 Apr 1730, [12] and was buried on 26 Apr 1730. [9]
- v. **Biata Mårtensdotter Jåfs** [9] was born on 7 Jul 1731 in Jörala, Vörå, Finland, [9] was christened on 11 Jul 1731, [9] died on 9 May 1797 in Jörala, Vörå, Finland [10] at age 65, and was buried on 14 May 1797. [9] Biata married **Anders Jöransson** [9] on 8 Dec 1751. [9]
- vi. **Anna Mårtensdotter Jåfs** [9] was born on 29 Aug 1732 in Jörala, Vörå, Finland, [9] was christened on 1 Sep 1732, [9] died on 26 Apr 1734 [9] at age 1, and was buried on 5 May 1734. [9]
- vii. **Mårten Mårtensson Jåfs** [9] was born on 16 Nov 1733 in Jörala, Vörå, Finland, [9] was christened on 18 Nov 1733, [9] died on 4 Mar 1798 in Jörala, Vörå, Finland [10] at age 64, and was buried on 11 Mar 1798. [9] Mårten married **Margeta Mårtensdotter** on 9 Jun 1756. [9]
- viii. **Brita Mårtensdotter Jåfs** [9] was born on 15 Jan 1735 in Jörala, Vörå, Finland, [9] was christened on 19 Jan 1735, [9] died on 5 Sep 1811 in Rejpelt, Vörå, Finland [9] at age 76, and was buried on 8 Sep 1811. [9] Brita married **Mårten Johansson Wäst**, [9] son of **Juho Matinpoika** and **Maria Sigfredsdotter Wäst**, on 7 Dec 1755. [9]
- ix. **Anna Mårtensdotter Jåfs** [9] was born on 13 Feb 1737 in Jörala, Vörå, Finland, [9] was christened on 20 Feb 1737, [9] died on 7 Jul 1737, [9] and was buried on 10 Jul 1737. [9]
- 33 x. **Lisa Mårtensdotter Jåfs**. [8] Lisa married **Johan Isaksson Knus**, [13] son of **Isack Isaksson** and **Maria Johansdotter,** on 18 Dec 1757. [9]
- xi. **Margeta Mårtensdotter Jåfs** [9] was born on 24 May 1739 in Jörala, Vörå, Finland, [9] was christened on 27 May 1739, [9] died on 28 Nov 1739, [9] and was buried on 9 Dec 1739. [9]
- xii. **Anna Mårtensdotter Jåfs** [9] was born on 6 Oct 1740 in Jörala, Vörå, Finland, [9] was christened on 7 Oct 1740, [9] died on 11 Mar 1742 [9] at age 1, and was buried on 17 Mar 1742. [9]

Mårten next married **Margeta Bertilsdotter Antus** [14] on 9 Dec 1744. [9]

Children from this marriage were:

- i. **Anna Mårtensdotter Jåfs** [9] was born on 29 Aug 1745 in Jörala, Vörå, Finland, [9] was christened on 1 Sep 1745, [9] and died on 24 Jan 1831 in Rejpelt, Vörå, Finland [11] at age 85. Anna married **Johan Eriksson Lång** on 22 Dec 1765.
- ii. **Margareta Mårtensotter Jåfs** [13] was born on 8 Jul 1748 in Jörala, Vörå, Finland, [13] was christened on 10 Jul 1748, [9] died on 31 Mar 1825 in Kaitsor, Vörå, Finland [9] at age 76, and was buried on 3 Apr 1825. [9] Margareta married **Johan Johansson Finnas** [9] on 10 Dec 1769. [9]
- iii. **Maria Mårtensdotter Jåfs** [13] was born on 6 Jul 1750 in Jörala, Vörå, Finland, [13] was christened on 8 Jul 1750, [9] died on 14 Jun 1751 in Jörala, Vörå, Finland, [13] and was buried on 23 Jun 1751. [9]

---

8. Hiski database (http://hiski.genealogia.fi). .... Anders Enders, Några sidor på nätet om släktforskning (http://www.enges.org/gene/).
9. Hiski database (http://hiski.genealogia.fi).
10. Hiski database (http://hiski.genealogia.fi). .... Email from Torbjörn Nikus.
11. Email from Torbjörn Nikus.
12. Email from Torbjörn Nikus. .... Hiski database (http://hiski.genealogia.fi).
13. Anders Enders, Några sidor på nätet om släktforskning (http://www.enges.org/gene/). .... Hiski database (http://hiski.genealogia.fi).
14. Anders Enders, Några sidor på nätet om släktforskning (http://www.enges.org/gene/). .... Email from Torbjörn Nikus. .... Hiski database (http://hiski.genealogia.fi).

67. Anna Johansdotter[15] was born about 1704 in Rökiö, Vörå, Finland,[15] died on 2 Apr 1741 in Jörala, Vörå, Finland[15] about age 37, and was buried on 12 Apr 1741.[16] Another name for Anna was Anna Michelsson.

Anna married **Mårten Michelsson Jåfs**[17] on 5 Dec 1725.[16]

70. Matts Påhlsson.[16]

Research Notes: Records are incomplete during his lifetime.

Matts married **Lisa Johansdotter**.[16]

The child from this marriage was:
35   i.   **Lisa Mattsdotter**.[16] Lisa married someone **Johan Mårtensson**[16] on 7 Dec 1746.[16]

71. Lisa Johansdotter.[16]

Lisa married **Matts Påhlsson**.[16]

72. Isack Sigfersson[18] was born in Feb 1692[18] and died in 1765[18] at age 73.

Research Notes: Birth date may be between 1689 ans 1698.[18]

Isack married **Brita Esajasdotter Trött**[18] before 1723.[18]

Children from this marriage were:
    i.   **Johan Isaksson Bengs**[18] was born on 23 May 1723 in Kåskeby, Vörå, Finland.[18]
    ii.   **Anders Isaksson Bengs**[18] was born on 5 Dec 1725 in Kåskeby, Vörå, Finland[18] and died on 22 Feb 1730[18] at age 4.
    iii. **Isac Isaksson Bengs**[18] was born on 22 May 1728 in Kåskeby, Vörå, Finland[18] and died on 22 May 1814 in Kåskeby, Vörå, Finland[18] at age 86. Isac married **Lisa Mårtensdotter Förars**[18] on 24 Dec 1797.[18]
    iv. **Erik Isaksson Bengs**[18] was born on 25 Apr 1731 in Kåskeby, Vörå, Finland.[18]
36   v.   **Esajas Isaksson Bengs**.[15] Esajas married someone **Maria Bertilsdotter Pörnull**,[15] daughter of **Bertel Bertilsson** and **Margareta Hendersdotter**, on 3 Jun 1764 in Kåskeby, Vörå, Finland.[16]

73. Brita Esajasdotter Trött,[18] daughter of **Esaias Erichsson Trött** and **Beata Mattsdotter**, was born in Feb 1692 in Bertby, Vörå, Finland[18] and died on 16 Feb 1753 in Kåskeby, Vörå, Finland[18] at age 61.

Brita married **Isack Sigfersson**[18] before 1723.[18]

74. Bertel Bertilsson,[18] son of **Bertill Bertilsson** and **Lisa Sigfridsdotter**, was born in Apr 1693,[18] was christened on 2 Apr 1699 in Lapua, Finland,[16] died on 22 Oct 1758 in Rejpelt, Vörå, Finland[18] at age 65, and was buried on 29 Oct 1758.[16]

Noted events in his life were:
• Language: Finnish.[18]

• Moved from: After 1724, Lapua, Finland.[16]

15. *Hiski database (http://hiski.genealogia.fi). .... Anders Enders, Några sidor på nätet om släktforskning (http://www.enges.org/gene/).*
16. *Hiski database (http://hiski.genealogia.fi).*
17. *Anders Enders, Några sidor på nätet om släktforskning (http://www.enges.org/gene/). .... Hiski database (http://hiski.genealogia.fi). .... Email from Torbjörn Nikus.*
18. *Anders Enders, Några sidor på nätet om släktforskning (http://www.enges.org/gene/).*

- Moved to: Between 1724 and 1729, Vörå, Finland. [19] to Pörnull homestead which was deserted by previous owner, Eric, in 1723

- Cause of death: stroke. [20]

Bertel married **Margareta Hendersdotter**[19] on 19 Apr 1724 in Lapua, Finland. [21]

Marriage Notes: on the Titula farm[20]

Children from this marriage were:
    i.   **Erich Bertilsson Pörnull**[21] was born on 3 May 1725 in Rejpelt, Vörå, Finland,[21] was christened on 6 May 1725,[21] and died on 4 Jul 1725 in Rejpelt, Vörå, Finland. [20]
    ii.   **Lisa Bertilsdotter Pörnull**[20] was born on 15 Sep 1726 in Rejpelt, Vörå, Finland[20] and was christened on 19 Sep 1726.[20]
    iii.   **Johan Bertilsson Pörnull**[20] was born on 24 Mar 1729 in Rejpelt, Vörå, Finland,[20] was christened on 25 Mar 1729,[20] and died on 12 Oct 1799[20] at age 70. Johan married **Maria Michelsdotter**[20] on 19 Nov 1749.[20]
    iv.   **Margeta Bertilsdotter Pörnull**[20] was born on 4 Apr 1733 in Rejpelt, Vörå, Finland,[20] was christened on 8 Apr 1733,[20] and died on 24 Aug 1733.[20]
    v.   **Hendrich Bertilsson Pörnull**[20] was born on 26 Dec 1734 in Rejpelt, Vörå, Finland,[20] was christened on 28 Dec 1734,[20] and died on 23 May 1737[20] at age 2.
    vi.   **Anders Bertilsson Pörnull**[20] was born on 28 Nov 1736 in Rejpelt, Vörå, Finland,[20] was christened on 30 Nov 1736,[20] and died on 29 Nov 1794 in Bergby, Vörå, Finland[20] at age 58. Anders married **Anna Jöransdotter** on 9 Dec 1759.[20]
37 vii.   **Maria Bertilsdotter Pörnull**.[22] Maria married someone **Esajas Isaksson Bengs**,[22] son of **Isack Sigfersson** and **Brita Esajasdotter Trött**, on 3 Jun 1764 in Kåskeby, Vörå, Finland. [20]

75. Margareta Hendersdotter[19] was born in Nov 1695,[19] died on 8 Apr 1764 in Rejpelt, Vörå, Finland[20] at age 68, and was buried on 15 Apr 1764. [20]

Noted events in her life were:
• Resided: Titula farm, Lapua, Finland. [21]

Margareta married **Bertel Bertilsson**[19] on 19 Apr 1724 in Lapua, Finland. [21]

76. Carl Johansson,[20] son of **Johan Johansson** and **Maria Johansdotter,** was born on 16 Aug 1710 in Oravais, Oravais, Finland,[20] was christened on 17 Aug 1710,[20] died on 2 Nov 1751 in Oravais, Finland[20] at age 41, and was buried on 10 Nov 1751.[20]

Noted events in his life were:
• Occupation: foundry dayworker, 1739.[20]

Carl married **Maria Andersdotter** on 23 Oct 1737 in Oravais, Finland.[20]

Children from this marriage were:
    i.   **Johannes Carlsson**[20] was born on 14 May 1739 in Oravais, Oravais, Finland[20] and was christened on 14 May 1739.[20]
38 ii.   **Mårten Carlsson**.[20] Mårten married **Lisa Hansdotter**[20] on 10 Nov 1765 in Oravais, Finland. [20]
    iii.   **Michael Carlsson**[20] was born on 27 Sep 1742 in Oravais, Oravais, Finland,[20] was christened on 28 Sep 1742,[20] died on 20 Apr 1803 in Oravais, Oravais, Finland[20] at age 60, and was buried on 1 May 1803.[20]
    iv.   **Carl Carlsson**[20] was born on 7 Feb 1745 in Oravais, Oravais, Finland[20] and was christened on 8 Feb 1745.[20]

19. Anders Enders, Några sidor på nätet om släktforskning (http://www.enges.org/gene/).
20. Hiski database (http://hiski.genealogia.fi).
21. Anders Enders, Några sidor på nätet om släktforskning (http://www.enges.org/gene/). .... Hiski database (http://hiski.genealogia.fi).
22. Hiski database (http://hiski.genealogia.fi). .... Anders Enders, Några sidor på nätet om släktforskning (http://www.enges.org/gene/).

    v.   **Carl Carlsson**[20] was born on 18 Feb 1746 in Oravais, Oravais, Finland[20] and was christened on 21 Feb 1746.[20]

    vi.   **Maria Carlsdotter**[23] was born on 1 Jan 1750 in Oravais, Oravais, Finland[23] and was christened on 3 Jan 1750.[23]

77. Maria Andersdotter.

Noted events in her life were:
- Occupation: servant, 1737.[23]

Maria married **Carl Johansson**[23] on 23 Oct 1737 in Oravais, Finland.[23]

---

23. Hiski database (http://hiski.genealogia.fi).

Ancestor Report for Johan Eriksson Wäst

Eighth Generation

128. Isak Isaksson.

Isak married **Maria Mattsdotter**.[1]

Children from this marriage were:

	i.	**Mattz Isaksson** was born on 26 Jun 1701 in Kåskeby, Vörå, Finland and died in 1711 at age 10.
	ii.	**Isaak Isaksson**[1] was born on 5 Jan 1703 in Kåskeby, Vörå, Finland[1] and died in 1703.[1]
64	iii.	**Isack Isaksson**.[1] Isack married **Maria Johansdotter**[1] on 14 Jan 1733 in Kåskeby, Vörå, Finland.[1]

129. Maria Mattsdotter.[1]

Maria married **Isak Isaksson**.

132. Mickel Michelsson[2] was born about 1671,[3] died on 13 Jun 1741 in Jörala, Vörå, Finland[4] about age 70, and was buried on 21 Jun 1741.[1]

Noted events in his life were:
• Occupation: bonde of Jåfs farm, 1719.[5]

Mickel married **Kirstin Larsdotter Jåfs**.[2]

Children from this marriage were:

	i.	**Anna Michelsdotter Jåfs**[1] was born on 27 Aug 1692 in Jörala, Vörå, Finland[1] and died in 1692.[1]
	ii.	**Mårten Michelsson Jåfs**[1] was born in 1693 in Jörala, Vörå, Finland[1] and died in 1693 in Jörala, Vörå, Finland.[1]
	iii.	**Margeta Michelsdotter Jåfs**[1] was born on 21 Jun 1694 in Jörala, Vörå, Finland[1] and died in 1711[1] at age 17.
	iv.	**Johan Michelsson Jåfs**[1] was born on 27 Oct 1695 in Jörala, Vörå, Finland.[1]
	v.	**Brita Michelsdotter Jåfs**[1] was born on 21 Jun 1698 in Jörala, Vörå, Finland[1] and died on 9 Jul 1698 in Jörala, Vörå, Finland.[1]
	vi.	**Lisa Michelsdotter Jåfs**[1] was born on 21 Jun 1698 in Jörala, Vörå, Finland.[1]
	vii.	**Maria Michelsdotter Jåfs**[1] was born on 11 Oct 1699 in Jörala, Vörå, Finland[1] and died on 17 Dec 1727 in Lålax, Vörå, Finland[1] at age 28. Maria married **Abraham Hendersson** on 17 Dec 1727.[1]
66	viii.	**Mårten Michelsson Jåfs**.[2] Mårten married **Anna Johansdotter**[6] on 5 Dec 1725.[1] Mårten next married **Margeta Bertilsdotter Antus**[4] on 9 Dec 1744.[1]
	ix.	**Anna Michelsson Jåfs**[1] was born about 1702 in Jörala, Vörå, Finland[1] and died on 10 Jul 1748 in Mäkipää, Vörå, Finland[1] about age 46. Anna married **Isak Isaksson Seppas**[5] on 20 Dec 1730.[5]
	x.	**Brita Michelsson Jåfs**[5] was born in 1704 in Jörala, Vörå, Finland[5] and died on 29 Jan 1771 in Kåskeby, Vörå, Finland[5] at age 67. Brita married **Mickel Johansson Knubb**[1] on 12 Jan 1729.[1]

133. Kirstin Larsdotter Jåfs,[2] daughter of **Lars Mårtensson** and **Brijta Mattsdotter,** was born in 1667[5] and died in 1722 in Jörala, Vörå, Finland[5] at age 55. Another name for Kirstin was Kirstin Michelsson.

Kirstin married **Mickel Michelsson**.[2]

---

1. *Hiski database (http://hiski.genealogia.fi).*

2. *Anders Enders, Några sidor på nätet om släktforskning (http://www.enges.org/gene/). .... Hiski database (http://hiski.genealogia.fi). .... Email from Torbjörn Nikus.*

3. *Anders Enders, Några sidor på nätet om släktforskning (http://www.enges.org/gene/). .... Hiski database (http://hiski.genealogia.fi).*

4. *Anders Enders, Några sidor på nätet om släktforskning (http://www.enges.org/gene/). .... Email from Torbjörn Nikus. .... Hiski database (http://hiski.genealogia.fi).*

5. *Email from Torbjörn Nikus.*

6. *Hiski database (http://hiski.genealogia.fi). .... Anders Enders, Några sidor på nätet om släktforskning (http://www.enges.org/gene/).*

146. Esaias Erichsson Trött.[7]

Esaias married **Beata Mattsdotter**.[7]

Children from this marriage were:
73	i.	**Brita Esajasdotter Trött**.[7] Brita married **Isack Sigfersson**[7] before 1723.[7]
	ii.	**Erich Esajasson Trött**[8] was born on 19 Mar 1692 in Bertby, Vörå, Finland.[8]
	iii.	**Kirstin Esajasdotter Trött**[8] was born on 25 Aug 1693 in Bertby, Vörå, Finland[8] and died on 3 Sep 1693.[8]
	iv.	**Michell Esajasson Trött**[8] was born on 17 Sep 1695 in Bertby, Vörå, Finland[8] and died in 1695.[8]

Esaias next married **Brita Andersdotter**.[8]

Children from this marriage were:
	i.	**Johan Esajasson**[8] was born on 4 May 1701 in Bertby, Vörå, Finland[8] and died in 1701.[8]
	ii.	**Esajasson**[8] was born on 16 Dec 1702 in Bertby, Vörå, Finland[8] and died on 23 Dec 1702.[8]

147. Beata Mattsdotter[7] was born about 1654[8] and died on 8 Mar 1699 in Bertby, Vörå, Finland[8] about age 45.

Beata married **Esaias Erichsson Trött**.[7]

148. Bertill Bertilsson.[8]

Noted events in his life were:
• Resided: 1699, Lapua, Finland.

Bertill had a relationship with **Lisa Sigfridsdotter**.[7] This couple did not marry.

The child from this marriage was:
74	i.	**Bertel Bertilsson**.[7] Bertel married **Margareta Hendersdotter**[7] on 19 Apr 1724 in Lapua, Finland.[9]

149. Lisa Sigfridsdotter[7] was born about 1666,[7] died on 7 May 1734 in Rejpelt, Vörå, Finland[7] about age 68, and was buried on 12 May 1734.[7] Another name for Lisa was Lijsala Sigfersdotter.[8]

Research Notes: She may have been born on the Suutarla farm to Sigfrid Sigfridsson. Many of her relatives were killed in the plague of and famine 1697 and 1698, which killed one third of the population of Finland. He husband may have been Jöran Henrichsson, married 1701. Her child Bertil was born out of wedlock.[8]

Noted events in her life were:
• Resided: 1699, Lapua, Finland.

Lisa had a relationship with **Bertill Bertilsson**.[8] This couple did not marry.

152. Johan Johansson[8] was born about 1666[8] and died on 26 Aug 1713 in Kimo, Oravais, Finland[8] about age 47.

Noted events in his life were:
• Resided: 1704, Kimo, Oravais, Finland.[8]

• Occupation: parish clerk, 1713.

Johan married **Maria Johansdotter**[8] on 27 Nov 1704 in Oravais, Finland.[8]

---

7. Anders Enders, Några sidor på nätet om släktforskning (http://www.enges.org/gene/).
8. Hiski database (http://hiski.genealogia.fi).
9. Anders Enders, Några sidor på nätet om släktforskning (http://www.enges.org/gene/). .... Hiski database (http://hiski.genealogia.fi).

Children from this marriage were:

i. **Gustaf Johansson**[10] was born on 5 Aug 1705 in Oravais, Oravais, Finland,[10] died on 17 Aug 1705 in Oravais, Oravais, Finland,[10] and was buried on 20 Aug 1705.[10] Another name for Gustaf was Giösta Johansson.

ii. **Anna Johansdotter**[10] was born on 30 Sep 1706 in Oravais, Oravais, Finland[10] and was christened on 30 Sep 1706.[10]

iii. **Mårten Johansson**[10] was born on 15 Sep 1708 in Oravais, Oravais, Finland[10] and was christened on 18 Sep 1708.[10]

76 iv. **Carl Johansson**.[10] Carl married **Maria Andersdotter** on 23 Oct 1737 in Oravais, Finland.[10]

v. **Simon Johansson**[10] was born on 18 Oct 1713 in Oravais, Oravais, Finland[10] and was christened on 19 Oct 1713.[10]

153. Maria Johansdotter[10] was born about 1670[10] and died in 1766 in Kimo, Oravais, Finland[10] about age 96.

Noted events in her life were:
• Resided: 1704, Oravais, Oravais, Finland.[10]

Maria married **Johan Johansson**[10] on 27 Nov 1704 in Oravais, Finland.[10]

---

10. *Hiski database (http://hiski.genealogia.fi).*

Ancestor Report for Johan Eriksson Wäst

Ninth Generation

266. Lars Mårtensson[1] died after 1696 in Jörala, Vörå, Finland.[2]

Noted events in his life were:
• Occupation: bonde (farm owner) of Jåfs, 1690-1696, Jörala, Vörå, Finland.[3]

Lars married **Brijta Mattsdotter**.[4]

Children from this marriage were:

	i.	**Valborg Larsdotter Jåfs**[5] was born in 1662 in Jörala, Vörå, Finland,[6] died on 10 Mar 1741 in Jörala, Vörå, Finland[6] at age 79, and was buried on 29 Mar 1741.[6] Valborg married **Lars Mårtensson**.[5] Valborg next married **Lars Andersson**.[5]
133	ii.	**Kirstin Larsdotter Jåfs**.[7] Kirstin married **Mickel Michelsson**.[7]
	iii.	**Mickel Larsson Jåfs**[8]
	iv.	**Anna Larsdotter Jåfs**.[5] Anna married **Mårten Mickelsson Lillund**.[5]

267. Brijta Mattsdotter[4] died in 1691 in Jörala, Vörå, Finland.[5]

Brijta married **Lars Mårtensson**.[1]

---

1. *Vörå Kommunionsboken 1750-56 (http://www.enges.org). .... Email from Torbjörn Nikus.*
2. *Email from Torbjörn Nikus. .... Vörå Mantalslängden 1695-96 (http://www.enges.org).*
3. *Vörå Jordeboken 1695-96 (http://www.enges.org). .... Vörå Mantalslängden 1695-96 (http://www.enges.org). .... Vörå Mantalslängden 1690-91 (http://www.enges.org).*
4. *Vörå Mantalslängden 1690-91 (http://www.enges.org). .... Email from Torbjörn Nikus.*
5. *Email from Torbjörn Nikus.*
6. *Hiski database (http://hiski.genealogia.fi).*
7. *Anders Enders, Några sidor på nätet om släktforskning (http://www.enges.org/gene/). .... Hiski database (http://hiski.genealogia.fi). .... Email from Torbjörn Nikus.*
8. *Vörå Jordeboken 1709-10 (http://www.enges.org).*

Pedigree Chart for Johan Eriksson Wäst

No. 1 on this chart is the same as no. 10 on chart no. 1

8 Isak Isaksson Knus
b. 20 Jul 1792 cont. __13__
p. Rökiö, Vörå, Finland
m. 23 Apr 1821
p. Oravais, Finland
d.
p.

4 Johan Isaksson Knuts
b. 22 Jun 1833
p. Rökiö, Vörå, Finland
m. 18 Dec 1757
p. Rökiö, Vörå, Finland
d.
p.

9 Lisa Esajasdotter Wäst
b. 1 Oct 1798 cont. __14__
p. Oravais, Oravais, Finland
d.
p.

2 Erik Johansson Knuts
b. 10 Feb 1774
p. Rökiö, Vörå, Finland
m. 10 Nov 1805
p. Rejpelt, Vörå, Finland
d.
p.

10 Mårten Isaksson
b.
p.
m.
p.
d.
p.

5 Lisa Mårtensdotter
b. 25 Mar 1732
p. Kåskeby, Vörå, Finland
d.
p.

11 Maria Mattsdotter
b.
p.
d.
p.

1 Johan Eriksson Wäst
b. 10 Mar 1799
p. Rejpelt, Vörå, Finland
m. 28 Dec 1819
p. Rejpelt, Vörå, Finland
d. 9 Jun 1878
p. Rejpelt, Vörå, Finland
sp. Lisa Johansdotter Wäst

12 Mårten Johansson
b. 20 Mar 1692 cont. __15__
p. Lomby, Vörå, Finland
m.
p.
d. 1 Oct 1764
p. Rejpelt, Vörå, Finland

6 Johan Mårtensson
b. 3 Jan 1731
p. Rejpelt, Vörå, Finland
m. 5 Dec 1756
p.
d. 1 Jun 1803
p. Rejpelt, Vörå, Finland

13 Anna Johansdotter
b. Abt 1705
p.
d. 8 Jun 1766
p. Rejpelt, Vörå, Finland

3 Margeta Johansdotter Kårvolain
b. 2 Dec 1776
p. Rejpelt, Vörå, Finland
d. 6 Jun 1850
p. Rejpelt, Vörå, Finland

14 Erich Åkesson
b. Abt 1697 cont. __16__
p. Kaitsor, Vörå, Finland
m.
p.
d. 15 Dec 1772
p. Mäkipää, Vörå, Finland

7 Brita Eriksdotter
b. 12 Feb 1734
p. Mäkipää, Vörå, Finland
d. 28 Aug 1791
p. Rejpelt, Vörå, Finland

15 Brita Simonsdotter
b. Abt 1684
p.
d. 9 Nov 1736
p. Mäkipää, Vörå, Finland

Pedigree Chart for Isak Isaksson Knus

No. 1 on this chart is the same as no. 8 on chart no. 12

8 Isack Isaksson
b. Abt 1708   cont. __17__
p. Kåskeby, Vörå, Finland
m. 14 Jan 1733
p. Kåskeby, Vörå, Finland
d. 24 Sep 1754
p. Rökiö, Vörå, Finland

4 Johan Isaksson Knus
b. 3 Nov 1735
p. Rökiö, Vörå, Finland
m. 18 Dec 1757
p.
d. 16 Jan 1809
p. Rökiö, Vörå, Finland

9 Maria Johansdotter
b. Abt 1712
p. Rejpelt, Vörå, Finland
d. 9 Mar 1758
p. Rökiö, Vörå, Finland

2 Isak Johansson Knus
b. 25 Jan 1760
p. Rökiö, Vörå, Finland
m. 18 May 1783
p. Rökiö, Vörå, Finland
d. 15 May 1809
p. Rökiö, Vörå, Finland

10 Mårten Michelsson Jåfs
b. 17 Oct 1702   cont. __18__
p. Jörala, Vörå, Finland
m. 5 Dec 1725
p.
d. 27 Feb 1788
p. Jörala, Vörå, Finland

5 Lisa Mårtensdotter Jåfs
b. 3 May 1738
p. Jörala, Vörå, Finland
d. 11 Apr 1788
p.

11 Anna Johansdotter
b. Abt 1704
p. Rökiö, Vörå, Finland
d. 2 Apr 1741
p. Jörala, Vörå, Finland

1 Isak Isaksson Knus
b. 20 Jul 1792
p. Rökiö, Vörå, Finland
m. 23 Apr 1821
p. Oravais, Finland
d.
p.
sp. Lisa Esajasdotter Wäst

12
b.
p.
m.
p.
d.
p.

6 Johan Mårtensson
b.
p.
m. 7 Dec 1746
p.
d.
p.

13
b.
p.
d.
p.

3 Maria Johansdotter Skått
b. 9 May 1759
p. Tuckor, Vörå, Finland
d. 22 Feb 1843
p. Rökiö, Vörå, Finland

14 Matts Påhlsson
b.
p.
m.
p.
d.
p.

7 Lisa Mattsdotter
b. 17 Jan 1723
p. Lomby, Vörå, Finland
d. 28 Jul 1766
p. Tuckor, Vörå, Finland

15 Lisa Johansdotter
b.
p.
d.
p.

Pedigree Chart for Lisa Esajasdotter Wäst

No. 1 on this chart is the same as no. 9 on chart no. 12

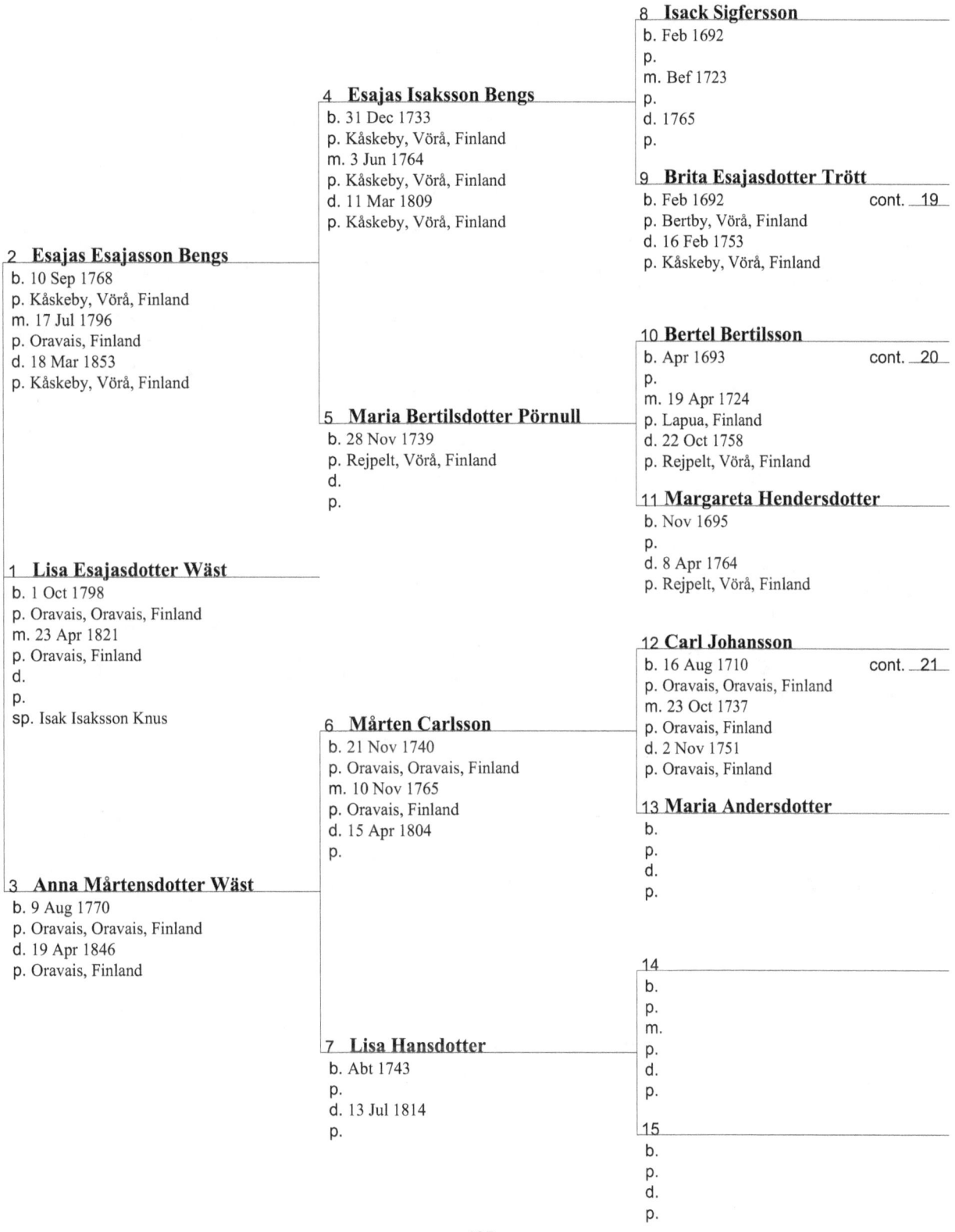

8 Isack Sigfersson
b. Feb 1692
p.
m. Bef 1723
p.
d. 1765
p.

4 Esajas Isaksson Bengs
b. 31 Dec 1733
p. Kåskeby, Vörå, Finland
m. 3 Jun 1764
p. Kåskeby, Vörå, Finland
d. 11 Mar 1809
p. Kåskeby, Vörå, Finland

9 Brita Esajasdotter Trött cont. 19
b. Feb 1692
p. Bertby, Vörå, Finland
d. 16 Feb 1753
p. Kåskeby, Vörå, Finland

2 Esajas Esajasson Bengs
b. 10 Sep 1768
p. Kåskeby, Vörå, Finland
m. 17 Jul 1796
p. Oravais, Finland
d. 18 Mar 1853
p. Kåskeby, Vörå, Finland

10 Bertel Bertilsson cont. 20
b. Apr 1693
p.
m. 19 Apr 1724
p. Lapua, Finland
d. 22 Oct 1758
p. Rejpelt, Vörå, Finland

5 Maria Bertilsdotter Pörnull
b. 28 Nov 1739
p. Rejpelt, Vörå, Finland
d.
p.

11 Margareta Hendersdotter
b. Nov 1695
p.
d. 8 Apr 1764
p. Rejpelt, Vörå, Finland

1 Lisa Esajasdotter Wäst
b. 1 Oct 1798
p. Oravais, Oravais, Finland
m. 23 Apr 1821
p. Oravais, Finland
d.
p.
sp. Isak Isaksson Knus

12 Carl Johansson cont. 21
b. 16 Aug 1710
p. Oravais, Oravais, Finland
m. 23 Oct 1737
p. Oravais, Finland
d. 2 Nov 1751
p. Oravais, Finland

6 Mårten Carlsson
b. 21 Nov 1740
p. Oravais, Oravais, Finland
m. 10 Nov 1765
p. Oravais, Finland
d. 15 Apr 1804
p.

13 Maria Andersdotter
b.
p.
d.
p.

3 Anna Mårtensdotter Wäst
b. 9 Aug 1770
p. Oravais, Oravais, Finland
d. 19 Apr 1846
p. Oravais, Finland

14
b.
p.
m.
p.
d.
p.

7 Lisa Hansdotter
b. Abt 1743
p.
d. 13 Jul 1814
p.

15
b.
p.
d.
p.

Pedigree Chart for Mårten Johansson

No. 1 on this chart is the same as no. 12 on chart no. 12

2 Johan Mårtensson
b.
p.
m.
p.
d.
p.

1 Mårten Johansson
b. 20 Mar 1692
p. Lomby, Vörå, Finland
m.
p.
d. 1 Oct 1764
p. Rejpelt, Vörå, Finland
sp. Anna Johansdotter

3 Brita Mårtensdotter
b.
p.
d.
p.

4
b.
p.
m.
p.
d.
p.

5
b.
p.
d.
p.

6
b.
p.
m.
p.
d.
p.

7
b.
p.
d.
p.

8
b.
p.
m.
p.
d.
p.

9
b.
p.
d.
p.

10
b.
p.
m.
p.
d.
p.

11
b.
p.
d.
p.

12
b.
p.
m.
p.
d.
p.

13
b.
p.
d.
p.

14
b.
p.
m.
p.
d.
p.

15
b.
p.
d.
p.

Pedigree Chart for Erich Åkesson

No. 1 on this chart is the same as no. 14 on chart no. 12

2 Åke Sigfersson
b.
p.
m.
p.
d.
p.

1 Erich Åkesson
b. Abt 1697
p. Kaitsor, Vörå, Finland
m.
p.
d. 15 Dec 1772
p. Mäkipää, Vörå, Finland
sp. Brita Simonsdotter

3 Maria Andersdotter
b.
p.
d.
p.

4
b.
p.
m.
p.
d.
p.

5
b.
p.
d.
p.

6
b.
p.
m.
p.
d.
p.

7
b.
p.
d.
p.

8
b.
p.
m.
p.
d.
p.

9
b.
p.
d.
p.

10
b.
p.
m.
p.
d.
p.

11
b.
p.
d.
p.

12
b.
p.
m.
p.
d.
p.

13
b.
p.
d.
p.

14
b.
p.
m.
p.
d.
p.

15
b.
p.
d.
p.

Pedigree Chart for Isack Isaksson

No. 1 on this chart is the same as no. 8 on chart no. 13

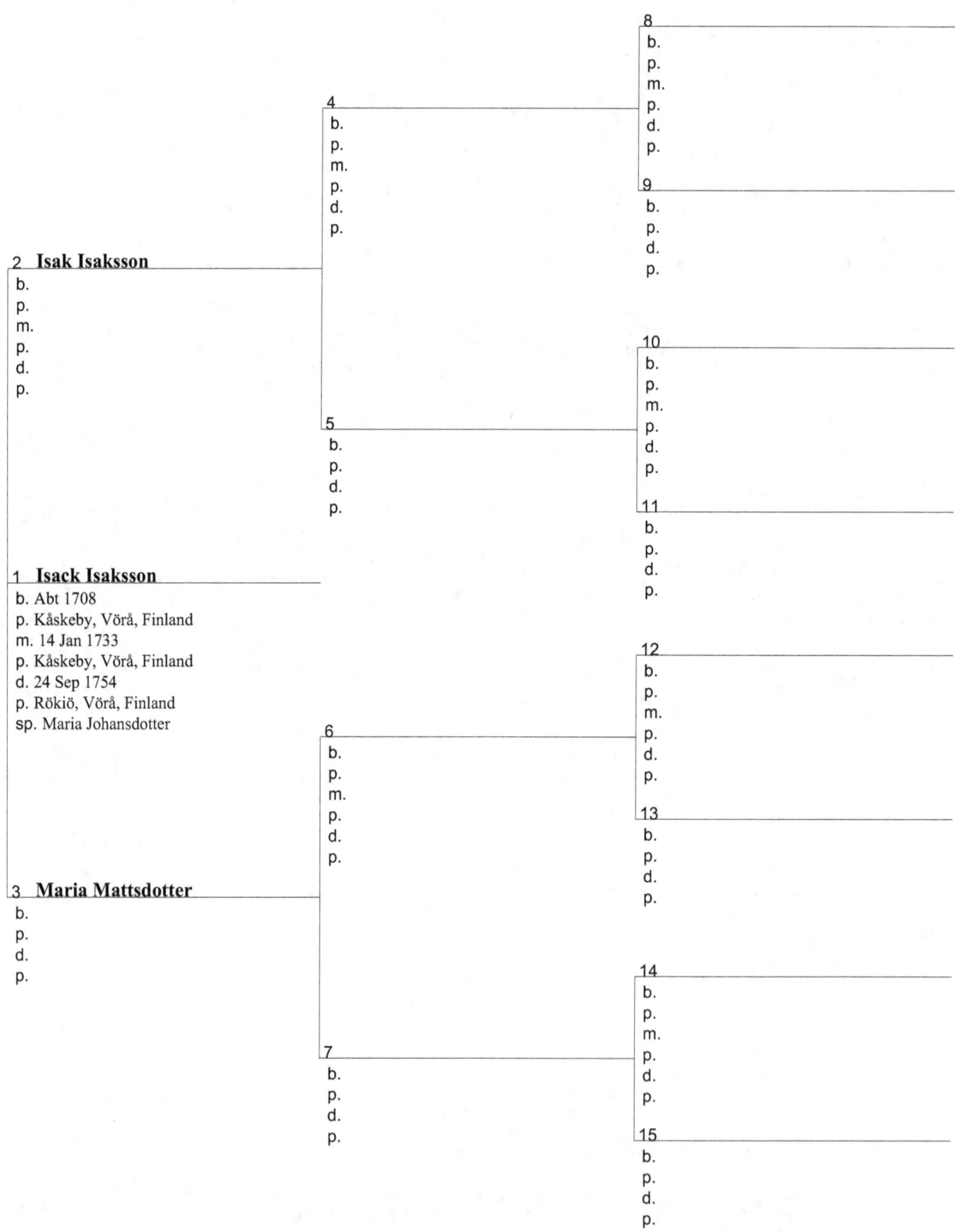

8
b.
p.
m.
p.
d.
p.

4
b.
p.
m.
p.
d.
p.

9
b.
p.
d.
p.

2 **Isak Isaksson**
b.
p.
m.
p.
d.
p.

10
b.
p.
m.
p.
d.
p.

5
b.
p.
d.
p.

11
b.
p.
d.
p.

1 **Isack Isaksson**
b. Abt 1708
p. Kåskeby, Vörå, Finland
m. 14 Jan 1733
p. Kåskeby, Vörå, Finland
d. 24 Sep 1754
p. Rökiö, Vörå, Finland
sp. Maria Johansdotter

12
b.
p.
m.
p.
d.
p.

6
b.
p.
m.
p.
d.
p.

13
b.
p.
d.
p.

3 **Maria Mattsdotter**
b.
p.
d.
p.

14
b.
p.
m.
p.
d.
p.

7
b.
p.
d.
p.

15
b.
p.
d.
p.

Pedigree Chart for Mårten Michelsson Jåfs

No. 1 on this chart is the same as no. 10 on chart no. 13

2 Mickel Michelsson
b. Abt 1671
p.
m.
p.
d. 13 Jun 1741
p. Jörala, Vörå, Finland

1 Mårten Michelsson Jåfs
b. 17 Oct 1702
p. Jörala, Vörå, Finland
m. 5 Dec 1725
p.
d. 27 Feb 1788
p. Jörala, Vörå, Finland
sp. Anna Johansdotter

3 Kirstin Larsdotter Jåfs
b. 1667
p.
d. 1722
p. Jörala, Vörå, Finland

4
b.
p.
m.
p.
d.
p.

5
b.
p.
d.
p.

6 Lars Mårtensson
b.
p.
m.
p.
d. After 1696
p. Jörala, Vörå, Finland

7 Brijta Mattsdotter
b.
p.
d. 1691
p. Jörala, Vörå, Finland

8
b.
p.
m.
p.
d.
p.

9
b.
p.
d.
p.

10
b.
p.
m.
p.
d.
p.

11
b.
p.
d.
p.

12
b.
p.
m.
p.
d.
p.

13
b.
p.
d.
p.

14
b.
p.
m.
p.
d.
p.

15
b.
p.
d.
p.

Pedigree Chart for Brita Esajasdotter Trött

No. 1 on this chart is the same as no. 9 on chart no. 14

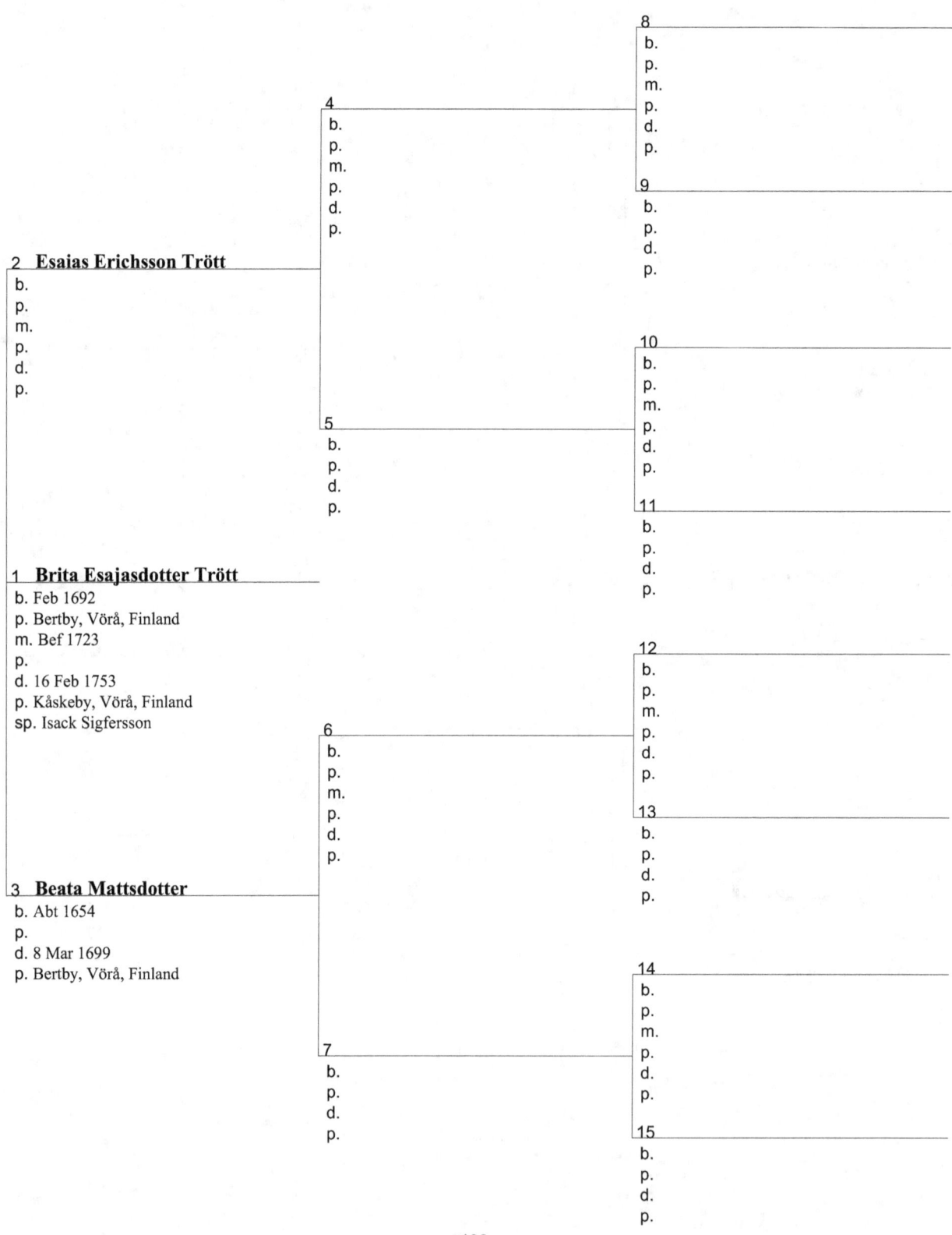

8
b.
p.
m.
p.
d.
p.

4
b.
p.
m.
p.
d.
p.

9
b.
p.
d.
p.

2 Esaias Erichsson Trött
b.
p.
m.
p.
d.
p.

10
b.
p.
m.
p.
d.
p.

5
b.
p.
d.
p.

11
b.
p.
d.
p.

1 Brita Esajasdotter Trött
b. Feb 1692
p. Bertby, Vörå, Finland
m. Bef 1723
p.
d. 16 Feb 1753
p. Kåskeby, Vörå, Finland
sp. Isack Sigfersson

12
b.
p.
m.
p.
d.
p.

6
b.
p.
m.
p.
d.
p.

13
b.
p.
d.
p.

3 Beata Mattsdotter
b. Abt 1654
p.
d. 8 Mar 1699
p. Bertby, Vörå, Finland

14
b.
p.
m.
p.
d.
p.

7
b.
p.
d.
p.

15
b.
p.
d.
p.

132

Pedigree Chart for Bertel Bertilsson

No. 1 on this chart is the same as no. 10 on chart no. 14

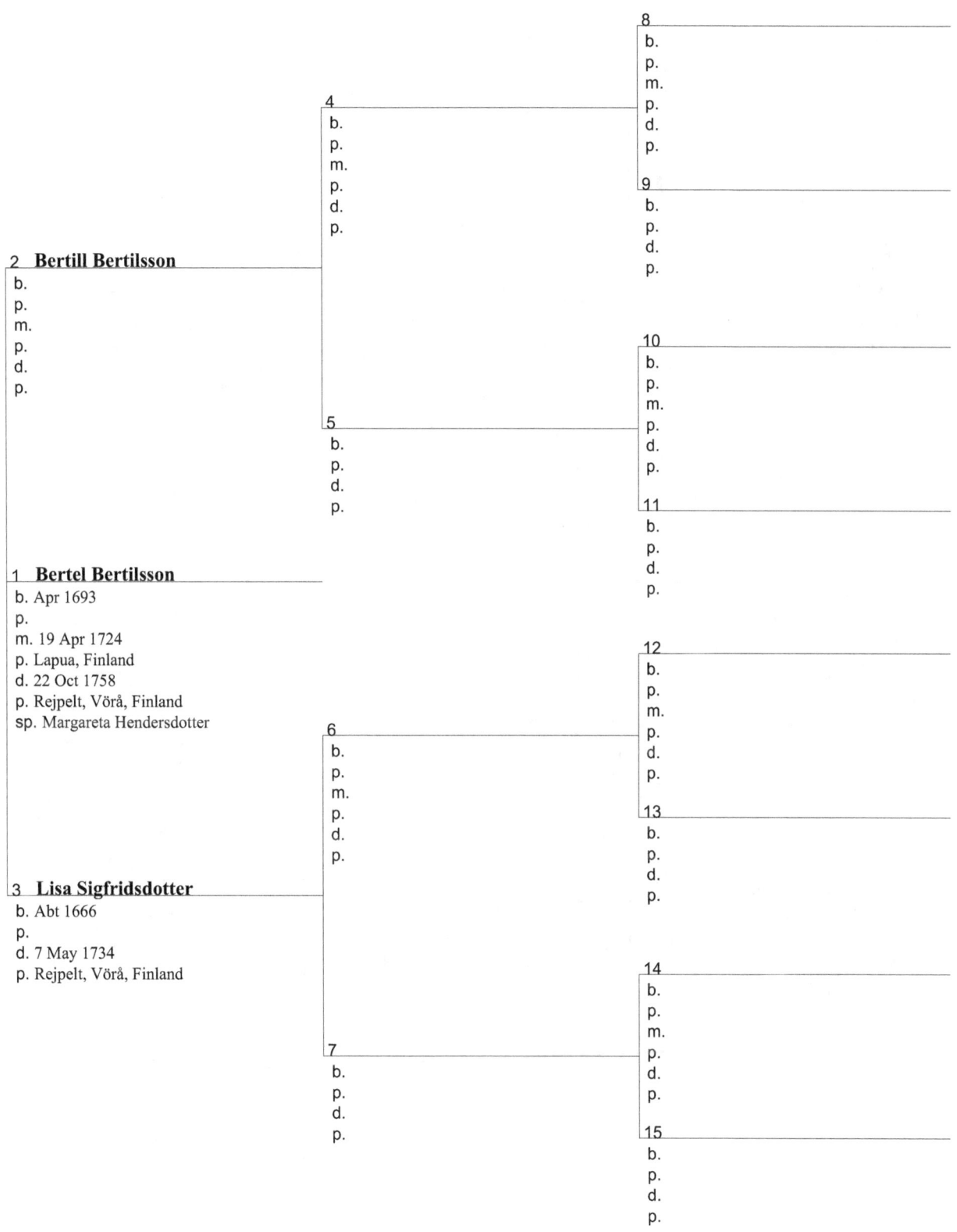

8
b.
p.
m.
p.
d.
p.

4
b.
p.
m.
p.
d.
p.

9
b.
p.
d.
p.

2 Bertill Bertilsson
b.
p.
m.
p.
d.
p.

10
b.
p.
m.
p.
d.
p.

5
b.
p.
d.
p.

11
b.
p.
d.
p.

1 Bertel Bertilsson
b. Apr 1693
p.
m. 19 Apr 1724
p. Lapua, Finland
d. 22 Oct 1758
p. Rejpelt, Vörå, Finland
sp. Margareta Hendersdotter

12
b.
p.
m.
p.
d.
p.

6
b.
p.
m.
p.
d.
p.

13
b.
p.
d.
p.

3 Lisa Sigfridsdotter
b. Abt 1666
p.
d. 7 May 1734
p. Rejpelt, Vörå, Finland

14
b.
p.
m.
p.
d.
p.

7
b.
p.
d.
p.

15
b.
p.
d.
p.

133

Pedigree Chart for Carl Johansson

No. 1 on this chart is the same as no. 12 on chart no. 14

8
b.
p.
m.
p.
d.
p.

4
b.
p.
m.
p.
d.
p.

9
b.
p.
d.
p.

2 **Johan Johansson**
b. Abt 1666
p.
m. 27 Nov 1704
p. Oravais, Finland
d. 26 Aug 1713
p. Kimo, Oravais, Finland

10
b.
p.
m.
p.
d.
p.

5
b.
p.
d.
p.

11
b.
p.
d.
p.

1 **Carl Johansson**
b. 16 Aug 1710
p. Oravais, Oravais, Finland
m. 23 Oct 1737
p. Oravais, Finland
d. 2 Nov 1751
p. Oravais, Finland
sp. Maria Andersdotter

12
b.
p.
m.
p.
d.
p.

6
b.
p.
m.
p.
d.
p.

13
b.
p.
d.
p.

3 **Maria Johansdotter**
b. Abt 1670
p.
d. 1766
p. Kimo, Oravais, Finland

14
b.
p.
m.
p.
d.
p.

7
b.
p.
d.
p.

15
b.
p.
d.
p.

Chapter 5. Ancestor Report for Lisa Johansdotter Wäst

First Generation

1. Lisa Johansdotter Wäst,[1] daughter of **Johan Mårtensson Wäst** and **Margaretha Johansdotter Kattil,** was born on 19 Sep 1789 in Rejpelt, Vörå, Finland,[1] was christened on 20 Sep 1789,[2] and died on 1 Jan 1856 in Rejpelt, Vörå, Finland[3] at age 66.

General Notes: daughter of a farm owner (bonde)[4]

Lisa married **Johan Eriksson Wäst**,[4] son of **Erik Johansson Knuts** and **Margeta Johansdotter Kårvolain,** on 28 Dec 1819 in Rejpelt, Vörå, Finland.[1]

General Notes: Born on the Wäst farm and was later bonde at Svens and Klemets farm.[4]

Children from this marriage were:

    i.   **Brita Stina Johansdotter Wäst**[2] was born on 30 Nov 1822 in Rejpelt, Vörå, Finland,[2] was christened on 1 Dec 1822,[2] died on 13 May 1847 in Rejpelt, Vörå, Finland[2] at age 24, and was buried on 16 May 1847.[5] Another name for Brita was Brita Johansdotter Klemets. Brita married **Mårten Mårtensson Långs**[2] on 1 Jul 1845.[2]

    ii.   **Erik Johansson Wäst**[2] was born on 13 Aug 1825 in Rejpelt, Vörå, Finland[2] and was christened on 14 Aug 1825.[2] Another name for Erik was Erik Johansson Svens.[2] Erik married someone **Brita Mickelsdotter Klafvus**[2] on 6 Feb 1846.[2]

    iii.   **Johan Johansson Wäst**[2] was born on 14 Jan 1828 in Rejpelt, Vörå, Finland[2] and was christened on 16 Jan 1828.[2]

    iv.   **Lisa Johansdotter Wäst**[1] was born on 28 Nov 1829 in Rejpelt, Vörå, Finland,[1] was christened on 29 Nov 1829,[2] and died on 14 Feb 1901 in Rejpelt, Vörå, Finland[4] at age 71. Another name for Lisa was Lisa Johansdotter Dala. Lisa married **Mickel Mårtensson Storkarhu**,[4] son of **Mårten Mårtensson Storkarhu** and **Lisa Samuelsdotter Miemois,** on 8 Jul 1852 in Rejpelt, Vörå, Finland.[4]

1. *Torbjörn Nikus, Storkarhu (unpublish document, 2008). .... Hiski database (http://hiski.genealogia.fi).*
2. *Hiski database (http://hiski.genealogia.fi).*
3. *Email from Torbjörn Nikus.*
4. *Torbjörn Nikus, Storkarhu (unpublish document, 2008).*
5. *Anders Enders, Några sidor på nätet om släktforskning (http://www.enges.org/gene/).*

Ancestor Report for Lisa Johansdotter Wäst

Second Generation

2. Johan Mårtensson Wäst,[1] son of **Mårten Johansson Wäst** and **Brita Mårtensdotter Jåfs,** was born on 1 Mar 1758 in Rejpelt, Vörå, Finland,[1] was christened on 5 Mar 1758,[1] and died in 1796[2] at age 38.

Johan married **Margaretha Johansdotter Kattil**[1] on 7 Dec 1786 in Rejpelt, Vörå, Finland.[1]

Children from this marriage were:
  i.   **Brita Johansdotter Wäst**[1] was born on 18 Aug 1787 in Rejpelt, Vörå, Finland[1] and was christened on 19 Aug 1787.[1]

1   ii.   **Lisa Johansdotter Wäst**.[3] Lisa married **Johan Eriksson Wäst**,[4] son of **Erik Johansson Knuts** and **Margeta Johansdotter Kårvolain,** on 28 Dec 1819 in Rejpelt, Vörå, Finland.[3]

  iii.   **Maria Johansdotter Wäst**[1] was born on 10 Sep 1791 in Rejpelt, Vörå, Finland,[1] was christened on 9 Oct 1791,[1] died on 3 Dec 1840 in Rejpelt, Vörå, Finland[1] at age 49, and was buried on 6 Dec 1840.[1] Maria married **Anders Mattsson Rex**[1] on 7 Feb 1811.[1]

  iv.   **Margeta Johansdotter Wäst**[1] was born on 5 Jan 1794 in Rejpelt, Vörå, Finland,[1] was christened on 6 Jan 1794,[1] died on 11 Jul 1811 in Rejpelt, Vörå, Finland[1] at age 17, and was buried on 14 Jul 1811.[1]

  v.   **Brita Mårtensdotter Wäst**[1] was born on 1 Sep 1795 in Rejpelt, Vörå, Finland[1] and was christened on 6 Sep 1795.[1]

3. Margaretha Johansdotter Kattil,[1] daughter of **Johan Jacobsson** and **Lisa Mårtensdotter Heinull,** was born on 17 Nov 1762 in Jörala, Vörå, Finland,[1] was christened on 21 Nov 1762,[1] died on 12 Jan 1804 in Rejpelt, Vörå, Finland[1] at age 41, and was buried on 22 Jan 1804.[1] Another name for Margaretha was Margaretha Johansdotter Wäst.

Noted events in her life were:
• Note: daughter of farm owner.[1]

Margaretha married **Johan Mårtensson Wäst**[1] on 7 Dec 1786 in Rejpelt, Vörå, Finland.[1]

1. Hiski database (http://hiski.genealogia.fi).
2. Anders Enders, Några sidor på nätet om släktforskning (http://www.enges.org/gene/).
3. Torbjörn Nikus, Storkarhu (unpublish document, 2008). .... Hiski database (http://hiski.genealogia.fi).
4. Torbjörn Nikus, Storkarhu (unpublish document, 2008).

Ancestor Report for Lisa Johansdotter Wäst

Third Generation

4. Mårten Johansson Wäst,[1] son of **Juho Matinpoika** and **Maria Sigfredsdotter Wäst,** was born on 28 Sep 1732 in Rejpelt, Vörå, Finland,[1] was christened on 1 Oct 1732,[1] died on 2 Sep 1788 in Rejpelt, Vörå, Finland[1] at age 55, and was buried on 7 Sep 1788.[1]

Mårten married **Brita Mårtensdotter Jåfs**[1] on 7 Dec 1755.[1]

Children from this marriage were:
-    i.   **Marja Mårtensdotter Wäst**[1] was born on 2 Jan 1757 in Rejpelt, Vörå, Finland[1] and was christened on 6 Jan 1757.[1]
- 2   ii.   **Johan Mårtensson Wäst**.[1] Johan married **Margaretha Johansdotter Kattil**,[1] daughter of **Johan Jacobsson** and **Lisa Mårtensdotter Heinull,** on 7 Dec 1786 in Rejpelt, Vörå, Finland.[1]
-    iii.   **Anna Mårtensdotter Wäst**[1] was born on 15 Sep 1759 in Rejpelt, Vörå, Finland,[1] was christened on 19 Sep 1759,[1] died on 23 Aug 1825 in Rejpelt, Vörå, Finland[1] at age 65, and was buried on 28 Aug 1825.[1] Anna married someone **Carl Carlsson**[1] on 7 Dec 1780.[1]
-    iv.   **Margeta Mårtensdotter Wäst**[1] was born on 22 Aug 1761 in Rejpelt, Vörå, Finland,[1] was christened on 25 Aug 1761,[1] died on 9 Jun 1819 in Rejpelt, Vörå, Finland[1] at age 57, and was buried on 13 Jun 1819.[1] Margeta married **Erik Eriksson Antbrams**[1] on 3 Jul 1783.[1]
-    v.   **Mårten Mårtensson Wäst**[1] was born on 23 Mar 1763 in Rejpelt, Vörå, Finland[1] and was christened on 25 Mar 1763.[1]
-    vi.   **Lisa Mårtensdotter Wäst**[1] was born on 25 Aug 1764 in Rejpelt, Vörå, Finland,[1] was christened on 26 Aug 1764,[1] died on 3 Aug 1806 in Rökiö, Vörå, Finland[1] at age 41, and was buried on 5 Aug 1806.[1] Lisa married someone **Matts Eriksson Antbrams**[1] on 13 Dec 1798.[1]
-    vii.   **Brita Mårtensdotter Wäst**[1] was born on 7 Nov 1768 in Rejpelt, Vörå, Finland[1] and was christened on 13 Nov 1768.[1]
-    viii.   **Beata Mårtensdotter Wäst**[1] was born on 1 Nov 1772 in Rejpelt, Vörå, Finland.[1]
-    ix.   **Erich Mårtensson Wäst**[1] was born on 21 Apr 1774 in Rejpelt, Vörå, Finland.[1]
-    x.   **Beata Mårtensdotter Wäst**[1] was born on 21 Oct 1776 in Rejpelt, Vörå, Finland[1] and was christened on 27 Oct 1776.[1] Beata married **Anders Eriksson Svens**[1] on 23 Nov 1800.[1]

5. Brita Mårtensdotter Jåfs,[1] daughter of **Mårten Michelsson Jåfs** and **Anna Johansdotter,** was born on 15 Jan 1735 in Jörala, Vörå, Finland,[1] was christened on 19 Jan 1735,[1] died on 5 Sep 1811 in Rejpelt, Vörå, Finland[1] at age 76, and was buried on 8 Sep 1811.[1]

Brita married **Mårten Johansson Wäst**[1] on 7 Dec 1755.[1]

6. Johan Jacobsson[2] was born in May 1726,[1] died on 29 Mar 1795 in Jörala, Vörå, Finland[1] at age 68, and was buried on 12 Apr 1795.[1]

Noted events in his life were:
- Occupation: laborer at Katill farm, 1750-1795, Jörala, Vörå, Finland. [3]

Johan married **Brita Hendriksdotter Kattil** on 14 Dec 1746.[4]

Research Notes: Named Kristin in Kommunionsboken 1750-56 but Hiski birth records matches Brita.

Children from this marriage were:
-    i.   **Hendrik Johansson Kattil**[4] was born on 9 Oct 1747 in Jörala, Vörå, Finland[4] and was christened on 11 Oct 1747.[1]
-    ii.   **Jacob Johansson Kattil**[4] was born on 6 Aug 1749 in Jörala, Vörå, Finland,[4] was christened on 6 Aug 1749,[1] died on 20 Dec 1818 in Jörala, Vörå, Finland[1] at age 69, and was buried on 27 Dec 1818.[1] Jacob

---

1. *Hiski database (http://hiski.genealogia.fi).*
2. *Hiski database (http://hiski.genealogia.fi). .... Anders Enders, Några sidor på nätet om släktforskning (http://www.enges.org/gene/).*
3. *Hiski database (http://hiski.genealogia.fi). .... Vörå Kommunionsboken 1750-56 (http://www.enges.org).*
4. *Anders Enders, Några sidor på nätet om släktforskning (http://www.enges.org/gene/).*

married **Maria Carlsdotter**[1] on 14 Sep 1780.[1]

   iii.   **Maria Johansdotter Kattil**[5] was born on 15 Nov 1752 in Jörala, Vörå, Finland,[6] died on 8 Apr 1823 in Bertby, Vörå, Finland[6] at age 70, and was buried on 13 Apr 1823.[6] Maria married **Elof Löfqvist**[7] on 11 Feb 1777 in Vörå, Finland.

   iv.   **Mickel Jacobsson Kattil**[6] was born on 18 Sep 1755 in Jörala, Vörå, Finland,[6] was christened on 21 Sep 1755,[6] and died on 27 Sep 1755.[6]

Johan next married **Lisa Mårtensdotter Heinull**[7] on 24 Jun 1756.[7]

Children from this marriage were:

   i.   **Anna Johansdotter Kattil**[6] was born on 18 Feb 1757 in Jörala, Vörå, Finland[6] and was christened on 20 Feb 1757.[6]

   ii.   **Mårten Johansdotter Kattil**[6] was born on 20 Apr 1758 in Jörala, Vörå, Finland[6] and was christened on 21 Apr 1758.[6] Mårten married **Margeta Mårtensdotter** on 16 Nov 1788 in Vörå, Finland.[6]

   iii.   **Brita Johansdotter Kattil**[6] was born on 12 Aug 1761 in Jörala, Vörå, Finland[6] and was christened on 16 Aug 1761.[6]

3   iv.   **Margaretha Johansdotter Kattil**.[6] Margaretha married **Johan Mårtensson Wäst**,[6] son of **Mårten Johansson Wäst** and **Brita Mårtensdotter Jåfs,** on 7 Dec 1786 in Rejpelt, Vörå, Finland.[6]

   v.   **Anna Johansdotter Kattil**[6] was born on 19 Sep 1767 in Jörala, Vörå, Finland[6] and was christened on 20 Sep 1767.[6] Anna married **Michel Abramsson Ströms**[5] on 19 Dec 1790.[6]

   vi.   **Carin Johansdotter Kattil**[6] was born on 25 Aug 1769 in Jörala, Vörå, Finland[6] and was christened on 27 Aug 1769.[6]

   vii.   **Brita Johansdotter Kattil**[6] was born on 11 Jan 1772 in Jörala, Vörå, Finland[6] and was christened on 12 Jan 1772.[6] Brita married **Anders Mattsson Wäst**[6] on 13 Dec 1792.[6]

7. Lisa Mårtensdotter Heinull,[7] daughter of **Mårten Andersson Heinull** and **Lisa Mattsdotter,** was born on 12 Aug 1734 in Jörala, Vörå, Finland,[7] was christened on 18 Aug 1734,[6] died on 23 Apr 1791 in Jörala, Vörå, Finland[5] at age 56, and was buried on 1 May 1791.[6]

Lisa married **Johan Jacobsson**[8] on 24 Jun 1756.[7]

5. *Anders Enders, Några sidor på nätet om släktforskning (http://www.enges.org/gene/). .... Hiski database (http://hiski.genealogia.fi).*
6. *Hiski database (http://hiski.genealogia.fi).*
7. *Anders Enders, Några sidor på nätet om släktforskning (http://www.enges.org/gene/).*
8. *Hiski database (http://hiski.genealogia.fi). .... Anders Enders, Några sidor på nätet om släktforskning (http://www.enges.org/gene/).*

Ancestor Report for Lisa Johansdotter Wäst

Fourth Generation

8. Juho Matinpoika[1] was born in Jun 1697,[1] died on 12 Mar 1754 in Rejpelt, Vörå, Finland[1] at age 56, and was buried on 25 Mar 1754.[1] Another name for Juho was Johan Mattsson Wäst.

Noted events in his life were:
- Language: probably Finnish.[1]

- Resided: After 1712, Keuruu, Finland.[2]

- Moved from: Cir 1723, Liesjärfvi, Keuruu, Finland.[1] possibly Korkatti farm.

Juho married **Maria Sigfredsdotter Wäst**[1] on 9 Dec 1723.[1]

Children from this marriage were:
	i.	**Lisa Johansdotter Wäst** was born on 25 Jul 1724 in Rejpelt, Vörå, Finland and was christened on 26 Jul 1724.
	ii.	**Mattz Johansson Wäst**[1] was born on 4 Feb 1726 in Rejpelt, Vörå, Finland,[1] was christened on 6 Feb 1726,[1] died on 4 Aug 1794 in Rejpelt, Vörå, Finland[1] at age 68, and was buried on 10 Aug 1794.[1] Mattz married **Maria Mårtensdotter**[1] on 4 Dec 1748.[1]
	iii.	**Erich Johansson Wäst**[1] was born on 16 Sep 1727 in Rejpelt, Vörå, Finland[1] and was christened on 17 Sep 1727.[1]
	iv.	**Johan Johansson Wäst**[1] was born on 1 Apr 1729 in Rejpelt, Vörå, Finland[1] and was christened on 4 Apr 1729.[1]
	v.	**Maria Johansdotter Wäst**[1] was born on 5 Aug 1730 in Rejpelt, Vörå, Finland[1] and was christened on 9 Aug 1730.[1]
4	vi.	**Mårten Johansson Wäst**.[1] Mårten married **Brita Mårtensdotter Jåfs**,[1] daughter of **Mårten Michelsson Jåfs** and **Anna Johansdotter,** on 7 Dec 1755.[1]
	vii.	**Johan Johansson Wäst**[1] was born on 29 Dec 1734 in Rejpelt, Vörå, Finland[1] and was christened on 1 Jan 1735.[1]

9. Maria Sigfredsdotter Wäst,[1] daughter of **Sigfred Påhlsson** and **Lisa Erichsdotter Wäst,** was born on 31 Aug 1692 in Rejpelt, Vörå, Finland,[1] died on 25 Mar 1752[1] at age 59, and was buried on 5 Apr 1752.[1]

Maria married **Juho Matinpoika**[1] on 9 Dec 1723.[1]

10. Mårten Michelsson Jåfs,[3] son of **Mickel Michelsson** and **Kirstin Larsdotter Jåfs,** was born on 17 Oct 1702 in Jörala, Vörå, Finland,[4] died on 27 Feb 1788 in Jörala, Vörå, Finland[5] at age 85, and was buried on 27 Feb 1788.[1]

Noted events in his life were:
- Occupation: owner of Jåfs farm, 1750, Jörala, Vörå, Finland.[6]

Mårten married **Anna Johansdotter**[7] on 5 Dec 1725.[1]

Marriage Notes: Possibly received permission to marry outside Vörå.[1]

---

1. Hiski database (http://hiski.genealogia.fi).

2. Keuruu, Rippikirja, 1712-1736 (http://www.sukuhistoria.fi). .... Hiski database (http://hiski.genealogia.fi).

3. Anders Enders, Några sidor på nätet om släktforskning (http://www.enges.org/gene/). .... Hiski database (http://hiski.genealogia.fi). .... Email from Torbjörn Nikus.

4. Hiski database (http://hiski.genealogia.fi). .... Anders Enders, Några sidor på nätet om släktforskning (http://www.enges.org/gene/). .... Vörå Kommunionsboken 1750-56 (http://www.enges.org). .... Email from Torbjörn Nikus.

5. Anders Enders, Några sidor på nätet om släktforskning (http://www.enges.org/gene/). .... Email from Torbjörn Nikus. .... Hiski database (http://hiski.genealogia.fi).

6. Vörå Kommunionsboken 1750-56 (http://www.enges.org). .... Email from Torbjörn Nikus. .... Hiski database (http://hiski.genealogia.fi).

7. Hiski database (http://hiski.genealogia.fi). .... Anders Enders, Några sidor på nätet om släktforskning (http://www.enges.org/gene/).

Ancestor Report for Lisa Johansdotter Wäst

Children from this marriage were:

i. **Lars Mårtensson Jåfs**[8] was born on 20 Dec 1726 in Jörala, Vörå, Finland,[8] was christened on 21 Dec 1726,[8] died on 29 Jul 1808 in Jörala, Vörå, Finland[9] at age 81, and was buried on 31 Jul 1808.[10]

ii. **Maria Mårtensdotter Jåfs**[8] was born on 26 Dec 1727 in Jörala, Vörå, Finland,[8] was christened on 27 Dec 1727,[10] and died on 16 Dec 1808 in Rejpelt, Vörå, Finland[9] at age 80.

iii. **Michel Mårtensson Jåfs**[10] was born on 7 Mar 1729 in Jörala, Vörå, Finland,[10] was christened on 9 Mar 1729,[10] died on 16 Mar 1729,[10] and was buried on 23 Mar 1729.[10]

iv. **Johan Mårtensson Jåfs**[10] was born on 8 Apr 1730 in Jörala, Vörå, Finland,[10] was christened on 12 Apr 1730,[10] died on 21 Apr 1730,[11] and was buried on 26 Apr 1730.[10]

v. **Biata Mårtensdotter Jåfs**[10] was born on 7 Jul 1731 in Jörala, Vörå, Finland,[10] was christened on 11 Jul 1731,[10] died on 9 May 1797 in Jörala, Vörå, Finland[8] at age 65, and was buried on 14 May 1797.[10] Biata married **Anders Jöransson**[10] on 8 Dec 1751.[10]

vi. **Anna Mårtensdotter Jåfs**[10] was born on 29 Aug 1732 in Jörala, Vörå, Finland,[10] was christened on 1 Sep 1732,[10] died on 26 Apr 1734[10] at age 1, and was buried on 5 May 1734.[10]

vii. **Mårten Mårtensson Jåfs**[10] was born on 16 Nov 1733 in Jörala, Vörå, Finland,[10] was christened on 18 Nov 1733,[10] died on 4 Mar 1798 in Jörala, Vörå, Finland[8] at age 64, and was buried on 11 Mar 1798.[10] Mårten married **Margeta Mårtensdotter** on 9 Jun 1756.[10]

5 viii. **Brita Mårtensdotter Jåfs**.[10] Brita married **Mårten Johansson Wäst**,[10] son of **Juho Matinpoika** and **Maria Sigfredsdotter Wäst,** on 7 Dec 1755.[10]

ix. **Anna Mårtensdotter Jåfs**[10] was born on 13 Feb 1737 in Jörala, Vörå, Finland,[10] was christened on 20 Feb 1737,[10] died on 7 Jul 1737,[10] and was buried on 10 Jul 1737.[10]

x. **Lisa Mårtensdotter Jåfs**[12] was born on 3 May 1738 in Jörala, Vörå, Finland,[13] was christened on 5 May 1738,[10] and died on 11 Apr 1788[13] at age 49. Lisa married **Johan Isaksson Knus**,[14] son of **Isack Isaksson** and **Maria Johansdotter,** on 18 Dec 1757.[10]

xi. **Margeta Mårtensdotter Jåfs**[10] was born on 24 May 1739 in Jörala, Vörå, Finland,[10] was christened on 27 May 1739,[10] died on 28 Nov 1739,[10] and was buried on 9 Dec 1739.[10]

xii. **Anna Mårtensdotter Jåfs**[10] was born on 6 Oct 1740 in Jörala, Vörå, Finland,[10] was christened on 7 Oct 1740,[10] died on 11 Mar 1742[10] at age 1, and was buried on 17 Mar 1742.[10]

Mårten next married **Margeta Bertilsdotter Antus**[15] on 9 Dec 1744.[10]

Children from this marriage were:

i. **Anna Mårtensdotter Jåfs**[10] was born on 29 Aug 1745 in Jörala, Vörå, Finland,[10] was christened on 1 Sep 1745,[10] and died on 24 Jan 1831 in Rejpelt, Vörå, Finland[9] at age 85. Anna married **Johan Eriksson Lång** on 22 Dec 1765.

ii. **Margareta Mårtensotter Jåfs**[14] was born on 8 Jul 1748 in Jörala, Vörå, Finland,[14] was christened on 10 Jul 1748,[10] died on 31 Mar 1825 in Kaitsor, Vörå, Finland[10] at age 76, and was buried on 3 Apr 1825.[10] Margareta married **Johan Johansson Finnas**[10] on 10 Dec 1769.[10]

iii. **Maria Mårtensdotter Jåfs**[14] was born on 6 Jul 1750 in Jörala, Vörå, Finland,[14] was christened on 8 Jul 1750,[10] died on 14 Jun 1751 in Jörala, Vörå, Finland,[14] and was buried on 23 Jun 1751.[10]

11. Anna Johansdotter[12] was born about 1704 in Rökiö, Vörå, Finland,[12] died on 2 Apr 1741 in Jörala, Vörå, Finland[12] about age 37, and was buried on 12 Apr 1741.[10] Another name for Anna was Anna Michelsson.

Anna married **Mårten Michelsson Jåfs**[16] on 5 Dec 1725.[10]

---

8. *Hiski database (http://hiski.genealogia.fi). .... Email from Torbjörn Nikus.*

9. *Email from Torbjörn Nikus.*

10. *Hiski database (http://hiski.genealogia.fi).*

11. *Email from Torbjörn Nikus. .... Hiski database (http://hiski.genealogia.fi).*

12. *Hiski database (http://hiski.genealogia.fi). .... Anders Enders, Några sidor på nätet om släktforskning (http://www.enges.org/gene/).*

13. *Anders Enders, Några sidor på nätet om släktforskning (http://www.enges.org/gene/).*

14. *Anders Enders, Några sidor på nätet om släktforskning (http://www.enges.org/gene/). .... Hiski database (http://hiski.genealogia.fi).*

15. *Anders Enders, Några sidor på nätet om släktforskning (http://www.enges.org/gene/). .... Email from Torbjörn Nikus. .... Hiski database (http://hiski.genealogia.fi).*

16. *Anders Enders, Några sidor på nätet om släktforskning (http://www.enges.org/gene/). .... Hiski database (http://hiski.genealogia.fi). .... Email from Torbjörn Nikus.*

Ancestor Report for Lisa Johansdotter Wäst

14. Mårten Andersson Heinull,[17] son of **Anders Eriksson Heinull** and **Karin Michelsdotter,** was born on 29 Jun 1700 in Jörala, Vörå, Finland,[17] died on 5 Oct 1761 in Jörala, Vörå, Finland[17] at age 61, and was buried on 16 Oct 1761.[18]

Mårten married **Lisa Mattsdotter**[17] on 4 Dec 1726.[17]

Children from this marriage were:

i. **Anders Mårtensson Heinull**[17] was born on 4 Dec 1727 in Jörala, Vörå, Finland[17] and died on 4 May 1784 in Jörala, Vörå, Finland[17] at age 56. Anders married **Maria Eriksdotter Gråbbil**[17] on 27 Nov 1748.[17]

ii. **Matts Mårtensson Heinull**[17] was born on 12 Sep 1729 in Jörala, Vörå, Finland,[17] died on 5 Sep 1761 in Jörala, Vörå, Finland[18] at age 31, and was buried on 13 Sep 1761.[18] Matts married **Brita Isaksdotter**[17] on 4 Dec 1757.[17]

iii. **Erich Mårtensson Heinull**[17] was born on 27 Oct 1731 in Jörala, Vörå, Finland[17] and was christened on 31 Oct 1731.[18]

7 iv. **Lisa Mårtensdotter Heinull**.[17] Lisa married **Johan Jacobsson**[19] on 24 Jun 1756.[17]

v. **Johan Mårtensson Heinull**[17] was born on 29 Dec 1738 in Jörala, Vörå, Finland.[17] Johan married **Susanna Isaksdotter**[17] on 14 Nov 1762.[17] Johan next married **Kristin Jacobsdotter**[17] on 24 Oct 1764.

vi. **Maria Mårtensdotter Heinull**[17] was born on 23 Jan 1744 in Jörala, Vörå, Finland,[17] died on 1 Feb 1759 in Jörala, Vörå, Finland[18] at age 15, and was buried on 4 Feb 1759.[18]

vii. **Mårten Mårtensson Henull**[17] was born on 3 Oct 1746 in Jörala, Vörå, Finland.[17]

viii. **Anna Mårtensdotter Heinull**[17] was born on 25 Dec 1749 in Jörala, Vörå, Finland.[17]

15. Lisa Mattsdotter[17] was born on 28 Mar 1703 in Vörå, Finland[17] and died about 1775 in Jörala, Vörå, Finland[17] about age 72.

Lisa married **Mårten Andersson Heinull**[17] on 4 Dec 1726.[17]

17. *Anders Enders, Några sidor på nätet om släktforskning (http://www.enges.org/gene/).*
18. *Hiski database (http://hiski.genealogia.fi).*
19. *Hiski database (http://hiski.genealogia.fi). .... Anders Enders, Några sidor på nätet om släktforskning (http://www.enges.org/gene/).*

Fifth Generation

18. Sigfred Påhlsson.[1]

Research Notes: His parents may be Påhl Erichsson and Brijta Bertillsdotter.

Noted events in his life were:
• Occupation: bonde (farm owner) of Wäst, 1695-1696, Rejpelt, Vörå, Finland. [2]

Sigfred married **Lisa Erichsdotter Wäst**.[3]

Children from this marriage were:
	i.	**Anna Sigfersdotter Wäst**[3] died on 23 May 1689 in Rejpelt, Vörå, Finland[3] and was buried on 23 May 1689.[3]
	ii.	**Erich Sigfredsson Wäst**[3] was born on 8 May 1690 in Rejpelt, Vörå, Finland[3] and died in 1690 in Rejpelt, Vörå, Finland.[3]
9	iii.	**Maria Sigfredsdotter Wäst**.[3] Maria married **Juho Matinpoika**[3] on 9 Dec 1723.[3]
	iv.	**Lisa Johansdotter Wäst**[3] was born on 24 Aug 1694 in Rejpelt, Vörå, Finland,[3] died on 5 Sep 1694 in Rejpelt, Vörå, Finland,[3] and was buried on 5 Sep 1694.[3]
	v.	**Beata Sigfredsdotter Wäst**[3] was born on 26 Sep 1695 in Rejpelt, Vörå, Finland,[3] died on 18 May 1696 in Rejpelt, Vörå, Finland,[3] and was buried on 18 May 1696.[3]
	vi.	**Margeta Sigfredsdotter Wäst**[3] was born on 28 Dec 1696 in Rejpelt, Vörå, Finland[3] and died in 1705 in Rejpelt, Vörå, Finland[3] at age 9.
	vii.	**Sigfred Sigfredsson Wäst**[3] was born on 18 Mar 1698 in Rejpelt, Vörå, Finland,[3] died on 26 Mar 1698 in Rejpelt, Vörå, Finland,[3] and was buried on 2 Apr 1698.[3]

19. Lisa Erichsdotter Wäst,[3] daughter of **Erik Hansson** and **Brita Markusdotter**, was born about 1668,[3] died on 6 Jan 1741 in Rejpelt, Vörå, Finland[3] about age 73, and was buried on 18 Jan 1741.[3]

Lisa married **Sigfred Påhlsson**.[1]

Lisa next married **Mårten Mårtensson**.[3]

The child from this marriage was:
	i.	**Mårten Mårtensson Wäst** was born on 16 Dec 1702 in Rejpelt, Vörå, Finland and died in 1703 at age 1.

20. Mickel Michelsson[4] was born about 1671,[5] died on 13 Jun 1741 in Jörala, Vörå, Finland[6] about age 70, and was buried on 21 Jun 1741.[3]

Noted events in his life were:
• Occupation: bonde of Jåfs farm, 1719. [7]

Mickel married **Kirstin Larsdotter Jåfs**.[4]

Children from this marriage were:
	i.	**Anna Michelsdotter Jåfs**[3] was born on 27 Aug 1692 in Jörala, Vörå, Finland[3] and died in 1692.[3]
	ii.	**Mårten Michelsson Jåfs**[3] was born in 1693 in Jörala, Vörå, Finland[3] and died in 1693 in Jörala, Vörå, Finland.[3]

---

1. Hiski database (http://hiski.genealogia.fi). .... Vörå Jordeboken 1695-96 (http://www.enges.org).
2. Vörå Jordeboken 1695-96 (http://www.enges.org).
3. Hiski database (http://hiski.genealogia.fi).
4. Anders Enders, Några sidor på nätet om släktforskning (http://www.enges.org/gene/). .... Hiski database (http://hiski.genealogia.fi). .... Email from Torbjörn Nikus.
5. Anders Enders, Några sidor på nätet om släktforskning (http://www.enges.org/gene/). .... Hiski database (http://hiski.genealogia.fi).
6. Anders Enders, Några sidor på nätet om släktforskning (http://www.enges.org/gene/). .... Email from Torbjörn Nikus. .... Hiski database (http://hiski.genealogia.fi).
7. Email from Torbjörn Nikus.

Ancestor Report for Lisa Johansdotter Wäst

    iii.   **Margeta Michelsdotter Jåfs**[3] was born on 21 Jun 1694 in Jörala, Vörå, Finland[3] and died in 1711[3] at age 17.

    iv.   **Johan Michelsson Jåfs**[8] was born on 27 Oct 1695 in Jörala, Vörå, Finland.[8]

    v.   **Brita Michelsdotter Jåfs**[8] was born on 21 Jun 1698 in Jörala, Vörå, Finland[8] and died on 9 Jul 1698 in Jörala, Vörå, Finland.[8]

    vi.   **Lisa Michelsdotter Jåfs**[8] was born on 21 Jun 1698 in Jörala, Vörå, Finland.[8]

    vii.   **Maria Michelsdotter Jåfs**[8] was born on 11 Oct 1699 in Jörala, Vörå, Finland[8] and died on 17 Dec 1727 in Lålax, Vörå, Finland[8] at age 28. Maria married **Abraham Hendersson** on 17 Dec 1727.[8]

10   viii.   **Mårten Michelsson Jåfs**.[9] Mårten married **Anna Johansdotter**[10] on 5 Dec 1725.[8] Mårten next married **Margeta Bertilsdotter Antus**[11] on 9 Dec 1744.[8]

    ix.   **Anna Michelsson Jåfs**[8] was born about 1702 in Jörala, Vörå, Finland[8] and died on 10 Jul 1748 in Mäkipää, Vörå, Finland[8] about age 46. Anna married **Isak Isaksson Seppas**[12] on 20 Dec 1730.[12]

    x.   **Brita Michelsson Jåfs**[12] was born in 1704 in Jörala, Vörå, Finland[12] and died on 29 Jan 1771 in Kåskeby, Vörå, Finland[12] at age 67. Brita married **Mickel Johansson Knubb**[8] on 12 Jan 1729.[8]

21. Kirstin Larsdotter Jåfs,[9] daughter of **Lars Mårtensson** and **Brijta Mattsdotter,** was born in 1667[12] and died in 1722 in Jörala, Vörå, Finland[12] at age 55. Another name for Kirstin was Kirstin Michelsson.

Kirstin married **Mickel Michelsson**.[9]

28. Anders Eriksson Heinull,[13] son of **Erik Andersson Heinull** and **Karin Olsdotter,** was born about 1667[13] and died on 21 Mar 1704 in Jörala, Vörå, Finland[13] about age 37.

Death Notes: Buried in church

Noted events in his life were:
• Occupation: bonde (farm owner) of Heinull.[8]

Anders married **Karin Michelsdotter**.[13]

Children from this marriage were:

    i.   **Barbru Andersdotter Heinull**[13] was born on 13 Sep 1691 in Jörala, Vörå, Finland[13] and died on 18 Jan 1754[13] at age 62.

    ii.   **Anna Andersdotter Heinull**[13] was born on 1 Sep 1692 in Jörala, Vörå, Finland[13] and died on 14 Sep 1695 in Jörala, Vörå, Finland[13] at age 3.

    iii.   **Erich Andersson Heinull**[13] was born on 10 Dec 1693 in Jörala, Vörå, Finland.[13]

    iv.   **Margeta Andersdotter Heinull**[13] was born on 28 Mar 1695 in Jörala, Vörå, Finland.[13] Margeta married **Mickel Mattsson Råndman**[13] on 20 Dec 1724.[13]

    v.   **Mickel Andersson Heinull**[13] was born on 6 Jan 1697 in Jörala, Vörå, Finland,[13] died on 29 Dec 1755 in Kåskeby, Vörå, Finland[13] at age 58, and was buried on 11 Jan 1756.[8] Mickel married **Maria Johansdotter Strand**.[13]

    vi.   **Anna Andersdotter Heinull**[13] was born on 17 Jul 1699 in Jörala, Vörå, Finland[13] and died in 1699.[13]

14   vii.   **Mårten Andersson Heinull**.[13] Mårten married **Lisa Mattsdotter**[13] on 4 Dec 1726.[13]

    viii.   **Maria Andersdotter Heinull**[13] was born on 12 Aug 1702 in Jörala, Vörå, Finland[13] and died on 29 Jun 1703.[13]

    ix.   **Anders Andersson Heinull**[13] was born on 19 Jan 1704 in Jörala, Vörå, Finland[13] and died in 1705[13] at age 1.

---

8. Hiski database (http://hiski.genealogia.fi).

9. Anders Enders, Några sidor på nätet om släktforskning (http://www.enges.org/gene/). .... Hiski database (http://hiski.genealogia.fi). .... Email from Torbjörn Nikus.

10. Hiski database (http://hiski.genealogia.fi). .... Anders Enders, Några sidor på nätet om släktforskning (http://www.enges.org/gene/).

11. Anders Enders, Några sidor på nätet om släktforskning (http://www.enges.org/gene/). .... Email from Torbjörn Nikus. .... Hiski database (http://hiski.genealogia.fi).

12. Email from Torbjörn Nikus.

13. Anders Enders, Några sidor på nätet om släktforskning (http://www.enges.org/gene/).

29. Karin Michelsdotter [14] was born in Sep 1659 in Vörå, Finland, [14] died on 5 Feb 1737 in Jörala, Vörå, Finland [14] at age 77, and was buried on 13 Feb 1737. [15]

Death Notes: Buried in the church

Research Notes: Enges places her on the Råndman farm.

Noted events in her life were:
• Resided: with her brother Eric Mickelsson, 1675-1676, Kåskeby, Vörå, Finland. [16]

Karin married **Anders Eriksson Heinull**. [14]

---

14. Anders Enders, Några sidor på nätet om släktforskning (http://www.enges.org/gene/).
15. Hiski database (http://hiski.genealogia.fi).
16. Vörå Mantalslängden 1675-76 (http://www.enges.org).

Ancestor Report for Lisa Johansdotter Wäst

Sixth Generation

38. Erik Hansson[1] died on 30 Jan 1690 in Rejpelt, Vörå, Finland[2] and was buried on 16 Feb 1690.[2]

Noted events in his life were:
• Occupation: bonde (farm owner) at Wäst.

Erik married **Brita Markusdotter**.[3]

The child from this marriage was:
   19   i.   **Lisa Erichsdotter Wäst**.[2] Lisa married **Sigfred Påhlsson**.[4] Lisa next married **Mårten Mårtensson**.[2]

39. Brita Markusdotter[3] was born about 1634,[2] died on 26 Dec 1694 in Rejpelt, Vörå, Finland[2] about age 60, and was buried on 26 Dec 1694.[2]

Brita married **Erik Hansson**.[1]

42. Lars Mårtensson[5] died after 1696 in Jörala, Vörå, Finland.[6]

Noted events in his life were:
• Occupation: bonde (farm owner) of Jåfs, 1690-1696, Jörala, Vörå, Finland.[7]

Lars married **Brijta Mattsdotter**.[8]

Children from this marriage were:
        i.   **Valborg Larsdotter Jåfs**[9] was born in 1662 in Jörala, Vörå, Finland,[2] died on 10 Mar 1741 in Jörala, Vörå, Finland[2] at age 79, and was buried on 29 Mar 1741.[2] Valborg married **Lars Mårtensson**.[9] Valborg next married **Lars Andersson**.[9]
   21   ii.   **Kirstin Larsdotter Jåfs**.[10] Kirstin married **Mickel Michelsson**.[10]
       iii.   **Mickel Larsson Jåfs**[11]
       iv.   **Anna Larsdotter Jåfs**.[9] Anna married **Mårten Mickelsson Lillund**.[9]

43. Brijta Mattsdotter[8] died in 1691 in Jörala, Vörå, Finland.[9]

Brijta married **Lars Mårtensson**.[5]

56. Erik Andersson Heinull,[12] son of **Anders Eriksson Heinull** and **Unknown**,.

---

1. *Hiski database (http://hiski.genealogia.fi). .... Vörå Mantalslängden 1690-91 (http://www.enges.org).*
2. *Hiski database (http://hiski.genealogia.fi).*
3. *Vörå Mantalslängden 1690-91 (http://www.enges.org). .... Hiski database (http://hiski.genealogia.fi).*
4. *Hiski database (http://hiski.genealogia.fi). .... Vörå Jordeboken 1695-96 (http://www.enges.org).*
5. *Vörå Kommunionsboken 1750-56 (http://www.enges.org). .... Email from Torbjörn Nikus.*
6. *Email from Torbjörn Nikus. .... Vörå Mantalslängden 1695-96 (http://www.enges.org).*
7. *Vörå Jordeboken 1695-96 (http://www.enges.org). .... Vörå Mantalslängden 1695-96 (http://www.enges.org). .... Vörå Mantalslängden 1690-91 (http://www.enges.org).*
8. *Vörå Mantalslängden 1690-91 (http://www.enges.org). .... Email from Torbjörn Nikus.*
9. *Email from Torbjörn Nikus.*
10. *Anders Enders, Några sidor på nätet om släktforskning (http://www.enges.org/gene/). .... Hiski database (http://hiski.genealogia.fi). .... Email from Torbjörn Nikus.*
11. *Vörå Jordeboken 1709-10 (http://www.enges.org).*
12. *Anders Enders, Några sidor på nätet om släktforskning (http://www.enges.org/gene/).*

Noted events in his life were:
• Occupation: bonde (farm owner) of Heinull, 1675-1690, Jörala, Vörå, Finland. [13]

Erik married **Karin Olsdotter**.[13]

The child from this marriage was:
28   i.   **Anders Eriksson Heinull**.[13] Anders married **Karin Michelsdotter**.[13]

57. Karin Olsdotter[13] died on 7 Nov 1689.[13]

Karin married **Erik Andersson Heinull**.[13]

13. Anders Enders, Några sidor på nätet om släktforskning (http://www.enges.org/gene/).

Seventh Generation

112. Anders Eriksson Heinull,[1] son of **Erik Andersson Heinull** and **Unknown,**.

Noted events in his life were:
• Occupation: bonde (farm owner) of Heinull, 1653, Jörala, Vörå, Finland. [1]

Anders married someone.

The child from this marriage was:

56   i.   **Erik Andersson Heinull.**[1] Erik married **Karin Olsdotter.**[1]

1. Anders Enders, Några sidor på nätet om släktforskning (http://www.enges.org/gene/).

Eighth Generation

224. Erik Andersson Heinull, son of **Anders Jöransson Heinull** and **Unknown,**.

Noted events in his life were:
• Occupation: bonde (farm owner) of Heinull, 1623-1650, Jörala, Vörå, Finland. [1]

Erik married someone.

His child was:
112   i.   **Anders Eriksson Heinull.**[1] Anders married someone.

---

1. Anders Enders, Några sidor på nätet om släktforskning (http://www.enges.org/gene/).

Ancestor Report for Lisa Johansdotter Wäst

Ninth Generation

448. Anders Jöransson Heinull,[1] son of **Jöran Hendersson** and **Unknown,**.

Noted events in his life were:
• Occupation: bonde (farm owner) of Heinull, 1585-1619, Jörala, Vörå, Finland. [1]

Anders married someone.

His child was:
224   i.   **Erik Andersson Heinull**. Erik married someone.

---

1. Anders Enders, Några sidor på nätet om släktforskning (http://www.enges.org/gene/).

Ancestor Report for Lisa Johansdotter Wäst

Tenth Generation

896. Jöran Hendersson,[1] son of **Henrik Olsson** and **Unknown**,.

Noted events in his life were:
• Occupation: bonde (farm owner), 1557-1579, Jörala, Vörå, Finland. [1]

Jöran married someone.

His child was:
448   i.   **Anders Jöransson Heinull**.[1] Anders married someone.

---

1. Anders Enders, Några sidor på nätet om släktforskning (http://www.enges.org/gene/).

1792. Henrik Olsson.[1]

Noted events in his life were:
- Office: juryman, 1543-1546.[1]

- Occupation: bonde (farm owner), 1548-1556, Vörå, Finland. [1]

Henrik married someone.

His child was:

896   i.   **Jöran Hendersson.**[1] Jöran married someone.

1. *Anders Enders, Några sidor på nätet om släktforskning (http://www.enges.org/gene/).*

Pedigree Chart for Lisa Johansdotter Wäst

No. 1 on this chart is the same as no. 11 on chart no. 1

8 Juho Matinpoika
b. Jun 1697
p.
m. 9 Dec 1723
p.
d. 12 Mar 1754
p. Rejpelt, Vörå, Finland

4 Mårten Johansson Wäst
b. 28 Sep 1732
p. Rejpelt, Vörå, Finland
m. 7 Dec 1755
p.
d. 2 Sep 1788
p. Rejpelt, Vörå, Finland

9 Maria Sigfredsdotter Wäst
b. 31 Aug 1692   cont. __23__
p. Rejpelt, Vörå, Finland
d. 25 Mar 1752
p.

2 Johan Mårtensson Wäst
b. 1 Mar 1758
p. Rejpelt, Vörå, Finland
m. 7 Dec 1786
p. Rejpelt, Vörå, Finland
d. 1796
p.

10 Mårten Michelsson Jåfs
b. 17 Oct 1702   cont. __24__
p. Jörala, Vörå, Finland
m. 5 Dec 1725
p.
d. 27 Feb 1788
p. Jörala, Vörå, Finland

5 Brita Mårtensdotter Jåfs
b. 15 Jan 1735
p. Jörala, Vörå, Finland
d. 5 Sep 1811
p. Rejpelt, Vörå, Finland

11 Anna Johansdotter
b. Abt 1704
p. Rökiö, Vörå, Finland
d. 2 Apr 1741
p. Jörala, Vörå, Finland

1 Lisa Johansdotter Wäst
b. 19 Sep 1789
p. Rejpelt, Vörå, Finland
m. 28 Dec 1819
p. Rejpelt, Vörå, Finland
d. 1 Jan 1856
p. Rejpelt, Vörå, Finland
sp. Johan Eriksson Wäst

12
b.
p.
m.
p.
d.
p.

6 Johan Jacobsson
b. May 1726
p.
m. 24 Jun 1756
p.
d. 29 Mar 1795
p. Jörala, Vörå, Finland

13
b.
p.
d.
p.

3 Margaretha Johansdotter Kattil
b. 17 Nov 1762
p. Jörala, Vörå, Finland
d. 12 Jan 1804
p. Rejpelt, Vörå, Finland

14 Mårten Andersson Heinull
b. 29 Jun 1700   cont. __25__
p. Jörala, Vörå, Finland
m. 4 Dec 1726
p.
d. 5 Oct 1761
p. Jörala, Vörå, Finland

7 Lisa Mårtensdotter Heinull
b. 12 Aug 1734
p. Jörala, Vörå, Finland
d. 23 Apr 1791
p. Jörala, Vörå, Finland

15 Lisa Mattsdotter
b. 28 Mar 1703
p. Vörå, Finland
d. Abt 1775
p. Jörala, Vörå, Finland

Pedigree Chart for Maria Sigfredsdotter Wäst

No. 1 on this chart is the same as no. 9 on chart no. 22

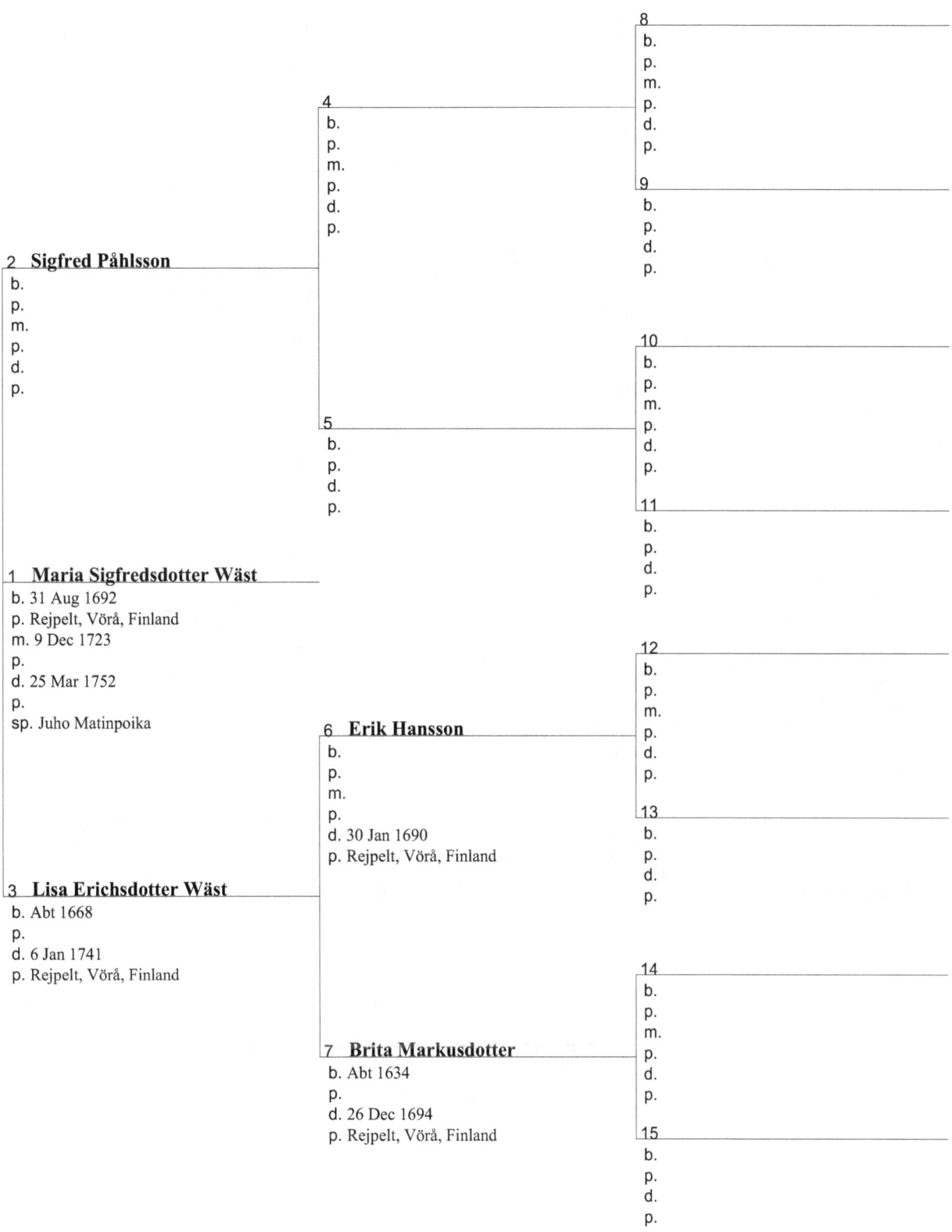

8 _____
b.
p.
m.
p.
d.
p.

4 _____
b.
p.
m.
p.
d.
p.

9 _____
b.
p.
d.
p.

2 Sigfred Påhlsson
b.
p.
m.
p.
d.
p.

10 _____
b.
p.
m.
p.
d.
p.

5 _____
b.
p.
d.
p.

11 _____
b.
p.
d.
p.

1 Maria Sigfredsdotter Wäst
b. 31 Aug 1692
p. Rejpelt, Vörå, Finland
m. 9 Dec 1723
p.
d. 25 Mar 1752
p.
sp. Juho Matinpoika

12 _____
b.
p.
m.
p.
d.
p.

6 Erik Hansson
b.
p.
m.
p.
d. 30 Jan 1690
p. Rejpelt, Vörå, Finland

13 _____
b.
p.
d.
p.

3 Lisa Erichsdotter Wäst
b. Abt 1668
p.
d. 6 Jan 1741
p. Rejpelt, Vörå, Finland

14 _____
b.
p.
m.
p.
d.
p.

7 Brita Markusdotter
b. Abt 1634
p.
d. 26 Dec 1694
p. Rejpelt, Vörå, Finland

15 _____
b.
p.
d.
p.

153

Pedigree Chart for Mårten Michelsson Jåfs

No. 1 on this chart is the same as no. 10 on chart no. 22

8 _____
b.
p.
m.
p.
d.
p.

4 _____
b.
p.
m.
p.
d.
p.

9 _____
b.
p.
d.
p.

2 **Mickel Michelsson**
b. Abt 1671
p.
m.
p.
d. 13 Jun 1741
p. Jörala, Vörå, Finland

10 _____
b.
p.
m.
p.
d.
p.

5 _____
b.
p.
d.
p.

11 _____
b.
p.
d.
p.

1 **Mårten Michelsson Jåfs**
b. 17 Oct 1702
p. Jörala, Vörå, Finland
m. 5 Dec 1725
p.
d. 27 Feb 1788
p. Jörala, Vörå, Finland
sp. Anna Johansdotter

12 _____
b.
p.
m.
p.
d.
p.

6 **Lars Mårtensson**
b.
p.
m.
p.
d. After 1696
p. Jörala, Vörå, Finland

13 _____
b.
p.
d.
p.

3 **Kirstin Larsdotter Jåfs**
b. 1667
p.
d. 1722
p. Jörala, Vörå, Finland

14 _____
b.
p.
m.
p.
d.
p.

7 **Brijta Mattsdotter**
b.
p.
d. 1691
p. Jörala, Vörå, Finland

15 _____
b.
p.
d.
p.

Pedigree Chart for Mårten Andersson Heinull

No. 1 on this chart is the same as no. 14 on chart no. 22

8 Anders Eriksson Heinull
b.   cont. __26__
p.
m.
p.
d.
p.

4 Erik Andersson Heinull
b.
p.
m.
p.
d.
p.

9 _____
b.
p.
d.
p.

2 Anders Eriksson Heinull
b. Abt 1667
p.
m.
p.
d. 21 Mar 1704
p. Jörala, Vörå, Finland

10 _____
b.
p.
m.
p.
d.
p.

5 Karin Olsdotter
b.
p.
d. 7 Nov 1689
p.

11 _____
b.
p.
d.
p.

1 Mårten Andersson Heinull
b. 29 Jun 1700
p. Jörala, Vörå, Finland
m. 4 Dec 1726
p.
d. 5 Oct 1761
p. Jörala, Vörå, Finland
sp. Lisa Mattsdotter

12 _____
b.
p.
m.
p.
d.
p.

6 _____
b.
p.
m.
p.
d.
p.

13 _____
b.
p.
d.
p.

3 Karin Michelsdotter
b. Sep 1659
p. Vörå, Finland
d. 5 Feb 1737
p. Jörala, Vörå, Finland

14 _____
b.
p.
m.
p.
d.
p.

7 _____
b.
p.
d.
p.

15 _____
b.
p.
d.
p.

Pedigree Chart for Anders Eriksson Heinull

No. 1 on this chart is the same as no. 8 on chart no. 25

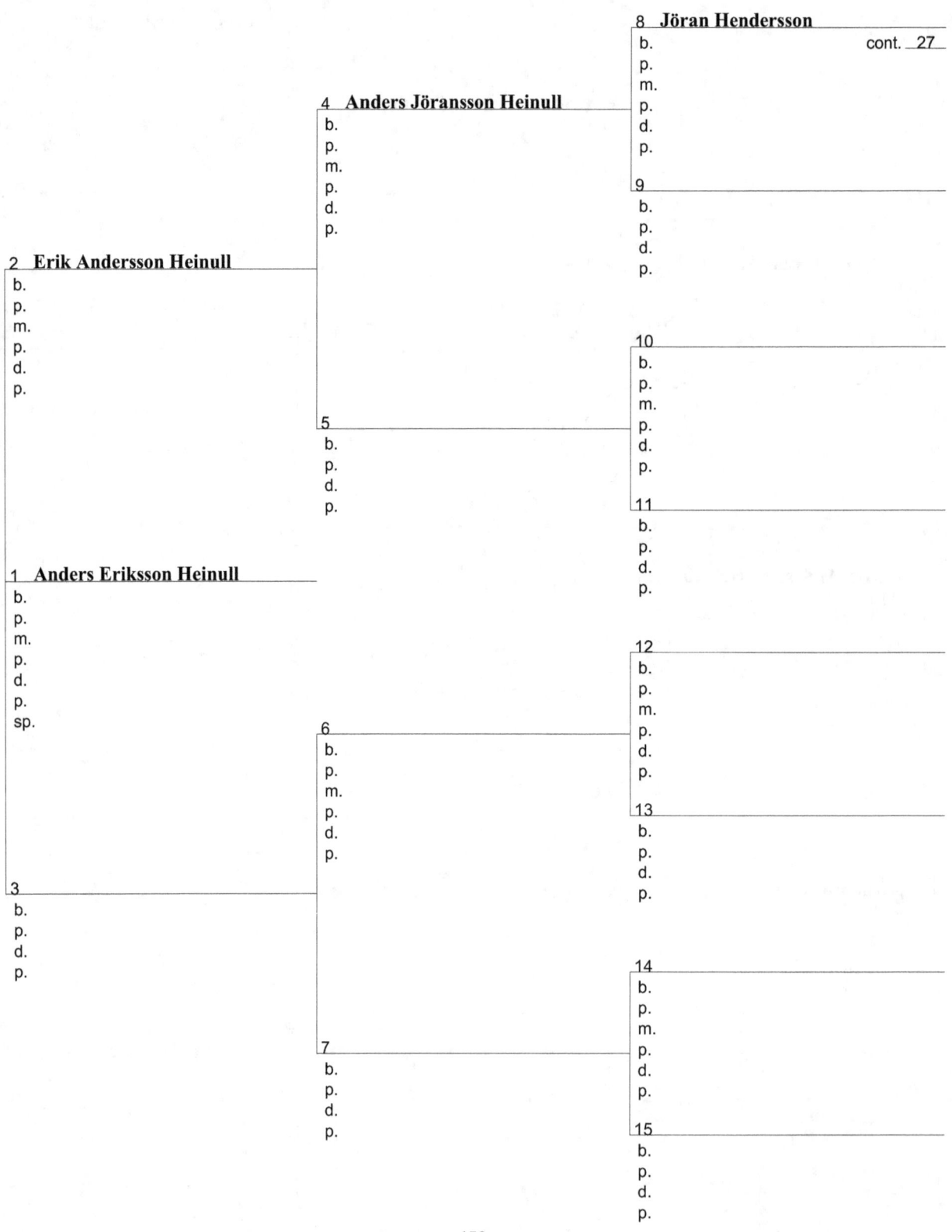

1　Anders Eriksson Heinull
b.
p.
m.
p.
d.
p.
sp.

2　Erik Andersson Heinull
b.
p.
m.
p.
d.
p.

3
b.
p.
d.
p.

4　Anders Jöransson Heinull
b.
p.
m.
p.
d.
p.

5
b.
p.
d.
p.

6
b.
p.
m.
p.
d.
p.

7
b.
p.
d.
p.

8　Jöran Hendersson
b.　　　　cont. __27__
p.
m.
p.
d.
p.

9
b.
p.
d.
p.

10
b.
p.
m.
p.
d.
p.

11
b.
p.
d.
p.

12
b.
p.
m.
p.
d.
p.

13
b.
p.
d.
p.

14
b.
p.
m.
p.
d.
p.

15
b.
p.
d.
p.

Pedigree Chart for Jöran Hendersson

No. 1 on this chart is the same as no. 8 on chart no. 26

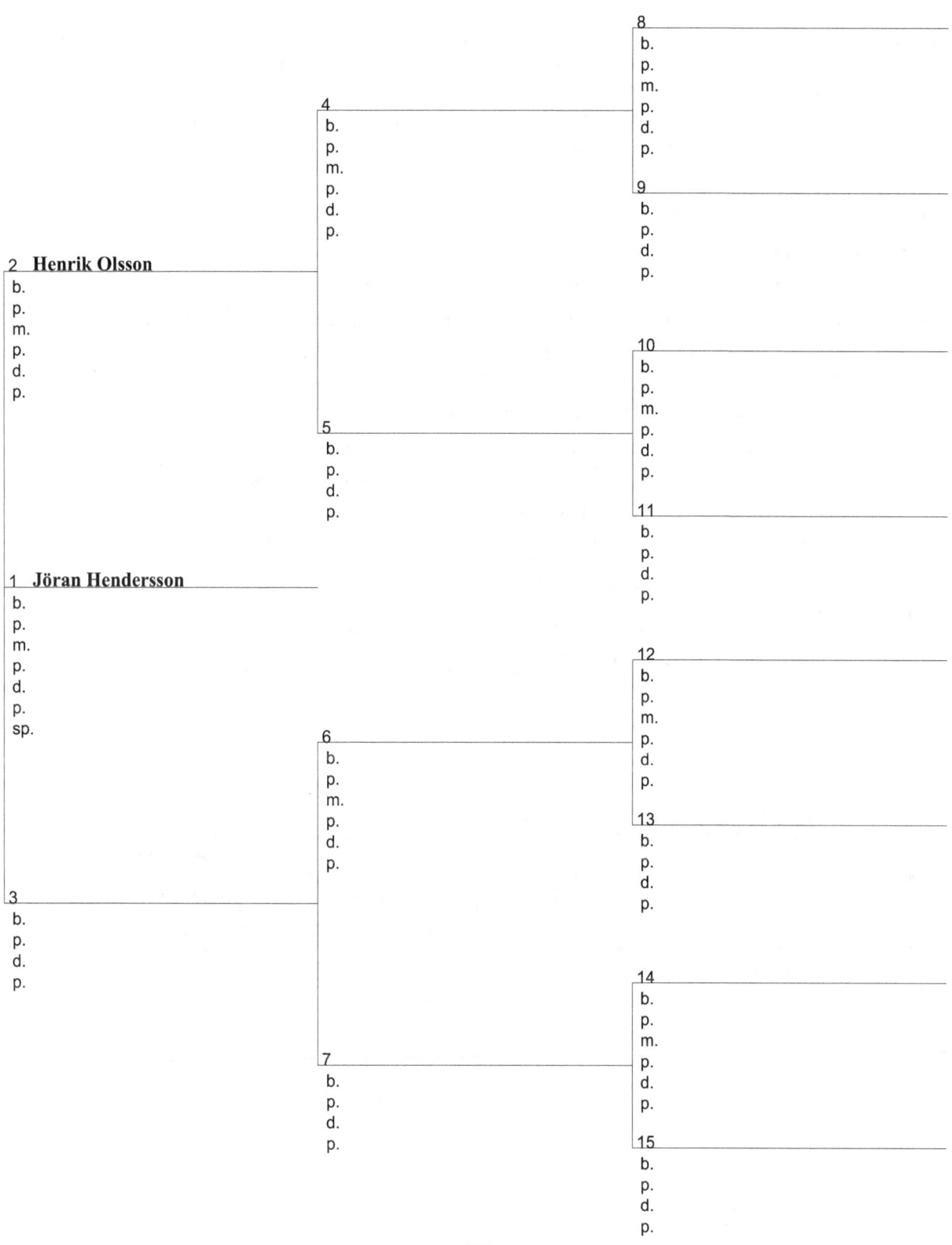

8
b.
p.
m.
p.
d.
p.

4
b.
p.
m.
p.
d.
p.

9
b.
p.
d.
p.

2 **Henrik Olsson**
b.
p.
m.
p.
d.
p.

10
b.
p.
m.
p.
d.
p.

5
b.
p.
d.
p.

11
b.
p.
d.
p.

1 **Jöran Hendersson**
b.
p.
m.
p.
d.
p.
sp.

12
b.
p.
m.
p.
d.
p.

6
b.
p.
m.
p.
d.
p.

13
b.
p.
d.
p.

3
b.
p.
d.
p.

14
b.
p.
m.
p.
d.
p.

7
b.
p.
d.
p.

15
b.
p.
d.
p.

Chapter 6. Ancestor Report for Jan Ersson

First Generation

1. Jan Ersson,[1] son of **Erik Nilsson** and **Catharina Jonasdotter,** was born on 14 Jan 1808 in Finhyttan, Grythyttan, Örebro, Sweden[2] and died on 31 May 1857 in Skärhyttan, Nora, Örebro, Sweden[3] at age 49. Another name for Jan was Jan Ersson Spångberg.[4]

Research Notes: Jan Ersson was a iron smelting master and land bonde (homestead owner). He employed several farmhands and iron workers. He and his descendents took Spångberg as a surname. [4]

Noted events in his life were:
- Resided: 1808-1812, Finhyttan, Grythyttan, Örebro, Sweden.[5]

- Resided: 1812-1829, Spångtorp, Grythyttan, Örebro, Sweden.[6]

- Occupation: blast furnace worker, Bef 1830, Grythyttan, Örebro, Sweden.[7]

- Moved to: 26 Dec 1831, Skärhyttan, Nora, Örebro, Sweden.[8] Leaves his mother Catrina Jonsdotter and siblings. He took over his father-in-law's homestead in 1831 (his father-in-law had no sons).

- Status: land bonde (farm owner), After 1831, Skärhyttan, Nora, Örebro, Sweden.[9]

- Occupation: hyttarbetare (smelter), 1834, Skärhyttan, Nora, Örebro, Sweden.[10]

- Occupation: masmästare (smelting master), 1836, Skärhyttan, Nora, Örebro, Sweden.[11]

- Status: topare (tenant farmer), Abt 1834-1841, Skärhyttan, Nora, Örebro, Sweden.[12]

- Name change: to Spångberg, Cir 1838.[12] He was born Jan Ersson. He used the surname Spångberg in the the Nora parish baptism for his child born in 1839 but not in 1836 or earlier.   In the communion book the word Spångberg was written in over his name sometime between 1831 and 1839.   The name Spångberg may have alluded to his childhood homestead "Spångtorp" in Grythyttan parish. Jan Spångberg continued to use his patronym "Ersson" in most records, i.e., "Jon Ersson Spångberg," and that is how it appears in his death record. His children use Spångberg sometimes with their patronym Jansson or Jansdotter.

- Status: land bonde (farm owner), 1841-1851, Skärhyttan, Nora, Örebro, Sweden.[13]

- Resided: 1852, Koppartorp, Skärhyttan, Nora, Örebro, Sweden.[14]

---

1. Grythyttan AIa:14b (1830-1840) Image 168 / page 446 (AID: v51206.b168.s446, NAD: SE/ULA/10337) .

2. Grythyttan AIa:14b (1830-1840) Image 168 / page 446 (AID: v51206.b168.s446, NAD: SE/ULA/10337) . .... Grythyttan AIa:13b (1820-1830) Image 174 / page 169 (AID: v51204.b174.s169, NAD: SE/ULA/10337) . .... Nora bergsförsamling AI:14bb (1841-1850) Image 49 / page 195 (AID: v52007.b49.s195, NAD: SE/ULA/11098) . .... Nora bergsförsamling AI:13b (1828-1841) Image 97 / page 92 (AID: v51997.b97.s92, NAD: SE/ULA/11098) . .... Grythyttan AIa:12b (1812-1820) Image 120 / page 110 (AID: v51202.b120.s110, NAD: SE/ULA/10337) . .... Grythyttan CI:7 (1797-1817) Image 118 / page 224 (AID: v53140.b118.s224, NAD: SE/ULA/10337) .

3. Nora bergsförsamling AI:15eb (1851-1861) Image 69 / page 223 (AID: v52013.b69.s223, NAD: SE/ULA/11098) .

4. Nora bergsförsamling AI:14bb (1841-1850) Image 49 / page 195 (AID: v52007.b49.s195, NAD: SE/ULA/11098) .

5. Grythyttan AIa:11b (1809-1812) Image 97 / page 89 (AID: v51200.b97.s89, NAD: SE/ULA/10337) . .... (Grythyttan AIa:9 (1798-1808) Image 198 / page 191 (AID: v51197.b198.s191, NAD: SE/ULA/10337)).

6. Grythyttan AIa:12b (1812-1820) Image 120 / page 110 (AID: v51202.b120.s110, NAD: SE/ULA/10337) . .... Grythyttan AIa:11b (1809-1812) Image 97 / page 89 (AID: v51200.b97.s89, NAD: SE/ULA/10337) . .... Grythyttan AIa:13b (1820-1830) Image 174 / page 169 (AID: v51204.b174.s169, NAD: SE/ULA/10337) .

7. Nora bergsförsamling EI:5 (1827-1842) Image 22 (AID: v53636.b22, NAD: SE/ULA/11098) .

8. Grythyttan AIa:14b (1830-1840) Image 168 / page 446 (AID: v51206.b168.s446, NAD: SE/ULA/10337) . .... Nora bergsförsamling AI:14bb (1841-1850) Image 49 / page 195 (AID: v52007.b49.s195, NAD: SE/ULA/11098) .

9. Nora bergsförsamling AI:13b (1828-1841) Image 97 / page 92 (AID: v51997.b97.s92, NAD: SE/ULA/11098) .

10. Nora bergsförsamling C:7 (1828-1842) Image 102 (AID: v53622.b102, NAD: SE/ULA/11098) .

11. Nora bergsförsamling C:7 (1828-1842) Image 134 (AID: v53622.b134, NAD: SE/ULA/11098) .

12. Nora bergsförsamling C:7 (1828-1842) Image 212 (AID: v53622.b212, NAD: SE/ULA/11098) .

13. Nora bergsförsamling C:8b (1842-1858) Image 17 (AID: v53624.b17, NAD: SE/ULA/11098) . .... Nora bergsförsamling AI:14bb (1841-1850) Image 49 / page 195 (AID: v52007.b49.s195, NAD: SE/ULA/11098) .

14. Nora bergsförsamling AI:15eb (1851-1861) Image 59 / page 213 (AID: v52013.b59.s213, NAD: SE/ULA/11098) .

Ancestor Report for Jan Ersson

- Resided: 1852-1857, Björnbo, Skärhyttan, Nora, Örebro, Sweden. [15]

Jan married **Maria Helena Persdotter**,[16] daughter of **Petter Jacobsson** and **Christina Jacobsdotter,** on 26 Dec 1830 in Hällefors, Örebro, Sweden. [17]

Noted events in her life were:
- Occupation: maid, 1830, Skärhyttan, Nora, Örebro, Sweden. [17]

- Resided: 1852, Koppartorp, Skärhyttan, Nora, Örebro, Sweden. [18]

- Resided: Björnbo, 1852-1871, Skärhyttan, Nora, Örebro, Sweden. [15]

Children from this marriage were:
i. **Jan Gustaf Jansson**[19] was born on 17 Nov 1832 in Skärhyttan, Nora, Örebro, Sweden.[20] Another name for Jan was Jan Gustaf Spångberg. Jan married **Maria Charlina Andersson** on 25 Nov 1855 in Hällefors, Örebro, Sweden.[21]
ii. **Eric Wilhelm Jansson** was born on 1 Apr 1834 in Skärhyttan, Nora, Örebro, Sweden.[22] Another name for Eric was Erich Wilhelm Spångberg.
iii. **Erik August Jansson**[19] was born on 14 May 1836 in Skärhyttan, Nora, Örebro, Sweden[23] and died after 1900 in USA.[24] Other names for Erik were Erick Erikson and Erik August Spångberg. Erik married **Christina Ersdotter** on 12 Apr 1857.[25]
iv. **Pehr Axel Jansson Spångberg**[19] was born on 9 May 1839 in Skärhyttan, Nora, Örebro, Sweden[26] and died on 12 Mar 1868 in Ås, Grythyttan, Örebro, Sweden[27] at age 28. Another name for Pehr was Pehr Axel Spångberg. Pehr married **Carolina Andersdotter** on 25 Mar 1862 in Hällefors, Örebro, Sweden. [28]
v. **Carolina Jansdotter Spångberg**[19] was born on 2 Nov 1841 in Skärhyttan, Nora, Örebro, Sweden[29] and died on 19 Feb 1854 in Skärhyttan, Nora, Örebro, Sweden[30] at age 12. Another name for Carolina was Carolina Spångberg.
vi. **Carl Fredrik Jansson Spångberg**[19] was born on 19 Feb 1844 in Skärhyttan, Nora, Örebro,

15. Nora bergsförsamling AI:16e (1861-1871) Image 289 / page 282 (AID: v52018.b289.s282, NAD: SE/ULA/11098) . .... Nora bergsförsamling AI:15eb (1851-1861) Image 73 / page 227 (AID: v52013.b73.s227, NAD: SE/ULA/11098) . .... Nora bergsförsamling AI:15eb (1851-1861) Image 69 / page 223 (AID: v52013.b69.s223, NAD: SE/ULA/11098) .
16. Nora bergsförsamling AI:14bb (1841-1850) Image 49 / page 195 (AID: v52007.b49.s195, NAD: SE/ULA/11098) . .... Nora bergsförsamling AI:15eb (1851-1861) Image 59 / page 213 (AID: v52013.b59.s213, NAD: SE/ULA/11098) .
17. Nora bergsförsamling EI:5 (1827-1842) Image 22 (AID: v53636.b22, NAD: SE/ULA/11098) .
18. Nora bergsförsamling AI:15eb (1851-1861) Image 59 / page 213 (AID: v52013.b59.s213, NAD: SE/ULA/11098) .
19. Nora bergsförsamling AI:14bb (1841-1850) Image 49 / page 195 (AID: v52007.b49.s195, NAD: SE/ULA/11098) .
20. Nora bergsförsamling AI:14bb (1841-1850) Image 49 / page 195 (AID: v52007.b49.s195, NAD: SE/ULA/11098) . .... Nora bergsförsamling AI:15eb (1851-1861) Image 59 / page 213 (AID: v52013.b59.s213, NAD: SE/ULA/11098) . .... Nora bergsförsamling AI:13b (1828-1841) Image 97 / page 92 (AID: v51997.b97.s92, NAD: SE/ULA/11098) . .... Nora bergsförsamling AI:19b (1892-1901) Image 282 / page 269 (AID: v52028.b282.s269, NAD: SE/ULA/11098) .
21. Nora bergsförsamling AI:18c (1882-1891) Image 238 / page 224 (AID: v52025.b238.s224, NAD: SE/ULA/11098) .
22. Nora bergsförsamling AI:13b (1828-1841) Image 97 / page 92 (AID: v51997.b97.s92, NAD: SE/ULA/11098) . .... Nora bergsförsamling C:7 (1828-1842) Image 102 (AID: v53622.b102, NAD: SE/ULA/11098) .
23. Nora bergsförsamling AI:14bb (1841-1850) Image 49 / page 195 (AID: v52007.b49.s195, NAD: SE/ULA/11098) . .... Nora bergsförsamling AI:15eb (1851-1861) Image 59 / page 213 (AID: v52013.b59.s213, NAD: SE/ULA/11098) . .... Nora bergsförsamling AI:13b (1828-1841) Image 97 / page 92 (AID: v51997.b97.s92, NAD: SE/ULA/11098) . .... Nora bergsförsamling C:7 (1828-1842) Image 134 (AID: v53622.b134, NAD: SE/ULA/11098) .
24. 1900 US Census.
25. Nora bergsförsamling AI:15eb (1851-1861) Image 94 / page 247 (AID: v52013.b94.s247, NAD: SE/ULA/11098) .
26. Nora bergsförsamling AI:14bb (1841-1850) Image 49 / page 195 (AID: v52007.b49.s195, NAD: SE/ULA/11098) . .... Nora bergsförsamling AI:15eb (1851-1861) Image 59 / page 213 (AID: v52013.b59.s213, NAD: SE/ULA/11098) . .... Nora bergsförsamling AI:13b (1828-1841) Image 97 / page 92 (AID: v51997.b97.s92, NAD: SE/ULA/11098) . .... Nora bergsförsamling C:7 (1828-1842) Image 176 (AID: v53622.b176, NAD: SE/ULA/11098) .
27. Grythyttan F:3 (1840-1871) Image 264 (AID: v53161.b264, NAD: SE/ULA/10337) .
28. Nora bergsförsamling AI:16e (1861-1871) Image 289 / page 282 (AID: v52018.b289.s282, NAD: SE/ULA/11098) .
29. Nora bergsförsamling AI:14bb (1841-1850) Image 49 / page 195 (AID: v52007.b49.s195, NAD: SE/ULA/11098) . .... Nora bergsförsamling AI:15eb (1851-1861) Image 59 / page 213 (AID: v52013.b59.s213, NAD: SE/ULA/11098) . .... Nora bergsförsamling C:7 (1828-1842) Image 212 (AID: v53622.b212, NAD: SE/ULA/11098) .
30. Nora bergsförsamling AI:15eb (1851-1861) Image 69 / page 223 (AID: v52013.b69.s223, NAD: SE/ULA/11098) .
31. Arkion 1890. .... August Spångberg, Stream of Time (1966). .... Duane & Jacquelyn Hargis, Headstones at Forest Home Cemetery, Newberry, Luce County, Michigan (http://files.usgwarchives.net/mi/luce/cemeteries/f62302.txt). .... Nora bergsförsamling AI:14bb (1841-1850) Image 49 / page 195 (AID: v52007.b49.s195, NAD: SE/ULA/11098) . .... Nora bergsförsamling AI:15eb (1851-1861) Image 59 / page

Sweden[31] and died on 31 Jul 1917 in Newberry, Luce, Michigan[32] at age 73. Another name for Carl was Carl Fredrik Spångberg. Carl married **Christina Elisabet Andersdotter,** daughter of **Anders Jansson** and **Anna Helena Persdotter,** on 21 Jun 1870 in Hällefors, Örebro, Sweden.[33]

vii. **Anders Albert Jansson Spångberg**[34] was born on 8 Aug 1847 in Skärhyttan, Nora, Örebro, Sweden[35] and died on 4 Jun 1851[36] at age 3. Another name for Anders was Anders Albert Spångberg.

---

213 (AID: v52013.b59.s213, NAD: SE/ULA/11098). .... Nora bergsförsamling AI:18d (1882-1891) Image 364 / page 762 (AID: v52026.b364.s762, NAD: SE/ULA/11098). .... Nora bergsförsamling C:9b (1843-1856) Image 19 (AID: v53626.b19, NAD: SE/ULA/11098) . .... Nora bergsförsamling C:8b (1842-1858) Image 17 (AID: v53624.b17, NAD: SE/ULA/11098) .

32. Duane & Jacquelyn Hargis, Headstones at Forest Home Cemetery, Newberry, Luce County, Michigan (http://files.usgwarchives.net/mi/luce/cemeteries/f62302.txt).

33. Nora bergsförsamling AI:18d (1882-1891) Image 364 / page 762 (AID: v52026.b364.s762, NAD: SE/ULA/11098) .

34. Nora bergsförsamling AI:14bb (1841-1850) Image 49 / page 195 (AID: v52007.b49.s195, NAD: SE/ULA/11098) . .... Nora bergsförsamling AI:15eb (1851-1861) Image 59 / page 213 (AID: v52013.b59.s213, NAD: SE/ULA/11098) .

35. Nora bergsförsamling AI:14bb (1841-1850) Image 49 / page 195 (AID: v52007.b49.s195, NAD: SE/ULA/11098) . .... Nora bergsförsamling AI:15eb (1851-1861) Image 59 / page 213 (AID: v52013.b59.s213, NAD: SE/ULA/11098) . .... Nora bergsförsamling C:8b (1842-1858) Image 36 (AID: v53624.b36, NAD: SE/ULA/11098) .

36. Nora bergsförsamling AI:15eb (1851-1861) Image 59 / page 213 (AID: v52013.b59.s213, NAD: SE/ULA/11098) .

Ancestor Report for Jan Ersson

Second Generation

2. Erik Nilsson,[1] son of **Nils Jansson** and **Maria Nilsdotter,** was born on 6 Mar 1776 in Västgötetorp, Grythyttan, Örebro, Sweden,[2] was christened on 10 Mar 1776,[3] and died on 1 Apr 1829 in Spångtorp, Grythyttan, Örebro, Sweden[4] at age 53.

Birth Notes: Finnhyttan (a.k.a. Lill Hälltorp) homestead. It appears all siblings were born at this homestead.

Research Notes: Incorrectly referred to as Erik Carlsson in the book, Stream of Time, by his great grandson, August Spångberg.

Noted events in his life were:
- Resided: Finhytta homestead, 1784-1812, Västgötetorp, Grythyttan, Örebro, Sweden.[5]

- Resided: After 1812, Spångtorp, Grythyttan, Örebro, Sweden.[6] Takes over the homestead of Jonas Ersson (d. 1809) and his widow Catherine (d. 1816).

- Occupation: foreman at an iron foundry, 1809-1812, Grythyttan, Örebro, Sweden.[7]

Erik married **Catharina Jonasdotter**[8] on 11 Jan 1807.[9]

Children from this marriage were:

1	i.	**Jan Ersson.**[10] Jan married **Maria Helena Persdotter,**[11] daughter of **Petter Jacobsson** and **Christina Jacobsdotter,** on 26 Dec 1830 in Hällefors, Örebro, Sweden.[12]
	ii.	**Erik Ersson**[10] was born on 28 Apr 1809 in Finhyttan, Grythyttan, Örebro, Sweden.[13] Erik married **Stina Lovisa Andersdotter Hälltorp**[13] on 27 Oct 1839.[10]
	iii.	**Carolina Ersdotter**[10] was born on 9 May 1813 in Spångtorp, Grythyttan, Örebro, Sweden.[14]
	iv.	**Lovisa Ersdotter**[10] was born on 21 Apr 1815 in Spångtorp, Grythyttan, Örebro, Sweden.[15]

3. Catharina Jonasdotter,[8] daughter of **Jonas Jonsson** and **Christina Johansdotter,** was born on 16 May 1776 in Grythyttan, Örebro, Sweden[16] and died on 23 Apr 1852 in Spången, Grythyttan, Örebro, Sweden[17] at age 75.

Birth Notes: In later records her birth date is given as 16 May 1776.

---

1. *Grythyttan AIa:6b (1775-1784) Image 80 / page 75 (AID: v51194.b80.s75, NAD: SE/ULA/10337)* .

2. *Grythyttan AIa:13b (1820-1830) Image 174 / page 169 (AID: v51204.b174.s169, NAD: SE/ULA/10337) . .... Grythyttan CI:6 (1775-1796) Image 20 / page 27 (AID: v53139.b20.s27, NAD: SE/ULA/10337) . .... Grythyttan AIa:6b (1775-1784) Image 80 / page 75 (AID: v51194.b80.s75, NAD: SE/ULA/10337) . .... Grythyttan AIa:8 (1785-1797) Image 185 / page 179 (AID: v51196.b185.s179, NAD: SE/ULA/10337).*

3. *Grythyttan CI:6 (1775-1796) Image 20 / page 27 (AID: v53139.b20.s27, NAD: SE/ULA/10337)* .

4. *Grythyttan AIa:13b (1820-1830) Image 174 / page 169 (AID: v51204.b174.s169, NAD: SE/ULA/10337) . .... Grythyttan F:2 (1821-1840) Image 57 (AID: v53160.b57, NAD: SE/ULA/10337)* .

5. *Grythyttan AIa:6b (1775-1784) Image 80 / page 75 (AID: v51194.b80.s75, NAD: SE/ULA/10337) . .... Grythyttan AIa:11b (1809-1812) Image 97 / page 89 (AID: v51200.b97.s89, NAD: SE/ULA/10337)* .

6. *Grythyttan AIa:11b (1809-1812) Image 97 / page 89 (AID: v51200.b97.s89, NAD: SE/ULA/10337) . .... Grythyttan AIa:12b (1812-1820) Image 120 / page 110 (AID: v51202.b120.s110, NAD: SE/ULA/10337)* .

7. *Grythyttan AIa:11b (1809-1812) Image 97 / page 89 (AID: v51200.b97.s89, NAD: SE/ULA/10337)* .

8. *Grythyttan AIa:14b (1830-1840) Image 168 / page 446 (AID: v51206.b168.s446, NAD: SE/ULA/10337) . .... Grythyttan AIa:8 (1785-1797) Image 188 / page 182 (AID: v51196.b188.s182, NAD: SE/ULA/10337)* .

9. *Grythyttan F:2 (1821-1840) Image 57 (AID: v53160.b57, NAD: SE/ULA/10337)* .

10. *Grythyttan AIa:14b (1830-1840) Image 168 / page 446 (AID: v51206.b168.s446, NAD: SE/ULA/10337)* .

11. *Nora bergsförsamling AI:14bb (1841-1850) Image 49 / page 195 (AID: v52007.b49.s195, NAD: SE/ULA/11098) . .... Nora bergsförsamling AI:15eb (1851-1861) Image 59 / page 213 (AID: v52013.b59.s213, NAD: SE/ULA/11098)* .

12. *Nora bergsförsamling EI:5 (1827-1842) Image 22 (AID: v53636.b22, NAD: SE/ULA/11098)* .

13. *Grythyttan AIa:14b (1830-1840) Image 168 / page 446 (AID: v51206.b168.s446, NAD: SE/ULA/10337) . .... Grythyttan AIa:13b (1820-1830) Image 174 / page 169 (AID: v51204.b174.s169, NAD: SE/ULA/10337)* .

14. *Grythyttan AIa:14b (1830-1840) Image 168 / page 446 (AID: v51206.b168.s446, NAD: SE/ULA/10337) . .... Grythyttan AIa:13b (1820-1830) Image 174 / page 169 (AID: v51204.b174.s169, NAD: SE/ULA/10337) . .... (Grythyttan CI:7 (1797-1817) Image 166 / page 319 (AID: v53140.b166.s319, NAD: SE/ULA/10337))*.

15. *Grythyttan AIa:14b (1830-1840) Image 168 / page 446 (AID: v51206.b168.s446, NAD: SE/ULA/10337) . .... Grythyttan AIa:13b (1820-1830) Image 174 / page 169 (AID: v51204.b174.s169, NAD: SE/ULA/10337) . .... Grythyttan CI:7 (1797-1817) Image 182 / page 351 (AID: v53140.b182.s351, NAD: SE/ULA/10337)* .

16. *Grythyttan AIa:13b (1820-1830) Image 174 / page 169 (AID: v51204.b174.s169, NAD: SE/ULA/10337) . .... Grythyttan AIa:14b (1830-1840) Image 168 / page 446 (AID: v51206.b168.s446, NAD: SE/ULA/10337) . .... Grythyttan AIa:15b (1841-1850) Image 331 / page*

Ancestor Report for Jan Ersson

Noted events in her life were:

- Resided: Långtjärnshöjden, 1781, Grythyttan, Örebro, Sweden. [18]

- Resided: Bef 1812, Finnhyttan, Västgötetorp, Grythyttan, Örebro, Sweden. [19]

- Resided: After 1812, Spångtorp, Grythyttan, Örebro, Sweden. [20]

Catharina married **Erik Nilsson**[21] on 11 Jan 1807.[22]

707 (AID: v51208.b331.s707, NAD: SE/ULA/10337) . .... Grythyttan AIa:8 (1785-1797) Image 188 / page 182 (AID: v51196.b188.s182, NAD: SE/ULA/10337). .... Grythyttan CI:6 (1775-1796) Image 22 / page 31 (AID: v53139.b22.s31, NAD: SE/ULA/10337) .

17. Grythyttan AIa:16e (1851-1861) Image 111 / page 712 (AID: v51213.b111.s712, NAD: SE/ULA/10337) .

18. Grythyttan AIa:6b (1775-1784) Image 83 / page 78 (AID: v51194.b83.s78, NAD: SE/ULA/10337) .

19. Grythyttan AIa:11b (1809-1812) Image 97 / page 89 (AID: v51200.b97.s89, NAD: SE/ULA/10337) .

20. Grythyttan AIa:11b (1809-1812) Image 97 / page 89 (AID: v51200.b97.s89, NAD: SE/ULA/10337) . .... Grythyttan AIa:12b (1812-1820) Image 120 / page 110 (AID: v51202.b120.s110, NAD: SE/ULA/10337) .

21. Grythyttan AIa:6b (1775-1784) Image 80 / page 75 (AID: v51194.b80.s75, NAD: SE/ULA/10337) .

22. Grythyttan F:2 (1821-1840) Image 57 (AID: v53160.b57, NAD: SE/ULA/10337) .

Ancestor Report for Jan Ersson

Third Generation

4. Nils Jansson,[1] son of **Johan Ersson** and **Sara Hansdotter,** was born on 12 May 1750 in Granbergsdalshyttetorp, Karlskoga, Örebro, Sweden[2] and died on 28 May 1828 in Finnhyttan, Västgötetorp, Grythyttan, Örebro, Sweden[3] at age 78.

Noted events in his life were:

- Resided: 1750-1760, Granbergsdalshyttetorp, Karlskoga, Örebro, Sweden. [4]

- Resided: After 1771, Västgötetorp, Grythyttan, Örebro, Sweden. [5]

- Resided: Finnhyttan (a.k.a. Lill Hälltorp) homestead, After 1774, Västgötetorp, Grythyttan, Örebro, Sweden. [6]

- Occupation: forrman at an iron foundry, After 1796, Grythyttan, Örebro, Sweden. [7]

Nils married **Maria Nilsdotter** on 26 Dec 1774 in Grythyttan, Örebro, Sweden.[8]

Children from this marriage were:

	i.	**Jan Nilsson**[9] was born on 26 Feb 1775 in Västgötetorp, Grythyttan, Örebro, Sweden. [10]
2	ii.	**Erik Nilsson.**[9] Erik married **Catharina Jonasdotter,**[11] daughter of **Jonas Jonsson** and **Christina Johansdotter,** on 11 Jan 1807.[12]
	iii.	**Maria Nilsdotter**[9] was born on 29 Apr 1778 in Lill Hälltorp, Västgötetorp, Grythyttan, Örebro, Sweden.[13]
	iv.	**Carl Nilsson**[9] was born on 12 Jun 1780 in Lill Hälltorp, Västgötetorp, Grythyttan, Örebro, Sweden. [14]
	v.	**Ander Nilsson**[9] was born on 5 Feb 1783 in Lill Hälltorp, Västgötetorp, Grythyttan, Örebro, Sweden [15] and died in 1786[16] at age 3.
	vi.	**Joseph Nilsson**[9] was born on 12 May 1784 in Lill Hälltorp, Västgötetorp, Grythyttan, Örebro, Sweden.[17] Joseph married **Anna Jacobsdotter**.[18]

1. *Karlskoga AI:1 (1757-1763) Image 84 / page 76 (AID: v51531.b84.s76, NAD: SE/ULA/10513) .*

2. *Goran Ekberg, Register och avskrifter - Göran Ekberg (http://www.gorek.se). .... Karlskoga AI:1 (1757-1763) Image 84 / page 76 (AID: v51531.b84.s76, NAD: SE/ULA/10513). .... Grythyttan AIa:8 (1785-1797) Image 185 / page 179 (AID: v51196.b185.s179, NAD: SE/ULA/10337). .... Karlskoga C:5 (1740-1752) Image 104 (AID: v53365.b104, NAD: SE/ULA/10513) .*

3. *Grythyttan F:2 (1821-1840) Image 48 (AID: v53160.b48, NAD: SE/ULA/10337) .*

4. *Karlskoga AI:1 (1757-1763) Image 84 / page 76 (AID: v51531.b84.s76, NAD: SE/ULA/10513) . .... Karlskoga C:5 (1740-1752) Image 104 (AID: v53365.b104, NAD: SE/ULA/10513).*

5. *Grythyttan AIa:5 (1771-1776) Image 144 / page 136 (AID: v51192.b144.s136, NAD: SE/ULA/10337) .*

6. *Grythyttan AIa:6b (1775-1784) Image 80 / page 75 (AID: v51194.b80.s75, NAD: SE/ULA/10337) . .... Grythyttan AIa:11b (1809-1812) Image 97 / page 89 (AID: v51200.b97.s89, NAD: SE/ULA/10337). .... Grythyttan AIa:9 (1798-1808) Image 198 / page 191 (AID: v51197.b198.s191, NAD: SE/ULA/10337). .... Grythyttan AIa:12b (1812-1820) Image 129 / page 119 (AID: v51202.b129.s119, NAD: SE/ULA/10337). .... Grythyttan AIa:13b (1820-1830) Image 183 / page 177b (AID: v51204.b183.s177b, NAD: SE/ULA/10337) .*

7. *Grythyttan AIa:11b (1809-1812) Image 97 / page 89 (AID: v51200.b97.s89, NAD: SE/ULA/10337) . .... Grythyttan AIa:6b (1775-1784) Image 80 / page 75 (AID: v51194.b80.s75, NAD: SE/ULA/10337).*

8. *Grythyttan AIa:6b (1775-1784) Image 80 / page 75 (AID: v51194.b80.s75, NAD: SE/ULA/10337) . .... Grythyttan AIa:11b (1809-1812) Image 97 / page 89 (AID: v51200.b97.s89, NAD: SE/ULA/10337) . .... Grythyttan CI:5 (1770-1774) Image 44 / page 78 (AID: v53138.b44.s78, NAD: SE/ULA/10337).*

9. *Grythyttan AIa:6b (1775-1784) Image 80 / page 75 (AID: v51194.b80.s75, NAD: SE/ULA/10337) .*

10. *Grythyttan AIa:6b (1775-1784) Image 80 / page 75 (AID: v51194.b80.s75, NAD: SE/ULA/10337) . .... Grythyttan AIa:8 (1785-1797) Image 185 / page 179 (AID: v51196.b185.s179, NAD: SE/ULA/10337) . .... Grythyttan CI:6 (1775-1796) Image 10 / page 7 (AID: v53139.b10.s7, NAD: SE/ULA/10337).*

11. *Grythyttan AIa:14b (1830-1840) Image 168 / page 446 (AID: v51206.b168.s446, NAD: SE/ULA/10337) . .... Grythyttan AIa:8 (1785-1797) Image 188 / page 182 (AID: v51196.b188.s182, NAD: SE/ULA/10337) .*

12. *Grythyttan F:2 (1821-1840) Image 57 (AID: v53160.b57, NAD: SE/ULA/10337) .*

13. *Grythyttan AIa:6b (1775-1784) Image 80 / page 75 (AID: v51194.b80.s75, NAD: SE/ULA/10337) . .... Grythyttan AIa:8 (1785-1797) Image 185 / page 179 (AID: v51196.b185.s179, NAD: SE/ULA/10337) . .... Grythyttan CI:6 (1775-1796) Image 39 / page 65 (AID: v53139.b39.s65, NAD: SE/ULA/10337).*

14. *Grythyttan AIa:6b (1775-1784) Image 80 / page 75 (AID: v51194.b80.s75, NAD: SE/ULA/10337) . .... Grythyttan AIa:8 (1785-1797) Image 185 / page 179 (AID: v51196.b185.s179, NAD: SE/ULA/10337) . .... Grythyttan CI:6 (1775-1796) Image 58 / page 103 (AID: v53139.b58.s103, NAD: SE/ULA/10337).*

15. *Grythyttan AIa:6b (1775-1784) Image 80 / page 75 (AID: v51194.b80.s75, NAD: SE/ULA/10337) . .... Grythyttan AIa:8 (1785-1797) Image 185 / page 179 (AID: v51196.b185.s179, NAD: SE/ULA/10337) . .... Grythyttan CI:6 (1775-1796) Image 78 / page 143 (AID: v53139.b78.s143, NAD: SE/ULA/10337).*

16. *Grythyttan AIa:8 (1785-1797) Image 185 / page 179 (AID: v51196.b185.s179, NAD: SE/ULA/10337) .*

17. *Grythyttan AIa:6b (1775-1784) Image 80 / page 75 (AID: v51194.b80.s75, NAD: SE/ULA/10337) . .... Grythyttan AIa:8 (1785-*

Ancestor Report for Jan Ersson

vii.   **Nils Nilsson**[9] was born on 16 Jun 1786 in Lill Hälltorp, Västgötetorp, Grythyttan, Örebro, Sweden [19] and died in 1789[16] at age 3.

viii.   **Olof Nilsson**[20] was born on 5 Feb 1789 in Lill Hälltorp, Västgötetorp, Grythyttan, Örebro, Sweden. [21] Olof married **Cajsa Jansdotter**[18] in 1811.[18]

5. Maria Nilsdotter, daughter of **Nils Jansson** and **Cherstin Jansdotter,** was born on 8 Sep 1746 in Brunsjötorp, Grythyttan, Örebro, Sweden[22] and died on 9 Jul 1821 in Bergslund, Grythyttan, Örebro, Sweden [23] at age 74.

Noted events in her life were:
• Resided: 1760, Granbergsdalshyttetorp, Karlskoga, Örebro, Sweden. [24]

• Resided: After 1771, Västgötetorp, Grythyttan, Örebro, Sweden.[25]

• Resided: Finnhyttan (a.k.a. Lill Hälltorp) homestead, After 1774, Västgötetorp, Grythyttan, Örebro, Sweden. [26]

Maria married **Nils Jansson**[27] on 26 Dec 1774 in Grythyttan, Örebro, Sweden.[28]

6. Jonas Jonsson[29] was born in 1745 in Karlskoga, Örebro, Sweden [30] and died in 1812 in Långtjärnshöjden, Grythyttan, Örebro, Sweden[31] at age 67.

Research Notes: Possible birth date 2 Jan 1746 at Gräsmossen to Kerstin Persdotter and Jonas Jansson. There are two there other families born in 1745 with a child of the same name. [32]

1797) Image 185 / page 179 (AID: v51196.b185.s179, NAD: SE/ULA/10337) . .... Grythyttan AIa:11b (1809-1812) Image 97 / page 89 (AID: v51200.b97.s89, NAD: SE/ULA/10337). .... Grythyttan AIa:12b (1812-1820) Image 129 / page 119 (AID: v51202.b129.s119, NAD: SE/ULA/10337). .... Grythyttan CI:6 (1775-1796) Image 86 / page 159 (AID: v53139.b86.s159, NAD: SE/ULA/10337) .

18. Grythyttan AIa:12b (1812-1820) Image 129 / page 119 (AID: v51202.b129.s119, NAD: SE/ULA/10337) .

19. Grythyttan AIa:6b (1775-1784) Image 80 / page 75 (AID: v51194.b80.s75, NAD: SE/ULA/10337) . .... Grythyttan AIa:8 (1785-1797) Image 185 / page 179 (AID: v51196.b185.s179, NAD: SE/ULA/10337) . .... Grythyttan CI:6 (1775-1796) Image 106 / page 199 (AID: v53139.b106.s199, NAD: SE/ULA/10337).

20. Grythyttan AIa:8 (1785-1797) Image 185 / page 179 (AID: v51196.b185.s179, NAD: SE/ULA/10337) .

21. Grythyttan AIa:8 (1785-1797) Image 185 / page 179 (AID: v51196.b185.s179, NAD: SE/ULA/10337) . .... Grythyttan AIa:11b (1809-1812) Image 97 / page 89 (AID: v51200.b97.s89, NAD: SE/ULA/10337) . .... Grythyttan CI:6 (1775-1796) Image 127 / page 241 (AID: v53139.b127.s241, NAD: SE/ULA/10337).

22. Grythyttan AIa:11b (1809-1812) Image 97 / page 89 (AID: v51200.b97.s89, NAD: SE/ULA/10337) . .... Grythyttan CI:3 (1737-1757) Image 197 (AID: v53136.b197, NAD: SE/ULA/10337).

23. Grythyttan F:2 (1821-1840) Image 10 (AID: v53160.b10, NAD: SE/ULA/10337) .

24. Goran Ekberg, Register och avskrifter - Göran Ekberg (http://www.gorek.se). .... Karlskoga AI:1 (1757-1763) Image 84 / page 76 (AID: v51531.b84.s76, NAD: SE/ULA/10513).

25. Grythyttan AIa:5 (1771-1776) Image 144 / page 136 (AID: v51192.b144.s136, NAD: SE/ULA/10337) .

26. Grythyttan AIa:6b (1775-1784) Image 80 / page 75 (AID: v51194.b80.s75, NAD: SE/ULA/10337) . .... Grythyttan AIa:11b (1809-1812) Image 97 / page 89 (AID: v51200.b97.s89, NAD: SE/ULA/10337) . .... Grythyttan AIa:9 (1798-1808) Image 198 / page 191 (AID: v51197.b198.s191, NAD: SE/ULA/10337). .... Grythyttan AIa:12b (1812-1820) Image 129 / page 119 (AID: v51202.b129.s119, NAD: SE/ULA/10337). .... Grythyttan AIa:13b (1820-1830) Image 183 / page 177b (AID: v51204.b183.s177b, NAD: SE/ULA/10337) .

27. Karlskoga AI:1 (1757-1763) Image 84 / page 76 (AID: v51531.b84.s76, NAD: SE/ULA/10513) .

28. Grythyttan AIa:6b (1775-1784) Image 80 / page 75 (AID: v51194.b80.s75, NAD: SE/ULA/10337) . .... Grythyttan AIa:11b (1809-1812) Image 97 / page 89 (AID: v51200.b97.s89, NAD: SE/ULA/10337) . .... Grythyttan CI:5 (1770-1774) Image 44 / page 78 (AID: v53138.b44.s78, NAD: SE/ULA/10337).

29. Grythyttan AIa:6b (1775-1784) Image 83 / page 78 (AID: v51194.b83.s78, NAD: SE/ULA/10337) . .... Grythyttan AIa:8 (1785-1797) Image 188 / page 182 (AID: v51196.b188.s182, NAD: SE/ULA/10337) . .... Grythyttan F:1 (1799-1820) Image 169 / page 164 (AID: v53159.b169.s164, NAD: SE/ULA/10337).

30. Grythyttan AIa:6b (1775-1784) Image 83 / page 78 (AID: v51194.b83.s78, NAD: SE/ULA/10337) . .... Grythyttan AIa:8 (1785-1797) Image 188 / page 182 (AID: v51196.b188.s182, NAD: SE/ULA/10337) .

31. Åke Norgrens Hemsida (http://leon.amaroq.se).

32. Karlskoga AI:1 (1757-1763) Image 49 / page 41 (AID: v51531.b49.s41, NAD: SE/ULA/10513) . .... Goran Ekberg, Register och avskrifter - Göran Ekberg (http://www.gorek.se).

33. Grythyttan AIa:6b (1775-1784) Image 83 / page 78 (AID: v51194.b83.s78, NAD: SE/ULA/10337) .

Ancestor Report for Jan Ersson

Noted events in his life were:
- Moved to: 1773, Grythyttan, Örebro, Sweden.[33]

- Resided: 9th homestead, 1781, Långtjärnshöjden, Grythyttan, Örebro, Sweden.[34]

Jonas married **Christina Johansdotter**[35] on 13 Jun 1762 in Kroppa, Värmland, Sweden.[36]

Children from this marriage were:
	i.	**Jonas Jonasson**[37] was born in 1764 in Grythyttan, Örebro, Sweden.[37]

- i. **Jonas Jonasson**[37] was born in 1764 in Grythyttan, Örebro, Sweden.[37]
- ii. **Jon Jonasson**[34] was born in 1766 in Grythyttan, Örebro, Sweden.[34]
- iii. **Anders Jonasson**[34] was born in 1767 in Grythyttan, Örebro, Sweden[37] and died on 3 Jan 1821 in Loka, Grythyttan, Örebro, Sweden[38] at age 54. Anders married **Elisabet Olofsdotter**[38] on 25 Jul 1793 in Grythyttan, Örebro, Sweden.[38] Anders next married **Katarina Johansdotter**[38] on 12 Mar 1802 in Hällefors, Örebro, Sweden.[38] Anders next married **Maria Andersdotter**.[38]
- iv. **Anna Jonsdotter**[37] was born in 1771 in Kroppa, Värmland, Sweden.[37]
- v. **Eric Jonasson**[37] was born in 1773 in Grythyttan, Örebro, Sweden.[37]
- vi. **Stina Jonasdotter**[34] was born on 27 Apr 1775 in Grythyttan, Örebro, Sweden[34] and died in 1776[34] at age 1.
- 3 vii. **Catharina Jonasdotter**.[39] Catharina married **Erik Nilsson**,[40] son of **Nils Jansson** and **Maria Nilsdotter**, on 11 Jan 1807.[41]
- viii. **Stina Jonasdotter**[37] was born in 1778 in Grythyttan, Örebro, Sweden.[37]
- ix. **Lars Jonasdotter**[37] was born in 1781 in Grythyttan, Örebro, Sweden.[37]
- x. **Olof Jonasdotter**[42] was born on 30 Sep 1785 in Grythyttan, Örebro, Sweden.[42]

7. Christina Johansdotter,[35] daughter of **Johan Johansson** and **Christina Eriksdotter**, was born in 1747 in Nybygget, Kroppa, Värmland, Sweden[43] and died on 12 Jan 1813 in Långtjärnshöjden, Grythyttan, Örebro, Sweden[44] at age 66.

Christina married **Jonas Jonsson**[45] on 13 Jun 1762 in Kroppa, Värmland, Sweden.[36]

---

34. Grythyttan AIa:6b (1775-1784) Image 83 / page 78 (AID: v51194.b83.s78, NAD: SE/ULA/10337).

35. Grythyttan AIa:6b (1775-1784) Image 83 / page 78 (AID: v51194.b83.s78, NAD: SE/ULA/10337). .... Åke Norgrens Hemsida (http://leon.amaroq.se). .... Grythyttan AIa:8 (1785-1797) Image 188 / page 182 (AID: v51196.b188.s182, NAD: SE/ULA/10337).

36. Sweden Marriages, 1630-1920 (familysearch.org). .... Åke Norgrens Hemsida (http://leon.amaroq.se). .... Grythyttan AIa:8 (1785-1797) Image 188 / page 182 (AID: v51196.b188.s182, NAD: SE/ULA/10337). .... Kroppa C:4 (1760-1810) Image 18 / page 27 (AID: v7308.b18.s27, NAD: SE/VA/13291).

37. Grythyttan AIa:6b (1775-1784) Image 83 / page 78 (AID: v51194.b83.s78, NAD: SE/ULA/10337). .... Grythyttan AIa:8 (1785-1797) Image 188 / page 182 (AID: v51196.b188.s182, NAD: SE/ULA/10337).

38. Åke Norgrens Hemsida (http://leon.amaroq.se).

39. Grythyttan AIa:14b (1830-1840) Image 168 / page 446 (AID: v51206.b168.s446, NAD: SE/ULA/10337). .... Grythyttan AIa:8 (1785-1797) Image 188 / page 182 (AID: v51196.b188.s182, NAD: SE/ULA/10337).

40. Grythyttan AIa:6b (1775-1784) Image 80 / page 75 (AID: v51194.b80.s75, NAD: SE/ULA/10337).

41. Grythyttan F:2 (1821-1840) Image 57 (AID: v53160.b57, NAD: SE/ULA/10337).

42. Grythyttan AIa:8 (1785-1797) Image 188 / page 182 (AID: v51196.b188.s182, NAD: SE/ULA/10337).

43. Grythyttan AIa:6b (1775-1784) Image 83 / page 78 (AID: v51194.b83.s78, NAD: SE/ULA/10337). .... Åke Norgrens Hemsida (http://leon.amaroq.se). .... Grythyttan AIa:8 (1785-1797) Image 188 / page 182 (AID: v51196.b188.s182, NAD: SE/ULA/10337). .... Kroppa AI:2 (1751-1760) Image 22 / page 16 (AID: v11902.b22.s16, NAD: SE/VA/13291).

44. Åke Norgrens Hemsida (http://leon.amaroq.se). .... Grythyttan F:1 (1799-1820) Image 169 / page 164 (AID: v53159.b169.s164, NAD: SE/ULA/10337).

45. Grythyttan AIa:6b (1775-1784) Image 83 / page 78 (AID: v51194.b83.s78, NAD: SE/ULA/10337). .... Grythyttan AIa:8 (1785-1797) Image 188 / page 182 (AID: v51196.b188.s182, NAD: SE/ULA/10337). .... Grythyttan F:1 (1799-1820) Image 169 / page 164 (AID: v53159.b169.s164, NAD: SE/ULA/10337).

Ancestor Report for Jan Ersson

Fourth Generation

8. Johan Ersson,[1] son of **Unknown** and **Annika Jonsdotter,** was born on 12 May 1712 in Rishöjden, Karlskoga, Örebro, Sweden[2] and died on 6 Mar 1773 in Norra Granbergsdalshyttetorp, Karlskoga, Örebro, Sweden[3] at age 60.

Research Notes: Johan's mother is clearly Annika Jonsdotter, based on the only birth recorded for a Johan Ersson in 1712. The birth record does not list the father, as was the practice at that time even for married parents. Several genealogists believe that the father of Johan is Eric Ersson, born 1695/6 probably because he appears as head of the farm where Johan and his children live. But I doubt the parentage for two reasons: (1) the father would have benn under 16 years old and (2) there is no marriage record for Eric Errson and Annika Jonsdotter before 1712. There is a marriage record for Annika Jonsdotter of Östra Lonntorp and another man, Eric Persson, 24 September 1711. Eric Persson is from Granbergsdalshyttetorp, but he does not appear in the later house books. I believe that Eric Persson is the father, and that Annika later marries Eric Persson, born 1696, and that he is Johan Ersson's step-father. But I lack firm proof because the earlier house records are not available.

Noted events in his life were:
- Resided: Norra Granbergsdalshyttetorp homestead, 1760-1773, Karlskoga, Örebro, Sweden.[4]

- Occupation: bergsman (miner).[5]

Johan married **Sara Hansdotter**.[1]

Children from this marriage were:

	i.	**Maria Jansdotter** was born on 27 Jun 1738 in Granbergsdalshyttetorp, Karlskoga, Örebro, Sweden.[6]
	ii.	**Erik Jansson**[1] was born on 8 Nov 1739 in Granbergsdalshyttetorp, Karlskoga, Örebro, Sweden[7] and died in 1824 in Karlskoga, Örebro, Sweden at age 85.
	iii.	**Lisa Jansdotter**[1] was born on 27 Jan 1744 in Norra Granbergsdalshyttetorp, Karlskoga, Örebro, Sweden.[8]
	iv.	**Brita Jansdotter** was born on 17 Jun 1746 in Granbergsdalshyttetorp, Karlskoga, Örebro, Sweden[9] and died in 1746 in Karlskoga, Örebro, Sweden.
	v.	**Carl Ersson** was born on 26 Feb 1747 in Fallet, Karlskoga, Örebro, Sweden.[1]
4	vi.	**Nils Jansson**.[1] Nils married **Maria Nilsdotter,** daughter of **Nils Jansson** and **Cherstin Jansdotter,** on 26 Dec 1774 in Grythyttan, Örebro, Sweden.[10]
	vii.	**Olof Jansson**[1] was born on 6 Jul 1752 in Granbergsdalshyttetorp, Karlskoga, Örebro, Sweden[11] and died on 28 May 1818[5] at age 65. Olof married **Catharina Gustafsdotter**.[5]
	viii.	**Jan Jansson** was born on 6 Jul 1752 in Granbergsdalshyttetorp, Karlskoga, Örebro, Sweden.[12]

---

1. *Karlskoga AI:1 (1757-1763) Image 84 / page 76 (AID: v51531.b84.s76, NAD: SE/ULA/10513) .*

2. *Karlskoga AI:1 (1757-1763) Image 84 / page 76 (AID: v51531.b84.s76, NAD: SE/ULA/10513) . .... Sven-Erik Lilja's website (http://www.svenlilja.com). .... Karlskoga C:1 (1679-1718) Image 148 / page 137 (AID: v53361.b148.s137, NAD: SE/ULA/10513) . .... Karlskoga AI:2 (1771-1776) Image 180 / page 172 (AID: v51532.b180.s172, NAD: SE/ULA/10513) .*

3. *Sven-Erik Lilja's website (http://www.svenlilja.com). .... Karlskoga F:1 (1740-1832) Image 63 / page 59 (AID: v53392.b63.s59, NAD: SE/ULA/10513).*

4. *Karlskoga AI:1 (1757-1763) Image 84 / page 76 (AID: v51531.b84.s76, NAD: SE/ULA/10513) . .... Karlskoga AI:2 (1771-1776) Image 180 / page 172 (AID: v51532.b180.s172, NAD: SE/ULA/10513) .*

5. *Sven-Erik Lilja's website (http://www.svenlilja.com).*

6. *Göran Ekberg website (http://www.gorek.se/). .... Karlskoga C:4 (1730-1739) Image 133 (AID: v53364.b133, NAD: SE/ULA/10513) .*

7. *Karlskoga AI:1 (1757-1763) Image 84 / page 76 (AID: v51531.b84.s76, NAD: SE/ULA/10513) . .... Karlskoga C:4 (1730-1739) Image 156 (AID: v53364.b156, NAD: SE/ULA/10513) . .... Karlskoga AI:2 (1771-1776) Image 180 / page 172 (AID: v51532.b180.s172, NAD: SE/ULA/10513).*

8. *Karlskoga AI:1 (1757-1763) Image 84 / page 76 (AID: v51531.b84.s76, NAD: SE/ULA/10513) . .... Karlskoga C:5 (1740-1752) Image 41 (AID: v53365.b41, NAD: SE/ULA/10513).*

9. *Karlskoga C:5 (1740-1752) Image 62 (AID: v53365.b62, NAD: SE/ULA/10513).*

10. *Grythyttan AIa:6b (1775-1784) Image 80 / page 75 (AID: v51194.b80.s75, NAD: SE/ULA/10337) . .... Grythyttan AIa:11b (1809-1812) Image 97 / page 89 (AID: v51200.b97.s89, NAD: SE/ULA/10337) . .... Grythyttan CI:5 (1770-1774) Image 44 / page 78 (AID: v53138.b44.s78, NAD: SE/ULA/10337).*

11. *Karlskoga AI:1 (1757-1763) Image 84 / page 76 (AID: v51531.b84.s76, NAD: SE/ULA/10513) . .... Sven-Erik Lilja's website (http://www.svenlilja.com). .... Karlskoga C:5 (1740-1752) Image 127 (AID: v53365.b127, NAD: SE/ULA/10513) .*

12. *Karlskoga C:5 (1740-1752) Image 127 (AID: v53365.b127, NAD: SE/ULA/10513) .*

Ancestor Report for Jan Ersson

ix.   **Joseph Jansson**[1] was born on 21 Apr 1755 in Granbergsdalshyttetorp, Karlskoga, Örebro, Sweden. [13]

x.   **Cathrina Jansdotter**[14] was born on 12 Jun 1756 in Granbergsdalshyttetorp, Karlskoga, Örebro, Sweden.[15]

Johan next married **Annika Arvidsdotter**.

Noted events in her life were:
• Resided: Norra Granbergsdalshyttetorp homestead, 1771-1776, Karlskoga, Örebro, Sweden. [16]

The child from this marriage was:

i.   **Olof Ersdotter** was born in 1759 in Norra Granbergsdalshyttetorp, Karlskoga, Örebro, Sweden. [16]

9. Sara Hansdotter[14] was born about 1711[17] and died on 9 Mar 1758 in Granbergsdalshyttetorp, Karlskoga, Örebro, Sweden[18] about age 47.

Research Notes: Some geneaologists argue that the parents of Sara Handsdotter are Hans Olsson and Sara Bengsdotter. But the birth date they give, 14 August, 1711 is for a Sarah Olsdotter, not Hansdotter. So I do not see any solid proof for their claim.

Noted events in her life were:
• Resided: Cir 1750, Granbergsdalshyttetorp, Karlskoga, Örebro, Sweden. [14]

Sara married **Johan Ersson**.[14]

10. Nils Jansson,[19] son of **Johan Nilsson** and **Maria Nilsdotter,** was born on 14 Jun 1710 in Grythyttan, Örebro, Sweden.[20]

Noted events in his life were:
• Resided: 1737-1771, Brunsjötorp, Grythyttan, Örebro, Sweden. [21]

• Occupation: laborer, After 1740, Långtjärnshöjden, Grythyttan, Örebro, Sweden. [22]

• Status: topare (tenant farmer), 1771-1783, Västgötetorp, Grythyttan, Örebro, Sweden. [23]

Nils married **Cherstin Jansdotter**[19] on 17 Apr 1737 in Grythyttan, Örebro, Sweden.[24]

---

   14. *Karlskoga AI:1 (1757-1763) Image 84 / page 76 (AID: v51531.b84.s76, NAD: SE/ULA/10513) .*

   15. *Karlskoga AI:1 (1757-1763) Image 84 / page 76 (AID: v51531.b84.s76, NAD: SE/ULA/10513) . .... Karlskoga C:6 (1753-1774) Image 44 (AID: v53366.b44, NAD: SE/ULA/10513) . .... Karlskoga AI:2 (1771-1776) Image 180 / page 172 (AID: v51532.b180.s172, NAD: SE/ULA/10513).*

   16. *Karlskoga AI:2 (1771-1776) Image 180 / page 172 (AID: v51532.b180.s172, NAD: SE/ULA/10513) .*

   17. *Karlskoga AI:1 (1757-1763) Image 84 / page 76 (AID: v51531.b84.s76, NAD: SE/ULA/10513) . .... Karlskoga F:1 (1740-1832) Image 41 / page 37 (AID: v53392.b41.s37, NAD: SE/ULA/10513) .*

   18. *Sven-Erik Lilja's website (http://www.svenlilja.com). .... Karlskoga F:1 (1740-1832) Image 41 / page 37 (AID: v53392.b41.s37, NAD: SE/ULA/10513).*

   19. *Grythyttan CI:3 (1737-1757) Image 197 (AID: v53136.b197, NAD: SE/ULA/10337) .*

   20. *Grythyttan AIa:4 (1740-1767) Image 137 / page 129 (AID: v51191.b137.s129, NAD: SE/ULA/10337) . .... (Grythyttan AIa:5 (1771-1776) Image 144 / page 136 (AID: v51192.b144.s136, NAD: SE/ULA/10337)). .... Grythyttan AIa:6b (1775-1784) Image 80 / page 75 (AID: v51194.b80.s75, NAD: SE/ULA/10337). .... Grythyttan CI:1 (1699-1715) Image 55 / page 49 (AID: v53134.b55.s49, NAD: SE/ULA/10337).*

   21. *Grythyttan CI:3 (1737-1757) Image 108 (AID: v53136.b108, NAD: SE/ULA/10337) . .... Grythyttan AIa:4 (1740-1767) Image 137 / page 129 (AID: v51191.b137.s129, NAD: SE/ULA/10337) . .... Grythyttan AIa:6b (1775-1784) Image 80 / page 75 (AID: v51194.b80.s75, NAD: SE/ULA/10337).*

   22. *Grythyttan AIa:4 (1740-1767) Image 141 / page 133 (AID: v51191.b141.s133, NAD: SE/ULA/10337) . .... Grythyttan AIa:3 (1737-1743) Image 36 / page 26 (AID: v51190.b36.s26, NAD: SE/ULA/10337) .*

   23. *(Grythyttan AIa:5 (1771-1776) Image 144 / page 136 (AID: v51192.b144.s136, NAD: SE/ULA/10337)). .... Grythyttan CI:5 (1770-1774) Image 122 (AID: v53138.b122, NAD: SE/ULA/10337) .*

   24. *Grythyttan CI:3 (1737-1757) Image 108 (AID: v53136.b108, NAD: SE/ULA/10337) . .... Grythyttan AIa:6b (1775-1784) Image 80 / page 75 (AID: v51194.b80.s75, NAD: SE/ULA/10337) .*

Ancestor Report for Jan Ersson

Children from this marriage were:

      i.   **Olof Nilsson** was born on 7 Jan 1740 in Brunsjötorp, Grythyttan, Örebro, Sweden. [25]

      ii.   **Johan Nilsson** was born on 23 Aug 1743 in Brunsjötorp, Grythyttan, Örebro, Sweden.

5   iii. **Maria Nilsdotter**. Maria married **Nils Jansson**,[27] son of **Johan Ersson** and **Sara Hansdotter,** on 26 Dec 1774 in Grythyttan, Örebro, Sweden.[28]

     iv. **Stina Nilsdotter** was born on 8 Jul 1749 in Långtjärnshöjden, Grythyttan, Örebro, Sweden. [29]

      v.   **Eric Nilsson** was born in 1751 [30] and died in 1754 [30] at age 3.

     vi. **Anders Nilsson** was born in 1759.[30]

11. Cherstin Jansdotter[31] was born in 1713 in Karlskoga, Örebro, Sweden [32] and died on 27 Oct 1783 in Västgötetorp, Grythyttan, Örebro, Sweden[33] at age 70.

Research Notes: Kerstin's death record indicates she was born in Björn, Karlskoga. There are two Kerstin Jansdotters born in 1713, and neither were born at place continuing the word "Björn."

Noted events in her life were:

• Resided: 1737-1771, Brunsjötorp, Grythyttan, Örebro, Sweden. [34]

• Resided: 1771-1783, Västgötetorp, Grythyttan, Örebro, Sweden. [35]

Cherstin married **Nils Jansson**[31] on 17 Apr 1737 in Grythyttan, Örebro, Sweden.[36]

14. Johan Johansson.[37]

Johan married **Christina Eriksdotter**.[37]

Children from this marriage were:

      i.   **Per Johansson**[38]

      ii.   **Catherina Johansdotter**[38]

7   iii. **Christina Johansdotter**.[39] Christina married **Jonas Jonsson**[40] on 13 Jun 1762 in Kroppa, Värmland, Sweden.[41]

---

25. *Grythyttan CI:3 (1737-1757) Image 140 (AID: v53136.b140, NAD: SE/ULA/10337)* .

26. *Grythyttan CI:3 (1737-1757) Image 175 (AID: v53136.b175, NAD: SE/ULA/10337)* .

27. *Karlskoga AI:1 (1757-1763) Image 84 / page 76 (AID: v51531.b84.s76, NAD: SE/ULA/10513)* .

28. *Grythyttan AIa:6b (1775-1784) Image 80 / page 75 (AID: v51194.b80.s75, NAD: SE/ULA/10337) . .... Grythyttan AIa:11b (1809-1812) Image 97 / page 89 (AID: v51200.b97.s89, NAD: SE/ULA/10337) . .... Grythyttan CI:5 (1770-1774) Image 44 / page 78 (AID: v53138.b44.s78, NAD: SE/ULA/10337)* .

29. *Grythyttan CI:3 (1737-1757) Image 216 (AID: v53136.b216, NAD: SE/ULA/10337)* .

30. *(Grythyttan AIa:5 (1771-1776) Image 144 / page 136 (AID: v51192.b144.s136, NAD: SE/ULA/10337))* .

31. *Grythyttan CI:3 (1737-1757) Image 197 (AID: v53136.b197, NAD: SE/ULA/10337)* .

32. *Grythyttan AIa:4 (1740-1767) Image 137 / page 129 (AID: v51191.b137.s129, NAD: SE/ULA/10337) . .... Grythyttan CI:3 (1737-1757) Image 108 (AID: v53136.b108, NAD: SE/ULA/10337) . .... (Grythyttan AIa:5 (1771-1776) Image 144 / page 136 (AID: v51192.b144.s136, NAD: SE/ULA/10337)). .... Grythyttan CI:5 (1770-1774) Image 122 (AID: v53138.b122, NAD: SE/ULA/10337)* .

33. *Grythyttan AIa:6b (1775-1784) Image 80 / page 75 (AID: v51194.b80.s75, NAD: SE/ULA/10337) . .... Grythyttan CI:5 (1770-1774) Image 122 (AID: v53138.b122, NAD: SE/ULA/10337)* .

34. *Grythyttan CI:3 (1737-1757) Image 108 (AID: v53136.b108, NAD: SE/ULA/10337) . .... Grythyttan AIa:4 (1740-1767) Image 137 / page 129 (AID: v51191.b137.s129, NAD: SE/ULA/10337) . .... Grythyttan AIa:6b (1775-1784) Image 80 / page 75 (AID: v51194.b80.s75, NAD: SE/ULA/10337)* .

35. *(Grythyttan AIa:5 (1771-1776) Image 144 / page 136 (AID: v51192.b144.s136, NAD: SE/ULA/10337)). .... Grythyttan CI:5 (1770-1774) Image 122 (AID: v53138.b122, NAD: SE/ULA/10337)* .

36. *Grythyttan CI:3 (1737-1757) Image 108 (AID: v53136.b108, NAD: SE/ULA/10337) . .... Grythyttan AIa:6b (1775-1784) Image 80 / page 75 (AID: v51194.b80.s75, NAD: SE/ULA/10337)* .

37. *Grythyttan F:1 (1799-1820) Image 169 / page 164 (AID: v53159.b169.s164, NAD: SE/ULA/10337)* .

38. *Kroppa AI:1 (1738-1744) Image 132 / page 255 (AID: v11901.b132.s255, NAD: SE/VA/13291)* .

39. *Grythyttan AIa:6b (1775-1784) Image 83 / page 78 (AID: v51194.b83.s78, NAD: SE/ULA/10337) . .... Åke Norgrens Hemsida (http://leon.amaroq.se). .... Grythyttan AIa:8 (1785-1797) Image 188 / page 182 (AID: v51196.b188.s182, NAD: SE/ULA/10337)* .

40. *Grythyttan AIa:6b (1775-1784) Image 83 / page 78 (AID: v51194.b83.s78, NAD: SE/ULA/10337) . .... Grythyttan AIa:8 (1785-1797) Image 188 / page 182 (AID: v51196.b188.s182, NAD: SE/ULA/10337) . .... Grythyttan F:1 (1799-1820) Image 169 / page 164 (AID: v53159.b169.s164, NAD: SE/ULA/10337)* .

41. *Sweden Marriages, 1630-1920 (familysearch.org). .... Åke Norgrens Hemsida (http://leon.amaroq.se). .... Grythyttan AIa:8 (1785-1797) Image 188 / page 182 (AID: v51196.b188.s182, NAD: SE/ULA/10337) . .... Kroppa C:4 (1760-1810) Image 18 / page 27 (AID: v7308.b18.s27, NAD: SE/VA/13291)* .

15. Christina Eriksdotter[42] was born in 1715 in Kroppa, Värmland, Sweden. [43]

Christina married **Johan Johansson**.[42]

42. *Grythyttan F:1 (1799-1820) Image 169 / page 164 (AID: v53159.b169.s164, NAD: SE/ULA/10337)* .
43. *Åke Norgrens Hemsida (http://leon.amaroq.se).*

Fifth Generation

17. Annika Jonsdotter.[1]

Research Notes: She is posibly from Lonntorp.

Annika married someone.

The child from this marriage was:
8   i.   **Johan Ersson.**[2] Johan married **Sara Hansdotter.**[2] Johan next married **Annika Arvidsdotter.**

20. Johan Nilsson.[3]

Research Notes: Possibly residing at Kerfvingeborn in Gyrthyttan.[4]

Johan married **Maria Nilsdotter.**[3]

The child from this marriage was:
10   i.   **Nils Jansson.**[5] Nils married **Cherstin Jansdotter**[5] on 17 Apr 1737 in Grythyttan, Örebro, Sweden.[6]

21. Maria Nilsdotter.[3]

Maria married **Johan Nilsson.**[3]

---

   1. Karlskoga C:1 (1679-1718) Image 148 / page 137 (AID: v53361.b148.s137, NAD: SE/ULA/10513) .
   2. Karlskoga AI:1 (1757-1763) Image 84 / page 76 (AID: v51531.b84.s76, NAD: SE/ULA/10513) .
   3. Grythyttan CI:1 (1699-1715) Image 55 / page 49 (AID: v53134.b55.s49, NAD: SE/ULA/10337) .
   4. Grythyttan AIa:2 (1727-1740) Image 38 / page 56 (AID: v51189.b38.s56, NAD: SE/ULA/10337) .
   5. Grythyttan CI:3 (1737-1757) Image 197 (AID: v53136.b197, NAD: SE/ULA/10337) .
   6. Grythyttan CI:3 (1737-1757) Image 108 (AID: v53136.b108, NAD: SE/ULA/10337) . .... Grythyttan AIa:6b (1775-1784) Image 80 / page 75 (AID: v51194.b80.s75, NAD: SE/ULA/10337) .

Pedigree Chart for Jan Ersson

No. 1 on this chart is the same as no. 12 on chart no. 1

8 Johan Ersson
b. 12 May 1712 cont. 29
p. Rishöjden, Karlskoga, Örebro, Sweden
m.
p.
d. 6 Mar 1773
p. Norra Granbergsdalshyttetorp, Karlskoga~

4 Nils Jansson
b. 12 May 1750
p. Granbergsdalshyttetorp, Karlskoga, Öre~
m. 26 Dec 1774
p. Grythyttan, Örebro, Sweden
d. 28 May 1828
p. Finnhyttan, Västgötetorp, Grythyttan, Ör~

9 Sara Hansdotter
b. Abt 1711
p.
d. 9 Mar 1758
p. Granbergsdalshyttetorp, Karlskoga, Öre~

2 Erik Nilsson
b. 6 Mar 1776
p. Västgötetorp, Grythyttan, Örebro, Sweden
m. 11 Jan 1807
p.
d. 1 Apr 1829
p. Spångtorp, Grythyttan, Örebro, Sweden

10 Nils Jansson
b. 14 Jun 1710 cont. 30
p. Grythyttan, Örebro, Sweden
m. 17 Apr 1737
p. Grythyttan, Örebro, Sweden
d.
p.

5 Maria Nilsdotter
b. 8 Sep 1746
p. Brunsjötorp, Grythyttan, Örebro, Sweden
d. 9 Jul 1821
p. Bergslund, Grythyttan, Örebro, Sweden

11 Cherstin Jansdotter
b. 1713
p. Karlskoga, Örebro, Sweden
d. 27 Oct 1783
p. Västgötetorp, Grythyttan, Örebro, Sweden

1 Jan Ersson
b. 14 Jan 1808
p. Finhyttan, Grythyttan, Örebro, Sweden
m. 26 Dec 1830
p. Hällefors, Örebro, Sweden
d. 31 May 1857
p. Skärhyttan, Nora, Örebro, Sweden
sp. Maria Helena Persdotter

12
b.
p.
m.
p.
d.
p.

6 Jonas Jonsson
b. 1745
p. Karlskoga, Örebro, Sweden
m. 13 Jun 1762
p. Kroppa, Värmland, Sweden
d. 1812
p. Långtjärnshöjden, Grythyttan, Örebro, ~

13
b.
p.
d.
p.

3 Catharina Jonasdotter
b. 16 May 1776
p. Grythyttan, Örebro, Sweden
d. 23 Apr 1852
p. Spången, Grythyttan, Örebro, Sweden

14 Johan Johansson
b.
p.
m.
p.
d.
p.

7 Christina Johansdotter
b. 1747
p. Nybygget, Kroppa, Värmland, Sweden
d. 12 Jan 1813
p. Långtjärnshöjden, Grythyttan, Örebro, ~

15 Christina Eriksdotter
b. 1715
p. Kroppa, Värmland, Sweden
d.
p.

Pedigree Chart for Johan Ersson

No. 1 on this chart is the same as no. 8 on chart no. 28

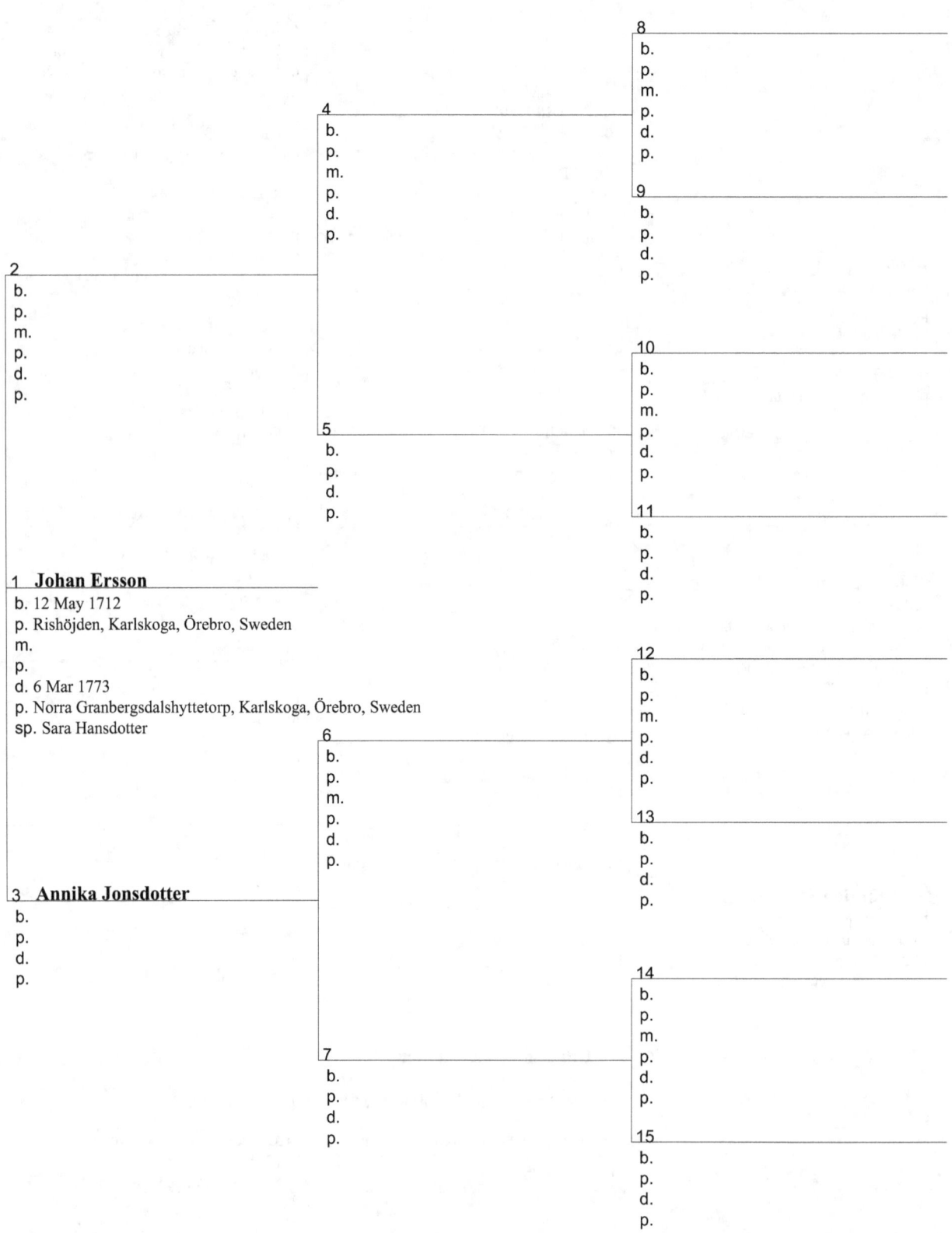

8 _____
b.
p.
m.
p.
d.
p.

4 _____
b.
p.
m.
p.
d.
p.

9 _____
b.
p.
d.
p.

2 _____
b.
p.
m.
p.
d.
p.

10 _____
b.
p.
m.
p.
d.
p.

5 _____
b.
p.
d.
p.

11 _____
b.
p.
d.
p.

1   **Johan Ersson** _____
b. 12 May 1712
p. Rishöjden, Karlskoga, Örebro, Sweden
m.
p.
d. 6 Mar 1773
p. Norra Granbergsdalshyttetorp, Karlskoga, Örebro, Sweden
sp. Sara Hansdotter

12 _____
b.
p.
m.
p.
d.
p.

6 _____
b.
p.
m.
p.
d.
p.

13 _____
b.
p.
d.
p.

3   **Annika Jonsdotter** _____
b.
p.
d.
p.

14 _____
b.
p.
m.
p.
d.
p.

7 _____
b.
p.
d.
p.

15 _____
b.
p.
d.
p.

Pedigree Chart for Nils Jansson

No. 1 on this chart is the same as no. 10 on chart no. 28

8 _____
b.
p.
m.
p.
d.
p.

4 _____
b.
p.
m.
p.
d.
p.

9 _____
b.
p.
d.
p.

2 **Johan Nilsson** _____
b.
p.
m.
p.
d.
p.

10 _____
b.
p.
m.
p.
d.
p.

5 _____
b.
p.
d.
p.

11 _____
b.
p.
d.
p.

1   **Nils Jansson** _____
b. 14 Jun 1710
p. Grythyttan, Örebro, Sweden
m. 17 Apr 1737
p. Grythyttan, Örebro, Sweden
d.
p.
sp. Cherstin Jansdotter

12 _____
b.
p.
m.
p.
d.
p.

6 _____
b.
p.
m.
p.
d.
p.

13 _____
b.
p.
d.
p.

3 **Maria Nilsdotter** _____
b.
p.
d.
p.

14 _____
b.
p.
m.
p.
d.
p.

7 _____
b.
p.
d.
p.

15 _____
b.
p.
d.
p.

Chapter 7. Ancestor Report for Maria Helena Persdotter

First Generation

1. Maria Helena Persdotter,[1] daughter of **Petter Jacobsson** and **Christina Jacobsdotter,** was born on 5 Mar 1811 in Skärhyttan, Nora, Örebro, Sweden,[2] died on 18 Mar 1887 in Skärhyttan, Nora, Örebro, Sweden[3] at age 76, and was buried on 25 Mar 1887 in Rockesholm, Nora, Örebro, Sweden. [4]

Noted events in her life were:
- Occupation: maid, 1830, Skärhyttan, Nora, Örebro, Sweden.[5]

- Resided: 1852, Koppartorp, Skärhyttan, Nora, Örebro, Sweden. [6]

- Resided: Björnbo, 1852-1871, Skärhyttan, Nora, Örebro, Sweden. [7]

Maria had a child

The child from this marriage was:
    i.   **Maja Christina Mariasdotter**[8] was born on 17 Nov 1827 in Skärhyttan, Nora, Örebro, Sweden.[9] Another name for Maja was Maja Stina Spångberg. [10] Maja married **Carl Andersson** on 11 Sep 1859.[11]

Maria next married **Jan Ersson**,[12] son of **Erik Nilsson** and **Catharina Jonasdotter,** on 26 Dec 1830 in Hällefors, Örebro, Sweden.[5]

Research Notes: Jan Ersson was a iron smelting master and land bonde (homestead owner). He employed several farmhands and iron workers. He and his descendents took Spångberg as a surname. [8]

Noted events in his life were:
- Resided: 1808-1812, Finhyttan, Grythyttan, Örebro, Sweden. [13]

- Resided: 1812-1829, Spångtorp, Grythyttan, Örebro, Sweden. [14]

---

1. Nora bergsförsamling AI:14bb (1841-1850) Image 49 / page 195 (AID: v52007.b49.s195, NAD: SE/ULA/11098) . .... Nora bergsförsamling AI:15eb (1851-1861) Image 59 / page 213 (AID: v52013.b59.s213, NAD: SE/ULA/11098) .

2. Nora bergsförsamling AI:14bb (1841-1850) Image 49 / page 195 (AID: v52007.b49.s195, NAD: SE/ULA/11098) . .... Nora bergsförsamling AI:15eb (1851-1861) Image 59 / page 213 (AID: v52013.b59.s213, NAD: SE/ULA/11098) . .... Nora bergsförsamling AI:15eb (1851-1861) Image 69 / page 223 (AID: v52013.b69.s223, NAD: SE/ULA/11098) . .... Nora bergsförsamling AI:15eb (1851-1861) Image 73 / page 227 (AID: v52013.b73.s227, NAD: SE/ULA/11098) . .... Nora bergsförsamling AI:11a (1811-1820) Image 243 / page 235 (AID: v51992.b243.s235, NAD: SE/ULA/11098) . .... Nora bergsförsamling AI:12a (1821-1829) Image 251 / page 244 (AID: v51994.b251.s244, NAD: SE/ULA/11098). .... Nora bergsförsamling AI:13b (1828-1841) Image 97 / page 92 (AID: v51997.b97.s92, NAD: SE/ULA/11098) . .... Nora bergsförsamling AI:18d (1882-1891) Image 374 / page 773 (AID: v52026.b374.s773, NAD: SE/ULA/11098) .

3. Nora bergsförsamling F:10 (1861-1894) Image 249 (AID: v53653.b249, NAD: SE/ULA/11098) . .... Nora bergsförsamling AI:18d (1882-1891) Image 374 / page 773 (AID: v52026.b374.s773, NAD: SE/ULA/11098) .

4. Nora bergsförsamling F:10 (1861-1894) Image 249 (AID: v53653.b249, NAD: SE/ULA/11098) .

5. Nora bergsförsamling EI:5 (1827-1842) Image 22 (AID: v53636.b22, NAD: SE/ULA/11098) .

6. Nora bergsförsamling AI:15eb (1851-1861) Image 59 / page 213 (AID: v52013.b59.s213, NAD: SE/ULA/11098) .

7. Nora bergsförsamling AI:16e (1861-1871) Image 289 / page 282 (AID: v52018.b289.s282, NAD: SE/ULA/11098) . .... Nora bergsförsamling AI:15eb (1851-1861) Image 73 / page 227 (AID: v52013.b73.s227, NAD: SE/ULA/11098) . .... Nora bergsförsamling AI:15eb (1851-1861) Image 69 / page 223 (AID: v52013.b69.s223, NAD: SE/ULA/11098) .

8. Nora bergsförsamling AI:14bb (1841-1850) Image 49 / page 195 (AID: v52007.b49.s195, NAD: SE/ULA/11098) .

9. Nora bergsförsamling AI:14bb (1841-1850) Image 49 / page 195 (AID: v52007.b49.s195, NAD: SE/ULA/11098) . .... Nora bergsförsamling AI:13b (1828-1841) Image 97 / page 92 (AID: v51997.b97.s92, NAD: SE/ULA/11098) . .... Nora bergsförsamling C:6 (1824-1827) Image 91 / page 86 (AID: v53621.b91.s86, NAD: SE/ULA/11098) . .... Nora bergsförsamling AI:17d (1872-1881) Image 322 / page 668 (AID: v52022.b322.s668, NAD: SE/ULA/11098) .

10. Nora bergsförsamling AI:13b (1828-1841) Image 97 / page 92 (AID: v51997.b97.s92, NAD: SE/ULA/11098) .

11. Nora bergsförsamling AI:15eb (1851-1861) Image 87 / page 240 (AID: v52013.b87.s240, NAD: SE/ULA/11098) .

12. Grythyttan AIa:14b (1830-1840) Image 168 / page 446 (AID: v51206.b168.s446, NAD: SE/ULA/10337) .

13. Grythyttan AIa:11b (1809-1812) Image 97 / page 89 (AID: v51200.b97.s89, NAD: SE/ULA/10337) . .... (Grythyttan AIa:9 (1798-1808) Image 198 / page 191 (AID: v51197.b198.s191, NAD: SE/ULA/10337)).

14. Grythyttan AIa:12b (1812-1820) Image 120 / page 110 (AID: v51202.b120.s110, NAD: SE/ULA/10337) . .... Grythyttan AIa:11b (1809-1812) Image 97 / page 89 (AID: v51200.b97.s89, NAD: SE/ULA/10337) . .... Grythyttan AIa:13b (1820-1830) Image 174 / page 169 (AID: v51204.b174.s169, NAD: SE/ULA/10337).

Ancestor Report for Maria Helena Persdotter

- Occupation: blast furnace worker, Bef 1830, Grythyttan, Örebro, Sweden.[15]

- Moved to: 26 Dec 1831, Skärhyttan, Nora, Örebro, Sweden.[16] Leaves his mother Catrina Jonsdotter and siblings. He took over his father-in-law's homestead in 1831 (his father-in-law had no sons).

- Status: land bonde (farm owner), After 1831, Skärhyttan, Nora, Örebro, Sweden.[17]

- Occupation: hyttarbetare (smelter), 1834, Skärhyttan, Nora, Örebro, Sweden.[18]

- Occupation: masmästare (smelting master), 1836, Skärhyttan, Nora, Örebro, Sweden.[19]

- Status: topare (tenant farmer), Abt 1834-1841, Skärhyttan, Nora, Örebro, Sweden.[20]

- Name change: to Spångberg, Cir 1838.[20] He was born Jan Ersson. He used the surname Spångberg in the the Nora parish baptism for his child born in 1839 but not in 1836 or earlier. In the communion book the word Spångberg was written in over his name sometime between 1831 and 1839. The name Spångberg may have alluded to his childhood homestead "Spångtorp" in Grythyttan parish. Jan Spångberg continued to use his patronym "Ersson" in most records, i.e., "Jon Ersson Spångberg," and that is how it appears in his death record. His children use Spångberg sometimes with their patronym Jansson or Jansdotter.

- Status: land bonde (farm owner), 1841-1851, Skärhyttan, Nora, Örebro, Sweden.[21]

- Resided: 1852, Koppartorp, Skärhyttan, Nora, Örebro, Sweden.[22]

- Resided: 1852-1857, Björnbo, Skärhyttan, Nora, Örebro, Sweden.[23]

Children from this marriage were:

    i.   **Jan Gustaf Jansson**[24] was born on 17 Nov 1832 in Skärhyttan, Nora, Örebro, Sweden.[25] Another name for Jan was Jan Gustaf Spångberg. Jan married **Maria Charlina Andersson** on 25 Nov 1855 in Hällefors, Örebro, Sweden.[26]

    ii.   **Eric Wilhelm Jansson** was born on 1 Apr 1834 in Skärhyttan, Nora, Örebro, Sweden.[27] Another name for Eric was Erich Wilhelm Spångberg.

    iii.   **Erik August Jansson**[24] was born on 14 May 1836 in Skärhyttan, Nora, Örebro, Sweden[28] and died after 1900 in USA.[29] Other names for Erik were Erick Erikson and Erik August Spångberg. Erik married **Christina Ersdotter** on 12 Apr 1857.[30]

    iv.   **Pehr Axel Jansson Spångberg**[24] was born on 9 May 1839 in Skärhyttan, Nora, Örebro, Sweden[31] and died on 12 Mar 1868 in Ås, Grythyttan, Örebro, Sweden[32] at age 28. Another name for Pehr was Pehr Axel

15. *Nora bergsförsamling EI:5 (1827-1842) Image 22 (AID: v53636.b22, NAD: SE/ULA/11098)* .

16. *Grythyttan AIa:14b (1830-1840) Image 168 / page 446 (AID: v51206.b168.s446, NAD: SE/ULA/10337) . .... Nora bergsförsamling AI:14bb (1841-1850) Image 49 / page 195 (AID: v52007.b49.s195, NAD: SE/ULA/11098)* .

17. *Nora bergsförsamling AI:13b (1828-1841) Image 97 / page 92 (AID: v51997.b97.s92, NAD: SE/ULA/11098)* .

18. *Nora bergsförsamling C:7 (1828-1842) Image 102 (AID: v53622.b102, NAD: SE/ULA/11098)* .

19. *Nora bergsförsamling C:7 (1828-1842) Image 134 (AID: v53622.b134, NAD: SE/ULA/11098)* .

20. *Nora bergsförsamling C:7 (1828-1842) Image 212 (AID: v53622.b212, NAD: SE/ULA/11098)* .

21. *Nora bergsförsamling C:8b (1842-1858) Image 17 (AID: v53624.b17, NAD: SE/ULA/11098) . .... Nora bergsförsamling AI:14bb (1841-1850) Image 49 / page 195 (AID: v52007.b49.s195, NAD: SE/ULA/11098)* .

22. *Nora bergsförsamling AI:15eb (1851-1861) Image 59 / page 213 (AID: v52013.b59.s213, NAD: SE/ULA/11098)* .

23. *Nora bergsförsamling AI:16e (1861-1871) Image 289 / page 282 (AID: v52018.b289.s282, NAD: SE/ULA/11098) . .... Nora bergsförsamling AI:15eb (1851-1861) Image 73 / page 227 (AID: v52013.b73.s227, NAD: SE/ULA/11098) . .... Nora bergsförsamling AI:15eb (1851-1861) Image 69 / page 223 (AID: v52013.b69.s223, NAD: SE/ULA/11098)* .

24. *Nora bergsförsamling AI:14bb (1841-1850) Image 49 / page 195 (AID: v52007.b49.s195, NAD: SE/ULA/11098)* .

25. *Nora bergsförsamling AI:14bb (1841-1850) Image 49 / page 195 (AID: v52007.b49.s195, NAD: SE/ULA/11098) . .... Nora bergsförsamling AI:15eb (1851-1861) Image 59 / page 213 (AID: v52013.b59.s213, NAD: SE/ULA/11098) . .... Nora bergsförsamling AI:13b (1828-1841) Image 97 / page 92 (AID: v51997.b97.s92, NAD: SE/ULA/11098) . .... Nora bergsförsamling AI:19b (1892-1901) Image 282 / page 269 (AID: v52028.b282.s269, NAD: SE/ULA/11098)* .

26. *Nora bergsförsamling AI:18c (1882-1891) Image 238 / page 224 (AID: v52025.b238.s224, NAD: SE/ULA/11098)* .

27. *Nora bergsförsamling AI:13b (1828-1841) Image 97 / page 92 (AID: v51997.b97.s92, NAD: SE/ULA/11098) . .... Nora bergsförsamling C:7 (1828-1842) Image 102 (AID: v53622.b102, NAD: SE/ULA/11098)* .

28. *Nora bergsförsamling AI:14bb (1841-1850) Image 49 / page 195 (AID: v52007.b49.s195, NAD: SE/ULA/11098) . .... Nora bergsförsamling AI:15eb (1851-1861) Image 59 / page 213 (AID: v52013.b59.s213, NAD: SE/ULA/11098) . .... Nora bergsförsamling AI:13b (1828-1841) Image 97 / page 92 (AID: v51997.b97.s92, NAD: SE/ULA/11098) . .... Nora bergsförsamling C:7 (1828-1842) Image 134 (AID: v53622.b134, NAD: SE/ULA/11098)* .

29. *1900 US Census.*

30. *Nora bergsförsamling AI:15eb (1851-1861) Image 94 / page 247 (AID: v52013.b94.s247, NAD: SE/ULA/11098)* .

31. *Nora bergsförsamling AI:14bb (1841-1850) Image 49 / page 195 (AID: v52007.b49.s195, NAD: SE/ULA/11098) . .... Nora*

Spångberg. Pehr married **Carolina Andersdotter** on 25 Mar 1862 in Hällefors, Örebro, Sweden. [33]

 v. **Carolina Jansdotter Spångberg**[34] was born on 2 Nov 1841 in Skärhyttan, Nora, Örebro, Sweden[35] and died on 19 Feb 1854 in Skärhyttan, Nora, Örebro, Sweden[36] at age 12. Another name for Carolina was Carolina Spångberg.

 vi. **Carl Fredrik Jansson Spångberg**[34] was born on 19 Feb 1844 in Skärhyttan, Nora, Örebro, Sweden[37] and died on 31 Jul 1917 in Newberry, Luce, Michigan[38] at age 73. Another name for Carl was Carl Fredrik Spångberg. Carl married **Christina Elisabet Andersdotter,** daughter of **Anders Jansson** and **Anna Helena Persdotter,** on 21 Jun 1870 in Hällefors, Örebro, Sweden. [39]

 vii. **Anders Albert Jansson Spångberg**[40] was born on 8 Aug 1847 in Skärhyttan, Nora, Örebro, Sweden[41] and died on 4 Jun 1851[42] at age 3. Another name for Anders was Anders Albert Spångberg.

---

bergsförsamling AI:15eb (1851-1861) Image 59 / page 213 (AID: v52013.b59.s213, NAD: SE/ULA/11098) . .... Nora bergsförsamling AI:13b (1828-1841) Image 97 / page 92 (AID: v51997.b97.s92, NAD: SE/ULA/11098) . .... Nora bergsförsamling C:7 (1828-1842) Image 176 (AID: v53622.b176, NAD: SE/ULA/11098) .

32. Grythyttan F:3 (1840-1871) Image 264 (AID: v53161.b264, NAD: SE/ULA/10337) .

33. Nora bergsförsamling AI:16e (1861-1871) Image 289 / page 282 (AID: v52018.b289.s282, NAD: SE/ULA/11098) .

34. Nora bergsförsamling AI:14bb (1841-1850) Image 49 / page 195 (AID: v52007.b49.s195, NAD: SE/ULA/11098) .

35. Nora bergsförsamling AI:14bb (1841-1850) Image 49 / page 195 (AID: v52007.b49.s195, NAD: SE/ULA/11098) . .... Nora bergsförsamling AI:15eb (1851-1861) Image 59 / page 213 (AID: v52013.b59.s213, NAD: SE/ULA/11098) . .... Nora bergsförsamling C:7 (1828-1842) Image 212 (AID: v53622.b212, NAD: SE/ULA/11098) .

36. Nora bergsförsamling AI:15eb (1851-1861) Image 69 / page 223 (AID: v52013.b69.s223, NAD: SE/ULA/11098) .

37. Arkion 1890. .... August Spångberg, Stream of Time (1966). .... Duane & Jacquelyn Hargis, Headstones at Forest Home Cemetery, Newberry, Luce County, Michigan (http://files.usgwarchives.net/mi/luce/cemeteries/f62302.txt). .... Nora bergsförsamling AI:14bb (1841-1850) Image 49 / page 195 (AID: v52007.b49.s195, NAD: SE/ULA/11098) . .... Nora bergsförsamling AI:15eb (1851-1861) Image 59 / page 213 (AID: v52013.b59.s213, NAD: SE/ULA/11098) . .... Nora bergsförsamling AI:18d (1882-1891) Image 364 / page 762 (AID: v52026.b364.s762, NAD: SE/ULA/11098) . .... Nora bergsförsamling C:9b (1843-1856) Image 19 (AID: v53626.b19, NAD: SE/ULA/11098) . .... Nora bergsförsamling C:8b (1842-1858) Image 17 (AID: v53624.b17, NAD: SE/ULA/11098) .

38. Duane & Jacquelyn Hargis, Headstones at Forest Home Cemetery, Newberry, Luce County, Michigan (http://files.usgwarchives.net/mi/luce/cemeteries/f62302.txt).

39. Nora bergsförsamling AI:18d (1882-1891) Image 364 / page 762 (AID: v52026.b364.s762, NAD: SE/ULA/11098) .

40. Nora bergsförsamling AI:14bb (1841-1850) Image 49 / page 195 (AID: v52007.b49.s195, NAD: SE/ULA/11098) . .... Nora bergsförsamling AI:15eb (1851-1861) Image 59 / page 213 (AID: v52013.b59.s213, NAD: SE/ULA/11098) .

41. Nora bergsförsamling AI:14bb (1841-1850) Image 49 / page 195 (AID: v52007.b49.s195, NAD: SE/ULA/11098) . .... Nora bergsförsamling AI:15eb (1851-1861) Image 59 / page 213 (AID: v52013.b59.s213, NAD: SE/ULA/11098) . .... Nora bergsförsamling C:8b (1842-1858) Image 36 (AID: v53624.b36, NAD: SE/ULA/11098) .

42. Nora bergsförsamling AI:15eb (1851-1861) Image 59 / page 213 (AID: v52013.b59.s213, NAD: SE/ULA/11098) .

Second Generation

2. Petter Jacobsson,[1] son of **Jacob Nilsson** and **Christina Andersdotter,** was born on 18 Feb 1780 in Brötorp, Nora, Örebro, Sweden[2] and died on 4 Jan 1854 in Skärhyttan, Nora, Örebro, Sweden[3] at age 73.

Noted events in his life were:
- Status: hemmansbrukaren (user of a homestead), 1802, Skärhyttan, Nora, Örebro, Sweden. [4]
- Status: land bonde (farm owner), 1821, Skärhyttan, Nora, Örebro, Sweden. [5]
- Resided: with his son-in-law's family, After 1851, Skärhyttan, Nora, Örebro, Sweden. [6]

Petter married **Christina Jacobsdotter**[1] on 4 Jun 1802 in Hällefors, Örebro, Sweden. [7]

Children from this marriage were:
    i.   **Christina Persdotter** was born on 27 Feb 1809 in Skärhyttan, Nora, Örebro, Sweden[8] and died in 1825[5] at age 16.

1   ii.   **Maria Helena Persdotter**.[9] Maria had a child. Maria married **Jan Ersson,**[10] son of **Erik Nilsson** and **Catharina Jonasdotter,** on 26 Dec 1830 in Hällefors, Örebro, Sweden. [11]

    iii.   **Brita Persdotter** was born on 10 Nov 1812 in Skärhyttan, Nora, Örebro, Sweden[12] and died in 1812.[12]

    iv.   **Brita Cathrina Persdotter** was born on 5 Apr 1818 in Skärhyttan, Nora, Örebro, Sweden. [13]

3. Christina Jacobsdotter,[1] daughter of **Jakob Olsson** and **Kristina Jansdotter,** was born on 28 Sep 1774 in Grekskog, Nora, Örebro, Sweden[14] and died on 23 Nov 1859 in Skärhyttan, Nora, Örebro, Sweden[15] at age 85.

Christina married **Petter Jacobsson**[1] on 4 Jun 1802 in Hällefors, Örebro, Sweden. [7]

1. Nora bergsförsamling AI:14bb (1841-1850) Image 49 / page 195 (AID: v52007.b49.s195, NAD: SE/ULA/11098) .

2. Nora bergsförsamling AI:14bb (1841-1850) Image 49 / page 195 (AID: v52007.b49.s195, NAD: SE/ULA/11098) . .... Nora bergsförsamling AI:8a (1775-1784) Image 244 / page 237 (AID: v51986.b244.s237, NAD: SE/ULA/11098) . .... Nora bergsförsamling AI:7a (1771-1790) Image 341 / page 157 (AID: v51984.b341.s157, NAD: SE/ULA/11098) . .... Nora bergsförsamling C:3 (1770-1788) Image 177 (AID: v53618.b177, NAD: SE/ULA/11098). .... Nora bergsförsamling AI:11a (1811-1820) Image 243 / page 235 (AID: v51992.b243.s235, NAD: SE/ULA/11098). .... Nora bergsförsamling AI:12a (1821-1829) Image 251 / page 244 (AID: v51994.b251.s244, NAD: SE/ULA/11098) . .... Nora bergsförsamling AI:13b (1828-1841) Image 97 / page 92 (AID: v51997.b97.s92, NAD: SE/ULA/11098) . .... Nora bergsförsamling AI:15eb (1851-1861) Image 59 / page 213 (AID: v52013.b59.s213, NAD: SE/ULA/11098) .

3. Nora bergsförsamling F:8b (1843-1859) Image 58 (AID: v53651.b58, NAD: SE/ULA/11098) .

4. Nora bergsförsamling EI:3 (1775-1804) Image 130 (AID: v53634.b130, NAD: SE/ULA/11098) .

5. Nora bergsförsamling AI:12a (1821-1829) Image 251 / page 244 (AID: v51994.b251.s244, NAD: SE/ULA/11098) .

6. Nora bergsförsamling AI:15eb (1851-1861) Image 59 / page 213 (AID: v52013.b59.s213, NAD: SE/ULA/11098) .

7. Nora bergsförsamling AI:14bb (1841-1850) Image 49 / page 195 (AID: v52007.b49.s195, NAD: SE/ULA/11098) . .... Nora bergsförsamling EI:3 (1775-1804) Image 130 (AID: v53634.b130, NAD: SE/ULA/11098) .

8. Nora bergsförsamling AI:11a (1811-1820) Image 243 / page 235 (AID: v51992.b243.s235, NAD: SE/ULA/11098) . .... Nora bergsförsamling AI:12a (1821-1829) Image 251 / page 244 (AID: v51994.b251.s244, NAD: SE/ULA/11098) .

9. Nora bergsförsamling AI:14bb (1841-1850) Image 49 / page 195 (AID: v52007.b49.s195, NAD: SE/ULA/11098) . .... Nora bergsförsamling AI:15eb (1851-1861) Image 59 / page 213 (AID: v52013.b59.s213, NAD: SE/ULA/11098) .

10. Grythyttan AIa:14b (1830-1840) Image 168 / page 446 (AID: v51206.b168.s446, NAD: SE/ULA/10337) .

11. Nora bergsförsamling EI:5 (1827-1842) Image 22 (AID: v53636.b22, NAD: SE/ULA/11098) .

12. Nora bergsförsamling AI:11a (1811-1820) Image 243 / page 235 (AID: v51992.b243.s235, NAD: SE/ULA/11098) .

13. Nora bergsförsamling AI:11a (1811-1820) Image 243 / page 235 (AID: v51992.b243.s235, NAD: SE/ULA/11098) . .... Nora bergsförsamling AI:12a (1821-1829) Image 251 / page 244 (AID: v51994.b251.s244, NAD: SE/ULA/11098) . .... Nora bergsförsamling AI:13b (1828-1841) Image 97 / page 92 (AID: v51997.b97.s92, NAD: SE/ULA/11098) .

14. Nora bergsförsamling AI:14bb (1841-1850) Image 49 / page 195 (AID: v52007.b49.s195, NAD: SE/ULA/11098) . .... Nora bergsförsamling C:3 (1770-1788) Image 73 (AID: v53618.b73, NAD: SE/ULA/11098) . .... Nora bergsförsamling AI:8a (1775-1784) Image 251 / page 244 (AID: v51986.b251.s244, NAD: SE/ULA/11098) . .... Nora bergsförsamling AI:11a (1811-1820) Image 243 / page 235 (AID: v51992.b243.s235, NAD: SE/ULA/11098) . .... Nora bergsförsamling AI:12a (1821-1829) Image 251 / page 244 (AID: v51994.b251.s244, NAD: SE/ULA/11098) . .... Nora bergsförsamling AI:13b (1828-1841) Image 97 / page 92 (AID: v51997.b97.s92, NAD: SE/ULA/11098) .

15. Nora bergsförsamling AI:15eb (1851-1861) Image 69 / page 223 (AID: v52013.b69.s223, NAD: SE/ULA/11098) . .... Nora bergsförsamling F:8b (1843-1859) Image 89 (AID: v53651.b89, NAD: SE/ULA/11098) .

Ancestor Report for Maria Helena Persdotter

Third Generation

4. Jacob Nilsson,[1] son of **Nils Nilsson** and **Karin Larsdotter,** was born on 2 Jan 1749 in Brötorp, Nora, Örebro, Sweden[2] and died on 15 Apr 1807 in Skärhyttan, Nora, Örebro, Sweden[4] at age 58.

Noted events in his life were:

• Resided: 1776, Höjden, Nora, Örebro, Sweden.[5]

• Occupation: miner, Hällefors, Örebro, Sweden.[6]

• Occupation: tenant ("torpare"), 1780, Brötorp, Nora, Örebro, Sweden.[1]

Jacob married **Christina Andersdotter**[1] on 6 Oct 1776 in Hällefors, Örebro, Sweden.[7]

Children from this marriage were:

	i.	**Anders Jacobsson** was born on 14 Oct 1777 in Brötorp, Nora, Örebro, Sweden.[8]
2	ii.	**Petter Jacobsson.**[9] Petter married **Christina Jacobsdotter,**[9] daughter of **Jakob Olsson** and **Kristina Jansdotter,** on 4 Jun 1802 in Hällefors, Örebro, Sweden.[10]
	iii.	**Eric Jacobsson** was born on 15 Jul 1782.[11]
	iv.	**Nils Jacobsson** was born on 15 Oct 1785 in Brötorp, Nora, Örebro, Sweden[12] and died on 6 Oct 1796 in Skärhyttan ägor, Nora, Örebro, Sweden[13] at age 10.

5. Christina Andersdotter,[1] daughter of **Anders Olsson** and **Margareta Hindersdotter,** was born on 7 Oct 1748 in Botiern, Resta, Ramsberg, Örebro, Sweden,[14] was christened on 9 Oct 1748,[15] and died on 10 Jan 1801 in Skärhyttan, Nora, Örebro, Sweden[16] at age 52.

---

1. Nora bergsförsamling C:3 (1770-1788) Image 177 (AID: v53618.b177, NAD: SE/ULA/11098) .

2. Nora bergsförsamling AI:8a (1775-1784) Image 244 / page 237 (AID: v51986.b244.s237, NAD: SE/ULA/11098) . .... Nora bergsförsamling AI:6b (1761-1770) Image 232 / page 226 (AID: v51983.b232.s226, NAD: SE/ULA/11098) . .... Nora bergsförsamling C:1 (1737-1756) Image 152 / page 299 (AID: v53616.b152.s299, NAD: SE/ULA/11098) . .... Nora bergsförsamling AI:7a (1771-1790) Image 127 / page 121 (AID: v51984.b127.s121, NAD: SE/ULA/11098) . .... Nora bergsförsamling AI:5b (1751-1760) Image 74 / page 65 (AID: v51981.b74.s65, NAD: SE/ULA/11098) .

3. Nora bergsförsamling AI:7a (1771-1790) Image 341 / page 157 (AID: v51984.b341.s157, NAD: SE/ULA/11098) .

4. Nora bergsförsamling F:4 (1795-1810) Image 180 / page 176 (AID: v53645.b180.s176, NAD: SE/ULA/11098) .

5. Nora bergsförsamling EI:3 (1775-1804) Image 11 / page 16 (AID: v53634.b11.s16, NAD: SE/ULA/11098) .

6. Nora bergsförsamling F:4 (1795-1810) Image 180 / page 176 (AID: v53645.b180.s176, NAD: SE/ULA/11098) . .... Nora bergsförsamling EI:3 (1775-1804) Image 11 / page 16 (AID: v53634.b11.s16, NAD: SE/ULA/11098) .

7. Nora bergsförsamling AI:8a (1775-1784) Image 244 / page 237 (AID: v51986.b244.s237, NAD: SE/ULA/11098) . .... Nora bergsförsamling EI:3 (1775-1804) Image 11 / page 16 (AID: v53634.b11.s16, NAD: SE/ULA/11098) .

8. Nora bergsförsamling AI:8a (1775-1784) Image 244 / page 237 (AID: v51986.b244.s237, NAD: SE/ULA/11098) . .... Nora bergsförsamling C:3 (1770-1788) Image 130 (AID: v53618.b130, NAD: SE/ULA/11098) . .... Nora bergsförsamling AI:7a (1771-1790) Image 341 / page 157 (AID: v51984.b341.s157, NAD: SE/ULA/11098) .

9. Nora bergsförsamling AI:14bb (1841-1850) Image 49 / page 195 (AID: v52007.b49.s195, NAD: SE/ULA/11098) .

10. Nora bergsförsamling AI:14bb (1841-1850) Image 49 / page 195 (AID: v52007.b49.s195, NAD: SE/ULA/11098) . .... Nora bergsförsamling EI:3 (1775-1804) Image 130 (AID: v53634.b130, NAD: SE/ULA/11098) .

11. Nora bergsförsamling AI:8a (1775-1784) Image 244 / page 237 (AID: v51986.b244.s237, NAD: SE/ULA/11098) . .... Nora bergsförsamling AI:7a (1771-1790) Image 341 / page 157 (AID: v51984.b341.s157, NAD: SE/ULA/11098) .

12. Nora bergsförsamling AI:7a (1771-1790) Image 341 / page 157 (AID: v51984.b341.s157, NAD: SE/ULA/11098) . .... Nora bergsförsamling C:3 (1770-1788) Image 273 (AID: v53618.b273, NAD: SE/ULA/11098) .

13. Nora bergsförsamling F:4 (1795-1810) Image 31 / page 27 (AID: v53645.b31.s27, NAD: SE/ULA/11098) .

14. Nora bergsförsamling AI:8a (1775-1784) Image 244 / page 237 (AID: v51986.b244.s237, NAD: SE/ULA/11098) . .... Ramsberg C:3 (1726-1749) Image 174 (AID: v53709.b174, NAD: SE/ULA/11259) . .... Ramsberg AI:7 (1750-1772) Image 42 / page 34 (AID: v52178.b42.s34, NAD: SE/ULA/11259) . .... Nora bergsförsamling AI:7a (1771-1790) Image 341 / page 157 (AID: v51984.b341.s157, NAD: SE/ULA/11098).

15. Ramsberg C:3 (1726-1749) Image 174 (AID: v53709.b174, NAD: SE/ULA/11259) .

16. Nora bergsförsamling F:4 (1795-1810) Image 95 / page 91 (AID: v53645.b95.s91, NAD: SE/ULA/11098) .

17. Nora bergsförsamling AI:8a (1775-1784) Image 244 / page 237 (AID: v51986.b244.s237, NAD: SE/ULA/11098) . .... Ramsberg B:1 (1750-1777) Image 89 (AID: v53702.b89, NAD: SE/ULA/11259) .

Ancestor Report for Maria Helena Persdotter

Noted events in her life were:
• Moved from: Ramsberg, 1771, Näsby, Örebro, Sweden.[17] Possibly moved Sept. 1772.

Christina married **Jacob Nilsson**[18] on 6 Oct 1776 in Hällefors, Örebro, Sweden.[19]

6. Jakob Olsson, son of **Olof Olsson** and **Christina Johansdotter,** was born on 7 Sep 1750 in Skärhyttan, Nora, Örebro, Sweden[20] and died on 30 Jan 1807 in Skärhyttan, Nora, Örebro, Sweden[21] at age 56.

Noted events in his life were:
• Resided: Skärhyttan, Nora, Örebro, Sweden.[22]

• Occupation: hemmansbrukare (farmer using homestead).

Jakob married **Kristina Jansdotter**[23] on 2 Jul 1771 in Grythyttan, Örebro, Sweden.[24]

Children from this marriage were:
	i.	**Olof Jakobsson**[25] was born on 4 Jan 1772 in Grekskog, Nora, Örebro, Sweden[26] and died in 1800 in Hällefors, Örebro, Sweden[27] at age 28. Olof married **Catharina Lundsdotter** on 30 Aug 1798.[27]
3	ii.	**Christina Jacobsdotter.**[28] Christina married **Petter Jacobsson,**[28] son of **Jacob Nilsson** and **Christina Andersdotter,** on 4 Jun 1802 in Hällefors, Örebro, Sweden.[29]
	iii.	**Erik Jakobsson**[25] was born on 3 Dec 1775 in Grekskog, Nora, Örebro, Sweden.[30]
	iv.	**Johan Jakobsson**[25] was born on 25 May 1777 in Grekskog, Nora, Örebro, Sweden.[31]
	v.	**Lars Jakobsson**[25] was born on 18 Sep 1778 in Grekskog, Nora, Örebro, Sweden[32] and died about 1799[33] about age 21.
	vi.	**Nils Jakobsson**[25] was born on 2 Apr 1780 in Grekskog, Nora, Örebro, Sweden.[32] Nils married **Helena Jansdotter** on 20 Jun 1807.[34]
	vii.	**Jakob Jakobsson**[25] was born on 4 Oct 1781 in Grekskog, Nora, Örebro, Sweden.[35]

---

18. *Nora bergsförsamling C:3 (1770-1788) Image 177 (AID: v53618.b177, NAD: SE/ULA/11098) .*

19. *Nora bergsförsamling AI:8a (1775-1784) Image 244 / page 237 (AID: v51986.b244.s237, NAD: SE/ULA/11098) . .... Nora bergsförsamling EI:3 (1775-1804) Image 11 / page 16 (AID: v53634.b11.s16, NAD: SE/ULA/11098) .*

20. *Nora bergsförsamling C:1 (1737-1756) Image 168 / page 331 (AID: v53616.b168.s331, NAD: SE/ULA/11098) . .... Nora bergsförsamling AI:5b (1751-1760) Image 71 / page 62 (AID: v51981.b71.s62, NAD: SE/ULA/11098) . .... Nora bergsförsamling AI:5b (1751-1760) Image 188 / page 178 (AID: v51981.b188.s178, NAD: SE/ULA/11098) . .... Nora bergsförsamling AI:6b (1761-1770) Image 81 / page 74 (AID: v51983.b81.s74, NAD: SE/ULA/11098) . .... Nora bergsförsamling AI:6b (1761-1770) Image 226 / page 220 (AID: v51983.b226.s220, NAD: SE/ULA/11098) . .... Nora bergsförsamling AI:7a (1771-1790) Image 120 / page 114 (AID: v51984.b120.s114, NAD: SE/ULA/11098) . .... Nora bergsförsamling AI:4b (1743-1752) Image 184 / page 178 (AID: v51979.b184.s178, NAD: SE/ULA/11098) .*

21. *Nora bergsförsamling F:4 (1795-1810) Image 177 / page 173 (AID: v53645.b177.s173, NAD: SE/ULA/11098) . .... Nora bergsförsamling AI:10b (1801-1810) Image 227 / page 221 (AID: v51991.b227.s221, NAD: SE/ULA/11098) .*

22. *Nora bergsförsamling AI:5b (1751-1760) Image 71 / page 62 (AID: v51981.b71.s62, NAD: SE/ULA/11098) . .... Nora bergsförsamling AI:5b (1751-1760) Image 188 / page 178 (AID: v51981.b188.s178, NAD: SE/ULA/11098) .*

23. *Grythyttan AIa:5 (1771-1776) Image 114 / page 106 (AID: v51192.b114.s106, NAD: SE/ULA/10337) .*

24. *Grythyttan CI:5 (1770-1774) Image 18 / page 28 (AID: v53138.b18.s28, NAD: SE/ULA/10337) . .... Nora bergsförsamling AI:8a (1775-1784) Image 251 / page 244 (AID: v51986.b251.s244, NAD: SE/ULA/11098) . .... Nora bergsförsamling AI:7a (1771-1790) Image 120 / page 114 (AID: v51984.b120.s114, NAD: SE/ULA/11098) .*

25. *Nora bergsförsamling AI:8a (1775-1784) Image 251 / page 244 (AID: v51986.b251.s244, NAD: SE/ULA/11098) .*

26. *Nora bergsförsamling C:3 (1770-1788) Image 35 (AID: v53618.b35, NAD: SE/ULA/11098) . .... Nora bergsförsamling AI:8a (1775-1784) Image 251 / page 244 (AID: v51986.b251.s244, NAD: SE/ULA/11098) .*

27. *Nora bergsförsamling AI:9a (1791-1800) Image 251 / page 245 (AID: v51988.b251.s245, NAD: SE/ULA/11098) .*

28. *Nora bergsförsamling AI:14bb (1841-1850) Image 49 / page 195 (AID: v52007.b49.s195, NAD: SE/ULA/11098) .*

29. *Nora bergsförsamling AI:14bb (1841-1850) Image 49 / page 195 (AID: v52007.b49.s195, NAD: SE/ULA/11098) . .... Nora bergsförsamling EI:3 (1775-1804) Image 130 (AID: v53634.b130, NAD: SE/ULA/11098) .*

30. *Nora bergsförsamling AI:8a (1775-1784) Image 251 / page 244 (AID: v51986.b251.s244, NAD: SE/ULA/11098) . .... Nora bergsförsamling C:3 (1770-1788) Image 97 (AID: v53618.b97, NAD: SE/ULA/11098) .*

31. *Nora bergsförsamling C:3 (1770-1788) Image 124 (AID: v53618.b124, NAD: SE/ULA/11098) . .... Nora bergsförsamling AI:8a (1775-1784) Image 251 / page 244 (AID: v51986.b251.s244, NAD: SE/ULA/11098) .*

32. *Nora bergsförsamling C:3 (1770-1788) Image 178 (AID: v53618.b178, NAD: SE/ULA/11098) . .... Nora bergsförsamling AI:8a (1775-1784) Image 251 / page 244 (AID: v51986.b251.s244, NAD: SE/ULA/11098) .*

33. *Nora bergsförsamling AI:9a (1791-1800) Image 212 / page 206 (AID: v51988.b212.s206, NAD: SE/ULA/11098) .*

34. *Nora bergsförsamling AI:10b (1801-1810) Image 227 / page 221 (AID: v51991.b227.s221, NAD: SE/ULA/11098) .*

35. *Nora bergsförsamling C:3 (1770-1788) Image 208 (AID: v53618.b208, NAD: SE/ULA/11098) . .... Nora bergsförsamling AI:8a (1775-1784) Image 251 / page 244 (AID: v51986.b251.s244, NAD: SE/ULA/11098) .*

viii.   **Brita Jakobsdotter**[25] was born on 21 Apr 1783 in Grekskog, Nora, Örebro, Sweden.[36] Brita married **Erik Johansson** on 27 Jun 1807.[34]

ix.   **Carl Jacobsson** was born on 8 Nov 1784 in Grekskog, Nora, Örebro, Sweden.[37]

7. Kristina Jansdotter,[38] daughter of **Johan Andersson** and **Brita Andersdotter,** was born on 23 Jul 1748 in Brunshyttan, Grythyttan, Orebro, Sweden[39] and died after 1820.[40]

Death Notes: May have returned to Hjulsjö parish.

Noted events in her life were:

• Residence: Cir 1753, Löfnäs, Grythyttan, Örebro, Sweden.[41]

• Occupation: servent at Rockesholm, 1771, Grythyttan, Örebro, Sweden.[41]

• Moved to: 1771, Hällefors, Örebro, Sweden.[38]

• Resided: After 1771, Grekskog, Nora, Örebro, Sweden.[42]

• Resided: After 1791, Skärhyttan, Nora, Örebro, Sweden.[43]

Kristina married **Jakob Olsson** on 2 Jul 1771 in Grythyttan, Örebro, Sweden.[44]

37. Nora bergsförsamling C:3 (1770-1788) Image 260 (AID: v53618.b260, NAD: SE/ULA/11098) .

38. Grythyttan AIa:5 (1771-1776) Image 114 / page 106 (AID: v51192.b114.s106, NAD: SE/ULA/10337) .

39. Grythyttan AIa:5 (1771-1776) Image 114 / page 106 (AID: v51192.b114.s106, NAD: SE/ULA/10337) . .... Grythyttan CI:3 (1737-1757) Image 210 (AID: v53136.b210, NAD: SE/ULA/10337) . .... Nora bergsförsamling AI:8a (1775-1784) Image 251 / page 244 (AID: v51986.b251.s244, NAD: SE/ULA/11098) . .... Nora bergsförsamling AI:7a (1771-1790) Image 120 / page 114 (AID: v51984.b120.s114, NAD: SE/ULA/11098) . .... Nora bergsförsamling AI:10b (1801-1810) Image 227 / page 221 (AID: v51991.b227.s221, NAD: SE/ULA/11098)

40. Nora bergsförsamling AI:11a (1811-1820) Image 245 / page 237 (AID: v51992.b245.s237, NAD: SE/ULA/11098) .

41. Grythyttan CI:5 (1770-1774) Image 18 / page 28 (AID: v53138.b18.s28, NAD: SE/ULA/10337) .

42. Nora bergsförsamling AI:8a (1775-1784) Image 251 / page 244 (AID: v51986.b251.s244, NAD: SE/ULA/11098) . .... Nora bergsförsamling AI:7a (1771-1790) Image 120 / page 114 (AID: v51984.b120.s114, NAD: SE/ULA/11098) .

43. Nora bergsförsamling AI:9a (1791-1800) Image 212 / page 206 (AID: v51988.b212.s206, NAD: SE/ULA/11098) .

44. Grythyttan CI:5 (1770-1774) Image 18 / page 28 (AID: v53138.b18.s28, NAD: SE/ULA/10337) . .... Nora bergsförsamling AI:8a (1775-1784) Image 251 / page 244 (AID: v51986.b251.s244, NAD: SE/ULA/11098) . .... Nora bergsförsamling AI:7a (1771-1790) Image 120 / page 114 (AID: v51984.b120.s114, NAD: SE/ULA/11098) .

Ancestor Report for Maria Helena Persdotter

Fourth Generation

8. Nils Nilsson[1] was born in 1709[2] and died on 25 Aug 1773 in Brötorp, Nora, Örebro, Sweden[3] at age 64.

Birth Notes: Birth listed as 1713 in household book.

Research Notes: There is a laborer named Nihls at the Strada estate in 1716-17, but he would have been too old to have been Nils Nilsson. It appears that Nils was not born at Strada, even though his marriage record says he lived there.[4]

Noted events in his life were:
- Resided: Bef 1748, Stadra, Nora, Örebro, Sweden.[5]

- Occupation: rower, 1748.[5]

- Occupation: miner, Bef 1773.[6]

Nils married **Karin Larsdotter**[1] on 16 Jul 1748 in Nora stadsförs, Nora, Örebro, Sweden.[5]

Marriage Notes: Married because of his/her illness ("för sin opasslighet") at the home of ("hemma hos") "Herr Norgren". This was probably town judge ("rådmannen") Magnus Norgren, and the "illness" may have been that she was four months pregnant and they wanted a private wedding.[5]

Children from this marriage were:
4	i.	**Jacob Nilsson.**[7] Jacob married **Christina Andersdotter**,[7] daughter of **Anders Olsson** and **Margareta Hindersdotter,** on 6 Oct 1776 in Hällefors, Örebro, Sweden.[8]
	ii.	**Brita Nilsdotter**[9] was born on 13 Nov 1750 in Brötorp, Nora, Örebro, Sweden.[10] Brita married **Eric Olofsson** on 5 Aug 1775 in Hällefors, Örebro, Sweden.[11]
	iii.	**Catherina Nilsdotter**[12] was born on 30 Nov 1752 in Brötorp, Nora, Örebro, Sweden.[13]
	iv.	**Christina Nilsdotter** was born in 1755 in Brötorp, Nora, Örebro, Sweden.[14]
	v.	**Anna Nilsdotter** was born in 1757 in Brötorp, Nora, Örebro, Sweden.[1]
	vi.	**Maria Nilsdotter** was born on 12 Sep 1762 in Brötorp, Nora, Örebro, Sweden.[15]
	vii.	**Abram Nilsson**[9] was born on 23 May 1765 in Brötorp, Nora, Örebro, Sweden[16] and died in 1784[9] at age 19.

---

1. *Nora bergsförsamling AI:6b (1761-1770) Image 232 / page 226 (AID: v51983.b232.s226, NAD: SE/ULA/11098)* .
2. *Nora bergsförsamling AI:6b (1761-1770) Image 232 / page 226 (AID: v51983.b232.s226, NAD: SE/ULA/11098)* . .... *Jimmy Freijs släktforskning webpage (http://gw2.geneanet.org/jimmyfreij).* .... *Nora bergsförsamling AI:5b (1751-1760) Image 74 / page 65 (AID: v51981.b74.s65, NAD: SE/ULA/11098).*
3. *Nora bergsförsamling F:2 (1751-1774) Image 209 / page 411 (AID: v53643.b209.s411, NAD: SE/ULA/11098)* . .... *Jimmy Freijs släktforskning webpage (http://gw2.geneanet.org/jimmyfreij).*
4. *Nora bergsförsamling AI:1a (1703-1717) Image 225 / page 220 (AID: v51972.b225.s220, NAD: SE/ULA/11098)* .
5. *Nora bergsförsamling EI:1 (1700-1750) Image 126 / page 244 (AID: v53632.b126.s244, NAD: SE/ULA/11098)* .
6. *Nora bergsförsamling F:2 (1751-1774) Image 209 / page 411 (AID: v53643.b209.s411, NAD: SE/ULA/11098)* .
7. *Nora bergsförsamling C:3 (1770-1788) Image 177 (AID: v53618.b177, NAD: SE/ULA/11098)* .
8. *Nora bergsförsamling AI:8a (1775-1784) Image 244 / page 237 (AID: v51986.b244.s237, NAD: SE/ULA/11098)* . .... *Nora bergsförsamling EI:3 (1775-1804) Image 11 / page 16 (AID: v53634.b11.s16, NAD: SE/ULA/11098)* .
9. *Nora bergsförsamling AI:8a (1775-1784) Image 244 / page 237 (AID: v51986.b244.s237, NAD: SE/ULA/11098)* .
10. *Nora bergsförsamling AI:8a (1775-1784) Image 244 / page 237 (AID: v51986.b244.s237, NAD: SE/ULA/11098)* . .... *Nora bergsförsamling C:1 (1737-1756) Image 171 / page 337 (AID: v53616.b171.s337, NAD: SE/ULA/11098)* . .... *Nora bergsförsamling AI:5b (1751-1760) Image 74 / page 65 (AID: v51981.b74.s65, NAD: SE/ULA/11098)* .
11. *Nora bergsförsamling AI:8a (1775-1784) Image 231 / page 224 (AID: v51986.b231.s224, NAD: SE/ULA/11098)* . .... *Nora bergsförsamling EI:3 (1775-1804) Image 8 / page 10 (AID: v53634.b8.s10, NAD: SE/ULA/11098)* .
12. *Jimmy Freijs släktforskning webpage (http://gw2.geneanet.org/jimmyfreij).*
13. *Nora bergsförsamling C:1 (1737-1756) Image 199 / page 393 (AID: v53616.b199.s393, NAD: SE/ULA/11098)* . .... *Nora bergsförsamling AI:5b (1751-1760) Image 74 / page 65 (AID: v51981.b74.s65, NAD: SE/ULA/11098)* .
14. *Nora bergsförsamling AI:7a (1771-1790) Image 127 / page 121 (AID: v51984.b127.s121, NAD: SE/ULA/11098)* .
15. *Nora bergsförsamling C:2 (1756-1770) Image 111 / page 215 (AID: v53617.b111.s215, NAD: SE/ULA/11098)* .
16. *Nora bergsförsamling AI:8a (1775-1784) Image 244 / page 237 (AID: v51986.b244.s237, NAD: SE/ULA/11098)* . .... *Nora bergsförsamling C:2 (1756-1770) Image 157 / page 307 (AID: v53617.b157.s307, NAD: SE/ULA/11098)* . .... *Jimmy Freijs släktforskning webpage (http://gw2.geneanet.org/jimmyfreij).*

viii.   **Isak Nilsson**[12] was born on 23 May 1765 in Brötorp, Nora, Örebro, Sweden. [17]

9. Karin Larsdotter,[18] daughter of **Lars Persson** and **Brita Olofsdotter,** was born in 1724 in Brötorp, Nora, Örebro, Sweden[19] and died on 14 Jul 1773 in Brötorp, Nora, Örebro, Sweden [20] at age 49.

Noted events in her life were:
• Occupation: maid, Bef 1748. [21]

Karin married **Nils Nilsson**[18] on 16 Jul 1748 in Nora stadsförs, Nora, Örebro, Sweden. [21]

10. Anders Olsson, son of **Olof Hansson** and **Brita Andersdotter,** was born on 2 Dec 1719 in Resta, Ramsberg, Örebro, Sweden,[22] was christened on 6 Dec 1719,[23] and died in 1770 in Botiern, Resta, Ramsberg, Örebro, Sweden [24] at age 51.

Anders married **Margareta Hindersdotter** on 9 Sep 1739 in Ramsberg, Örebro, Sweden. [24]

Children from this marriage were:
i.   **Petter Andersson** was born on 27 Sep 1739 in Resta, Ramsberg, Örebro, Sweden [25] and was christened on 30 Sep 1739.[26] Petter married someone **Stina Johansdotter**[24] in 1765.[24]
ii.   **Margreta Andersdotter** was born on 10 May 1741 in Resta, Ramsberg, Örebro, Sweden[27] and was christened on 13 May 1741.[28]
iii.   **Olof Andersson** was born on 3 May 1742 in Ramsberg, Örebro, Sweden[29] and was christened on 1 Jun 1742.[30]
iv.   **Anna Andersdotter** was born on 6 Oct 1743 in Ramsberg, Örebro, Sweden[31] and was christened on 7 Oct 1743.[31]
v.   **Anders Andersson** was born on 30 Mar 1746 in Ramsberg, Örebro, Sweden[32] and was christened on 2 Apr 1746.[33]
5   vi.   **Christina Andersdotter.**[34] Christina married **Jacob Nilsson,**[34] son of **Nils Nilsson** and **Karin Larsdotter,** on 6 Oct 1776 in Hällefors, Örebro, Sweden. [35]
vii.   **Eric Andersson** was born on 14 May 1751 in Botiern, Resta, Ramsberg, Örebro, Sweden[36] and was

18. Nora bergsförsamling AI:6b (1761-1770) Image 232 / page 226 (AID: v51983.b232.s226, NAD: SE/ULA/11098) .
19. Nora bergsförsamling AI:6b (1761-1770) Image 232 / page 226 (AID: v51983.b232.s226, NAD: SE/ULA/11098) . .... Nora bergsförsamling F:2 (1751-1774) Image 206 / page 405 (AID: v53643.b206.s405, NAD: SE/ULA/11098) . .... Jimmy Freijs släktforskning webpage (http://gw2.geneanet.org/jimmyfreij). .... Nora bergsförsamling AI:5b (1751-1760) Image 74 / page 65 (AID: v51981.b74.s65, NAD: SE/ULA/11098). .... Nora bergsförsamling AI:4b (1743-1752) Image 186 / page 180 (AID: v51979.b186.s180, NAD: SE/ULA/11098) .
20. Nora bergsförsamling F:2 (1751-1774) Image 206 / page 405 (AID: v53643.b206.s405, NAD: SE/ULA/11098) . .... Jimmy Freijs släktforskning webpage (http://gw2.geneanet.org/jimmyfreij).
21. Nora bergsförsamling EI:1 (1700-1750) Image 126 / page 244 (AID: v53632.b126.s244, NAD: SE/ULA/11098) .
22. Ramsberg AI:7 (1750-1772) Image 42 / page 34 (AID: v52178.b42.s34, NAD: SE/ULA/11259) . .... Ramsberg C:2 (1699-1725) Image 97 / page 93 (AID: v53708.b97.s93, NAD: SE/ULA/11259) .
23. Ramsberg C:2 (1699-1725) Image 97 / page 93 (AID: v53708.b97.s93, NAD: SE/ULA/11259) .
24. Ramsberg AI:7 (1750-1772) Image 42 / page 34 (AID: v52178.b42.s34, NAD: SE/ULA/11259) .
25. Ramsberg C:3 (1726-1749) Image 96 (AID: v53709.b96, NAD: SE/ULA/11259) . .... Ramsberg AI:7 (1750-1772) Image 42 / page 34 (AID: v52178.b42.s34, NAD: SE/ULA/11259) .
26. Ramsberg C:3 (1726-1749) Image 96 (AID: v53709.b96, NAD: SE/ULA/11259) .
27. Ramsberg C:3 (1726-1749) Image 108 (AID: v53709.b108, NAD: SE/ULA/11259) . .... Ramsberg AI:7 (1750-1772) Image 42 / page 34 (AID: v52178.b42.s34, NAD: SE/ULA/11259) .
28. Ramsberg C:3 (1726-1749) Image 108 (AID: v53709.b108, NAD: SE/ULA/11259) .
29. Ramsberg AI:7 (1750-1772) Image 42 / page 34 (AID: v52178.b42.s34, NAD: SE/ULA/11259) . .... Ramsberg C:3 (1726-1749) Image 117 (AID: v53709.b117, NAD: SE/ULA/11259) .
30. Ramsberg C:3 (1726-1749) Image 117 (AID: v53709.b117, NAD: SE/ULA/11259) .
31. Ramsberg C:3 (1726-1749) Image 129 (AID: v53709.b129, NAD: SE/ULA/11259).
32. Ramsberg C:3 (1726-1749) Image 151 (AID: v53709.b151, NAD: SE/ULA/11259) . .... Ramsberg AI:7 (1750-1772) Image 42 / page 34 (AID: v52178.b42.s34, NAD: SE/ULA/11259) .
33. Ramsberg C:3 (1726-1749) Image 151 (AID: v53709.b151, NAD: SE/ULA/11259) .
34. Nora bergsförsamling C:3 (1770-1788) Image 177 (AID: v53618.b177, NAD: SE/ULA/11098) .
35. Nora bergsförsamling AI:8a (1775-1784) Image 244 / page 237 (AID: v51986.b244.s237, NAD: SE/ULA/11098) . .... Nora bergsförsamling EI:3 (1775-1804) Image 11 / page 16 (AID: v53634.b11.s16, NAD: SE/ULA/11098) .
36. Ramsberg C:4 (1750-1774) Image 12 / page 15 (AID: v53710.b12.s15, NAD: SE/ULA/11259) . .... Ramsberg AI:7 (1750-1772) Image 42 / page 34 (AID: v52178.b42.s34, NAD: SE/ULA/11259) .
37. Ramsberg C:4 (1750-1774) Image 12 / page 15 (AID: v53710.b12.s15, NAD: SE/ULA/11259) .

christened on 19 May 1751.[37]

viii. **Maria Andersdotter** was born on 20 Oct 1753 in Botiern, Resta, Ramsberg, Örebro, Sweden [38] and died in 1753.[39]

ix. **Maria Andersdotter** was born on 7 Jul 1755 in Botiern, Resta, Ramsberg, Örebro, Sweden [40] and died on 7 May 1759[39] at age 3.

x. **Johan Andersson** was born on 9 Feb 1759 in Botiern, Resta, Ramsberg, Örebro, Sweden [41] and died on 9 Jun 1759.[39]

11. Margareta Hindersdotter, daughter of **Hendrik Hansson** and **Anna Persdotter,** was born on 7 Jul 1715 in Hägernäs, Ramsberg, Örebro, Sweden,[42] was christened on 12 Jul 1715,[43] and died in 1763 in Botiern, Resta, Ramsberg, Örebro, Sweden[39] at age 48.

Margareta married **Anders Olsson** on 9 Sep 1739 in Ramsberg, Örebro, Sweden.[39]

12. Olof Olsson, son of **Olof Persson** and **Anna Johansdotter,** was born on 3 Jun 1718 in Brudgumstorp, Grythyttan, Örebro, Sweden[44] and died on 30 Apr 1799 in Skärhyttan, Nora, Örebro, Sweden [45] at age 80.

Birth Notes: Lund, which is next to Brudgumstorp, is listed as birthplace in his death record.

Noted events in his life were:

• Resided: Bef 1741, Brudgumstorp, Grythyttan, Örebro, Sweden. [46]

• Moved from: 1746, Grythyttan, Örebro, Sweden.[47]

• Occupation: manager of iron mine, Skärhyttan, Nora, Örebro, Sweden. [48]

Olof married **Christina Johansdotter** on 19 Mar 1744 in Hällefors, Örebro, Sweden. [49]

Children from this marriage were:

i. **Olof Olsson** was born on 7 Nov 1746 in Skärhyttan, Nora, Örebro, Sweden. [50]

ii. **Erik Olsson** [51] was born on 1 Oct 1752 in Skärhyttan, Nora, Örebro, Sweden. [52] Erik married **Brita**

---

38. *Ramsberg C:4 (1750-1774) Image 28 / page 47 (AID: v53710.b28.s47, NAD: SE/ULA/11259) . .... Ramsberg AI:7 (1750-1772) Image 42 / page 34 (AID: v52178.b42.s34, NAD: SE/ULA/11259) .*

39. *Ramsberg AI:7 (1750-1772) Image 42 / page 34 (AID: v52178.b42.s34, NAD: SE/ULA/11259) .*

40. *Ramsberg C:4 (1750-1774) Image 42 / page 75 (AID: v53710.b42.s75, NAD: SE/ULA/11259) . .... Ramsberg AI:7 (1750-1772) Image 42 / page 34 (AID: v52178.b42.s34, NAD: SE/ULA/11259) .*

41. *Ramsberg C:4 (1750-1774) Image 66 / page 123 (AID: v53710.b66.s123, NAD: SE/ULA/11259) . .... Ramsberg AI:7 (1750-1772) Image 42 / page 34 (AID: v52178.b42.s34, NAD: SE/ULA/11259) .*

42. *Ramsberg AI:7 (1750-1772) Image 42 / page 34 (AID: v52178.b42.s34, NAD: SE/ULA/11259) . .... Ramsberg C:2 (1699-1725) Image 82 / page 78 (AID: v53708.b82.s78, NAD: SE/ULA/11259) .*

43. *Ramsberg C:2 (1699-1725) Image 82 / page 78 (AID: v53708.b82.s78, NAD: SE/ULA/11259) .*

44. *Nora bergsförsamling AI:5b (1751-1760) Image 71 / page 62 (AID: v51981.b71.s62, NAD: SE/ULA/11098) . .... Nora bergsförsamling AI:5b (1751-1760) Image 188 / page 178 (AID: v51981.b188.s178, NAD: SE/ULA/11098) . .... Nora bergsförsamling AI:6b (1761-1770) Image 81 / page 74 (AID: v51983.b81.s74, NAD: SE/ULA/11098) . .... Nora bergsförsamling AI:7a (1771-1790) Image 120 / page 114 (AID: v51984.b120.s114, NAD: SE/ULA/11098) . .... Nora bergsförsamling F:4 (1795-1810) Image 69 / page 65 (AID: v53645.b69.s65, NAD: SE/ULA/11098). .... Nora bergsförsamling AI:4b (1743-1752) Image 184 / page 178 (AID: v51979.b184.s178, NAD: SE/ULA/11098) .*

45. *Nora bergsförsamling F:4 (1795-1810) Image 69 / page 65 (AID: v53645.b69.s65, NAD: SE/ULA/11098) . .... Nora bergsförsamling AI:9a (1791-1800) Image 213 / page 207 (AID: v51988.b213.s207, NAD: SE/ULA/11098) .*

46. *Grythyttan AIa:3 (1737-1743) Image 93 / page 83 (AID: v51190.b93.s83, NAD: SE/ULA/10337) . .... Grythyttan AIa:2 (1727-1740) Image 120 / page 220 (AID: v51189.b120.s220, NAD: SE/ULA/10337) .*

47. *Nora bergsförsamling AI:6b (1761-1770) Image 226 / page 220 (AID: v51983.b226.s220, NAD: SE/ULA/11098) .*

48. *Nora bergsförsamling AI:6b (1761-1770) Image 81 / page 74 (AID: v51983.b81.s74, NAD: SE/ULA/11098) . .... Nora bergsförsamling F:3 (1775-1795) Image 309 / page 306 (AID: v53644.b309.s306, NAD: SE/ULA/11098) .*

49. *Nora bergsförsamling EI:1 (1700-1750) Image 111 / page 214 (AID: v53632.b111.s214, NAD: SE/ULA/11098) .*

50. *Nora bergsförsamling AI:5b (1751-1760) Image 188 / page 178 (AID: v51981.b188.s178, NAD: SE/ULA/11098) . .... Nora bergsförsamling AI:5b (1751-1760) Image 71 / page 62 (AID: v51981.b71.s62, NAD: SE/ULA/11098) . .... Nora bergsförsamling AI:6b (1761-1770) Image 225 / page 219 (AID: v51983.b225.s219, NAD: SE/ULA/11098) . .... Nora bergsförsamling AI:6b (1761-1770) Image 81 / page 74 (AID: v51983.b81.s74, NAD: SE/ULA/11098). .... Nora bergsförsamling C:1 (1737-1756) Image 129 / page 253 (AID: v53616.b129.s253, NAD: SE/ULA/11098). .... Nora bergsförsamling AI:6b (1761-1770) Image 226 / page 220 (AID: v51983.b226.s220, NAD: SE/ULA/11098) . .... Nora bergsförsamling AI:4b (1743-1752) Image 184 / page 178 (AID: v51979.b184.s178, NAD: SE/ULA/11098) .*

51. *Nora bergsförsamling AI:5b (1751-1760) Image 71 / page 62 (AID: v51981.b71.s62, NAD: SE/ULA/11098) .*

52. *Nora bergsförsamling C:1 (1737-1756) Image 196 / page 387 (AID: v53616.b196.s387, NAD: SE/ULA/11098) . .... Nora*

Ancestor Report for Maria Helena Persdotter

                Nilsdotter on 5 Aug 1775.[53]

6   iii.   **Jakob Olsson**. Jakob married **Kristina Jansdotter**,[54] daughter of **Johan Andersson** and **Brita Andersdotter,** on 2 Jul 1771 in Grythyttan, Örebro, Sweden.[55]

    iv.   **Lars Olsson**[56] was born on 6 Feb 1755 in Skärhyttan, Nora, Örebro, Sweden.[57] Lars married **Beata Nilsdotter**[53] in 1771.[53]

    v.   **Christina Olsdotter** was born on 21 Dec 1757 in Skärhyttan, Nora, Örebro, Sweden.[58]

    vi.   **Margareta Olsdotter** was born in 1761 in Skärhyttan, Nora, Örebro, Sweden.[59]

    vii.   **Johan Olsson**[53] was born on 25 May 1763 in Skärhyttan, Nora, Örebro, Sweden.[60]

    viii.   **Catherina Olsdotter** was born in 1766 in Skärhyttan, Nora, Örebro, Sweden[61] and died in 1773 in Skärhyttan, Nora, Örebro, Sweden[53] at age 7.

    ix.   **Nils Olsson** was born on 28 Apr 1769 in Skärhyttan, Nora, Örebro, Sweden.[61]

13. Christina Johansdotter was born in 1724[62] and died on 2 Jun 1791 in Skärhyttan, Nora, Örebro, Sweden[63] at age 67.

Noted events in her life were:
• Resided: Skärhyttan, Nora, Örebro, Sweden.[64]

Christina married **Olof Olsson** on 19 Mar 1744 in Hällefors, Örebro, Sweden.[65]

14. Johan Andersson[54] was born in 1708 in Hjulsjö, Örebro, Sweden[66] and died on 9 May 1775 in Löfnäs, Grythyttan, Örebro, Sweden[67] at age 67.

---

bergsförsamling AI:5b (1751-1760) Image 71 / page 62 (AID: v51981.b71.s62, NAD: SE/ULA/11098) . .... Nora bergsförsamling AI:5b (1751-1760) Image 188 / page 178 (AID: v51981.b188.s178, NAD: SE/ULA/11098) . .... Nora bergsförsamling AI:6b (1761-1770) Image 81 / page 74 (AID: v51983.b81.s74, NAD: SE/ULA/11098) . .... Nora bergsförsamling AI:6b (1761-1770) Image 226 / page 220 (AID: v51983.b226.s220, NAD: SE/ULA/11098). .... Nora bergsförsamling AI:7a (1771-1790) Image 120 / page 114 (AID: v51984.b120.s114, NAD: SE/ULA/11098) .

53. Nora bergsförsamling AI:7a (1771-1790) Image 120 / page 114 (AID: v51984.b120.s114, NAD: SE/ULA/11098) .

54. Grythyttan AIa:5 (1771-1776) Image 114 / page 106 (AID: v51192.b114.s106, NAD: SE/ULA/10337) .

55. Grythyttan CI:5 (1770-1774) Image 18 / page 28 (AID: v53138.b18.s28, NAD: SE/ULA/10337) . .... Nora bergsförsamling AI:8a (1775-1784) Image 251 / page 244 (AID: v51986.b251.s244, NAD: SE/ULA/11098) . .... Nora bergsförsamling AI:7a (1771-1790) Image 120 / page 114 (AID: v51984.b120.s114, NAD: SE/ULA/11098) .

56. Nora bergsförsamling AI:5b (1751-1760) Image 71 / page 62 (AID: v51981.b71.s62, NAD: SE/ULA/11098) .

57. Nora bergsförsamling AI:5b (1751-1760) Image 71 / page 62 (AID: v51981.b71.s62, NAD: SE/ULA/11098) . .... Nora bergsförsamling AI:5b (1751-1760) Image 187 / page 177 (AID: v51981.b187.s177, NAD: SE/ULA/11098) . .... Nora bergsförsamling AI:5b (1751-1760) Image 188 / page 178 (AID: v51981.b188.s178, NAD: SE/ULA/11098) . .... Nora bergsförsamling AI:6b (1761-1770) Image 81 / page 74 (AID: v51983.b81.s74, NAD: SE/ULA/11098) . .... Nora bergsförsamling AI:6b (1761-1770) Image 226 / page 220 (AID: v51983.b226.s220, NAD: SE/ULA/11098) . .... Nora bergsförsamling AI:7a (1771-1790) Image 120 / page 114 (AID: v51984.b120.s114, NAD: SE/ULA/11098) .

58. Nora bergsförsamling AI:5b (1751-1760) Image 188 / page 178 (AID: v51981.b188.s178, NAD: SE/ULA/11098) . .... Nora bergsförsamling C:2 (1756-1770) Image 32 / page 57 (AID: v53617.b32.s57, NAD: SE/ULA/11098) . .... Nora bergsförsamling AI:6b (1761-1770) Image 81 / page 74 (AID: v51983.b81.s74, NAD: SE/ULA/11098) . .... Nora bergsförsamling AI:6b (1761-1770) Image 226 / page 220 (AID: v51983.b226.s220, NAD: SE/ULA/11098). .... Nora bergsförsamling AI:7a (1771-1790) Image 120 / page 114 (AID: v51984.b120.s114, NAD: SE/ULA/11098).

59. Nora bergsförsamling AI:6b (1761-1770) Image 81 / page 74 (AID: v51983.b81.s74, NAD: SE/ULA/11098) . .... Nora bergsförsamling AI:6b (1761-1770) Image 226 / page 220 (AID: v51983.b226.s220, NAD: SE/ULA/11098). .... Nora bergsförsamling AI:7a (1771-1790) Image 120 / page 114 (AID: v51984.b120.s114, NAD: SE/ULA/11098) .

60. Nora bergsförsamling AI:7a (1771-1790) Image 120 / page 114 (AID: v51984.b120.s114, NAD: SE/ULA/11098) . .... Nora bergsförsamling AI:6b (1761-1770) Image 81 / page 74 (AID: v51983.b81.s74, NAD: SE/ULA/11098) . .... Nora bergsförsamling AI:6b (1761-1770) Image 226 / page 220 (AID: v51983.b226.s220, NAD: SE/ULA/11098) .

61. Nora bergsförsamling AI:6b (1761-1770) Image 226 / page 220 (AID: v51983.b226.s220, NAD: SE/ULA/11098) . .... Nora bergsförsamling AI:7a (1771-1790) Image 120 / page 114 (AID: v51984.b120.s114, NAD: SE/ULA/11098) .

62. Nora bergsförsamling AI:5b (1751-1760) Image 188 / page 178 (AID: v51981.b188.s178, NAD: SE/ULA/11098) . .... Nora bergsförsamling F:3 (1775-1795) Image 309 / page 306 (AID: v53644.b309.s306, NAD: SE/ULA/11098) . .... Nora bergsförsamling AI:6b (1761-1770) Image 81 / page 74 (AID: v51983.b81.s74, NAD: SE/ULA/11098) . .... Nora bergsförsamling AI:6b (1761-1770) Image 226 / page 220 (AID: v51983.b226.s220, NAD: SE/ULA/11098).

63. Nora bergsförsamling F:3 (1775-1795) Image 309 / page 306 (AID: v53644.b309.s306, NAD: SE/ULA/11098) . .... Nora bergsförsamling AI:9a (1791-1800) Image 213 / page 207 (AID: v51988.b213.s207, NAD: SE/ULA/11098) .

64. Nora bergsförsamling AI:5b (1751-1760) Image 188 / page 178 (AID: v51981.b188.s178, NAD: SE/ULA/11098) . .... Nora bergsförsamling AI:8a (1775-1784) Image 231 / page 224 (AID: v51986.b231.s224, NAD: SE/ULA/11098) . .... Nora bergsförsamling AI:9a (1791-1800) Image 213 / page 207 (AID: v51988.b213.s207, NAD: SE/ULA/11098) .

65. Nora bergsförsamling EI:1 (1700-1750) Image 111 / page 214 (AID: v53632.b111.s214, NAD: SE/ULA/11098) .

Noted events in his life were:
- Resided: Bef 1773, Rundbohöjden, Hjulsjö, Örebro, Sweden. [68]

- Resided: Cir 1775, Löfnäs, Grythyttan, Örebro, Sweden. [69]

Johan married **Brita Andersdotter**[69] on 14 Oct 1733 in Hjulsjö, Örebro, Sweden. [68]

Children from this marriage were:
7   i.   **Kristina Jansdotter**.[69] Kristina married **Jakob Olsson,** son of **Olof Olsson** and **Christina Johansdotter,** on 2 Jul 1771 in Grythyttan, Örebro, Sweden. [70]
     ii.   **Johan Jansson** was born on 22 Aug 1753 in Löfnäs, Grythyttan, Örebro, Sweden. [71]

15. Brita Andersdotter[69] was born in 1709 in Grångshyttan, Hjulsjö, Örebro, Sweden [72] and died on 13 Aug 1784 in Finhagen, Grythyttan, Örebro, Sweden[73] at age 75.

Noted events in her life were:
- Resided: Bef 1773, Nya Grångshyttan, Hjulsjö, Örebro, Sweden. [68]

- Resided: Cir 1775, Löfnäs, Grythyttan, Örebro, Sweden. [69]

Brita married **Johan Andersson**[69] on 14 Oct 1733 in Hjulsjö, Örebro, Sweden. [68]

68. Hjulsjö F:1 (1674-1772) Image 246 (AID: v53273.b246, NAD: SE/ULA/10404) .

69. Grythyttan AIa:5 (1771-1776) Image 114 / page 106 (AID: v51192.b114.s106, NAD: SE/ULA/10337) .

70. Grythyttan CI:5 (1770-1774) Image 18 / page 28 (AID: v53138.b18.s28, NAD: SE/ULA/10337) . .... Nora bergsförsamling AI:8a (1775-1784) Image 251 / page 244 (AID: v51986.b251.s244, NAD: SE/ULA/11098) . .... Nora bergsförsamling AI:7a (1771-1790) Image 120 / page 114 (AID: v51984.b120.s114, NAD: SE/ULA/11098) .

71. Grythyttan AIa:5 (1771-1776) Image 114 / page 106 (AID: v51192.b114.s106, NAD: SE/ULA/10337) . .... Grythyttan CI:3 (1737-1757) Image 245 (AID: v53136.b245, NAD: SE/ULA/10337) .

72. Grythyttan AIa:5 (1771-1776) Image 114 / page 106 (AID: v51192.b114.s106, NAD: SE/ULA/10337) . .... Grythyttan CI:5 (1770-1774) Image 128 (AID: v53138.b128, NAD: SE/ULA/10337) .

73. Nora bergsförsamling F:4 (1795-1810) Image 69 / page 65 (AID: v53645.b69.s65, NAD: SE/ULA/11098) . .... Grythyttan CI:5 (1770-1774) Image 128 (AID: v53138.b128, NAD: SE/ULA/10337) .

Fifth Generation

18. Lars Persson was born in 1693 in Hällefors, Örebro, Sweden,[1] died on 28 Jan 1763 in Brötorp, Nora, Örebro, Sweden[2] at age 70, and was buried on 13 Feb 1763.[2]

Birth Notes: Bith is 1691 in house book.

Research Notes: Father is likely Pehrs Larsson at Sund Fingerboda, Nora, Örebro.[3]

Noted events in his life were:
• Resided: Bef 1720, Västra Fingerboda, Nora, Örebro, Sweden.[4]

• Occupation: miner, Bef 1763.[2]

Lars married **Brita Olofsdotter** on 19 Sep 1720 in Hällefors, Örebro, Sweden.[4]

The child from this marriage was:
9   i.   **Karin Larsdotter**.[5] Karin married **Nils Nilsson**[5] on 16 Jul 1748 in Nora stadsförs, Nora, Örebro, Sweden.[6]

19. Brita Olofsdotter was born in 1693,[7] died on 20 Mar 1760 in Brötorp, Nora, Örebro, Sweden[8] at age 67, and was buried on 25 Mar 1760.[8]

Birth Notes: Birth is 1690 in housebook.

Research Notes: Brita's parents might be Olof Eliasson and Carin at Skärhyttan, Nora, Örebro. Brita appears to have only one surviving child in the housebooks; birth records are not available to discover other children.[9]

Noted events in her life were:
• Resided: Bef 1720, Skärhyttan, Nora, Örebro, Sweden.[4]

Brita married **Lars Persson** on 19 Sep 1720 in Hällefors, Örebro, Sweden.[4]

20. Olof Hansson, son of **Hans Nilsson** and **Karin Olofsdotter,** was born on 12 Dec 1696 in Resta torp, Ramsberg, Örebro, Sweden,[10] was christened on 25 Dec 1696,[11] and died on 10 Apr 1737 in Ramsberg, Örebro, Sweden[12] at age 40.

Birth Notes: The houshold name is spelled Botierna, Botinnan, or Boolinnan. The records have different spellings.

---

1. Nora bergsförsamling F:2 (1751-1774) Image 109 / page 211 (AID: v53643.b109.s211, NAD: SE/ULA/11098) . .... Nora bergsförsamling AI:5b (1751-1760) Image 74 / page 65 (AID: v51981.b74.s65, NAD: SE/ULA/11098) . .... Nora bergsförsamling AI:5b (1751-1760) Image 191 / page 181 (AID: v51981.b191.s181, NAD: SE/ULA/11098) . .... Nora bergsförsamling AI:4b (1743-1752) Image 186 / page 180 (AID: v51979.b186.s180, NAD: SE/ULA/11098).
2. Nora bergsförsamling F:2 (1751-1774) Image 109 / page 211 (AID: v53643.b109.s211, NAD: SE/ULA/11098) .
3. Nora bergsförsamling AI:1b (1703-1717) Image 258 / page 254 (AID: v51973.b258.s254, NAD: SE/ULA/11098) .
4. Nora bergsförsamling EI:1 (1700-1750) Image 38 / page 68 (AID: v53632.b38.s68, NAD: SE/ULA/11098) .
5. Nora bergsförsamling AI:6b (1761-1770) Image 232 / page 226 (AID: v51983.b232.s226, NAD: SE/ULA/11098) .
6. Nora bergsförsamling EI:1 (1700-1750) Image 126 / page 244 (AID: v53632.b126.s244, NAD: SE/ULA/11098) .
7. Nora bergsförsamling F:2 (1751-1774) Image 80 / page 153 (AID: v53643.b80.s153, NAD: SE/ULA/11098) . .... Nora bergsförsamling AI:5b (1751-1760) Image 74 / page 65 (AID: v51981.b74.s65, NAD: SE/ULA/11098) . .... Nora bergsförsamling AI:5b (1751-1760) Image 191 / page 181 (AID: v51981.b191.s181, NAD: SE/ULA/11098) . .... Nora bergsförsamling AI:4b (1743-1752) Image 186 / page 180 (AID: v51979.b186.s180, NAD: SE/ULA/11098).
8. Nora bergsförsamling F:2 (1751-1774) Image 80 / page 153 (AID: v53643.b80.s153, NAD: SE/ULA/11098) .
9. Nora bergsförsamling AI:1a (1703-1717) Image 226 / page 221 (AID: v51972.b226.s221, NAD: SE/ULA/11098) .
10. Ramsberg C:2 (1699-1725) Image 167 / page 163 (AID: v53708.b167.s163, NAD: SE/ULA/11259) . .... Ramsberg AI:7 (1750-1772) Image 42 / page 34 (AID: v52178.b42.s34, NAD: SE/ULA/11259) . .... Ramsberg C:1 (1679-1698) Image 67 / page 62 (AID: v53707.b67.s62, NAD: SE/ULA/11259). .... Ramsberg AI:3 (1699-1710) Image 22 / page 16 (AID: v52173.b22.s16, NAD: SE/ULA/11259) . .... Ramsberg AI:3 (1699-1710) Image 137 / page 131 (AID: v52173.b137.s131, NAD: SE/ULA/11259) . .... Ramsberg AI:4 (1711-1722) Image 20 / page 13 (AID: v52174.b20.s13, NAD: SE/ULA/11259). .... Ramsberg AI:5 (1723-1733) Image 20 / page 14 (AID: v52175.b20.s14, NAD: SE/ULA/11259).
11. Ramsberg C:1 (1679-1698) Image 67 / page 62 (AID: v53707.b67.s62, NAD: SE/ULA/11259) .
12. Ramsberg C:2 (1699-1725) Image 167 / page 163 (AID: v53708.b167.s163, NAD: SE/ULA/11259) .

Ancestor Report for Maria Helena Persdotter

Research Notes: His father and step mother are living with him in 1723. [13]

Noted events in his life were:
- Resided: 1717, Resta, Ramsberg, Örebro, Sweden. [14]

- Occupation: bergsman (miner). [15]

Olof married **Brita Andersdotter**[16] on 29 Sep 1717 in Ramsberg, Örebro, Sweden. [14]

Children from this marriage were:
- i. **Hans Olsson** was born on 19 Aug 1718 in Resta, Ramsberg, Örebro, Sweden [17] and died on 8 Feb 1719 in Resta, Ramsberg, Örebro, Sweden. [18]
- 10 ii. **Anders Olsson**. Anders married **Margareta Hindersdotter,** daughter of **Hendrik Hansson** and **Anna Persdotter,** on 9 Sep 1739 in Ramsberg, Örebro, Sweden. [19]
- iii. **Maria Olsdotter** was born on 21 Apr 1721 in Resta, Ramsberg, Örebro, Sweden [20] and died on 14 Jan 1728 in Resta, Ramsberg, Örebro, Sweden [21] at age 6.
- iv. **Lars Olsson** was born on 16 Jan 1725 in Resta, Ramsberg, Örebro, Sweden. [22]

Olof next married **Karin Jacobsdotter** on 3 Aug 1735 in Ramsberg, Örebro, Sweden. [23]

Children from this marriage were:
- i. **Maria Olsdotter** was born on 22 Nov 1735 in Resta, Ramsberg, Örebro, Sweden. [24]
- ii. **Cathrina Olsdotter** was born on 11 Mar 1737 in Resta, Ramsberg, Örebro, Sweden. [25]

21. Brita Andersdotter,[16] daughter of **Anders Andersson** and **Anna Larsdotter,** was born on 17 Jun 1683 in Glifsån, Ramsberg, Örebro, Sweden[26] and died on 9 Nov 1734 in Ramsberg, Örebro, Sweden [15] at age 51.

Birth Notes: Birth year is 1688 in household books.

Brita married **Olof Hansson** on 29 Sep 1717 in Ramsberg, Örebro, Sweden. [14]

22. Hendrik Hansson,[27] son of **Hans Henningsson** and **Brita Olsdotter,** was born on 28 Sep 1689 in Östra Hägernäs, Ramsberg, Örebro, Sweden[28] and died in 1765 in Hägernäs hammar, Ramsberg, Örebro, Sweden [29] at age 76.

Hendrik married **Anna Persdotter** on 3 Sep 1711 in Ramsberg, Örebro, Sweden. [30]

Children from this marriage were:
- i. **Hans Hindersson**[31] was born on 9 Mar 1712 in Hägernäs, Ramsberg, Örebro, Sweden. [32]

13. Ramsberg AI:5 (1723-1733) Image 20 / page 14 (AID: v52175.b20.s14, NAD: SE/ULA/11259) .
14. Ramsberg C:2 (1699-1725) Image 14 / page 10 (AID: v53708.b14.s10, NAD: SE/ULA/11259) .
15. Ramsberg C:2 (1699-1725) Image 162 / page 158 (AID: v53708.b162.s158, NAD: SE/ULA/11259) .
16. Ramsberg AI:3 (1699-1710) Image 84 / page 78 (AID: v52173.b84.s78, NAD: SE/ULA/11259) .
17. Ramsberg C:2 (1699-1725) Image 94 / page 90 (AID: v53708.b94.s90, NAD: SE/ULA/11259) .
18. Ramsberg C:2 (1699-1725) Image 141 / page 137 (AID: v53708.b141.s137, NAD: SE/ULA/11259) .
19. Ramsberg AI:7 (1750-1772) Image 42 / page 34 (AID: v52178.b42.s34, NAD: SE/ULA/11259) .
20. Ramsberg C:2 (1699-1725) Image 102 / page 98 (AID: v53708.b102.s98, NAD: SE/ULA/11259) .
21. Ramsberg C:2 (1699-1725) Image 151 / page 147 (AID: v53708.b151.s147, NAD: SE/ULA/11259) .
22. Ramsberg C:2 (1699-1725) Image 118 / page 114 (AID: v53708.b118.s114, NAD: SE/ULA/11259) .
23. Ramsberg C:2 (1699-1725) Image 24 / page 20 (AID: v53708.b24.s20, NAD: SE/ULA/11259) .
24. Ramsberg C:3 (1726-1749) Image 68 (AID: v53709.b68, NAD: SE/ULA/11259) .
25. Ramsberg C:3 (1726-1749) Image 77 (AID: v53709.b77, NAD: SE/ULA/11259) .
26. Ramsberg C:1 (1679-1698) Image 16 / page 11 (AID: v53707.b16.s11, NAD: SE/ULA/11259) . .... Ramsberg AI:6a (1734-1753) Image 14 / page 9 (AID: v52176.b14.s9, NAD: SE/ULA/11259) . .... Ramsberg AI:3 (1699-1710) Image 84 / page 78 (AID: v52173.b84.s78, NAD: SE/ULA/11259) . .... Ramsberg AI:5 (1723-1733) Image 20 / page 14 (AID: v52175.b20.s14, NAD: SE/ULA/11259) .
27. Ramsberg AI:1 (1664-1690) Image 56 / page 49 (AID: v52171.b56.s49, NAD: SE/ULA/11259) .
28. Ramsberg C:1 (1679-1698) Image 35 / page 30 (AID: v53707.b35.s30, NAD: SE/ULA/11259) . .... Ramsberg AI:8a (1754-1772) Image 129 / page 228 (AID: v52179.b129.s228, NAD: SE/ULA/11259) .
29. Ramsberg AI:8a (1754-1772) Image 129 / page 228 (AID: v52179.b129.s228, NAD: SE/ULA/11259) .
30. Ramsberg C:2 (1699-1725) Image 11 / page 7 (AID: v53708.b11.s7, NAD: SE/ULA/11259) .
31. Jimmy Freijs släktforskning webpage (http://gw2.geneanet.org/jimmyfreij).
32. Ramsberg C:2 (1699-1725) Image 70 / page 66 (AID: v53708.b70.s66, NAD: SE/ULA/11259) .

	ii.	**Pehr Hindersson**[31] was born on 18 Sep 1713 in Hägernäs, Ramsberg, Örebro, Sweden.

11 iii. **Margareta Hindersdotter**. Margareta married **Anders Olsson,** son of **Olof Hansson** and **Brita Andersdotter,** on 9 Sep 1739 in Ramsberg, Örebro, Sweden. [34]

iv. **Olof Hindersson** was born on 3 Jan 1717 in Hägernäs, Ramsberg, Örebro, Sweden and died on 19 Apr 1717.

v. **Erich Hindersson**[36] was born on 9 Jan 1718 in Hägernäs, Ramsberg, Örebro, Sweden. [37]

vi. **Anna Hindersdotter** was born on 25 Mar 1720 in Hägernäs, Ramsberg, Örebro, Sweden [38] and died on 19 Jun 1720.

vii. **Olof Hindersson**[36] was born on 12 May 1721 in Hägernäs, Ramsberg, Örebro, Sweden [39] and died in 1729[36] at age 8.

Hendrik next married **Maria Ersdotter**[40] on 1 Nov 1724 in Ramsberg, Örebro, Sweden. [41]

Children from this marriage were:

i. **Brita Hindersson** was born on 2 Apr 1727 in Hägernäs, Ramsberg, Örebro, Sweden [42] and died on 12 Apr 1727 in Hägernäs, Ramsberg, Örebro, Sweden. [43]

ii. **Lars Hindersson** was born on 4 May 1728 in Hägernäs, Ramsberg, Örebro, Sweden. [44]

iii. **Anders Hindersson** was born on 8 Jun 1732 in Hägernäs, Ramsberg, Örebro, Sweden. [45]

iv. **Olof Hindersson** was born on 21 Jan 1734 in Hägernäs, Ramsberg, Örebro, Sweden. [46] Olof married **Margaret Isaksdotter**.[40]

23. Anna Persdotter, daughter of **Petter Mattsson** and **Margareta Olsdotter,** was born on 6 Mar 1687 in Larsbo, Söderbärke, Kopparberg, Sweden[47] and died on 28 Jul 1723 in Ramsberg, Örebro, Sweden [48] at age 36.

Noted events in her life were:
• Resided: 1711-1716, Hägernäs, Ramsberg, Örebro, Sweden. [49]

Anna married **Hendrik Hansson**[50] on 3 Sep 1711 in Ramsberg, Örebro, Sweden. [51]

24. Olof Persson[52] was born in 1686[53] and died on 24 Feb 1750 in Brudgumstorp, Grythyttan, Örebro, Sweden [54] at age 64.

---

34. Ramsberg AI:7 (1750-1772) Image 42 / page 34 (AID: v52178.b42.s34, NAD: SE/ULA/11259) .

35. Ramsberg C:2 (1699-1725) Image 88 / page 84 (AID: v53708.b88.s84, NAD: SE/ULA/11259) .

36. Jimmy Freijs släktforskning webpage (http://gw2.geneanet.org/jimmyfreij).

37. Ramsberg C:2 (1699-1725) Image 92 / page 88 (AID: v53708.b92.s88, NAD: SE/ULA/11259) .

38. Ramsberg C:2 (1699-1725) Image 98 / page 94 (AID: v53708.b98.s94, NAD: SE/ULA/11259) .

39. Ramsberg C:2 (1699-1725) Image 102 / page 98 (AID: v53708.b102.s98, NAD: SE/ULA/11259) .

40. Ramsberg AI:8a (1754-1772) Image 129 / page 228 (AID: v52179.b129.s228, NAD: SE/ULA/11259) .

41. Ramsberg C:2 (1699-1725) Image 17 / page 13 (AID: v53708.b17.s13, NAD: SE/ULA/11259) .

42. Ramsberg C:3 (1726-1749) Image 11 (AID: v53709.b11, NAD: SE/ULA/11259) .

43. Ramsberg C:2 (1699-1725) Image 150 / page 146 (AID: v53708.b150.s146, NAD: SE/ULA/11259) .

44. Ramsberg C:3 (1726-1749) Image 16 (AID: v53709.b16, NAD: SE/ULA/11259) .

45. Ramsberg C:3 (1726-1749) Image 41 (AID: v53709.b41, NAD: SE/ULA/11259) .

46. Ramsberg C:3 (1726-1749) Image 54 (AID: v53709.b54, NAD: SE/ULA/11259) .... Ramsberg AI:8a (1754-1772) Image 129 / page 228 (AID: v52179.b129.s228, NAD: SE/ULA/11259) .

47. Söderbärke C:1 (1675-1694) Image 87 (AID: v132270.b87, NAD: SE/ULA/11521) .... Ramsberg AI:3 (1699-1710) Image 221 / page 215 (AID: v52173.b221.s215, NAD: SE/ULA/11259).

48. Ramsberg C:2 (1699-1725) Image 145 / page 141 (AID: v53708.b145.s141, NAD: SE/ULA/11259) .

49. Ramsberg C:2 (1699-1725) Image 11 / page 7 (AID: v53708.b11.s7, NAD: SE/ULA/11259) .... Ramsberg AI:4 (1711-1722) Image 111 / page 104 (AID: v52174.b111.s104, NAD: SE/ULA/11259) .

50. Ramsberg AI:1 (1664-1690) Image 56 / page 49 (AID: v52171.b56.s49, NAD: SE/ULA/11259) .

51. Ramsberg C:2 (1699-1725) Image 11 / page 7 (AID: v53708.b11.s7, NAD: SE/ULA/11259) .

52. Grythyttan AIa:3 (1737-1743) Image 93 / page 83 (AID: v51190.b93.s83, NAD: SE/ULA/10337) .

53. Grythyttan AIa:4 (1740-1767) Image 51 / page 44 (AID: v51191.b51.s44, NAD: SE/ULA/10337) .... Grythyttan CI:3 (1737-1757) Image 63 / page 59 (AID: v53136.b63.s59, NAD: SE/ULA/10337).

54. Grythyttan AIa:4 (1740-1767) Image 179 / page 171 (AID: v51191.b179.s171, NAD: SE/ULA/10337) .... Grythyttan CI:3 (1737-1757) Image 63 / page 59 (AID: v53136.b63.s59, NAD: SE/ULA/10337).

Ancestor Report for Maria Helena Persdotter

Noted events in his life were:
• Moved to: 1710, Brudgumstorp, Grythyttan, Örebro, Sweden. [55]

Olof married **Anna Johansdotter**[56] on 2 Jan 1710 in Grythyttan, Örebro, Sweden. [57]

Children from this marriage were:
- i.   **Johan Olsson**[58] was born on 7 Nov 1711 in Brudgumstorp, Grythyttan, Örebro, Sweden. [59] Johan married **Kerstin Hindersdotter**.[58]
- ii.   **Anna Olsdotter**[58] was born on 26 Feb 1713 in Brudgumstorp, Grythyttan, Örebro, Sweden. [60]
- 12   iii.   **Olof Olsson**. Olof married **Christina Johansdotter** on 19 Mar 1744 in Hällefors, Örebro, Sweden. [61]

Olof next married **Anna Ersdotter**.

25. Anna Johansdotter[56] was born in 1690[62] and died on 25 Feb 1740 in Brudgumstorp, Grythyttan, Örebro, Sweden[63] at age 50.

Noted events in her life were:
• Resided: 1710, Brudgumstorp, Grythyttan, Örebro, Sweden. [64]

Anna married **Olof Persson**[58] on 2 Jan 1710 in Grythyttan, Örebro, Sweden. [57]

---

55. Grythyttan AIa:3 (1737-1743) Image 93 / page 83 (AID: v51190.b93.s83, NAD: SE/ULA/10337) . .... Grythyttan CI:2 (1718-1737) Image 8 / page 4 (AID: v53135.b8.s4, NAD: SE/ULA/10337) . .... Grythyttan AIa:2 (1727-1740) Image 120 / page 220 (AID: v51189.b120.s220, NAD: SE/ULA/10337) . .... Grythyttan CI:1 (1699-1715) Image 53 / page 47 (AID: v53134.b53.s47, NAD: SE/ULA/10337).

56. Grythyttan CI:2 (1718-1737) Image 8 / page 4 (AID: v53135.b8.s4, NAD: SE/ULA/10337) . .... Grythyttan AIa:3 (1737-1743) Image 93 / page 83 (AID: v51190.b93.s83, NAD: SE/ULA/10337) .

57. Grythyttan CI:1 (1699-1715) Image 53 / page 47 (AID: v53134.b53.s47, NAD: SE/ULA/10337) .

58. Grythyttan AIa:3 (1737-1743) Image 93 / page 83 (AID: v51190.b93.s83, NAD: SE/ULA/10337) .

59. Grythyttan CI:1 (1699-1715) Image 61 / page 55 (AID: v53134.b61.s55, NAD: SE/ULA/10337) .

60. Grythyttan AIa:4 (1740-1767) Image 51 / page 44 (AID: v51191.b51.s44, NAD: SE/ULA/10337) . .... Grythyttan CI:1 (1699-1715) Image 70 / page 64 (AID: v53134.b70.s64, NAD: SE/ULA/10337) .

61. Nora bergsförsamling EI:1 (1700-1750) Image 111 / page 214 (AID: v53632.b111.s214, NAD: SE/ULA/11098) .

62. Grythyttan CI:3 (1737-1757) Image 17 / page 13 (AID: v53136.b17.s13, NAD: SE/ULA/10337) .

63. Grythyttan AIa:2 (1727-1740) Image 120 / page 220 (AID: v51189.b120.s220, NAD: SE/ULA/10337) . .... Grythyttan CI:3 (1737-1757) Image 17 / page 13 (AID: v53136.b17.s13, NAD: SE/ULA/10337) .

64. Grythyttan AIa:3 (1737-1743) Image 93 / page 83 (AID: v51190.b93.s83, NAD: SE/ULA/10337) . .... Grythyttan CI:2 (1718-1737) Image 8 / page 4 (AID: v53135.b8.s4, NAD: SE/ULA/10337) . .... Grythyttan CI:1 (1699-1715) Image 53 / page 47 (AID: v53134.b53.s47, NAD: SE/ULA/10337).

Sixth Generation

40. Hans Nilsson,[1] son of **Nils Olsson** and **Elin,** was born in 1651[2] and died on 15 Jun 1727 in Resta, Ramsberg, Örebro, Sweden at age 76.

Hans married **Karin Olofsdotter** on 20 Jun 1683 in Ramsberg, Örebro, Sweden.[3]

Marriage Notes: Date given as 2 Trin.

Children from this marriage were:

	i.	**Anna Hansdotter** was born on 24 Dec 1683 in Resta, Ramsberg, Örebro, Sweden.[4]
	ii.	**Nils Hansson** was born on 18 Mar 1686 in Resta, Ramsberg, Örebro, Sweden.[5]
	iii.	**Malin Hansdotter** was born on 20 May 1688 in Resta, Ramsberg, Örebro, Sweden.[6]
	iv.	**Carin Hansdotter** was born on 26 Jan 1693 in Resta torp, Ramsberg, Örebro, Sweden[7] and was christened on 29 Jan 1693.[8]
20	v.	**Olof Hansson.** Olof married **Brita Andersdotter,**[9] daughter of **Anders Andersson** and **Anna Larsdotter,** on 29 Sep 1717 in Ramsberg, Örebro, Sweden.[10] Olof next married **Karin Jacobsdotter** on 3 Aug 1735 in Ramsberg, Örebro, Sweden.[11]
	vi.	**Elisabet Hansdotter** was born on 23 Jun 1697 in Resta, Ramsberg, Örebro, Sweden.[12]

Hans next married **Cherstin Bengtsdotter**[13] on 26 Aug 1700 in Ramsberg, Örebro, Sweden.[14]

Children from this marriage were:

	i.	**Hans Hansson** was born on 17 Mar 1701 in Resta, Ramsberg, Örebro, Sweden[15] and died on 19 Jul 1703 in Resta, Ramsberg, Örebro, Sweden[16] at age 2.
	ii.	**Johan Hansson** was born on 16 Oct 1703 in Resta, Ramsberg, Örebro, Sweden.[17]

---

1. Ramsberg AI:1 (1664-1690) Image 11 / page 4 (AID: v52171.b11.s4, NAD: SE/ULA/11259) . .... Ramsberg AI:1 (1664-1690) Image 28 / page 21 (AID: v52171.b28.s21, NAD: SE/ULA/11259) . .... Ramsberg AI:1 (1664-1690) Image 46 / page 39 (AID: v52171.b46.s39, NAD: SE/ULA/11259).

2. Ramsberg AI:3 (1699-1710) Image 22 / page 16 (AID: v52173.b22.s16, NAD: SE/ULA/11259) . .... Ramsberg AI:3 (1699-1710) Image 137 / page 131 (AID: v52173.b137.s131, NAD: SE/ULA/11259) . .... Ramsberg AI:4 (1711-1722) Image 138 / page 131 (AID: v52174.b138.s131, NAD: SE/ULA/11259) . .... Ramsberg AI:5 (1723-1733) Image 20 / page 14 (AID: v52175.b20.s14, NAD: SE/ULA/11259)

3. Ramsberg C:1 (1679-1698) Image 17 / page 12 (AID: v53707.b17.s12, NAD: SE/ULA/11259) .

4. Ramsberg AI:3 (1699-1710) Image 22 / page 16 (AID: v52173.b22.s16, NAD: SE/ULA/11259) . .... Ramsberg AI:3 (1699-1710) Image 137 / page 131 (AID: v52173.b137.s131, NAD: SE/ULA/11259) . .... Ramsberg C:1 (1679-1698) Image 17 / page 12 (AID: v53707.b17.s12, NAD: SE/ULA/11259) . .... Ramsberg AI:4 (1711-1722) Image 20 / page 13 (AID: v52174.b20.s13, NAD: SE/ULA/11259) .

5. Ramsberg AI:3 (1699-1710) Image 22 / page 16 (AID: v52173.b22.s16, NAD: SE/ULA/11259) . .... Ramsberg AI:3 (1699-1710) Image 137 / page 131 (AID: v52173.b137.s131, NAD: SE/ULA/11259) . .... Ramsberg C:1 (1679-1698) Image 25 / page 20 (AID: v53707.b25.s20, NAD: SE/ULA/11259). .... Ramsberg AI:4 (1711-1722) Image 20 / page 13 (AID: v52174.b20.s13, NAD: SE/ULA/11259) .

6. Ramsberg AI:3 (1699-1710) Image 22 / page 16 (AID: v52173.b22.s16, NAD: SE/ULA/11259) . .... Ramsberg AI:3 (1699-1710) Image 137 / page 131 (AID: v52173.b137.s131, NAD: SE/ULA/11259) . .... Ramsberg C:1 (1679-1698) Image 30 / page 25 (AID: v53707.b30.s25, NAD: SE/ULA/11259). .... Ramsberg AI:4 (1711-1722) Image 20 / page 13 (AID: v52174.b20.s13, NAD: SE/ULA/11259) .

7. Ramsberg AI:3 (1699-1710) Image 137 / page 131 (AID: v52173.b137.s131, NAD: SE/ULA/11259) . .... Ramsberg AI:4 (1711-1722) Image 20 / page 13 (AID: v52174.b20.s13, NAD: SE/ULA/11259) . .... Ramsberg C:1 (1679-1698) Image 51 / page 46 (AID: v53707.b51.s46, NAD: SE/ULA/11259).

8. Ramsberg C:1 (1679-1698) Image 51 / page 46 (AID: v53707.b51.s46, NAD: SE/ULA/11259) .

9. Ramsberg AI:3 (1699-1710) Image 84 / page 78 (AID: v52173.b84.s78, NAD: SE/ULA/11259) .

10. Ramsberg C:2 (1699-1725) Image 14 / page 10 (AID: v53708.b14.s10, NAD: SE/ULA/11259) .

11. Ramsberg C:2 (1699-1725) Image 24 / page 20 (AID: v53708.b24.s20, NAD: SE/ULA/11259) .

12. Ramsberg AI:3 (1699-1710) Image 137 / page 131 (AID: v52173.b137.s131, NAD: SE/ULA/11259) . .... Ramsberg C:1 (1679-1698) Image 80 / page 75 (AID: v53707.b80.s75, NAD: SE/ULA/11259) . .... Ramsberg AI:4 (1711-1722) Image 20 / page 13 (AID: v52174.b20.s13, NAD: SE/ULA/11259).

13. Ramsberg AI:3 (1699-1710) Image 137 / page 131 (AID: v52173.b137.s131, NAD: SE/ULA/11259) . .... Ramsberg AI:5 (1723-1733) Image 20 / page 14 (AID: v52175.b20.s14, NAD: SE/ULA/11259) .

14. Ramsberg C:2 (1699-1725) Image 7 / page 3 (AID: v53708.b7.s3, NAD: SE/ULA/11259) .

15. Ramsberg C:2 (1699-1725) Image 32 / page 28 (AID: v53708.b32.s28, NAD: SE/ULA/11259) .

16. Ramsberg C:2 (1699-1725) Image 127 / page 123 (AID: v53708.b127.s123, NAD: SE/ULA/11259) .

17. Ramsberg C:2 (1699-1725) Image 41 / page 37 (AID: v53708.b41.s37, NAD: SE/ULA/11259) .

Ancestor Report for Maria Helena Persdotter

41. Karin Olofsdotter was born in 1662 [18] and died on 22 May 1698 in Resta, Ramsberg, Örebro, Sweden [18] at age 36.

Karin married **Hans Nilsson** [19] on 20 Jun 1683 in Ramsberg, Örebro, Sweden. [20]

42. Anders Andersson, [21] son of **Anders Embjörnsson** and **Karin Nilsdotter,** was born about 1647 [22] and died on 17 Nov 1715 in Glifsån, Ramsberg, Örebro, Sweden [23] about age 68.

Noted events in his life were:
- Resided: Abt 1672, Lögdeå, Nordmaling, Västerbotten, Sweden. [24]

- Resided: 1705, Glifsån, Ramsberg, Örebro, Sweden. [25] Probably moved to Ramsberg parish about 1679.

- Occupation: bergsman (miner), Glifsån, Ramsberg, Örebro, Sweden.

Anders married **Anna Larsdotter** [26] Est 1672.

Children from this marriage were:
    i.   **Olof Andersson** was born about Sep 1673, [27] died on 29 May 1751 in Bygdeå, Västerbotten, Sweden [27] about age 77, and was buried on 9 Jun 1751. [27]
    ii.   **Peder Andersson** [28] was born in 1675 [29] and died on 28 Nov 1679 in Ramsberg, Örebro, Sweden [29] at age 4.
    iii.   **Elsa Andersson** was born about 1678 [24] and died on 9 Feb 1757 in Bygdeå, Västerbotten, Sweden [24] about age 79. Elsa married **Daniel Olofsson** [24] in 1696. [24] Elsa next married **Mårten Johansson**. [24]
    iv.   **Anders Andersson** was born in 1679, [30] was christened on 26 Jan 1679 in Västra Vingåkers, Södermanland, Sweden, [31] and died on 13 Mar 1759 in Neder-Vannala, Västra Vingåkers, Södermanland, Sweden [32] at age 80.
    v.   **Carin Andersson** was born on 24 Nov 1680 in Glifsån, Ramsberg, Örebro, Sweden. [25] Carin married **Lars Larsson** [33] on 29 Sep 1698 in Ramsberg, Örebro, Sweden. [33]
    vi.   **Lars Andersson** [34] was born about 1681 in Glifsån, Ramsberg, Örebro, Sweden [34] and died on 11 Aug 1717 [35] about age 36.
    vii.   **Anna Andersson** was born about 1681 [36] and died on 30 May 1759 in Allmänningbo, Ramsberg, Örebro,

18. *Jimmy Freijs släktforskning webpage (http://gw2.geneanet.org/jimmyfreij). .... Ramsberg C:1 (1679-1698) Image 98 / page 93 (AID: v53707.b98.s93, NAD: SE/ULA/11259).*

19. *Ramsberg AI:1 (1664-1690) Image 11 / page 4 (AID: v52171.b11.s4, NAD: SE/ULA/11259) . .... Ramsberg AI:1 (1664-1690) Image 28 / page 21 (AID: v52171.b28.s21, NAD: SE/ULA/11259) . .... Ramsberg AI:1 (1664-1690) Image 46 / page 39 (AID: v52171.b46.s39, NAD: SE/ULA/11259).*

20. *Ramsberg C:1 (1679-1698) Image 17 / page 12 (AID: v53707.b17.s12, NAD: SE/ULA/11259) .*

21. *Ramsberg AI:2 (1691-1696) Image 62 / page 57 (AID: v52172.b62.s57, NAD: SE/ULA/11259) . .... Ramsberg AI:1 (1664-1690) Image 18 / page 11 (AID: v52171.b18.s11, NAD: SE/ULA/11259) . .... Svenska Antavlor V:8 nr 301. .... Ramsberg AI:1 (1664-1690) Image 6 (AID: v52171.b6, NAD: SE/ULA/11259).*

22. *Ramsberg C:2 (1699-1725) Image 137 / page 133 (AID: v53708.b137.s133, NAD: SE/ULA/11259) . .... Svenska Antavlor V:8 nr 301. .... Ramsberg AI:3 (1699-1710) Image 84 / page 78 (AID: v52173.b84.s78, NAD: SE/ULA/11259) .*

23. *Ramsberg C:2 (1699-1725) Image 137 / page 133 (AID: v53708.b137.s133, NAD: SE/ULA/11259) . .... Svenska Antavlor V:8 nr 301.*

24. *Bygdeå C:2 (1745-1780) Image 112 / page 229 (AID: v139127.b112.s229, NAD: SE/HLA/1010025) .*

25. *Ramsberg AI:3 (1699-1710) Image 84 / page 78 (AID: v52173.b84.s78, NAD: SE/ULA/11259) .*

26. *Ramsberg AI:2 (1691-1696) Image 62 / page 57 (AID: v52172.b62.s57, NAD: SE/ULA/11259) .*

27. *Bygdeå C:2 (1745-1780) Image 103 / page 211 (AID: v139127.b103.s211, NAD: SE/HLA/1010025) .*

28. *Ramsberg AI:1 (1664-1690) Image 6 (AID: v52171.b6, NAD: SE/ULA/11259) .*

29. *Ramsberg C:1 (1679-1698) Image 12 / page 7 (AID: v53707.b12.s7, NAD: SE/ULA/11259) .*

30. *Västra Vingåker C:4 (1748-1767) Image 152 / page 146 (AID: v63043.b152.s146, NAD: SE/ULA/11076) . .... Ramsberg AI:3 (1699-1710) Image 84 / page 78 (AID: v52173.b84.s78, NAD: SE/ULA/11259) .*

31. *Västra Vingåker C:1 (1666-1697) Image 66 / page 61 (AID: v63040.b66.s61, NAD: SE/ULA/11076) .*

32. *Västra Vingåker C:4 (1748-1767) Image 152 / page 146 (AID: v63043.b152.s146, NAD: SE/ULA/11076) .*

33. *Ramsberg C:1 (1679-1698) Image 96 / page 91 (AID: v53707.b96.s91, NAD: SE/ULA/11259) .*

34. *Ramsberg C:2 (1699-1725) Image 139 / page 135 (AID: v53708.b139.s135, NAD: SE/ULA/11259) . .... Ramsberg AI:3 (1699-1710) Image 84 / page 78 (AID: v52173.b84.s78, NAD: SE/ULA/11259) .*

35. *Ramsberg C:2 (1699-1725) Image 139 / page 135 (AID: v53708.b139.s135, NAD: SE/ULA/11259) .*

36. *Ramsberg EI:1 (1736-1774) Image 139 / page 8 (AID: v53719.b139.s8, NAD: SE/ULA/11259) . .... Ramsberg AI:3 (1699-1710) Image 84 / page 78 (AID: v52173.b84.s78, NAD: SE/ULA/11259) .*

37. *Ramsberg EI:1 (1736-1774) Image 139 / page 8 (AID: v53719.b139.s8, NAD: SE/ULA/11259) .*

Sweden[37] about age 78. Anna married **Anders Larsson**.[37]

  21   viii.   **Brita Andersdotter**.[38] Brita married **Olof Hansson**, son of **Hans Nilsson** and **Karin Olofsdotter**, on 29 Sep 1717 in Ramsberg, Örebro, Sweden. [39]

        ix.   **Pers Andersson** was born on 23 Aug 1685 in Glifsån, Ramsberg, Örebro, Sweden. [40]

        x.   **Johan Andersson** was born on 5 Jan 1688 in Glifsån, Ramsberg, Örebro, Sweden [41] and died before 1690.

        xi.   **Matts Andersson**[38] was born about 1689.[38]

        xii.   **Johan Andersson**[38] was born on 6 Dec 1690 in Glifsån, Ramsberg, Örebro, Sweden [42] and died on 4 Nov 1739 at age 48.

        xiii.   **Maria Andersson**[38] was born in 1695 in Glifsån, Ramsberg, Örebro, Sweden. [38]

43. Anna Larsdotter[43] was born in 1650[44] and died on 21 Dec 1718 in Glifsån, Ramsberg, Örebro, Sweden [45] at age 68.

Anna married **Anders Andersson**[46] Est 1672.

44. Hans Henningsson,[47] son of **Henning Hansson** and **Ingeborg,** was born in 1626 in Ramshyttan, Ramsberg, Örebro, Sweden[48] and died on 4 May 1690 in Hägernäs, Ramsberg, Örebro, Sweden [48] at age 64.

Hans married **Brita Olsdotter**[49] in Dec 1682 in Ramsberg, Örebro, Sweden. [48]

Children from this marriage were:

        i.   **Elias Hansson**[49]

        ii.   **Karin Hansdotter**[50]

        iii.   **Per Hansson**[49]

        iv.   **Hans Hansson**[50] was born in 1688 in Ramsberg, Örebro, Sweden. [50]

        v.   **Lars Hansson**[49]

  22   vi.   **Hendrik Hansson**.[50] Hendrik married **Anna Persdotter**, daughter of **Petter Mattsson** and **Margareta Olsdotter**, on 3 Sep 1711 in Ramsberg, Örebro, Sweden. [51] Hendrik next married **Maria Ersdotter**[52] on 1 Nov 1724 in Ramsberg, Örebro, Sweden. [53]

45. Brita Olsdotter[49] was born in 1661 in Ramsberg, Örebro, Sweden [48] and died on 25 Aug 1728 in Hägernäs, Ramsberg, Örebro, Sweden[48] at age 67.

Brita married **Hans Henningsson**[47] in Dec 1682 in Ramsberg, Örebro, Sweden. [48]

38. *Ramsberg AI:3 (1699-1710) Image 84 / page 78 (AID: v52173.b84.s78, NAD: SE/ULA/11259)* .

39. *Ramsberg C:2 (1699-1725) Image 14 / page 10 (AID: v53708.b14.s10, NAD: SE/ULA/11259)* .

40. *Ramsberg C:1 (1679-1698) Image 24 / page 19 (AID: v53707.b24.s19, NAD: SE/ULA/11259)* . .... *Ramsberg AI:3 (1699-1710) Image 84 / page 78 (AID: v52173.b84.s78, NAD: SE/ULA/11259)* .

41. *Ramsberg C:1 (1679-1698) Image 28 / page 23 (AID: v53707.b28.s23, NAD: SE/ULA/11259)* .

42. *Ramsberg C:1 (1679-1698) Image 40 / page 35 (AID: v53707.b40.s35, NAD: SE/ULA/11259)* . .... *Ramsberg AI:3 (1699-1710) Image 84 / page 78 (AID: v52173.b84.s78, NAD: SE/ULA/11259)* .

43. *Ramsberg AI:2 (1691-1696) Image 62 / page 57 (AID: v52172.b62.s57, NAD: SE/ULA/11259)* .

44. *Ramsberg C:2 (1699-1725) Image 140 / page 136 (AID: v53708.b140.s136, NAD: SE/ULA/11259)* . .... *Ramsberg AI:3 (1699-1710) Image 84 / page 78 (AID: v52173.b84.s78, NAD: SE/ULA/11259)* .

45. *Ramsberg C:2 (1699-1725) Image 140 / page 136 (AID: v53708.b140.s136, NAD: SE/ULA/11259)* .

46. *Ramsberg AI:2 (1691-1696) Image 62 / page 57 (AID: v52172.b62.s57, NAD: SE/ULA/11259)* . .... *Ramsberg AI:1 (1664-1690) Image 18 / page 11 (AID: v52171.b18.s11, NAD: SE/ULA/11259)* . .... *Svenska Antavlor V:8 nr 301.* .... *Ramsberg AI:1 (1664-1690) Image 6 (AID: v52171.b6, NAD: SE/ULA/11259)* .

47. *Ramsberg C:1 (1679-1698) Image 35 / page 30 (AID: v53707.b35.s30, NAD: SE/ULA/11259)* . .... *Ramsberg AI:1 (1664-1690) Image 38 / page 31 (AID: v52171.b38.s31, NAD: SE/ULA/11259)* . .... *Ramsberg AI:1 (1664-1690) Image 56 / page 49 (AID: v52171.b56.s49, NAD: SE/ULA/11259)* . .... *(Ramsberg AI:2 (1691-1696) Image 82 / page 77 (AID: v52172.b82.s77, NAD: SE/ULA/11259))* .

48. *Jimmy Freijs släktforskning webpage (http://gw2.geneanet.org/jimmyfreij)*.

49. *Ramsberg AI:1 (1664-1690) Image 56 / page 49 (AID: v52171.b56.s49, NAD: SE/ULA/11259)* . .... *(Ramsberg AI:2 (1691-1696) Image 82 / page 77 (AID: v52172.b82.s77, NAD: SE/ULA/11259))* .

50. *Ramsberg AI:1 (1664-1690) Image 56 / page 49 (AID: v52171.b56.s49, NAD: SE/ULA/11259)* .

51. *Ramsberg C:2 (1699-1725) Image 11 / page 7 (AID: v53708.b11.s7, NAD: SE/ULA/11259)* .

52. *Ramsberg AI:8a (1754-1772) Image 129 / page 228 (AID: v52179.b129.s228, NAD: SE/ULA/11259)* .

53. *Ramsberg C:2 (1699-1725) Image 17 / page 13 (AID: v53708.b17.s13, NAD: SE/ULA/11259)* .

46. Petter Mattsson was born Cal 1632[54] and died on 12 Apr 1734 in Hägernäs, Ramsberg, Örebro, Sweden[55] about age 102.

Research Notes: His father is possibly Matts Bengtsson at Larsbo, Söderbärke. [56]

Noted events in his life were:
* Resided: Bef 1689, Larsbo, Söderbärke, Kopparberg, Sweden. [57]
* Resided: After 1690, Hägernäs smeder, Ramsberg, Örebro, Sweden. [58]

Petter married **Margareta Olsdotter**.

Children from this marriage were:

23   i.   **Anna Persdotter**. Anna married **Hendrik Hansson**,[59] son of **Hans Henningsson** and **Brita Olsdotter**, on 3 Sep 1711 in Ramsberg, Örebro, Sweden. [60]

      ii.   **Anders Persson** was born on 14 Jul 1689 in Larsbo bruk, Söderbärke, Kopparberg, Sweden. [61]

47. Margareta Olsdotter was born Cal 1650[62] and died on 10 Nov 1728 in Hägernäs, Ramsberg, Örebro, Sweden[63] about age 78.

Noted events in her life were:
* Resided: Bef 1689, Larsbo, Söderbärke, Kopparberg, Sweden. [57]
* Resided: After 1699, Hägernäs smeder, Ramsberg, Örebro, Sweden. [64]

Margareta married **Petter Mattsson**.

54. *Ramsberg AI:3 (1699-1710) Image 221 / page 215 (AID: v52173.b221.s215, NAD: SE/ULA/11259) . .... Ramsberg C:2 (1699-1725) Image 161 / page 157 (AID: v53708.b161.s157, NAD: SE/ULA/11259) .*

55. *Ramsberg C:2 (1699-1725) Image 161 / page 157 (AID: v53708.b161.s157, NAD: SE/ULA/11259) .*

56. *Söderbärke AI:1 (1673-1673) Image 14 / page 13 (AID: v132222.b14.s13, NAD: SE/ULA/11521) .*

57. *Söderbärke AI:1 (1673-1673) Image 14 / page 13 (AID: v132222.b14.s13, NAD: SE/ULA/11521) . .... Ramsberg AI:3 (1699-1710) Image 112 / page 106 (AID: v52173.b112.s106, NAD: SE/ULA/11259) .*

58. *Ramsberg AI:3 (1699-1710) Image 221 / page 215 (AID: v52173.b221.s215, NAD: SE/ULA/11259) . .... Ramsberg AI:5 (1723-1733) Image 108 / page 102 (AID: v52175.b108.s102, NAD: SE/ULA/11259) . .... Ramsberg AI:4 (1711-1722) Image 111 / page 104 (AID: v52174.b111.s104, NAD: SE/ULA/11259) . .... Ramsberg AI:3 (1699-1710) Image 112 / page 106 (AID: v52173.b112.s106, NAD: SE/ULA/11259).*

59. *Ramsberg AI:1 (1664-1690) Image 56 / page 49 (AID: v52171.b56.s49, NAD: SE/ULA/11259) .*

60. *Ramsberg C:2 (1699-1725) Image 11 / page 7 (AID: v53708.b11.s7, NAD: SE/ULA/11259) .*

61. *Ramsberg AI:3 (1699-1710) Image 221 / page 215 (AID: v52173.b221.s215, NAD: SE/ULA/11259) . .... Söderbärke C:1 (1675-1694) Image 112 (AID: v132270.b112, NAD: SE/ULA/11521) .*

62. *Ramsberg AI:3 (1699-1710) Image 221 / page 215 (AID: v52173.b221.s215, NAD: SE/ULA/11259) . .... Ramsberg C:2 (1699-1725) Image 152 / page 148 (AID: v53708.b152.s148, NAD: SE/ULA/11259) .*

63. *Ramsberg C:2 (1699-1725) Image 152 / page 148 (AID: v53708.b152.s148, NAD: SE/ULA/11259) .*

64. *Ramsberg AI:5 (1723-1733) Image 108 / page 102 (AID: v52175.b108.s102, NAD: SE/ULA/11259) . .... Ramsberg AI:4 (1711-1722) Image 111 / page 104 (AID: v52174.b111.s104, NAD: SE/ULA/11259) . .... Ramsberg AI:3 (1699-1710) Image 112 / page 106 (AID: v52173.b112.s106, NAD: SE/ULA/11259) .*

Ancestor Report for Maria Helena Persdotter

Seventh Generation

80. Nils Olsson[1] died on 9 Jan 1698 in Ritan, Resta, Ramsberg, Örebro, Sweden. [2]

Noted events in his life were:
• Resided: Resta, Ramsberg, Örebro, Sweden. [3]

Nils married **Elin**. [1]

Children from this marriage were:

40	i.	**Hans Nilsson**.[4] Hans married **Karin Olofsdotter** on 20 Jun 1683 in Ramsberg, Örebro, Sweden. [5] Hans next married **Cherstin Bengtsdotter**[6] on 26 Aug 1700 in Ramsberg, Örebro, Sweden. [7]
	ii.	**Elizabets Nilsdotter**[8]
	iii.	**Johan Nilsson**[9] was born about 1665. [10]
	iv.	**Anna Nilsdotter**[3]
	v.	**Milan Nilsdotter**[11]
	vi.	**Olof Nilsson**[11]

81. Elin.[1]

Elin married **Nils Olsson**.[1]

84. Anders Embjörnsson,[12] son of **Embjörn Persson** and **Unknown,** died in 1674 in Glifsån, Ramsberg, Örebro, Sweden.[13]

Noted events in his life were:
• Occupation: miner.[14]

• Resided: Glifsån, Ramsberg, Örebro, Sweden. [14]

1. Ramsberg AI:1 (1664-1690) Image 11 / page 4 (AID: v52171.b11.s4, NAD: SE/ULA/11259) . .... Ramsberg AI:1 (1664-1690) Image 28 / page 21 (AID: v52171.b28.s21, NAD: SE/ULA/11259). .... Ramsberg AI:1 (1664-1690) Image 46 / page 39 (AID: v52171.b46.s39, NAD: SE/ULA/11259). .... Ramsberg AI:2 (1691-1696) Image 16 / page 11 (AID: v52172.b16.s11, NAD: SE/ULA/11259) .

2. Jimmy Freijs släktforskning webpage (http://gw2.geneanet.org/jimmyfreij). .... Ramsberg C:1 (1679-1698) Image 97 / page 92 (AID: v53707.b97.s92, NAD: SE/ULA/11259) .

3. Ramsberg AI:1 (1664-1690) Image 46 / page 39 (AID: v52171.b46.s39, NAD: SE/ULA/11259) .

4. Ramsberg AI:1 (1664-1690) Image 11 / page 4 (AID: v52171.b11.s4, NAD: SE/ULA/11259) . .... Ramsberg AI:1 (1664-1690) Image 28 / page 21 (AID: v52171.b28.s21, NAD: SE/ULA/11259). .... Ramsberg AI:1 (1664-1690) Image 46 / page 39 (AID: v52171.b46.s39, NAD: SE/ULA/11259).

5. Ramsberg C:1 (1679-1698) Image 17 / page 12 (AID: v53707.b17.s12, NAD: SE/ULA/11259) .

6. Ramsberg AI:3 (1699-1710) Image 137 / page 131 (AID: v52173.b137.s131, NAD: SE/ULA/11259) . .... Ramsberg AI:5 (1723-1733) Image 20 / page 14 (AID: v52175.b20.s14, NAD: SE/ULA/11259) .

7. Ramsberg C:2 (1699-1725) Image 7 / page 3 (AID: v53708.b7.s3, NAD: SE/ULA/11259) .

8. Ramsberg AI:1 (1664-1690) Image 11 / page 4 (AID: v52171.b11.s4, NAD: SE/ULA/11259) . .... Ramsberg AI:1 (1664-1690) Image 28 / page 21 (AID: v52171.b28.s21, NAD: SE/ULA/11259).

9. Ramsberg AI:1 (1664-1690) Image 28 / page 21 (AID: v52171.b28.s21, NAD: SE/ULA/11259) . .... Ramsberg AI:1 (1664-1690) Image 46 / page 39 (AID: v52171.b46.s39, NAD: SE/ULA/11259) . .... Ramsberg AI:2 (1691-1696) Image 16 / page 11 (AID: v52172.b16.s11, NAD: SE/ULA/11259).

10. Ramsberg AI:1 (1664-1690) Image 28 / page 21 (AID: v52171.b28.s21, NAD: SE/ULA/11259) .

11. Ramsberg AI:1 (1664-1690) Image 46 / page 39 (AID: v52171.b46.s39, NAD: SE/ULA/11259) . .... Ramsberg AI:2 (1691-1696) Image 16 / page 11 (AID: v52172.b16.s11, NAD: SE/ULA/11259) .

12. Svenska Antavlor V:8 nr 301. .... Ramsberg AI:1 (1664-1690) Image 18 / page 11 (AID: v52171.b18.s11, NAD: SE/ULA/11259) .

13. Svenska Antavlor V:8 nr 301.

14. Ramsberg AI:1 (1664-1690) Image 18 / page 11 (AID: v52171.b18.s11, NAD: SE/ULA/11259) .

- Court case: witness, 13 Apr 1670, Arboga, Arboga, Västmanland, Sweden. [15] Anders was asked by the authorities in 1669 to retrieve a woman named Malin, stepdaughter of Jon Stake of Arbago, from Stockholm. When Anders and the ship's crew found her and tried to force her on the boat, she lost her skirt. She took another boat back home, but the crew claimed they were not to blame for accosting Malin. The court disagreed.

Translated Court Record, Arboga rådhusrätt 13 april 1670: Larsson's step-daughter says Anders Hansson went after her in the city, and when she came in the boat, he took her skirt. Anders Hansson admits taking her skirt and throwing it in bed. But Malin on the second day resumed, and unclothed went from the coop [ships cabin?]. Mats Persson after taking an oath on the book testifies now that he word for word on March 17th did this: "Mats Persson captain testifies that Anders Hansson followed a miner after the maid in the city and when they came there, she pulled off her skirt and Anders Hansson took her skirt and lay in his bed in the cabin and then the maid left town on another boat. Mats Persson asked the miner where the skirt was and the miner said it is in storage in Anders Hansson's trunk. AndersEmbjörnsson, miner in Glifsa, testifed after taking the oath, that Malin Eriksdotter put her skirt in the cabin above the bed feet, then when the King would turn a knight (this was June 28, 1669) she took her skirt again and got dressed, then said Anders Hansson whither she shall take the road, she answers, I shall go away. Anders says, you can't go with the clothes you hath on, and he takes the skirt from her and throws it alone in bed at the head of the bed, when the maid says, thou hast got a better reason for them than I do, so keep them. The miner says he is appointed by Joe L Stake searching for his step-daughter and where she would travel, and to take her home with him, which he also planned to do, but he did not appoint Anders Hansson to forcibly take the girl home." Verdict: words of Anders Hansson are disproven with Nils Lars Menlöse's certificate dated Stockholm d 23 March 1670 as the certificate in the letter reads, however, that she is blameless for the force used against Malin Eriksdotter and for their person know nothing but good about her.

Anders married **Karin Nilsdotter**[16] in 1634.[17]

Children from this marriage were:

	i.	**Peder Andersson**[18]
	ii.	**Matts Andersson**[19]
42	iii.	**Anders Andersson**.[20] Anders married **Anna Larsdotter**[21] Est 1672.
	iv.	**Kerstin Andersdotter**[19]
	v.	**Karin Andersdotter**[22]

85. Karin Nilsdotter[16] was born in 1608[23] and died on 20 May 1688 in Glifsån, Ramsberg, Örebro, Sweden[23] at age 80.

General Notes: From Ramsberg death record: "Karin Nilsdotter in Glifsa Saft Anders who has been married 40 years, widow 14 years, the whole age 80 years. Burial on the graveyard opposite of Sungstefterna." [17]

Karin married **Anders Embjörnsson**[24] in 1634.[17]

88. Henning Hansson[25] was born in 1605[26] and died in Dec 1689 in Ramshyttan, Ramsberg, Örebro, Sweden[27] at age 84.

----

15. Goran Ekberg, Website: Jon Stake borgare i Arboga (www.gorek.se/skriftx/jonstake.pdf). .... Email from Goran Ekberg.

16. Ramsberg AI:1 (1664-1690) Image 18 / page 11 (AID: v52171.b18.s11, NAD: SE/ULA/11259) . .... Svenska Antavlor V:8 nr 301.

17. Ramsberg C:1 (1679-1698) Image 106 / page 101 (AID: v53707.b106.s101, NAD: SE/ULA/11259) .

18. Ramsberg AI:1 (1664-1690) Image 18 / page 11 (AID: v52171.b18.s11, NAD: SE/ULA/11259) .

19. Ramsberg AI:1 (1664-1690) Image 18 / page 11 (AID: v52171.b18.s11, NAD: SE/ULA/11259) . .... Ramsberg AI:1 (1664-1690) Image 6 (AID: v52171.b6, NAD: SE/ULA/11259).

20. Ramsberg AI:2 (1691-1696) Image 62 / page 57 (AID: v52172.b62.s57, NAD: SE/ULA/11259) . .... Ramsberg AI:1 (1664-1690) Image 18 / page 11 (AID: v52171.b18.s11, NAD: SE/ULA/11259) . .... Svenska Antavlor V:8 nr 301. .... Ramsberg AI:1 (1664-1690) Image 6 (AID: v52171.b6, NAD: SE/ULA/11259).

21. Ramsberg AI:2 (1691-1696) Image 62 / page 57 (AID: v52172.b62.s57, NAD: SE/ULA/11259) .

22. Ramsberg AI:1 (1664-1690) Image 6 (AID: v52171.b6, NAD: SE/ULA/11259) .

23. Svenska Antavlor V:8 nr 301. .... Ramsberg C:1 (1679-1698) Image 106 / page 101 (AID: v53707.b106.s101, NAD: SE/ULA/11259)

24. Svenska Antavlor V:8 nr 301. .... Ramsberg AI:1 (1664-1690) Image 18 / page 11 (AID: v52171.b18.s11, NAD: SE/ULA/11259) .

Ancestor Report for Maria Helena Persdotter

Henning married **Ingeborg**[28] in 1625 in Ramsberg, Örebro, Sweden.[29]

Children from this marriage were:

44	i.	**Hans Henningsson**.[30] Hans married **Brita Olsdotter**[31] in Dec 1682 in Ramsberg, Örebro, Sweden.[29]
	ii.	**Henning Henningsson**[32]
	iii.	**Henrik Henningsson**[29]
	iv.	**Anna Henningsdotter**[33]
	v.	**Derdi Henningsdotter**[32]
	vi.	**Marit Henningsdotter**[32]
	vii.	**Olof Henningsson**[32]

Henning next married **Elin Jonsdotter**[34] on 11 Jun 1682 in Ramsberg, Örebro, Sweden.[29]

89. Ingeborg[28] died in 1675 in Ramshyttan, Ramsberg, Örebro, Sweden.[29]

Ingeborg married **Henning Hansson**[28] in 1625 in Ramsberg, Örebro, Sweden.[29]

---

28. *Ramsberg AI:1 (1664-1690) Image 9 / page 2 (AID: v52171.b9.s2, NAD: SE/ULA/11259) . .... Ramsberg AI:1 (1664-1690) Image 26 / page 19 (AID: v52171.b26.s19, NAD: SE/ULA/11259) .*

29. *Jimmy Freijs släktforskning webpage (http://gw2.geneanet.org/jimmyfreij).*

30. *Ramsberg C:1 (1679-1698) Image 35 / page 30 (AID: v53707.b35.s30, NAD: SE/ULA/11259) . .... Ramsberg AI:1 (1664-1690) Image 38 / page 31 (AID: v52171.b38.s31, NAD: SE/ULA/11259) . .... Ramsberg AI:1 (1664-1690) Image 56 / page 49 (AID: v52171.b56.s49, NAD: SE/ULA/11259). .... (Ramsberg AI:2 (1691-1696) Image 82 / page 77 (AID: v52172.b82.s77, NAD: SE/ULA/11259)).*

31. *Ramsberg AI:1 (1664-1690) Image 56 / page 49 (AID: v52171.b56.s49, NAD: SE/ULA/11259) . .... (Ramsberg AI:2 (1691-1696) Image 82 / page 77 (AID: v52172.b82.s77, NAD: SE/ULA/11259)).*

32. *Jimmy Freijs släktforskning webpage (http://gw2.geneanet.org/jimmyfreij). .... Ramsberg AI:1 (1664-1690) Image 9 / page 2 (AID: v52171.b9.s2, NAD: SE/ULA/11259). .... Ramsberg AI:1 (1664-1690) Image 26 / page 19 (AID: v52171.b26.s19, NAD: SE/ULA/11259) . .... Ramsberg AI:1 (1664-1690) Image 38 / page 31 (AID: v52171.b38.s31, NAD: SE/ULA/11259) .*

33. *Jimmy Freijs släktforskning webpage (http://gw2.geneanet.org/jimmyfreij). .... Ramsberg AI:1 (1664-1690) Image 9 / page 2 (AID: v52171.b9.s2, NAD: SE/ULA/11259). .... Ramsberg AI:1 (1664-1690) Image 26 / page 19 (AID: v52171.b26.s19, NAD: SE/ULA/11259) .*

34. *Ramsberg AI:1 (1664-1690) Image 74 / page 67 (AID: v52171.b74.s67, NAD: SE/ULA/11259) .*

Eighth Generation

168. Embjörn Persson[1] died in 1649 in Glifsån, Ramsberg, Örebro, Sweden. [1]

Research Notes: Embjörn Persson may have been a founder of the villiage Glifsån which was established in 1629.

Noted events in his life were:
- Occupation: miner.[2]

- Legal action: mining dispute, 7 Sep 1624, Ramsberg, Örebro, Sweden. [2] Embjörn Persson had a dispute with Claes Christierson Horn about property boundaries and who had the right to take ore from the mines. Apparently the landmarks marking the property were in dispute, but Claes Christierson Horn had a history of mining violatios.

Embjörn married someone.

The child from this marriage was:

    84   i.   **Anders Embjörnsson**.[3] Anders married **Karin Nilsdotter**[4] in 1634.[5]

---

1. Svenska Antavlor V:8 nr 301.

2. Johan Johansson, Noraskogs arkiv: Berghistoriska samlingar och anteckningar (1891).

3. Svenska Antavlor V:8 nr 301. .... Ramsberg AI:1 (1664-1690) Image 18 / page 11 (AID: v52171.b18.s11, NAD: SE/ULA/11259) .

4. Ramsberg AI:1 (1664-1690) Image 18 / page 11 (AID: v52171.b18.s11, NAD: SE/ULA/11259) . .... Svenska Antavlor V:8 nr 301.

5. Ramsberg C:1 (1679-1698) Image 106 / page 101 (AID: v53707.b106.s101, NAD: SE/ULA/11259) .

Pedigree Chart for Maria Helena Persdotter

No. 1 on this chart is the same as no. 13 on chart no. 1

8 Nils Nilsson
b. 1709
p.
m. 16 Jul 1748
p. Nora stadsförs, Nora, Örebro, Sweden
d. 25 Aug 1773
p. Brötorp, Nora, Örebro, Sweden

4 Jacob Nilsson
b. 2 Jan 1749
p. Brötorp, Nora, Örebro, Sweden
m. 6 Oct 1776
p. Hällefors, Örebro, Sweden
d. 15 Apr 1807
p. Skärhyttan, Nora, Örebro, Sweden

9 Karin Larsdotter
b. 1724   cont. __32__
p. Brötorp, Nora, Örebro, Sweden
d. 14 Jul 1773
p. Brötorp, Nora, Örebro, Sweden

2 Petter Jacobsson
b. 18 Feb 1780
p. Brötorp, Nora, Örebro, Sweden
m. 4 Jun 1802
p. Hällefors, Örebro, Sweden
d. 4 Jan 1854
p. Skärhyttan, Nora, Örebro, Sweden

10 Anders Olsson
b. 2 Dec 1719   cont. __33__
p. Resta, Ramsberg, Örebro, Sweden
m. 9 Sep 1739
p. Ramsberg, Örebro, Sweden
d. 1770
p. Botiern, Resta, Ramsberg, Örebro, Swe~

5 Christina Andersdotter
b. 7 Oct 1748
p. Botiern, Resta, Ramsberg, Örebro, Swe~
d. 10 Jan 1801
p. Skärhyttan, Nora, Örebro, Sweden

11 Margareta Hindersdotter
b. 7 Jul 1715   cont. __34__
p. Hägernäs, Ramsberg, Örebro, Sweden
d. 1763
p. Botiern, Resta, Ramsberg, Örebro, Swe~

1 Maria Helena Persdotter
b. 5 Mar 1811
p. Skärhyttan, Nora, Örebro, Sweden
m. 26 Dec 1830
p. Hällefors, Örebro, Sweden
d. 18 Mar 1887
p. Skärhyttan, Nora, Örebro, Sweden
sp. Jan Ersson

12 Olof Olsson
b. 3 Jun 1718   cont. __35__
p. Brudgumstorp, Grythyttan, Örebro, Swe~
m. 19 Mar 1744
p. Hällefors, Örebro, Sweden
d. 30 Apr 1799
p. Skärhyttan, Nora, Örebro, Sweden

6 Jakob Olsson
b. 7 Sep 1750
p. Skärhyttan, Nora, Örebro, Sweden
m. 2 Jul 1771
p. Grythyttan, Örebro, Sweden
d. 30 Jan 1807
p. Skärhyttan, Nora, Örebro, Sweden

13 Christina Johansdotter
b. 1724
p.
d. 2 Jun 1791
p. Skärhyttan, Nora, Örebro, Sweden

3 Christina Jacobsdotter
b. 28 Sep 1774
p. Grekskog, Nora, Örebro, Sweden
d. 23 Nov 1859
p. Skärhyttan, Nora, Örebro, Sweden

14 Johan Andersson
b. 1708
p. Hjulsjö, Örebro, Sweden
m. 14 Oct 1733
p. Hjulsjö, Örebro, Sweden
d. 9 May 1775
p. Löfnäs, Grythyttan, Örebro, Sweden

7 Kristina Jansdotter
b. 23 Jul 1748
p. Brunshyttan, Grythyttan, Orebro, Sweden
d. After 1820
p.

15 Brita Andersdotter
b. 1709
p. Grångshyttan, Hjulsjö, Örebro, Sweden
d. 13 Aug 1784
p. Finhagen, Grythyttan, Örebro, Sweden

Pedigree Chart for Karin Larsdotter

No. 1 on this chart is the same as no. 9 on chart no. 31

8
b.
p.
m.
p.
d.
p.

4
b.
p.
m.
p.
d.
p.

9
b.
p.
d.
p.

2 **Lars Persson**
b. 1693
p. Hällefors, Örebro, Sweden
m. 19 Sep 1720
p. Hällefors, Örebro, Sweden
d. 28 Jan 1763
p. Brötorp, Nora, Örebro, Sweden

10
b.
p.
m.
p.
d.
p.

5
b.
p.
d.
p.

11
b.
p.
d.
p.

1 **Karin Larsdotter**
b. 1724
p. Brötorp, Nora, Örebro, Sweden
m. 16 Jul 1748
p. Nora stadsförs, Nora, Örebro, Sweden
d. 14 Jul 1773
p. Brötorp, Nora, Örebro, Sweden
sp. Nils Nilsson

12
b.
p.
m.
p.
d.
p.

6
b.
p.
m.
p.
d.
p.

13
b.
p.
d.
p.

3 **Brita Olofsdotter**
b. 1693
p.
d. 20 Mar 1760
p. Brötorp, Nora, Örebro, Sweden

14
b.
p.
m.
p.
d.
p.

7
b.
p.
d.
p.

15
b.
p.
d.
p.

Pedigree Chart for Anders Olsson

No. 1 on this chart is the same as no. 10 on chart no. 31

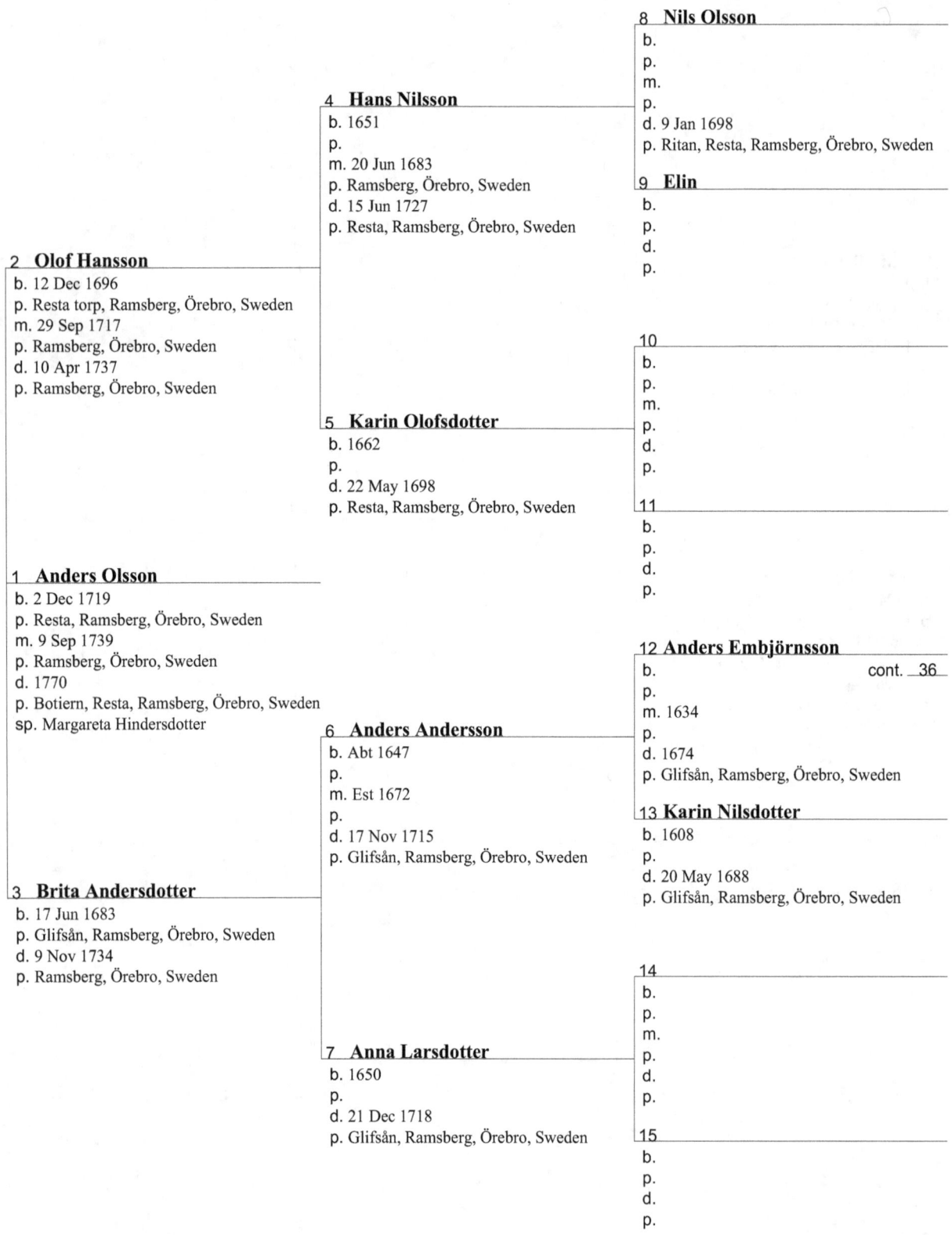

8 Nils Olsson
b.
p.
m.
p.
d. 9 Jan 1698
p. Ritan, Resta, Ramsberg, Örebro, Sweden

4 Hans Nilsson
b. 1651
p.
m. 20 Jun 1683
p. Ramsberg, Örebro, Sweden
d. 15 Jun 1727
p. Resta, Ramsberg, Örebro, Sweden

9 Elin
b.
p.
d.
p.

2 Olof Hansson
b. 12 Dec 1696
p. Resta torp, Ramsberg, Örebro, Sweden
m. 29 Sep 1717
p. Ramsberg, Örebro, Sweden
d. 10 Apr 1737
p. Ramsberg, Örebro, Sweden

10
b.
p.
m.
p.
d.
p.

5 Karin Olofsdotter
b. 1662
p.
d. 22 May 1698
p. Resta, Ramsberg, Örebro, Sweden

11
b.
p.
d.
p.

1 Anders Olsson
b. 2 Dec 1719
p. Resta, Ramsberg, Örebro, Sweden
m. 9 Sep 1739
p. Ramsberg, Örebro, Sweden
d. 1770
p. Botiern, Resta, Ramsberg, Örebro, Sweden
sp. Margareta Hindersdotter

12 Anders Embjörnsson
b.   cont. 36
p.
m. 1634
p.
d. 1674
p. Glifsån, Ramsberg, Örebro, Sweden

6 Anders Andersson
b. Abt 1647
p.
m. Est 1672
p.
d. 17 Nov 1715
p. Glifsån, Ramsberg, Örebro, Sweden

13 Karin Nilsdotter
b. 1608
p.
d. 20 May 1688
p. Glifsån, Ramsberg, Örebro, Sweden

3 Brita Andersdotter
b. 17 Jun 1683
p. Glifsån, Ramsberg, Örebro, Sweden
d. 9 Nov 1734
p. Ramsberg, Örebro, Sweden

14
b.
p.
m.
p.
d.
p.

7 Anna Larsdotter
b. 1650
p.
d. 21 Dec 1718
p. Glifsån, Ramsberg, Örebro, Sweden

15
b.
p.
d.
p.

Pedigree Chart for Margareta Hindersdotter

No. 1 on this chart is the same as no. 11 on chart no. 31

8 Henning Hansson
b. 1605
p.
m. 1625
p. Ramsberg, Örebro, Sweden
d. Dec 1689
p. Ramshyttan, Ramsberg, Örebro, Sweden

4 Hans Henningsson
b. 1626
p. Ramshyttan, Ramsberg, Örebro, Sweden
m. Dec 1682
p. Ramsberg, Örebro, Sweden
d. 4 May 1690
p. Hägernäs, Ramsberg, Örebro, Sweden

9 Ingeborg
b.
p.
d. 1675
p. Ramshyttan, Ramsberg, Örebro, Sweden

2 Hendrik Hansson
b. 28 Sep 1689
p. Östra Hägernäs, Ramsberg, Örebro, Sw~
m. 3 Sep 1711
p. Ramsberg, Örebro, Sweden
d. 1765
p. Hägernäs hammar, Ramsberg, Örebro, ~

10
b.
p.
m.

5 Brita Olsdotter
b. 1661
p. Ramsberg, Örebro, Sweden
d. 25 Aug 1728
p. Hägernäs, Ramsberg, Örebro, Sweden

p.
d.
p.

11
b.
p.
d.
p.

1 Margareta Hindersdotter
b. 7 Jul 1715
p. Hägernäs, Ramsberg, Örebro, Sweden
m. 9 Sep 1739
p. Ramsberg, Örebro, Sweden
d. 1763
p. Botiern, Resta, Ramsberg, Örebro, Sweden
sp. Anders Olsson

12
b.
p.
m.

6 Petter Mattsson
b. Cal 1632
p.
m.
p.
d. 12 Apr 1734
p. Hägernäs, Ramsberg, Örebro, Sweden

p.
d.
p.

13
b.
p.
d.
p.

3 Anna Persdotter
b. 6 Mar 1687
p. Larsbo, Söderbärke, Kopparberg, Sweden
d. 28 Jul 1723
p. Ramsberg, Örebro, Sweden

14
b.
p.
m.

7 Margareta Olsdotter
b. Cal 1650
p.
d. 10 Nov 1728
p. Hägernäs, Ramsberg, Örebro, Sweden

p.
d.
p.

15
b.
p.
d.
p.

Pedigree Chart for Olof Olsson

No. 1 on this chart is the same as no. 12 on chart no. 31

8
b.
p.
m.
p.
d.
p.

4
b.
p.
m.
p.
d.
p.

9
b.
p.
d.
p.

2   **Olof Persson**
b. 1686
p.
m. 2 Jan 1710
p. Grythyttan, Örebro, Sweden
d. 24 Feb 1750
p. Brudgumstorp, Grythyttan, Örebro, Swe~

10
b.
p.
m.
p.
d.
p.

5
b.
p.
d.
p.

11
b.
p.
d.
p.

1   **Olof Olsson**
b. 3 Jun 1718
p. Brudgumstorp, Grythyttan, Örebro, Sweden
m. 19 Mar 1744
p. Hällefors, Örebro, Sweden
d. 30 Apr 1799
p. Skärhyttan, Nora, Örebro, Sweden
sp. Christina Johansdotter

12
b.
p.
m.
p.
d.
p.

6
b.
p.
m.
p.
d.
p.

13
b.
p.
d.
p.

3   **Anna Johansdotter**
b. 1690
p.
d. 25 Feb 1740
p. Brudgumstorp, Grythyttan, Örebro, Swe~

14
b.
p.
m.
p.
d.
p.

7
b.
p.
d.
p.

15
b.
p.
d.
p.

Pedigree Chart for Anders Embjörnsson

No. 1 on this chart is the same as no. 12 on chart no. 33

8
b.
p.
m.
p.
d.
p.

4
b.
p.
m.
p.
d.
p.

9
b.
p.
d.
p.

2 Embjörn Persson
b.
p.
m.
p.
d. 1649
p. Glifsån, Ramsberg, Örebro, Sweden

10
b.
p.
m.
p.
d.
p.

5
b.
p.
d.
p.

11
b.
p.
d.
p.

1   Anders Embjörnsson
b.
p.
m. 1634
p.
d. 1674
p. Glifsån, Ramsberg, Örebro, Sweden
sp. Karin Nilsdotter

12
b.
p.
m.
p.
d.
p.

6
b.
p.
m.
p.
d.
p.

13
b.
p.
d.
p.

3
b.
p.
d.
p.

14
b.
p.
m.
p.
d.
p.

7
b.
p.
d.
p.

15
b.
p.
d.
p.

Chapter 8. Ancestor Report for Anders Jansson

First Generation

1. Anders Jansson,[1] son of **Jan Olsson** and **Catharina Hindersdotter,** was born on 23 Jun 1814 in Barken, Grythyttan, Örebro, Sweden[2] and died on 7 Mar 1851 in Blanka, Sandsjöhöjden, Nora, Örebro, Sweden at age 36. Another name for Anders was Anders Barkén.

Noted events in his life were:
- Moved from: 1841, Grythyttan, Örebro, Sweden.[3] Lived on same homestead as his future son-in-law, Carl Fredric Spångberg. Probably working for Carl's father, Jan Ersson Spångberg.

- Occupation: laborer, 1843, Skärhyttan, Nora, Örebro, Sweden.

- Occupation: laborer, 1845, Sandsjöhöjden, Nora, Örebro, Sweden. [4]

- Name change: to Barken, Cir 1849. Barken was the name of his father's homestead. Anders adopted the surname Barken, later spelled Barkén (accented e), about 1849 when his son Anders was born.

- Resided: 1851, Blanka, Sandsjöhöjden, Nora, Örebro, Sweden. [5]

Anders married **Anna Helena Persdotter,** daughter of **Petter Jacobsson** and **Catharina Olsdotter,** on 30 Sep 1843 in Grythyttan, Örebro, Sweden.[6]

Noted events in her life were:
- Moved to: 1825, Järnboås, Örebro, Sweden. [7]

- Resided: 1825-1835, Hammarhult, Järnboås, Örebro, Sweden. [8]

- Moved to: 1835, Sandsjöhöjden, Nora, Örebro, Sweden. [9]

- Occupation: maid to Gustaf Jansson, former inspector, 1843, Sandsjöhöjden, Nora, Örebro, Sweden. [9]

- Resided: 1845, Sandsjöhöjden, Nora, Örebro, Sweden. [4]

- Resided: Blanka homestead, 1851, Sandsjöhöjden, Nora, Örebro, Sweden. [5]

Children from this marriage were:

    i.   **Christina Elisabet Andersdotter** was born on 3 Jun 1845 in Sandsjöhöjden, Nora, Örebro, Sweden[10] and died on 16 Mar 1891 in Lämtjärnsfallet, Skärhyttan, Nora, Örebro, Sweden [11] at age 45. Other names for Christina were Christina Elisabet Andersdotter Barkén and Christina Elisabet Barkén. Christina had a child. Christina married **Carl Fredrik Jansson Spångberg,**[12] son of **Jan Ersson** and **Maria Helena Persdotter,** on 21 Jun 1870 in Hällefors, Örebro, Sweden. [11]

    ii.   **Jan Petter Andersson Barkén** was born on 12 May 1849 in Sandsjöhöjden, Nora, Örebro, Sweden. [13]

---

1. Grythyttan AIa:13a (1820-1830) Image 246 / page 240 (AID: v51203.b246.s240, NAD: SE/ULA/10337) .

2. Grythyttan AIa:13a (1820-1830) Image 246 / page 240 (AID: v51203.b246.s240, NAD: SE/ULA/10337) . .... Nora bergsförsamling AI:15eb (1851-1861) Image 113 / page 266 (AID: v52013.b113.s266, NAD: SE/ULA/11098) . .... Grythyttan CI:7 (1797-1817) Image 173 / page 333 (AID: v53140.b173.s333, NAD: SE/ULA/10337) .

3. Nora bergsförsamling AI:14bb (1841-1850) .

4. Nora bergsförsamling C:8b (1842-1858) .

5. Nora bergsförsamling AI:15eb (1851-1861) Image 113 / page 266 (AID: v52013.b113.s266, NAD: SE/ULA/11098) .

6. Nora bergsförsamling AI:15eb (1851-1861) Image 113 / page 266 (AID: v52013.b113.s266, NAD: SE/ULA/11098) . .... Nora bergsförsamling AI:14bb (1841-1850) Image 102 / page 248 (AID: v52007.b102.s248, NAD: SE/ULA/11098) .

7. Nora bergsförsamling AI:12a (1821-1829) Image 269 / page 262 (AID: v51994.b269.s262, NAD: SE/ULA/11098) .

8. Järnboås AI:12b (1835-1840) Image 66 / page 278 (AID: v51505.b66.s278, NAD: SE/ULA/10503) .

9. Nora bergsförsamling AI:14bb (1841-1850) Image 102 / page 248 (AID: v52007.b102.s248, NAD: SE/ULA/11098) .

10. Nora bergsförsamling AI:17d (1872-1881) Image 322 / page 668 (AID: v52022.b322.s668, NAD: SE/ULA/11098) . .... Nora bergsförsamling AI:18d (1882-1891) Image 364 / page 762 (AID: v52026.b364.s762, NAD: SE/ULA/11098) . .... Nora bergsförsamling AI:16e (1861-1871) Image 324 / page 317 (AID: v52018.b324.s317, NAD: SE/ULA/11098) . .... Nora bergsförsamling C:9b (1843-1856) Image 38 (AID: v53626.b38, NAD: SE/ULA/11098) .

11. Nora bergsförsamling AI:18d (1882-1891) Image 364 / page 762 (AID: v52026.b364.s762, NAD: SE/ULA/11098) .

12. Nora bergsförsamling AI:14bb (1841-1850) Image 49 / page 195 (AID: v52007.b49.s195, NAD: SE/ULA/11098) .

13. Nora bergsförsamling AI:15eb (1851-1861) . .... Nora bergsförsamling AI:19c (1892-1901) Image 467 / page 951 (AID: v52029.b467.s951, NAD: SE/ULA/11098) . .... Nora bergsförsamling C:9b (1843-1856) Image 88 (AID: v53626.b88, NAD: SE/ULA/11098) .

Ancestor Report for Anders Jansson

Another name for Jan was Jan Petter Barkén.

Ancestor Report for Anders Jansson

Second Generation

2. Jan Olsson,[1] son of **Olof Andersson** and **Märtha Jansdotter,** was born on 9 Apr 1774 in Furunäs, Grythyttan, Örebro, Sweden[2] and died on 22 Apr 1827 in Barken, Grythyttan, Örebro, Sweden[3] at age 53.

Research Notes: The surname Barken was adopted by some of Jan Olsson's ancestors. The Barken farm is not listed until 1812 in the housebooks, so Jan Olsson was probably among its first residents, although he did not own the farm. The Barken homestead was part of the larger Högborn farm in Erstorp, and was first known as Ullnäs Barken because it was part of the Ullnäs estate of Rockesholm manor. It was later divided into Lille Barkan and Stora Barken. The placename Barken might refer to Barken lake which lies to the northwest in Dalarnas Län, more than 100km away.[4]

Noted events in his life were:
- Resided: 1783-1798, Torrvarpsund, Grythyttan, Örebro, Sweden.[5]

- Occupation: dagkarl (day laborer), After 1812, Barken, Grythyttan, Örebro, Sweden.[6]

- Occupation: hemmansbrukare (farmer), Bef 1827, Barken, Grythyttan, Örebro, Sweden.[3]

Jan married **Catharina Hindersdotter**[1] on 30 Nov 1798 in Grythyttan, Örebro, Sweden.[5]

Their children were:
	i.	**Maria Jansdotter**[1] was born on 22 Nov 1799 in Torrvarpsund, Grythyttan, Örebro, Sweden[7] and died on 19 Nov 1847 in Sjöfallet, Grythyttan, Örebro, Sweden[8] at age 47. Maria married **Olof Olsson**.[9] Maria had a relationship with **Per**. This couple did not marry.
	ii.	**Catharina Jansdotter**[1] was born on 30 Oct 1802 in Hasselhöjden, Grythyttan, Örebro, Sweden[10] and was christened on 1 Nov 1802.[11]
	iii.	**Stina Jansdotter**[1] was born on 24 Dec 1806 in Grythyttan, Örebro, Sweden.[1]
	iv.	**Lisa Jansdotter**[1] was born on 5 Jul 1810 in Högborn, Grythyttan, Örebro, Sweden.[12]
	v.	**Anna Jansdotter**[1] was born on 8 Mar 1812 in Elfstorp, Grythyttan, Örebro, Sweden.[13]
1	vi.	**Anders Jansson**.[1] Anders married **Anna Helena Persdotter,** daughter of **Petter Jacobsson** and **Catharina Olsdotter,** on 30 Sep 1843 in Grythyttan, Örebro, Sweden.[14]
	vii.	**Anna Lisa Jansdotter**[1] was born on 1 Feb 1818 in Högborns Gruva, Grythyttan, Örebro, Sweden.[15]

---

1. *Grythyttan AIa:13a (1820-1830) Image 246 / page 240 (AID: v51203.b246.s240, NAD: SE/ULA/10337) .*

2. *Grythyttan AIa:13a (1820-1830) Image 246 / page 240 (AID: v51203.b246.s240, NAD: SE/ULA/10337) . .... Grythyttan AIa:6b (1775-1784) Image 72 / page 67 (AID: v51194.b72.s67, NAD: SE/ULA/10337) . .... Grythyttan CI:5 (1770-1774) Image 33 / page 57 (AID: v53138.b33.s57, NAD: SE/ULA/10337) .*

3. *Grythyttan F:2 (1821-1840) Image 42 (AID: v53160.b42, NAD: SE/ULA/10337) .*

4. *Sammanställd av Carl Geschwind, Trakten kring sjöarna Halvarsnoren och Skärjen och dess historia. Tillkomsten av Rockesholm. (http://hem.passagen.se, 1998).*

5. *Grythyttan EI:1 (1775-1828) Image 53 / page 48 (AID: v53155.b53.s48, NAD: SE/ULA/10337) .*

6. *Grythyttan AIa:13a (1820-1830) Image 246 / page 240 (AID: v51203.b246.s240, NAD: SE/ULA/10337) . .... Grythyttan EI:1 (1775-1828) Image 53 / page 48 (AID: v53155.b53.s48, NAD: SE/ULA/10337) . .... Grythyttan AIa:12a (1812-1819) Image 170 / page 171 (AID: v51201.b170.s171, NAD: SE/ULA/10337) .*

7. *Grythyttan AIa:13a (1820-1830) Image 246 / page 240 (AID: v51203.b246.s240, NAD: SE/ULA/10337) . .... Grythyttan CI:7 (1797-1817) Image 33 / page 57 (AID: v53140.b33.s57, NAD: SE/ULA/10337) .*

8. *Bo-Arne Östborg, Tree of Maja Jansdotter on GENI (http://www.geni.com).*

9. *Bo-Arne Östborg, Tree of Maja Jansdotter on GENI (http://www.geni.com). .... Grythyttan AIa:14a (1830-1840) Image 254 / page 248 (AID: v51205.b254.s248, NAD: SE/ULA/10337) .*

10. *Grythyttan AIa:13a (1820-1830) Image 246 / page 240 (AID: v51203.b246.s240, NAD: SE/ULA/10337) . .... Grythyttan CI:7 (1797-1817) Image 63 / page 115 (AID: v53140.b63.s115, NAD: SE/ULA/10337) .*

11. *Grythyttan CI:7 (1797-1817) Image 63 / page 115 (AID: v53140.b63.s115, NAD: SE/ULA/10337) .*

12. *Grythyttan AIa:13a (1820-1830) Image 246 / page 240 (AID: v51203.b246.s240, NAD: SE/ULA/10337) . .... Grythyttan CI:7 (1797-1817) Image 140 / page 267 (AID: v53140.b140.s267, NAD: SE/ULA/10337) .*

13. *Grythyttan AIa:13a (1820-1830) Image 246 / page 240 (AID: v51203.b246.s240, NAD: SE/ULA/10337) . .... Grythyttan CI:7 (1797-1817) Image 156 / page 299 (AID: v53140.b156.s299, NAD: SE/ULA/10337) .*

14. *Nora bergsförsamling AI:15eb (1851-1861) Image 113 / page 266 (AID: v52013.b113.s266, NAD: SE/ULA/11098) . .... Nora bergsförsamling AI:14bb (1841-1850) Image 102 / page 248 (AID: v52007.b102.s248, NAD: SE/ULA/11098) .*

15. *Grythyttan AIa:13a (1820-1830) Image 246 / page 240 (AID: v51203.b246.s240, NAD: SE/ULA/10337) . .... Grythyttan CI:8 (1818-1847) Image 4 / page 3 (AID: v53141.b4.s3, NAD: SE/ULA/10337) .*

  viii.   **Sara Greta Jansdotter**[1] was born on 4 Dec 1821 in Barken, Grythyttan, Örebro, Sweden.[16]

  ix.   **Johanna Jansdotter**[17] was born on 4 Dec 1821 in Barken, Grythyttan, Örebro, Sweden.[18]

3. Catharina Hindersdotter,[17] daughter of **Henrik Nilsson** and **Ingrid Olsdotter,** was born in 1777 in Knatten, Kroppa, Värmland, Sweden[19] and died on 29 Apr 1830 in Barken, Grythyttan, Örebro, Sweden[17] at age 53.

Research Notes: Some genealogies posit a son Carl, but he arrived at Barken in 1820 and his biological parents were Jan Olsson and Anna Bengtsdotter in Axberg.

Noted events in her life were:

• Resided: Bef 1788, Knatten, Kroppa, Värmland, Sweden.[20]

• Moved from: 1793, Abbortjärn, Kroppa, Värmland, Sweden.[21]

• Moved from: 1794, Åskagen, Kroppa, Värmland, Sweden.[22]

• Moved from: 1795, Fristjärn, Kroppa, Värmland, Sweden.[19]

• Occupation: maid, Bef 1798, Heden, Grythyttan, Örebro, Sweden.[23]

• Resided: After 1812, Barken, Grythyttan, Örebro, Sweden.[24]

Catharina married **Jan Olsson**[17] on 30 Nov 1798 in Grythyttan, Örebro, Sweden.[23]

17. Grythyttan AIa:13a (1820-1830) Image 246 / page 240 (AID: v51203.b246.s240, NAD: SE/ULA/10337) .

18. Grythyttan AIa:13a (1820-1830) Image 246 / page 240 (AID: v51203.b246.s240, NAD: SE/ULA/10337) . .... Grythyttan CI:8 (1818-1847) Image 42 / page 79 (AID: v53141.b42.s79, NAD: SE/ULA/10337) .

19. Grythyttan AIa:13a (1820-1830) Image 246 / page 240 (AID: v51203.b246.s240, NAD: SE/ULA/10337) . .... Grythyttan AIa:7 (1778-1798) Image 64 / page 60 (AID: v51195.b64.s60, NAD: SE/ULA/10337) . .... Kroppa AI:7 (1792-1797) Image 66 / page 60 (AID: v11907.b66.s60, NAD: SE/VA/13291) .

20. Kroppa AI:5 (1780-1786) Image 114 / page 107 (AID: v11905.b114.s107, NAD: SE/VA/13291) .

21. Kroppa AI:7 (1792-1797) Image 23 / page 17 (AID: v11907.b23.s17, NAD: SE/VA/13291) .

22. Kroppa AI:7 (1792-1797) Image 90 / page 84 (AID: v11907.b90.s84, NAD: SE/VA/13291) .

23. Grythyttan EI:1 (1775-1828) Image 53 / page 48 (AID: v53155.b53.s48, NAD: SE/ULA/10337) .

24. Grythyttan AIa:12a (1812-1819) Image 170 / page 171 (AID: v51201.b170.s171, NAD: SE/ULA/10337) .

Ancestor Report for Anders Jansson

Third Generation

4. Olof Andersson,[1] son of **Anders Andersson** and **Catharina Jansdotter,** was born on 19 Oct 1732 in Stensnäs, Grythyttan, Örebro, Sweden.[2] Another name for Olof was Unga Olof Andersson.

Noted events in his life were:

- Resided: with parents, Bef 1753, Stensnäs, Grythyttan, Örebro, Sweden. [3]

- Occupation: servant, After 1753, Björskogsnäs, Grythyttan, Örebro, Sweden. [4]

- Occupation: servant, Bef 1759, Västgötetorp, Grythyttan, Örebro, Sweden. [5]

- Resided: Cir 1759, Brunsjötorp, Grythyttan, Örebro, Sweden. [6]

- Resided: Abt 1783-1794, Torrvarpsund, Grythyttan, Örebro, Sweden. [7] Takes over the farm at Torrvarpsund when he marries a widower with several children.

Olof married **Märtha Jansdotter**[8] on 12 Aug 1759 in Grythyttan, Örebro, Sweden.[8]

His children were:

	i.	**Catherina Olsdotter**[9] was born on 27 Sep 1759 in Grythyttan, Örebro, Sweden. [10] Catherina married someone in 1783.[9]
	ii.	**Olof Olsson**[9] was born on 10 May 1767 in Grythyttan, Örebro, Sweden. [11]
2	iii.	**Jan Olsson**.[12] Jan married **Catharina Hindersdotter**,[12] daughter of **Henrik Nilsson** and **Ingrid Olsdotter,** on 30 Nov 1798 in Grythyttan, Örebro, Sweden.[13]
	iv.	**Ander Olsdotter**[9] was born on 4 Jan 1779 in Grythyttan, Örebro, Sweden[14] and died in 1779.[9]

Olof next married **Maja Persdotter**[1] in 1783.

5. Märtha Jansdotter,[8] daughter of **Jan Jansson** and **Maria Carlsdotter,** was born on 14 Mar 1736 in Gammelkroppa, Kroppa, Värmland, Sweden[15] and died on 30 May 1783 in Furunäs, Grythyttan, Örebro, Sweden[16] at age 47.

---

1. Grythyttan AIa:8 (1785-1797) Image 179 / page 173 (AID: v51196.b179.s173, NAD: SE/ULA/10337) .

2. Grythyttan AIa:8 (1785-1797) Image 179 / page 173 (AID: v51196.b179.s173, NAD: SE/ULA/10337) . .... Grythyttan CI:4 (1758-1769) Image 26 / page 22 (AID: v53137.b26.s22, NAD: SE/ULA/10337) . .... Grythyttan AIa:6b (1775-1784) Image 74 / page 69 (AID: v51194.b74.s69, NAD: SE/ULA/10337) . .... Grythyttan AIa:4 (1740-1767) Image 217 / page 209 (AID: v51191.b217.s209, NAD: SE/ULA/10337) . .... Grythyttan AIa:4 (1740-1767) Image 145 / page 137 (AID: v51191.b145.s137, NAD: SE/ULA/10337) . .... Grythyttan CI:2 (1718-1737) Image 74 / page 70 (AID: v53135.b74.s70, NAD: SE/ULA/10337) .

3. Grythyttan AIa:4 (1740-1767) Image 217 / page 209 (AID: v51191.b217.s209, NAD: SE/ULA/10337) .

4. Grythyttan AIa:4 (1740-1767) Image 224 / page 216 (AID: v51191.b224.s216, NAD: SE/ULA/10337) .

5. Grythyttan AIa:4 (1740-1767) Image 219 / page 211 (AID: v51191.b219.s211, NAD: SE/ULA/10337) .

6. Grythyttan CI:4 (1758-1769) Image 20 / page 16 (AID: v53137.b20.s16, NAD: SE/ULA/10337) .

7. Grythyttan EI:1 (1775-1828) Image 53 / page 48 (AID: v53155.b53.s48, NAD: SE/ULA/10337) . .... Grythyttan AIa:6b (1775-1784) Image 74 / page 69 (AID: v51194.b74.s69, NAD: SE/ULA/10337) .

8. Grythyttan AIa:6b (1775-1784) Image 72 / page 67 (AID: v51194.b72.s67, NAD: SE/ULA/10337) . .... Grythyttan CI:4 (1758-1769) Image 20 / page 16 (AID: v53137.b20.s16, NAD: SE/ULA/10337) .

9. Grythyttan AIa:6b (1775-1784) Image 72 / page 67 (AID: v51194.b72.s67, NAD: SE/ULA/10337) .

10. Grythyttan AIa:6b (1775-1784) Image 72 / page 67 (AID: v51194.b72.s67, NAD: SE/ULA/10337) . .... Grythyttan CI:4 (1758-1769) Image 17 / page 13 (AID: v53137.b17.s13, NAD: SE/ULA/10337) .

11. Grythyttan AIa:6b (1775-1784) Image 72 / page 67 (AID: v51194.b72.s67, NAD: SE/ULA/10337) . .... Grythyttan CI:4 (1758-1769) Image 69 / page 64 (AID: v53137.b69.s64, NAD: SE/ULA/10337) .

12. Grythyttan AIa:13a (1820-1830) Image 246 / page 240 (AID: v51203.b246.s240, NAD: SE/ULA/10337) .

13. Grythyttan EI:1 (1775-1828) Image 53 / page 48 (AID: v53155.b53.s48, NAD: SE/ULA/10337) .

14. Grythyttan AIa:6b (1775-1784) Image 72 / page 67 (AID: v51194.b72.s67, NAD: SE/ULA/10337) . .... Grythyttan CI:6 (1775-1796) Image 45 / page 77 (AID: v53139.b45.s77, NAD: SE/ULA/10337) .

15. Grythyttan AIa:6b (1775-1784) Image 72 / page 67 (AID: v51194.b72.s67, NAD: SE/ULA/10337) . .... Grythyttan CI:5 (1770-1774) Image 120 (AID: v53138.b120, NAD: SE/ULA/10337) . .... Kroppa C:2 (1722-1759) Image 52 / page 95 (AID: v7306.b52.s95, NAD: SE/VA/13291) . .... Kroppa AI:2 (1751-1760) Image 94 / page 86 (AID: v11902.b94.s86, NAD: SE/VA/13291) .

16. Grythyttan AIa:6b (1775-1784) Image 72 / page 67 (AID: v51194.b72.s67, NAD: SE/ULA/10337) . .... Grythyttan CI:5 (1770-1774) Image 120 (AID: v53138.b120, NAD: SE/ULA/10337) .

Ancestor Report for Anders Jansson

Noted events in her life were:
- Resided: Brunsjötorp, 1759, Grythyttan, Örebro, Sweden. [17]
- Resided: Abt 1783-1794, Torrvarpsund, Grythyttan, Örebro, Sweden. [18]

Märtha married **Olof Andersson**[19] on 12 Aug 1759 in Grythyttan, Örebro, Sweden.[20]

6. Henrik Nilsson[21] was born Cal 1733[22] and died on 18 Mar 1785 in Knatten, Kroppa, Värmland, Sweden [23] about age 52.

Research Notes: Possibly moved from Filipstad to Kroppa parish in 1751. [24]

Noted events in his life were:
- Resided: Bef 1785, Knatten, Kroppa, Värmland, Sweden. [25]

Henrik married **Ingrid Olsdotter**.[21]

Children from this marriage were:

	i.	**Maria Hindersdotter**[26] was born on 2 Feb 1761 in Lårhöjden, Kroppa, Värmland, Sweden. [26]
	ii.	**Stina Hindersdotter**[27] was born on 1 Oct 1763 in Gammelkroppa, Kroppa, Värmland, Sweden [28] and was christened on 2 Oct 1763. [29]
	iii.	**Nils Hindersson**[27] was born on 18 Apr 1766 in Knatten, Kroppa, Värmland, Sweden. [30]
	iv.	**Sara Hindersdotter**[25] was born in 1770 in Knatten, Kroppa, Värmland, Sweden. [25]
	v.	**Brita Hindersdotter**[25] was born on 23 May 1773 in Knatten, Kroppa, Värmland, Sweden. [31]
3	vi.	**Catharina Hindersdotter**.[32] Catharina married **Jan Olsson**,[32] son of **Olof Andersson** and **Märtha Jansdotter,** on 30 Nov 1798 in Grythyttan, Örebro, Sweden.[33]
	vii.	**Henric Hindersson**[25] was born on 5 May 1779 in Knatten, Kroppa, Värmland, Sweden. [34]
	viii.	**Ingrid Hindersdotter** was born on 9 Nov 1783 in Knatten, Kroppa, Värmland, Sweden. [35]

---

17. *Grythyttan CI:4 (1758-1769) Image 20 / page 16 (AID: v53137.b20.s16, NAD: SE/ULA/10337)* .

18. *Grythyttan EI:1 (1775-1828) Image 53 / page 48 (AID: v53155.b53.s48, NAD: SE/ULA/10337)* . .... *Grythyttan AIa:6b (1775-1784) Image 74 / page 69 (AID: v51194.b74.s69, NAD: SE/ULA/10337)* .

19. *Grythyttan AIa:8 (1785-1797) Image 179 / page 173 (AID: v51196.b179.s173, NAD: SE/ULA/10337)* .

20. *Grythyttan AIa:6b (1775-1784) Image 72 / page 67 (AID: v51194.b72.s67, NAD: SE/ULA/10337)* . .... *Grythyttan CI:4 (1758-1769) Image 20 / page 16 (AID: v53137.b20.s16, NAD: SE/ULA/10337)* .

21. *Kroppa AI:5 (1780-1786) Image 114 / page 107 (AID: v11905.b114.s107, NAD: SE/VA/13291)* . .... *Kroppa AI:3 (1759-1772) Image 164 / page 156 (AID: v11903.b164.s156, NAD: SE/VA/13291)* .

22. *Kroppa AI:5 (1780-1786) Image 114 / page 107 (AID: v11905.b114.s107, NAD: SE/VA/13291)* . .... *Kroppa C:4 (1760-1810) Image 101 / page 193 (AID: v7308.b101.s193, NAD: SE/VA/13291)* .

23. *Kroppa C:4 (1760-1810) Image 101 / page 193 (AID: v7308.b101.s193, NAD: SE/VA/13291)* .

24. *Kroppa AI:2 (1751-1760) Image 79 / page 72a (AID: v11902.b79.s72a, NAD: SE/VA/13291)* . .... *Filipstad C:5 (1717-1742) Image 216 / page 415 (AID: v5797.b216.s415, NAD: SE/VA/13110)* .

25. *Kroppa AI:5 (1780-1786) Image 114 / page 107 (AID: v11905.b114.s107, NAD: SE/VA/13291)* .

26. *Kroppa C:4 (1760-1810) Image 11 / page 13 (AID: v7308.b11.s13, NAD: SE/VA/13291)* .

27. *Kroppa AI:3 (1759-1772) Image 164 / page 156 (AID: v11903.b164.s156, NAD: SE/VA/13291)* .

28. *Kroppa AI:3 (1759-1772) Image 164 / page 156 (AID: v11903.b164.s156, NAD: SE/VA/13291)* . .... *Kroppa C:4 (1760-1810) Image 25 / page 41 (AID: v7308.b25.s41, NAD: SE/VA/13291)* .

29. *Kroppa C:4 (1760-1810) Image 25 / page 41 (AID: v7308.b25.s41, NAD: SE/VA/13291)* .

30. *Kroppa AI:3 (1759-1772) Image 164 / page 156 (AID: v11903.b164.s156, NAD: SE/VA/13291)* . .... *Kroppa C:4 (1760-1810) Image 36 / page 63 (AID: v7308.b36.s63, NAD: SE/VA/13291)* .

31. *Kroppa AI:5 (1780-1786) Image 114 / page 107 (AID: v11905.b114.s107, NAD: SE/VA/13291)* . .... *Kroppa C:4 (1760-1810) Image 66 / page 123 (AID: v7308.b66.s123, NAD: SE/VA/13291)* .

32. *Grythyttan AIa:13a (1820-1830) Image 246 / page 240 (AID: v51203.b246.s240, NAD: SE/ULA/10337)* .

33. *Grythyttan EI:1 (1775-1828) Image 53 / page 48 (AID: v53155.b53.s48, NAD: SE/ULA/10337)* .

34. *Kroppa AI:5 (1780-1786) Image 114 / page 107 (AID: v11905.b114.s107, NAD: SE/VA/13291)* . .... *Kroppa C:4 (1760-1810) Image 82 / page 155 (AID: v7308.b82.s155, NAD: SE/VA/13291)* .

35. *Kroppa C:4 (1760-1810) Image 94 / page 179 (AID: v7308.b94.s179, NAD: SE/VA/13291)* .

Ancestor Report for Anders Jansson

7. Ingrid Olsdotter,[36] daughter of **Olof Mattsson** and **Kjerstin Andersdotter,** was born on 20 Mar 1740 in Lårhöjden, Kroppa, Värmland, Sweden[37] and died on 8 Apr 1809 in Vargbon, Kroppa, Värmland, Sweden[38] at age 69.

Noted events in her life were:

- Resided: 1740-1761, Lårhöjden, Kroppa, Värmland, Sweden. [39]

- Resided: Bef 1783, Knatten, Kroppa, Värmland, Sweden. [40]

- Resided: 1798, Vargtorp, Kroppa, Värmland, Sweden. [41]

- Moved to: 1798, Grythyttan, Örebro, Sweden.[41] Apparently moves back before 1809.

Ingrid married **Henrik Nilsson**.[36]

---

36. Kroppa AI:5 (1780-1786) Image 114 / page 107 (AID: v11905.b114.s107, NAD: SE/VA/13291) . .... Kroppa AI:3 (1759-1772) Image 164 / page 156 (AID: v11903.b164.s156, NAD: SE/VA/13291) .

37. Kroppa AI:5 (1780-1786) Image 114 / page 107 (AID: v11905.b114.s107, NAD: SE/VA/13291) . .... Kroppa C:4 (1760-1810) Image 201 / page 393 (AID: v7308.b201.s393, NAD: SE/VA/13291) . .... Kroppa C:2 (1722-1759) Image 73 / page 137 (AID: v7306.b73.s137, NAD: SE/VA/13291).

38. Kroppa C:4 (1760-1810) Image 201 / page 393 (AID: v7308.b201.s393, NAD: SE/VA/13291) .

39. Kroppa C:4 (1760-1810) Image 11 / page 13 (AID: v7308.b11.s13, NAD: SE/VA/13291) . .... Kroppa AI:1 (1738-1744) Image 4 (AID: v11901.b4, NAD: SE/VA/13291) .

40. Kroppa AI:5 (1780-1786) Image 114 / page 107 (AID: v11905.b114.s107, NAD: SE/VA/13291) .

41. Kroppa AI:8 (1798-1804) Image 51 / page 46 (AID: v11908.b51.s46, NAD: SE/VA/13291) .

Fourth Generation

8. Anders Andersson, son of **Anders Andersson** and **Karin Nilsdotter,** was born Cal 1700[1] and died on 20 Aug 1773 in Stensnästorp, Grythyttan, Örebro, Sweden[2] about age 73.

Noted events in his life were:
- Occupation: ship's mate, 1730.[3]

- Occupation: ironworker, 1740, Varnäs, Grythyttan, Örebro, Sweden.[4]

- Resided: Bef 1753, Stensnäs, Grythyttan, Örebro, Sweden.[5]

- Resided: Bef 1773, Stensnästorp, Grythyttan, Örebro, Sweden.[6]

Anders married **Catharina Jansdotter** on 6 Oct 1728 in Grythyttan, Örebro, Sweden.[7]

Children from this marriage were:
	i.	**Anders Andersson** was born on 28 Nov 1728 in Finnhyttan, Västgötetorp, Grythyttan, Örebro, Sweden.[8]
	ii.	**Catharina Andersdotter**[9] was born on 6 Mar 1730 in Stensnäs, Grythyttan, Örebro, Sweden.[10]
4	iii.	**Olof Andersson.**[11] Olof married **Märtha Jansdotter**,[12] daughter of **Jan Jansson** and **Maria Carlsdotter,** on 12 Aug 1759 in Grythyttan, Örebro, Sweden.[12] Olof next married **Maja Persdotter**[11] in 1783.
	iv.	**Erik Andersson**[9] was born on 31 Jul 1739 in Stensnäs, Grythyttan, Örebro, Sweden.[13]

9. Catharina Jansdotter, daughter of **Unknown** and **Margreta Hansdotter,** was born Cal 1710[14] and died on 14 Oct 1773 in Stensnästorp, Grythyttan, Örebro, Sweden[15] about age 63.

Birth Notes: Possibly born 28 Nov in Kroppa, Värmland.

Noted events in her life were:
- Occupation: maid, 1728, Tröshyttan, Grythyttan, Örebro, Sweden.[16]

- Resided: Bef 1753, Stensnäs, Grythyttan, Örebro, Sweden.[9]

---

1. Grythyttan AIa:4 (1740-1767) Image 217 / page 209 (AID: v51191.b217.s209, NAD: SE/ULA/10337) . .... Grythyttan AIa:5 (1771-1776) Image 139 / page 131 (AID: v51192.b139.s131, NAD: SE/ULA/10337) . .... Grythyttan AIa:4 (1740-1767) Image 145 / page 137 (AID: v51191.b145.s137, NAD: SE/ULA/10337).

2. Grythyttan AIa:5 (1771-1776) Image 139 / page 131 (AID: v51192.b139.s131, NAD: SE/ULA/10337) . .... Grythyttan CI:5 (1770-1774) Image 66 (AID: v53138.b66, NAD: SE/ULA/10337) .

3. Grythyttan CI:2 (1718-1737) Image 61 / page 57 (AID: v53135.b61.s57, NAD: SE/ULA/10337) .

4. Grythyttan AIa:4 (1740-1767) Image 145 / page 137 (AID: v51191.b145.s137, NAD: SE/ULA/10337) .

5. Grythyttan AIa:4 (1740-1767) Image 217 / page 209 (AID: v51191.b217.s209, NAD: SE/ULA/10337) . .... Grythyttan AIa:2 (1727-1740) Image 70 / page 120 (AID: v51189.b70.s120, NAD: SE/ULA/10337) .

6. Grythyttan AIa:5 (1771-1776) Image 139 / page 131 (AID: v51192.b139.s131, NAD: SE/ULA/10337) .

7. Grythyttan AIa:2 (1727-1740) Image 24 / page 28 (AID: v51189.b24.s28, NAD: SE/ULA/10337) . .... Grythyttan CI:2 (1718-1737) Image 54 / page 50 (AID: v53135.b54.s50, NAD: SE/ULA/10337) .

8. Grythyttan CI:2 (1718-1737) Image 53 / page 49 (AID: v53135.b53.s49, NAD: SE/ULA/10337) .

9. Grythyttan AIa:4 (1740-1767) Image 217 / page 209 (AID: v51191.b217.s209, NAD: SE/ULA/10337) .

10. Grythyttan AIa:4 (1740-1767) Image 145 / page 137 (AID: v51191.b145.s137, NAD: SE/ULA/10337) . .... Grythyttan CI:2 (1718-1737) Image 61 / page 57 (AID: v53135.b61.s57, NAD: SE/ULA/10337) .

11. Grythyttan AIa:8 (1785-1797) Image 179 / page 173 (AID: v51196.b179.s173, NAD: SE/ULA/10337) .

12. Grythyttan AIa:6b (1775-1784) Image 72 / page 67 (AID: v51194.b72.s67, NAD: SE/ULA/10337) . .... Grythyttan CI:4 (1758-1769) Image 20 / page 16 (AID: v53137.b20.s16, NAD: SE/ULA/10337) .

13. Grythyttan AIa:4 (1740-1767) Image 217 / page 209 (AID: v51191.b217.s209, NAD: SE/ULA/10337) . .... Grythyttan CI:3 (1737-1757) Image 132 (AID: v53136.b132, NAD: SE/ULA/10337) .

14. Grythyttan AIa:4 (1740-1767) Image 217 / page 209 (AID: v51191.b217.s209, NAD: SE/ULA/10337) . .... Grythyttan AIa:4 (1740-1767) Image 145 / page 137 (AID: v51191.b145.s137, NAD: SE/ULA/10337) .

15. Grythyttan AIa:5 (1771-1776) Image 139 / page 131 (AID: v51192.b139.s131, NAD: SE/ULA/10337) . .... Grythyttan CI:5 (1770-1774) Image 68 (AID: v53138.b68, NAD: SE/ULA/10337) .

16. Grythyttan CI:2 (1718-1737) Image 54 / page 50 (AID: v53135.b54.s50, NAD: SE/ULA/10337) .

Ancestor Report for Anders Jansson

- Resided: Bef 1773, Stensnästorp, Grythyttan, Örebro, Sweden. [17]

Catharina married **Anders Andersson** on 6 Oct 1728 in Grythyttan, Örebro, Sweden. [18]

10. Jan Jansson [19] was born Cal 1689 [20] and died on 8 May 1753 in Gammelkroppa, Kroppa, Värmland, Sweden [20] about age 64.

Noted events in his life were:
- Resided: Gammelkroppa, Kroppa, Värmland, Sweden. [21]

Jan married **Maria Carlsdotter** [19] on 21 Sep 1713 in Kroppa, Värmland, Sweden. [22]

Children from this marriage were:
	i.	**Maria Jansdotter** [23] was born on 24 Oct 1713 in Gammelkroppa, Kroppa, Värmland, Sweden. [24]
	ii.	**Jan Jansson** [23] was born about 1717. [25]
	iii.	**Petter Jansson** was born on 3 Jan 1717 in Gammelkroppa, Kroppa, Värmland, Sweden. [26]
	iv.	**Cherstin Jansson** [23] was born on 5 Aug 1720 in Gammelkroppa, Kroppa, Värmland, Sweden. [27]
	v.	**Carl Jansson** was born on 30 Nov 1723 in Gammelkroppa, Kroppa, Värmland, Sweden. [28]
	vi.	**Nils Jansson** was born on 17 Aug 1726 in Gammelkroppa, Kroppa, Värmland, Sweden. [29]
	vii.	**Jansson** was born on 24 Feb 1731 in Gammelkroppa, Kroppa, Värmland, Sweden. [30]
	viii.	**Erik Jansson** [23] was born about 1733. [25]
	ix.	**Lisa Jansdotter** [23] was born about 1733. [25]
5	x.	**Märtha Jansdotter**. [31] Märtha married **Olof Andersson**, [32] son of **Anders Andersson** and **Catharina Jansdotter,** on 12 Aug 1759 in Grythyttan, Örebro, Sweden. [31]

11. Maria Carlsdotter, [19] daughter of **Carl Olofsson** and **Unknown,** was born on 19 Dec 1690 in Gammelkroppa, Kroppa, Värmland, Sweden [33] and died on 3 Mar 1773 in Gammelkroppa, Kroppa, Värmland, Sweden [34] at age 82.

Maria married **Jan Jansson** [19] on 21 Sep 1713 in Kroppa, Värmland, Sweden. [22]

14. Olof Mattsson, [35] son of **Matts Olofsson** and **Ingeborg Eriksdotter,** was born on 5 Jul 1693 in Lårhöjden, Kroppa, Värmland, Sweden [36] and died on 11 Dec 1748 in Lårhöjden, Kroppa, Värmland, Sweden [37] at age 55.

---

17. *Grythyttan AIa:5 (1771-1776) Image 139 / page 131 (AID: v51192.b139.s131, NAD: SE/ULA/10337) .*

18. *Grythyttan AIa:2 (1727-1740) Image 24 / page 28 (AID: v51189.b24.s28, NAD: SE/ULA/10337) . .... Grythyttan CI:2 (1718-1737) Image 54 / page 50 (AID: v53135.b54.s50, NAD: SE/ULA/10337) .*

19. *Grythyttan CI:5 (1770-1774) Image 120 (AID: v53138.b120, NAD: SE/ULA/10337) .*

20. *Kroppa AI:2 (1751-1760) Image 94 / page 86 (AID: v11902.b94.s86, NAD: SE/VA/13291) . .... Kroppa C:3 (1722-1759) Image 147 (AID: v7307.b147, NAD: SE/VA/13291) .*

21. *Kroppa C:3 (1722-1759) Image 13 (AID: v7307.b13, NAD: SE/VA/13291) . .... Kroppa AI:1 (1738-1744) Image 87 / page 165 (AID: v11901.b87.s165, NAD: SE/VA/13291) . .... Kroppa AI:2 (1751-1760) Image 94 / page 86 (AID: v11902.b94.s86, NAD: SE/VA/13291) .*

22. *Kroppa C:1 (1687-1721) Image 122 / page 235 (AID: v7305.b122.s235, NAD: SE/VA/13291) .*

23. *Kroppa AI:1 (1738-1744) Image 87 / page 165 (AID: v11901.b87.s165, NAD: SE/VA/13291) .*

24. *Kroppa C:1 (1687-1721) Image 123 / page 237 (AID: v7305.b123.s237, NAD: SE/VA/13291) .*

25. *Kroppa AI:2 (1751-1760) Image 94 / page 86 (AID: v11902.b94.s86, NAD: SE/VA/13291) .*

26. *Kroppa C:1 (1687-1721) Image 133 / page 257 (AID: v7305.b133.s257, NAD: SE/VA/13291) .*

27. *Kroppa C:1 (1687-1721) Image 144 / page 279 (AID: v7305.b144.s279, NAD: SE/VA/13291) .*

28. *Kroppa C:3 (1722-1759) Image 13 (AID: v7307.b13, NAD: SE/VA/13291) .*

29. *Kroppa C:2 (1722-1759) Image 20 / page 31 (AID: v7306.b20.s31, NAD: SE/VA/13291) .*

30. *Kroppa C:2 (1722-1759) Image 34 / page 59 (AID: v7306.b34.s59, NAD: SE/VA/13291) .*

31. *Grythyttan AIa:6b (1775-1784) Image 72 / page 67 (AID: v51194.b72.s67, NAD: SE/ULA/10337) . .... Grythyttan CI:4 (1758-1769) Image 20 / page 16 (AID: v53137.b20.s16, NAD: SE/ULA/10337) .*

32. *Grythyttan AIa:8 (1785-1797) Image 179 / page 173 (AID: v51196.b179.s173, NAD: SE/ULA/10337) .*

33. *Kroppa AI:2 (1751-1760) Image 94 / page 86 (AID: v11902.b94.s86, NAD: SE/VA/13291) . .... Kroppa C:4 (1760-1810) Image 66 / page 123 (AID: v7308.b66.s123, NAD: SE/VA/13291) . .... Kroppa C:1 (1687-1721) Image 22 / page 35 (AID: v7305.b22.s35, NAD: SE/VA/13291).*

34. *Kroppa C:4 (1760-1810) Image 66 / page 123 (AID: v7308.b66.s123, NAD: SE/VA/13291) .*

35. *Kroppa C:2 (1722-1759) Image 73 / page 137 (AID: v7306.b73.s137, NAD: SE/VA/13291) .*

36. *Kroppa C:3 (1722-1759) Image 119 (AID: v7307.b119, NAD: SE/VA/13291) . .... Stefan Björn, Kroppa och Lungsund förr i tiden*

Ancestor Report for Anders Jansson

Noted events in his life were:
• Resided: Lårhöjden, Kroppa, Värmland, Sweden. [38]

Olof married **Kjerstin Andersdotter**[39] on 13 Oct 1723 in Kroppa, Värmland, Sweden. [40]

Children from this marriage were:

	i.	**Erich Olsson** was born on 13 Aug 1724 in Lårhöjden, Kroppa, Värmland, Sweden. [41]
	ii.	**Catharina Olsdotter** was born on 12 Sep 1725 in Lårhöjden, Kroppa, Värmland, Sweden. [42]
	iii.	**Matts Olsson** was born on 8 Feb 1727 in Lårhöjden, Kroppa, Värmland, Sweden. [43]
	iv.	**Anders Olsson** was born on 11 Nov 1728 in Lårhöjden, Kroppa, Värmland, Sweden. [44]
	v.	**Carl Olsson** was born on 12 Jan 1730 in Lårhöjden, Kroppa, Värmland, Sweden. [45]
	vi.	**Maria Olsdotter** was born on 9 Apr 1731 in Lårhöjden, Kroppa, Värmland, Sweden.
	vii.	**Carl Olsson** was born on 20 Jan 1734 in Lårhöjden, Kroppa, Värmland, Sweden. [46]
	viii.	**Annika Olsdotter** was born on 29 Jun 1735 in Lårhöjden, Kroppa, Värmland, Sweden. [47]
	ix.	**Carl Olsson** was born on 11 Sep 1736 in Lårhöjden, Kroppa, Värmland, Sweden. [48]
	x.	**Olof Olsson** was born on 1 Dec 1738 in Lårhöjden, Kroppa, Värmland, Sweden. [49]
7	xi.	**Ingrid Olsdotter**.[50] Ingrid married **Henrik Nilsson**.[50]
	xii.	**Erich Olsson** was born on 17 Oct 1742 in Lårhöjden, Kroppa, Värmland, Sweden. [51]
	xiii.	**Nils Olsson** was born on 31 May 1748 in Lårhöjden, Kroppa, Värmland, Sweden. [52]

15. Kjerstin Andersdotter[39] was born Cal 1701[53] and died on 5 Jan 1779 in Lårhöjden, Kroppa, Värmland, Sweden[54] about age 78.

Noted events in her life were:
• Resided: Bef 1723, Lungsund, Kroppa, Värmland, Sweden. [40]

• Resided: After 1724, Lårhöjden, Kroppa, Värmland, Sweden. [38]

Kjerstin married **Olof Mattsson**[39] on 13 Oct 1723 in Kroppa, Värmland, Sweden. [40]

Kjerstin next married **Erik Engelbrektsson**.

(http://www.bondetorp.se/lungsund/). .... Kroppa C:1 (1687-1721) Image 31 / page 53 (AID: v7305.b31.s53, NAD: SE/VA/13291) .

37. Kroppa C:3 (1722-1759) Image 119 (AID: v7307.b119, NAD: SE/VA/13291) .

38. Kroppa AI:1 (1738-1744) Image 4 (AID: v11901.b4, NAD: SE/VA/13291) .

39. Kroppa C:2 (1722-1759) Image 73 / page 137 (AID: v7306.b73.s137, NAD: SE/VA/13291) .

40. Stefan Björn, Kroppa och Lungsund förr i tiden (http://www.bondetorp.se/lungsund/) .

41. Kroppa C:2 (1722-1759) Image 14 / page 19 (AID: v7306.b14.s19, NAD: SE/VA/13291) .

42. Kroppa C:2 (1722-1759) Image 16 / page 23 (AID: v7306.b16.s23, NAD: SE/VA/13291) .

43. Kroppa C:2 (1722-1759) Image 22 / page 35 (AID: v7306.b22.s35, NAD: SE/VA/13291) .

44. Kroppa C:2 (1722-1759) Image 26 / page 43 (AID: v7306.b26.s43, NAD: SE/VA/13291) .

45. Kroppa C:1 (1687-1721) Image 31 / page 53 (AID: v7305.b31.s53, NAD: SE/VA/13291) .

46. Kroppa C:1 (1687-1721) Image 41 / page 73 (AID: v7305.b41.s73, NAD: SE/VA/13291) .

47. Kroppa C:2 (1722-1759) Image 47 / page 85 (AID: v7306.b47.s85, NAD: SE/VA/13291) .

48. Kroppa C:2 (1722-1759) Image 54 / page 99 (AID: v7306.b54.s99, NAD: SE/VA/13291) .

49. Kroppa C:2 (1722-1759) Image 66 / page 123 (AID: v7306.b66.s123, NAD: SE/VA/13291) .

50. Kroppa AI:5 (1780-1786) Image 114 / page 107 (AID: v11905.b114.s107, NAD: SE/VA/13291) . .... Kroppa AI:3 (1759-1772) Image 164 / page 156 (AID: v11903.b164.s156, NAD: SE/VA/13291) .

51. Kroppa C:2 (1722-1759) Image 83 / page 157 (AID: v7306.b83.s157, NAD: SE/VA/13291) .

52. Kroppa C:2 (1722-1759) Image 105 / page 201 (AID: v7306.b105.s201, NAD: SE/VA/13291) .

53. Kroppa AI:2 (1751-1760) Image 28 / page 22 (AID: v11902.b28.s22, NAD: SE/VA/13291) . .... Kroppa AI:4 (1774-1779) Image 64 / page 59 (AID: v11904.b64.s59, NAD: SE/VA/13291) .

54. Kroppa AI:4 (1774-1779) Image 64 / page 59 (AID: v11904.b64.s59, NAD: SE/VA/13291) . .... Kroppa C:4 (1760-1810) Image 81 / page 153 (AID: v7308.b81.s153, NAD: SE/VA/13291) .

Ancestor Report for Anders Jansson

Fifth Generation

16. Anders Andersson, son of **Anders Gunnarsson** and **Merit Torkilsdotter,** was born Cal 1664 in Bovik, Grythyttan, Örebro, Sweden[1] and died on 21 Feb 1740 in Stensnäs, Grythyttan, Örebro, Sweden[2] about age 76.

Noted events in his life were:
• Resided: After 1727, Stensnäs, Grythyttan, Örebro, Sweden.[3]

Anders married **Karin Nilsdotter**[4] about 1692.[1]

Children from this marriage were:
        i.   **Maria Andersdotter**[3] died about 1737.[5]
        ii.   **Christina Andersdotter**[6]
        iii. **Per Andersson**[3] was born on 14 Sep 1699 in Stensnäs, Grythyttan, Örebro, Sweden.[7]
8   iv. **Anders Andersson.** Anders married **Catharina Jansdotter,** daughter of **Unknown** and **Margreta Hansdotter,** on 6 Oct 1728 in Grythyttan, Örebro, Sweden.[8]
        v.   **Johan Andersson** was born on 11 Feb 1705 in Stensnäs, Grythyttan, Örebro, Sweden.[9]
        vi. **Olof Andersson**[3] was born on 3 Oct 1706 in Stensnäs, Grythyttan, Örebro, Sweden.[10]
        vii. **Eric Andersson**[3] was born on 8 Oct 1711 in Stensnäs, Grythyttan, Örebro, Sweden.[11]

17. Karin Nilsdotter[4] was born in 1663 in Brunsjötorp, Grythyttan, Örebro, Sweden[12] and died on 3 Jun 1756 in Stensnäs, Grythyttan, Örebro, Sweden[13] at age 93. Another name for Karin was Catharina Nilsdotter.[14]

Noted events in her life were:
• Resided: After 1727, Stensnäs, Grythyttan, Örebro, Sweden.[3]

Karin married **Anders Andersson** about 1692.[1]

19. Margreta Hansdotter[15] was born in 1674[16] and died on 28 Mar 1748 in Stensnäs, Grythyttan, Örebro, Sweden[16] at age 74.

Death Notes: "Old widow Margreta Hansdotter of Stensnäs, ill for some time due to old age and ?, has lived a silent and Christian life, was 74, was buried without personal belongings".

Margreta married someone.

---

    1. Grythyttan CI:3 (1737-1757) Image 22 / page 18 (AID: v53136.b22.s18, NAD: SE/ULA/10337) .
    2. Grythyttan AIa:3 (1737-1743) Image 43 / page 33 (AID: v51190.b43.s33, NAD: SE/ULA/10337) . .... Grythyttan CI:3 (1737-1757) Image 22 / page 18 (AID: v53136.b22.s18, NAD: SE/ULA/10337) .
    3. Grythyttan AIa:2 (1727-1740) Image 24 / page 28 (AID: v51189.b24.s28, NAD: SE/ULA/10337) .
    4. Grythyttan AIa:2 (1727-1740) Image 24 / page 28 (AID: v51189.b24.s28, NAD: SE/ULA/10337) . .... Grythyttan CI:3 (1737-1757) Image 22 / page 18 (AID: v53136.b22.s18, NAD: SE/ULA/10337) .
    5. Grythyttan AIa:3 (1737-1743) Image 43 / page 33 (AID: v51190.b43.s33, NAD: SE/ULA/10337) .
    6. Grythyttan AIa:2 (1727-1740) Image 92 / page 164 (AID: v51189.b92.s164, NAD: SE/ULA/10337) .
    7. Grythyttan CI:1 (1699-1715) Image 8 / page 3 (AID: v53134.b8.s3, NAD: SE/ULA/10337) .
    8. Grythyttan AIa:2 (1727-1740) Image 24 / page 28 (AID: v51189.b24.s28, NAD: SE/ULA/10337) . .... Grythyttan CI:2 (1718-1737) Image 54 / page 50 (AID: v53135.b54.s50, NAD: SE/ULA/10337) .
    9. Grythyttan CI:1 (1699-1715) Image 27 / page 22 (AID: v53134.b27.s22, NAD: SE/ULA/10337) .
    10. Grythyttan CI:1 (1699-1715) Image 32 / page 27 (AID: v53134.b32.s27, NAD: SE/ULA/10337) .
    11. Grythyttan CI:1 (1699-1715) Image 61 / page 55 (AID: v53134.b61.s55, NAD: SE/ULA/10337) .
    12. Grythyttan AIa:4 (1740-1767) Image 216 / page 208 (AID: v51191.b216.s208, NAD: SE/ULA/10337) . .... Grythyttan CI:3 (1737-1757) Image 91 / page 87 (AID: v53136.b91.s87, NAD: SE/ULA/10337) .
    13. Grythyttan AIa:3 (1737-1743) Image 43 / page 33 (AID: v51190.b43.s33, NAD: SE/ULA/10337) . .... Grythyttan AIa:4 (1740-1767) Image 216 / page 208 (AID: v51191.b216.s208, NAD: SE/ULA/10337) . .... Grythyttan CI:3 (1737-1757) Image 91 / page 87 (AID: v53136.b91.s87, NAD: SE/ULA/10337).
    14. Grythyttan CI:3 (1737-1757) Image 91 / page 87 (AID: v53136.b91.s87, NAD: SE/ULA/10337) .
    15. Grythyttan AIa:4 (1740-1767) Image 145 / page 137 (AID: v51191.b145.s137, NAD: SE/ULA/10337) .
    16. Grythyttan AIa:4 (1740-1767) Image 145 / page 137 (AID: v51191.b145.s137, NAD: SE/ULA/10337) . .... Grythyttan CI:3 (1737-1757) Image 52 / page 48 (AID: v53136.b52.s48, NAD: SE/ULA/10337) .

Ancestor Report for Anders Jansson

The child from this marriage was:
9   i.   **Catharina Jansdotter**. Catharina married **Anders Andersson,** son of **Anders Andersson** and **Karin Nilsdotter,** on 6 Oct 1728 in Grythyttan, Örebro, Sweden.[17]

22. Carl Olofsson.[18]

Carl married someone.

The child from this marriage was:
11   i.   **Maria Carlsdotter**.[19] Maria married **Jan Jansson**[19] on 21 Sep 1713 in Kroppa, Värmland, Sweden.[20]

28. Matts Olofsson[21] was born calc 1649[22] and died on 13 Dec 1747 in Lårhöjden, Kroppa, Värmland, Sweden [22] about age 98.

Matts married **Ingeborg Eriksdotter**[21] on 6 Nov 1687 in Kroppa, Värmland, Sweden. [23]

Children from this marriage were:
    i.   **Annika Mattsdotter**[21] was born on 27 Nov 1689 in Lårhöjden, Kroppa, Värmland, Sweden. [24]
14   ii.   **Olof Mattsson**.[25] Olof married **Kjerstin Andersdotter**[25] on 13 Oct 1723 in Kroppa, Värmland, Sweden.[21]
    iii.   **Erik Mattsson**[21] was born on 30 Apr 1695 in Lårhöjden, Kroppa, Värmland, Sweden. [26]
    iv.   **Karl Mattsson**[21] was born on 27 Dec 1697 in Lårhöjden, Kroppa, Värmland, Sweden. [27]

29. Ingeborg Eriksdotter.[21]

Ingeborg married **Matts Olofsson**[21] on 6 Nov 1687 in Kroppa, Värmland, Sweden. [23]

---

17. *Grythyttan AIa:2 (1727-1740) Image 24 / page 28 (AID: v51189.b24.s28, NAD: SE/ULA/10337) . .... Grythyttan CI:2 (1718-1737) Image 54 / page 50 (AID: v53135.b54.s50, NAD: SE/ULA/10337) .*

18. *Kroppa C:1 (1687-1721) Image 22 / page 35 (AID: v7305.b22.s35, NAD: SE/VA/13291) .*

19. *Grythyttan CI:5 (1770-1774) Image 120 (AID: v53138.b120, NAD: SE/ULA/10337) .*

20. *Kroppa C:1 (1687-1721) Image 122 / page 235 (AID: v7305.b122.s235, NAD: SE/VA/13291) .*

21. *Stefan Björn, Kroppa och Lungsund förr i tiden (http://www.bondetorp.se/lungsund/).*

22. *Kroppa C:3 (1722-1759) Image 114 (AID: v7307.b114, NAD: SE/VA/13291) .*

23. *Stefan Björn, Kroppa och Lungsund förr i tiden (http://www.bondetorp.se/lungsund/). .... Kroppa C:1 (1687-1721) Image 6 / page 3 (AID: v7305.b6.s3, NAD: SE/VA/13291).*

24. *Stefan Björn, Kroppa och Lungsund förr i tiden (http://www.bondetorp.se/lungsund/). .... Kroppa C:1 (1687-1721) Image 19 / page 29 (AID: v7305.b19.s29, NAD: SE/VA/13291).*

25. *Kroppa C:2 (1722-1759) Image 73 / page 137 (AID: v7306.b73.s137, NAD: SE/VA/13291) .*

26. *Stefan Björn, Kroppa och Lungsund förr i tiden (http://www.bondetorp.se/lungsund/). .... Kroppa C:1 (1687-1721) Image 38 / page 67 (AID: v7305.b38.s67, NAD: SE/VA/13291).*

27. *Stefan Björn, Kroppa och Lungsund förr i tiden (http://www.bondetorp.se/lungsund/). .... Kroppa C:1 (1687-1721) Image 52 / page 95 (AID: v7305.b52.s95, NAD: SE/VA/13291).*

32. Anders Gunnarsson.[1]

Anders married **Merit Torkilsdotter**.[1]

The child from this marriage was:
    16   i.   **Anders Andersson**. Anders married **Karin Nilsdotter**[2] about 1692.[1]

33. Merit Torkilsdotter.[1]

Merit married **Anders Gunnarsson**.[1]

    1. *Grythyttan CI:3 (1737-1757) Image 22 / page 18 (AID: v53136.b22.s18, NAD: SE/ULA/10337)* .
    2. *Grythyttan AIa:2 (1727-1740) Image 24 / page 28 (AID: v51189.b24.s28, NAD: SE/ULA/10337)* . .... *Grythyttan CI:3 (1737-1757) Image 22 / page 18 (AID: v53136.b22.s18, NAD: SE/ULA/10337)* .

Pedigree Chart for Anders Jansson

No. 1 on this chart is the same as no. 14 on chart no. 1

8 Anders Andersson
b. Cal 1700   cont. __38__
p.
m. 6 Oct 1728
p. Grythyttan, Örebro, Sweden
d. 20 Aug 1773
p. Stensnästorp, Grythyttan, Örebro, Sweden

4 Olof Andersson
b. 19 Oct 1732
p. Stensnäs, Grythyttan, Örebro, Sweden
m. 12 Aug 1759
p. Grythyttan, Örebro, Sweden
d.
p.

9 Catharina Jansdotter
b. Cal 1710   cont. __39__
p.
d. 14 Oct 1773
p. Stensnästorp, Grythyttan, Örebro, Sweden

2 Jan Olsson
b. 9 Apr 1774
p. Furunäs, Grythyttan, Örebro, Sweden
m. 30 Nov 1798
p. Grythyttan, Örebro, Sweden
d. 22 Apr 1827
p. Barken, Grythyttan, Örebro, Sweden

10 Jan Jansson
b. Cal 1689
p.
m. 21 Sep 1713
p. Kroppa, Värmland, Sweden
d. 8 May 1753
p. Gammelkroppa, Kroppa, Värmland, Sw~

5 Märtha Jansdotter
b. 14 Mar 1736
p. Gammelkroppa, Kroppa, Värmland, Sw~
d. 30 May 1783
p. Furunäs, Grythyttan, Örebro, Sweden

11 Maria Carlsdotter
b. 19 Dec 1690   cont. __40__
p. Gammelkroppa, Kroppa, Värmland, Sw~
d. 3 Mar 1773
p. Gammelkroppa, Kroppa, Värmland, Sw~

1 Anders Jansson
b. 23 Jun 1814
p. Barken, Grythyttan, Örebro, Sweden
m. 30 Sep 1843
p. Grythyttan, Örebro, Sweden
d. 7 Mar 1851
p. Blanka, Sandsjöhöjden, Nora, Örebro, Sweden
sp. Anna Helena Persdotter

12
b.
p.
m.
p.
d.
p.

6 Henrik Nilsson
b. Cal 1733
p.
m.
p.
d. 18 Mar 1785
p. Knatten, Kroppa, Värmland, Sweden

13
b.
p.
d.
p.

3 Catharina Hindersdotter
b. 1777
p. Knatten, Kroppa, Värmland, Sweden
d. 29 Apr 1830
p. Barken, Grythyttan, Örebro, Sweden

14 Olof Mattsson
b. 5 Jul 1693   cont. __41__
p. Lårhöjden, Kroppa, Värmland, Sweden
m. 13 Oct 1723
p. Kroppa, Värmland, Sweden
d. 11 Dec 1748
p. Lårhöjden, Kroppa, Värmland, Sweden

7 Ingrid Olsdotter
b. 20 Mar 1740
p. Lårhöjden, Kroppa, Värmland, Sweden
d. 8 Apr 1809
p. Vargbon, Kroppa, Värmland, Sweden

15 Kjerstin Andersdotter
b. Cal 1701
p.
d. 5 Jan 1779
p. Lårhöjden, Kroppa, Värmland, Sweden

Pedigree Chart for Anders Andersson

No. 1 on this chart is the same as no. 8 on chart no. 37

8 _____
b.
p.
m.
p.
d.
p.

4 Anders Gunnarsson
b.
p.
m.
p.
d.
p.

9 _____
b.
p.
d.
p.

2 Anders Andersson
b. Cal 1664
p. Bovik, Grythyttan, Örebro, Sweden
m. Abt 1692
p.
d. 21 Feb 1740
p. Stensnäs, Grythyttan, Örebro, Sweden

10 _____
b.
p.
m.
p.
d.
p.

5 Merit Torkilsdotter
b.
p.
d.
p.

11 _____
b.
p.
d.
p.

1 Anders Andersson
b. Cal 1700
p.
m. 6 Oct 1728
p. Grythyttan, Örebro, Sweden
d. 20 Aug 1773
p. Stensnästorp, Grythyttan, Örebro, Sweden
sp. Catharina Jansdotter

12 _____
b.
p.
m.
p.
d.
p.

6 _____
b.
p.
m.
p.
d.
p.

13 _____
b.
p.
d.
p.

3 Karin Nilsdotter
b. 1663
p. Brunsjötorp, Grythyttan, Örebro, Sweden
d. 3 Jun 1756
p. Stensnäs, Grythyttan, Örebro, Sweden

14 _____
b.
p.
m.
p.
d.
p.

7 _____
b.
p.
d.
p.

15 _____
b.
p.
d.
p.

Pedigree Chart for Catharina Jansdotter

No. 1 on this chart is the same as no. 9 on chart no. 37

8
b.
p.
m.
p.
d.
p.

4
b.
p.
m.
p.
d.
p.

9
b.
p.
d.
p.

2
b.
p.
m.
p.
d.
p.

10
b.
p.
m.
p.
d.
p.

5
b.
p.
d.
p.

11
b.
p.
d.
p.

1 **Catharina Jansdotter**
b. Cal 1710
p.
m. 6 Oct 1728
p. Grythyttan, Örebro, Sweden
d. 14 Oct 1773
p. Stensnästorp, Grythyttan, Örebro, Sweden
sp. Anders Andersson

12
b.
p.
m.
p.
d.
p.

6
b.
p.
m.
p.
d.
p.

13
b.
p.
d.
p.

3 **Margreta Hansdotter**
b. 1674
p.
d. 28 Mar 1748
p. Stensnäs, Grythyttan, Örebro, Sweden

14
b.
p.
m.
p.
d.
p.

7
b.
p.
d.
p.

15
b.
p.
d.
p.

Pedigree Chart for Maria Carlsdotter

No. 1 on this chart is the same as no. 11 on chart no. 37

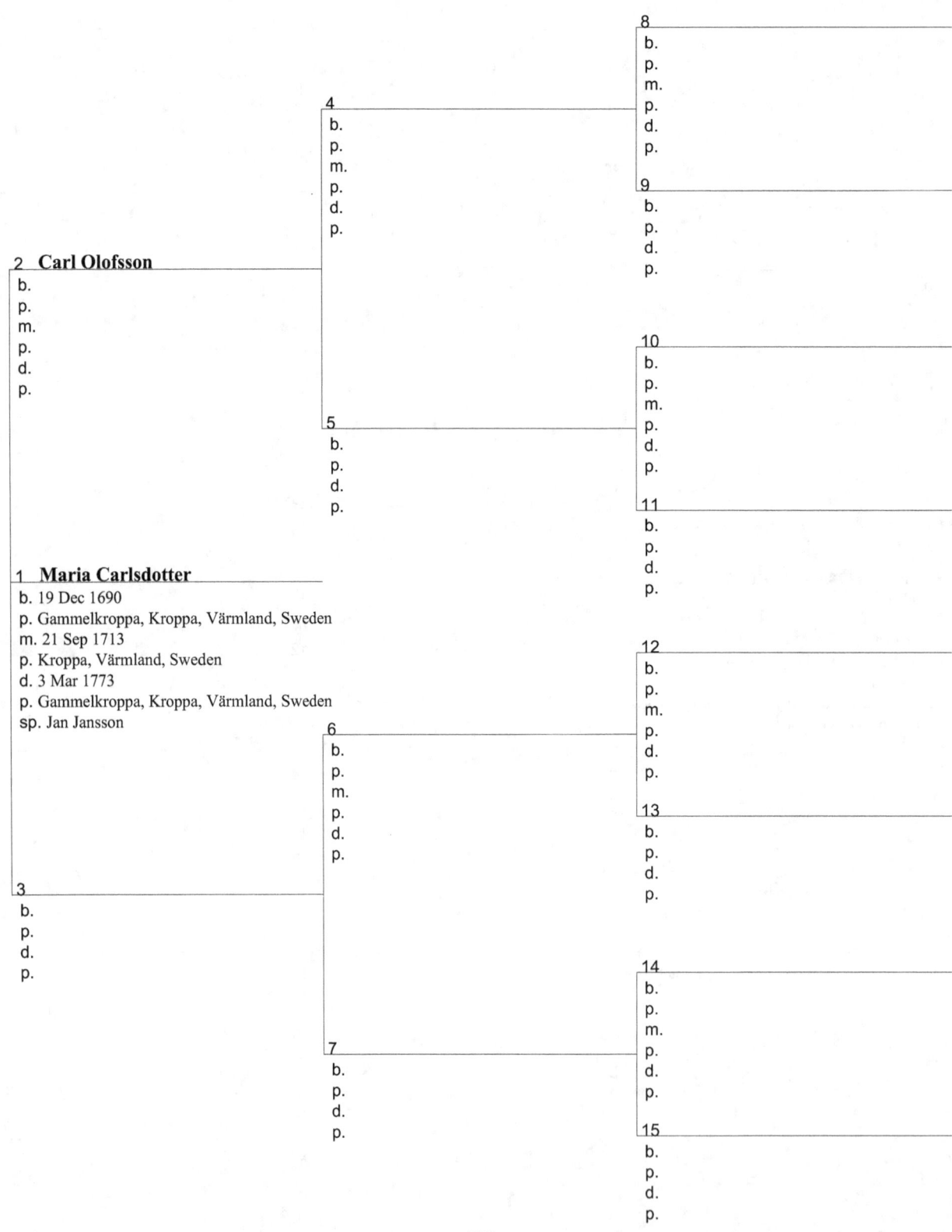

8 _____
b.
p.
m.
p.
d.
p.

4 _____
b.
p.
m.
p.
d.
p.

9 _____
b.
p.
d.
p.

2 Carl Olofsson _____
b.
p.
m.
p.
d.
p.

10 _____
b.
p.
m.
p.
d.
p.

5 _____
b.
p.
d.
p.

11 _____
b.
p.
d.
p.

1   Maria Carlsdotter _____
b. 19 Dec 1690
p. Gammelkroppa, Kroppa, Värmland, Sweden
m. 21 Sep 1713
p. Kroppa, Värmland, Sweden
d. 3 Mar 1773
p. Gammelkroppa, Kroppa, Värmland, Sweden
sp. Jan Jansson

12 _____
b.
p.
m.
p.
d.
p.

6 _____
b.
p.
m.
p.
d.
p.

13 _____
b.
p.
d.
p.

3 _____
b.
p.
d.
p.

14 _____
b.
p.
m.
p.
d.
p.

7 _____
b.
p.
d.
p.

15 _____
b.
p.
d.
p.

Pedigree Chart for Olof Mattsson

No. 1 on this chart is the same as no. 14 on chart no. 37

2 Matts Olofsson
b. calc 1649
p.
m. 6 Nov 1687
p. Kroppa, Värmland, Sweden
d. 13 Dec 1747
p. Lårhöjden, Kroppa, Värmland, Sweden

1 Olof Mattsson
b. 5 Jul 1693
p. Lårhöjden, Kroppa, Värmland, Sweden
m. 13 Oct 1723
p. Kroppa, Värmland, Sweden
d. 11 Dec 1748
p. Lårhöjden, Kroppa, Värmland, Sweden
sp. Kjerstin Andersdotter

3 Ingeborg Eriksdotter
b.
p.
d.
p.

4
b.
p.
m.
p.
d.
p.

5
b.
p.
d.
p.

6
b.
p.
m.
p.
d.
p.

7
b.
p.
d.
p.

8
b.
p.
m.
p.
d.
p.

9
b.
p.
d.
p.

10
b.
p.
m.
p.
d.
p.

11
b.
p.
d.
p.

12
b.
p.
m.
p.
d.
p.

13
b.
p.
d.
p.

14
b.
p.
m.
p.
d.
p.

15
b.
p.
d.
p.

Chapter 9. Ancestor Report for Anna Helena Persdotter

First Generation

1. Anna Helena Persdotter, daughter of **Petter Jacobsson** and **Catharina Olsdotter,** was born on 27 Nov 1816 in Ryttarbacken, Stadra, Nora, Örebro, Sweden[1] and died on 16 Apr 1887 in Skärhyttan, Nora, Örebro, Sweden[2] at age 70.

Noted events in her life were:
- Moved to: 1825, Järnboås, Örebro, Sweden. [3]

- Resided: 1825-1835, Hammarhult, Järnboås, Örebro, Sweden. [4]

- Moved to: 1835, Sandsjöhöjden, Nora, Örebro, Sweden. [5]

- Occupation: maid to Gustaf Jansson, former inspector, 1843, Sandsjöhöjden, Nora, Örebro, Sweden. [5]

- Resided: 1845, Sandsjöhöjden, Nora, Örebro, Sweden. [6]

- Resided: Blanka homestead, 1851, Sandsjöhöjden, Nora, Örebro, Sweden. [7]

Anna married **Anders Jansson,**[8] son of **Jan Olsson** and **Catharina Hindersdotter,** on 30 Sep 1843 in Grythyttan, Örebro, Sweden.[9]

Noted events in his life were:
- Moved from: 1841, Grythyttan, Örebro, Sweden.[10] Lived on same homestead as his future son-in-law, Carl Fredric Spångberg. Probably working for Carl's father, Jan Ersson Spångberg.

- Occupation: laborer, 1843, Skärhyttan, Nora, Örebro, Sweden.

- Occupation: laborer, 1845, Sandsjöhöjden, Nora, Örebro, Sweden. [6]

- Name change: to Barken, Cir 1849. Barken was the name of his father's homestead. Anders adopted the surname Barken, later spelled Barkén (accented e), about 1849 when his son Anders was born.

- Resided: 1851, Blanka, Sandsjöhöjden, Nora, Örebro, Sweden. [7]

Children from this marriage were:
  i.   **Christina Elisabet Andersdotter** was born on 3 Jun 1845 in Sandsjöhöjden, Nora, Örebro, Sweden[11] and died on 16 Mar 1891 in Lämtjärnsfallet, Skärhyttan, Nora, Örebro, Sweden [12] at age 45. Other names for Christina were Christina Elisabet Andersdotter Barkén and Christina Elisabet Barkén. Christina had a child. Christina married **Carl Fredrik Jansson Spångberg,**[13] son of **Jan Ersson** and **Maria Helena Persdotter,** on 21 Jun 1870 in Hällefors, Örebro, Sweden. [12]
  ii. **Jan Petter Andersson Barkén** was born on 12 May 1849 in Sandsjöhöjden, Nora, Örebro, Sweden. [14]

---

   1. Nora bergsförsamling AI:15eb (1851-1861) Image 113 / page 266 (AID: v52013.b113.s266, NAD: SE/ULA/11098) . .... Nora bergsförsamling C:5 (1806-1823) Image 231 / page 227 (AID: v53620.b231.s227, NAD: SE/ULA/11098) . .... Nora bergsförsamling AI:11a (1811-1820) Image 261 / page 253 (AID: v51992.b261.s253, NAD: SE/ULA/11098) .
   2. Nora bergsförsamling F:10 (1861-1894) Image 250 (AID: v53653.b250, NAD: SE/ULA/11098) .
   3. Nora bergsförsamling AI:12a (1821-1829) Image 269 / page 262 (AID: v51994.b269.s262, NAD: SE/ULA/11098) .
   4. Järnboås AI:12b (1835-1840) Image 66 / page 278 (AID: v51505.b66.s278, NAD: SE/ULA/10503) .
   5. Nora bergsförsamling AI:14bb (1841-1850) Image 102 / page 248 (AID: v52007.b102.s248, NAD: SE/ULA/11098) .
   6. Nora bergsförsamling C:8b (1842-1858) .
   7. Nora bergsförsamling AI:15eb (1851-1861) Image 113 / page 266 (AID: v52013.b113.s266, NAD: SE/ULA/11098) .
   8. Grythyttan AIa:13a (1820-1830) Image 246 / page 240 (AID: v51203.b246.s240, NAD: SE/ULA/10337) .
   9. Nora bergsförsamling AI:15eb (1851-1861) Image 113 / page 266 (AID: v52013.b113.s266, NAD: SE/ULA/11098) . .... Nora bergsförsamling AI:14bb (1841-1850) Image 102 / page 248 (AID: v52007.b102.s248, NAD: SE/ULA/11098) .
   10. Nora bergsförsamling AI:14bb (1841-1850) .
   11. Nora bergsförsamling AI:17d (1872-1881) Image 322 / page 668 (AID: v52022.b322.s668, NAD: SE/ULA/11098) . .... Nora bergsförsamling AI:18d (1882-1891) Image 364 / page 762 (AID: v52026.b364.s762, NAD: SE/ULA/11098) . .... Nora bergsförsamling AI:16e (1861-1871) Image 324 / page 317 (AID: v52018.b324.s317, NAD: SE/ULA/11098) . .... Nora bergsförsamling C:9b (1843-1856) Image 38 (AID: v53626.b38, NAD: SE/ULA/11098).
   12. Nora bergsförsamling AI:18d (1882-1891) Image 364 / page 762 (AID: v52026.b364.s762, NAD: SE/ULA/11098) .
   13. Nora bergsförsamling AI:14bb (1841-1850) Image 49 / page 195 (AID: v52007.b49.s195, NAD: SE/ULA/11098) .
   14. Nora bergsförsamling AI:15eb (1851-1861) . .... Nora bergsförsamling AI:19c (1892-1901) Image 467 / page 951 (AID: v52029.b467.s951, NAD: SE/ULA/11098) . .... Nora bergsförsamling C:9b (1843-1856) Image 88 (AID: v53626.b88, NAD: SE/ULA/11098) .

Ancestor Report for Anna Helena Persdotter

Another name for Jan was Jan Petter Barkén.

Ancestor Report for Anna Helena Persdotter

Second Generation

2. Petter Jacobsson, son of **Jacob Andersson** and **Catharina Persdotter Sundbohm,** was born on 23 Apr 1776 in Limåsen, Grythyttan, Örebro, Sweden[1] and died on 17 Jan 1837 in Hammarhult, Järnboås, Örebro, Sweden [2] at age 60.

Noted events in his life were:
- Resided: 1801, Grekskog, Grythyttan, Örebro, Sweden.[3]

- Moved from: 1802, Grythyttan, Örebro, Sweden.[4]

- Occupation: laborer, farm user, and tenant farmer, After 1802, Ryttarbacken, Nora, Örebro, Sweden. [5] He worked at several homestead in various capacities in the Stadra estate area. He seemed to spend the most time at Ryttarbacken.

- Moved to: 1825, Järnboås, Örebro, Sweden. [6]

- Status: topare (tenant farmer), After 1825, Hammarhult, Järnboås, Örebro, Sweden. [7]

Petter married **Catharina Olsdotter** on 11 Oct 1801 in Rockesholm, Grythyttan, Örebro, Sweden. [8]

Children from this marriage were:

	i.	**Jacob Persson** was born on 15 Aug 1802 in Stadra ägor, Nora, Örebro, Sweden. [9]
	ii.	**Elisabet Persdotter** was born on 30 Aug 1804 in Ryttarbacken, Stadra, Nora, Örebro, Sweden. [10]
	iii.	**Maria Helena Persdotter** [11] was born on 1 May 1807 in Skärhyttan, Nora, Örebro, Sweden [12] and died in 1809[11] at age 2.
	iv.	**Peter Persson** was born on 24 Aug 1809 in Ryttarbacken, Stadra, Nora, Örebro, Sweden. [13]
	v.	**Maria Persdotter** [11] was born on 30 Sep 1811 in Ryttarbacken, Stadra, Nora, Örebro, Sweden [14] and died in 1812[11] at age 1.
	vi.	**Olof Persson** was born on 12 Jul 1814 in Grekskog, Nora, Örebro, Sweden. [15]
1	vii.	**Anna Helena Persdotter**. Anna married **Anders Jansson**,[16] son of **Jan Olsson** and **Catharina Hindersdotter,** on 30 Sep 1843 in Grythyttan, Örebro, Sweden. [17]

---

1. Nora bergsförsamling AI:11a (1811-1820) Image 261 / page 253 (AID: v51992.b261.s253, NAD: SE/ULA/11098) . .... Grythyttan CI:6 (1775-1796) Image 22 / page 31 (AID: v53139.b22.s31, NAD: SE/ULA/10337) . .... Grythyttan AIa:6a (1775-1784) Image 114 / page 105 (AID: v51193.b114.s105, NAD: SE/ULA/10337) .

2. Järnboås F:5 (1832-1855) Image 34 (AID: v53342.b34, NAD: SE/ULA/10503) .

3. Grythyttan EI:1 (1775-1828) Image 59 / page 54 (AID: v53155.b59.s54, NAD: SE/ULA/10337) .

4. Nora bergsförsamling AI:11a (1811-1820) Image 261 / page 253 (AID: v51992.b261.s253, NAD: SE/ULA/11098) . .... Nora bergsförsamling AI:10b (1801-1810) Image 241 / page 235 (AID: v51991.b241.s235, NAD: SE/ULA/11098) .

5. Nora bergsförsamling AI:10b (1801-1810) Image 241 / page 235 (AID: v51991.b241.s235, NAD: SE/ULA/11098) . .... Nora bergsförsamling AI:12a (1821-1829) Image 269 / page 262 (AID: v51994.b269.s262, NAD: SE/ULA/11098) .

6. Nora bergsförsamling AI:12a (1821-1829) Image 269 / page 262 (AID: v51994.b269.s262, NAD: SE/ULA/11098) .

7. Järnboås F:5 (1832-1855) Image 34 (AID: v53342.b34, NAD: SE/ULA/10503) . .... Järnboås AI:12b (1835-1840) Image 66 / page 278 (AID: v51505.b66.s278, NAD: SE/ULA/10503) .

8. Nora bergsförsamling AI:11a (1811-1820) Image 261 / page 253 (AID: v51992.b261.s253, NAD: SE/ULA/11098) . .... Grythyttan EI:1 (1775-1828) Image 59 / page 54 (AID: v53155.b59.s54, NAD: SE/ULA/10337) .

9. Nora bergsförsamling AI:10b (1801-1810) Image 241 / page 235 (AID: v51991.b241.s235, NAD: SE/ULA/11098) . .... Nora bergsförsamling AI:11a (1811-1820) Image 261 / page 253 (AID: v51992.b261.s253, NAD: SE/ULA/11098) . .... Nora bergsförsamling C:4 (1788-1805) Image 315 (AID: v53619.b315, NAD: SE/ULA/11098) .

10. Nora bergsförsamling AI:10b (1801-1810) Image 241 / page 235 (AID: v51991.b241.s235, NAD: SE/ULA/11098) . .... Nora bergsförsamling C:4 (1788-1805) Image 354 (AID: v53619.b354, NAD: SE/ULA/11098) .

11. Nora bergsförsamling AI:11a (1811-1820) Image 261 / page 253 (AID: v51992.b261.s253, NAD: SE/ULA/11098) .

12. Nora bergsförsamling AI:10b (1801-1810) Image 241 / page 235 (AID: v51991.b241.s235, NAD: SE/ULA/11098) . .... Nora bergsförsamling AI:11a (1811-1820) Image 261 / page 253 (AID: v51992.b261.s253, NAD: SE/ULA/11098) . .... Nora bergsförsamling C:5 (1806-1823) Image 40 / page 36 (AID: v53620.b40.s36, NAD: SE/ULA/11098) .

13. Nora bergsförsamling AI:10b (1801-1810) Image 241 / page 235 (AID: v51991.b241.s235, NAD: SE/ULA/11098) . .... Nora bergsförsamling C:5 (1806-1823) Image 92 / page 88 (AID: v53620.b92.s88, NAD: SE/ULA/11098) .

14. Nora bergsförsamling AI:11a (1811-1820) Image 261 / page 253 (AID: v51992.b261.s253, NAD: SE/ULA/11098) . .... Nora bergsförsamling C:5 (1806-1823) Image 137 / page 133 (AID: v53620.b137.s133, NAD: SE/ULA/11098) .

15. Nora bergsförsamling AI:11a (1811-1820) Image 261 / page 253 (AID: v51992.b261.s253, NAD: SE/ULA/11098) . .... Nora bergsförsamling C:5 (1806-1823) Image 194 / page 190 (AID: v53620.b194.s190, NAD: SE/ULA/11098) .

16. Grythyttan AIa:13a (1820-1830) Image 246 / page 240 (AID: v51203.b246.s240, NAD: SE/ULA/10337) .

17. Nora bergsförsamling AI:15eb (1851-1861) Image 113 / page 266 (AID: v52013.b113.s266, NAD: SE/ULA/11098) . .... Nora bergsförsamling AI:14bb (1841-1850) Image 102 / page 248 (AID: v52007.b102.s248, NAD: SE/ULA/11098) .

Ancestor Report for Anna Helena Persdotter

3. Catharina Olsdotter, daughter of **Olof Persson** and **Lisa Larsdotter,** was born on 19 Apr 1776 in Grekstorp, Nora, Örebro, Sweden.[18]

Noted events in her life were:

• Resided: After 1776, Grekstorp, Nora, Örebro, Sweden.[19]

• Moved to: 1794, Grythyttan, Örebro, Sweden.[20]

• Moved from: 1802, Grythyttan, Örebro, Sweden.[21]

• Resided: After 1802, Stadra ägor, Nora, Örebro, Sweden.[22] Lived at various homesteads in the Stadra estate area including Skärhyttan, Ryttarbacken, Grekskog.

• Moved to: 1825, Järnboås, Örebro, Sweden.[23]

• Resided: 1836-1838, Hammarhult, Järnboås, Örebro, Sweden.[24]

Catharina married **Petter Jacobsson** on 11 Oct 1801 in Rockesholm, Grythyttan, Örebro, Sweden.[25]

---

18. *Nora bergsförsamling AI:11a (1811-1820) Image 261 / page 253 (AID: v51992.b261.s253, NAD: SE/ULA/11098) . .... Nora bergsförsamling C:3 (1770-1788) Image 104 (AID: v53618.b104, NAD: SE/ULA/11098). .... Nora bergsförsamling AI:9a (1791-1800) Image 229 / page 223 (AID: v51988.b229.s223, NAD: SE/ULA/11098) .*
19. *Nora bergsförsamling AI:9a (1791-1800) Image 229 / page 223 (AID: v51988.b229.s223, NAD: SE/ULA/11098) . .... Nora bergsförsamling AI:8a (1775-1784) Image 254 / page 247 (AID: v51986.b254.s247, NAD: SE/ULA/11098) .*
20. *Nora bergsförsamling AI:9a (1791-1800) Image 229 / page 223 (AID: v51988.b229.s223, NAD: SE/ULA/11098) .*
21. *Nora bergsförsamling AI:11a (1811-1820) Image 261 / page 253 (AID: v51992.b261.s253, NAD: SE/ULA/11098) . .... Nora bergsförsamling AI:10b (1801-1810) Image 241 / page 235 (AID: v51991.b241.s235, NAD: SE/ULA/11098) .*
22. *Nora bergsförsamling AI:10b (1801-1810) Image 241 / page 235 (AID: v51991.b241.s235, NAD: SE/ULA/11098) .*
23. *Nora bergsförsamling AI:12a (1821-1829) Image 269 / page 262 (AID: v51994.b269.s262, NAD: SE/ULA/11098) .*
24. *Järnboås F:5 (1832-1855) Image 34 (AID: v53342.b34, NAD: SE/ULA/10503) . .... Järnboås AI:12b (1835-1840) Image 66 / page 278 (AID: v51505.b66.s278, NAD: SE/ULA/10503) .*
25. *Nora bergsförsamling AI:11a (1811-1820) Image 261 / page 253 (AID: v51992.b261.s253, NAD: SE/ULA/11098) . .... Grythyttan EI:1 (1775-1828) Image 59 / page 54 (AID: v53155.b59.s54, NAD: SE/ULA/10337) .*

Ancestor Report for Anna Helena Persdotter

Third Generation

4. Jacob Andersson,[1] son of **Anders Persson** and **Kerstin Eriksson,** was born on 11 Nov 1730 in Greksnäs, Grythyttan, Örebro, Sweden,[2] was christened on 15 Nov 1730,[3] and died on 17 Feb 1800 in Grekskog, Nora, Örebro, Sweden[4] at age 69.

Research Notes: After Jakob's mother died after 1730 (she disappears from the house books) he and his brother Anders are sent to foster parents. His father died soon afterward, in 1735. [5]

Noted events in his life were:
* Resided: After 1730, Greksnäs, Grythyttan, Örebro, Sweden. [6]

* Resided: with foster parents Eric Ersson and Brita Nilsdotter, Cir 1740, Brunshyttan, Grythyttan, Orebro, Sweden. [7]

* Resided: with his brother Erik, Cir 1745, Greksnäs, Grythyttan, Örebro, Sweden. [8]

* Resided: Cir 1750, Ullnäshyttan, Grythyttan, Örebro, Sweden. [9]

* Resided: After 1766, Brunshyttan, Grythyttan, Orebro, Sweden. [10]

* Resided: torpare at homestead #9, After 1771, Kärvingeborn, Grythyttan, Örebro, Sweden. [11]

* Note: possibly worked at Kolarhagen, After 1771, Grythyttan, Örebro, Sweden. [11]

* Resided: 1773, Limåsen, Grythyttan, Örebro, Sweden. [12]

* Resided: After 1794, Grekskog, Nora, Örebro, Sweden. [13]

Jacob married **Catharina Persdotter Sundbohm**[14] on 9 Feb 1766 in Grythyttan, Örebro, Sweden.[15]

Children from this marriage were:
  i.   **Anders Jacobsson** was born on 16 Mar 1766 in Brunshyttan, Grythyttan, Orebro, Sweden. [10]
  ii. **Anders Jacobsson** was born on 10 Apr 1767 in Brunshyttan, Grythyttan, Orebro, Sweden. [16]
  iii. **Eric Jacobsson** was born in 1770 in Grythyttan, Örebro, Sweden. [17] Eric married **Stina Persdotter**.[13]
  iv. **Jacob Jacobsson** was born on 21 Jan 1773 in Limåsen, Grythyttan, Örebro, Sweden. [18]

---

1. Grythyttan CI:6 (1775-1796) Image 22 / page 31 (AID: v53139.b22.s31, NAD: SE/ULA/10337) .

2. Grythyttan AIa:6a (1775-1784) Image 114 / page 105 (AID: v51193.b114.s105, NAD: SE/ULA/10337) . .... Grythyttan AIa:5 (1771-1776) Image 74 / page 66 (AID: v51192.b74.s66, NAD: SE/ULA/10337) . .... Grythyttan CI:2 (1718-1737) Image 64 / page 60 (AID: v53135.b64.s60, NAD: SE/ULA/10337) .

3. Grythyttan CI:2 (1718-1737) Image 64 / page 60 (AID: v53135.b64.s60, NAD: SE/ULA/10337) .

4. Nora bergsförsamling F:4 (1795-1810) Image 80 / page 76 (AID: v53645.b80.s76, NAD: SE/ULA/11098) .

5. Grythyttan AIa:2 (1727-1740) Image 50 / page 80 (AID: v51189.b50.s80, NAD: SE/ULA/10337) . .... Grythyttan AIa:2 (1727-1740) Image 115 / page 210 (AID: v51189.b115.s210, NAD: SE/ULA/10337) .

6. Grythyttan AIa:2 (1727-1740) Image 50 / page 80 (AID: v51189.b50.s80, NAD: SE/ULA/10337) .

7. Grythyttan CI:4 (1758-1769) Image 63 / page 59 (AID: v53137.b63.s59, NAD: SE/ULA/10337) . .... Grythyttan AIa:4 (1740-1767) Image 185 / page 177 (AID: v51191.b185.s177, NAD: SE/ULA/10337) .

8. Grythyttan AIa:4 (1740-1767) Image 189 / page 181 (AID: v51191.b189.s181, NAD: SE/ULA/10337) .

9. Grythyttan AIa:4 (1740-1767) Image 199 / page 191 (AID: v51191.b199.s191, NAD: SE/ULA/10337) .

10. Grythyttan CI:4 (1758-1769) Image 63 / page 59 (AID: v53137.b63.s59, NAD: SE/ULA/10337) .

11. Grythyttan AIa:6a (1775-1784) Image 114 / page 105 (AID: v51193.b114.s105, NAD: SE/ULA/10337) .

12. Grythyttan CI:5 (1770-1774) Image 26 / page 43 (AID: v53138.b26.s43, NAD: SE/ULA/10337) .

13. Nora bergsförsamling AI:9a (1791-1800) Image 226 / page 220 (AID: v51988.b226.s220, NAD: SE/ULA/11098) .

14. Grythyttan CI:6 (1775-1796) Image 22 / page 31 (AID: v53139.b22.s31, NAD: SE/ULA/10337) . .... Grythyttan AIa:2 (1727-1740) Image 38 / page 56 (AID: v51189.b38.s56, NAD: SE/ULA/10337) . .... Grythyttan AIa:2 (1727-1740) Image 25 / page 30 (AID: v51189.b25.s30, NAD: SE/ULA/10337) .

15. Grythyttan AIa:6a (1775-1784) Image 114 / page 105 (AID: v51193.b114.s105, NAD: SE/ULA/10337) . .... Grythyttan CI:4 (1758-1769) Image 67 / page 63a (AID: v53137.b67.s63a, NAD: SE/ULA/10337) .

16. Grythyttan CI:4 (1758-1769) Image 69 / page 64 (AID: v53137.b69.s64, NAD: SE/ULA/10337) . .... Grythyttan AIa:6a (1775-1784) Image 114 / page 105 (AID: v51193.b114.s105, NAD: SE/ULA/10337) . .... Grythyttan AIa:5 (1771-1776) Image 74 / page 66 (AID: v51192.b74.s66, NAD: SE/ULA/10337) .

17. Grythyttan AIa:6a (1775-1784) Image 114 / page 105 (AID: v51193.b114.s105, NAD: SE/ULA/10337) . .... Grythyttan AIa:5 (1771-1776) Image 74 / page 66 (AID: v51192.b74.s66, NAD: SE/ULA/10337) .

18. Grythyttan CI:5 (1770-1774) Image 26 / page 43 (AID: v53138.b26.s43, NAD: SE/ULA/10337) . .... Grythyttan AIa:5 (1771-1776)

2   v.   **Petter Jacobsson**. Petter married **Catharina Olsdotter,** daughter of **Olof Persson** and **Lisa Larsdotter,** on 11 Oct 1801 in Rockesholm, Grythyttan, Örebro, Sweden. [19]

5. Catharina Persdotter Sundbohm,[20] daughter of **Petter Jakobsson Sundbohm** and **Ingrid Andersdotter,** was born on 5 Oct 1733 in Sundet, Grythyttan, Örebro, Sweden,[21] died on 9 Nov 1811 in Klingtorp, Nora, Örebro, Sweden[22] at age 78, and was buried on 11 Nov 1811 in Rockesholm, Nora, Örebro, Sweden.[23] Another name for Catharina was Catharina Persdotter Sundbom.

Noted events in her life were:
- Resided: 1733-1754, Torrvarpsund, Grythyttan, Örebro, Sweden.[24]

- Occupation: maid, Abt 1741, Brunsjötorp, Grythyttan, Örebro, Sweden.[25]

- Moved to: 1754, Karlskoga, Örebro, Sweden.[26]

- Resided: After 1766, Brunshyttan, Grythyttan, Orebro, Sweden.[27]

- Resided: torpare at homestead #9, After 1771, Kärvingeborn, Grythyttan, Örebro, Sweden.[28]

- Resided: 1773, Limåsen, Grythyttan, Örebro, Sweden.[29]

- Resided: After 1794, Grekskog, Nora, Örebro, Sweden.[30]

Catharina married **Jacob Andersson**[31] on 9 Feb 1766 in Grythyttan, Örebro, Sweden.[32]

6. Olof Persson was born in 1721[33] and died Est 1796-1800 in Nora, Örebro, Sweden[34] about age 75.

Research Notes: It is not clear where Olof was born. The Nora birth records don't cover 1721. According to the Grythyttan parish christening books, there is an Olof Persson born on 27 Feb 1721. The parents are Per Persson and Maria Andersdotter.[35]

Image 74 / page 66 (AID: v51192.b74.s66, NAD: SE/ULA/10337) . .... Grythyttan AIa:6a (1775-1784) Image 114 / page 105 (AID: v51193.b114.s105, NAD: SE/ULA/10337).

19. Nora bergsförsamling AI:11a (1811-1820) Image 261 / page 253 (AID: v51992.b261.s253, NAD: SE/ULA/11098) . .... Grythyttan EI:1 (1775-1828) Image 59 / page 54 (AID: v53155.b59.s54, NAD: SE/ULA/10337) .

20. Grythyttan CI:6 (1775-1796) Image 22 / page 31 (AID: v53139.b22.s31, NAD: SE/ULA/10337) . .... Grythyttan AIa:2 (1727-1740) Image 38 / page 56 (AID: v51189.b38.s56, NAD: SE/ULA/10337) . .... Grythyttan AIa:2 (1727-1740) Image 25 / page 30 (AID: v51189.b25.s30, NAD: SE/ULA/10337).

21. Grythyttan AIa:6a (1775-1784) Image 114 / page 105 (AID: v51193.b114.s105, NAD: SE/ULA/10337) . .... Grythyttan AIa:5 (1771-1776) Image 74 / page 66 (AID: v51192.b74.s66, NAD: SE/ULA/10337) . .... Grythyttan CI:2 (1718-1737) Image 83 / page 79 (AID: v53135.b83.s79, NAD: SE/ULA/10337).

22. Nora bergsförsamling AI:10b (1801-1810) Image 239 / page 233 (AID: v51991.b239.s233, NAD: SE/ULA/11098) . .... Nora bergsförsamling AI:11a (1811-1820) Image 257 / page 249 (AID: v51992.b257.s249, NAD: SE/ULA/11098) . .... Nora bergsförsamling F:5 (1811-1827) Image 15 (AID: v53646.b15, NAD: SE/ULA/11098).

23. Nora bergsförsamling F:5 (1811-1827) Image 15 (AID: v53646.b15, NAD: SE/ULA/11098).

24. Grythyttan AIa:4 (1740-1767) Image 149 / page 141 (AID: v51191.b149.s141, NAD: SE/ULA/10337) . .... Grythyttan AIa:4 (1740-1767) Image 217 / page 209 (AID: v51191.b217.s209, NAD: SE/ULA/10337).

25. Grythyttan AIa:4 (1740-1767) Image 136 / page 128 (AID: v51191.b136.s128, NAD: SE/ULA/10337) .

26. Grythyttan AIa:4 (1740-1767) Image 217 / page 209 (AID: v51191.b217.s209, NAD: SE/ULA/10337) .

27. Grythyttan CI:4 (1758-1769) Image 63 / page 59 (AID: v53137.b63.s59, NAD: SE/ULA/10337) .

28. Grythyttan AIa:6a (1775-1784) Image 114 / page 105 (AID: v51193.b114.s105, NAD: SE/ULA/10337) .

29. Grythyttan CI:5 (1770-1774) Image 26 / page 43 (AID: v53138.b26.s43, NAD: SE/ULA/10337).

30. Nora bergsförsamling AI:9a (1791-1800) Image 226 / page 220 (AID: v51988.b226.s220, NAD: SE/ULA/11098) . .... Nora bergsförsamling AI:10b (1801-1810) Image 239 / page 233 (AID: v51991.b239.s233, NAD: SE/ULA/11098) .

31. Grythyttan CI:6 (1775-1796) Image 22 / page 31 (AID: v53139.b22.s31, NAD: SE/ULA/10337) .

32. Grythyttan AIa:6a (1775-1784) Image 114 / page 105 (AID: v51193.b114.s105, NAD: SE/ULA/10337) . .... Grythyttan CI:4 (1758-1769) Image 67 / page 63a (AID: v53137.b67.s63a, NAD: SE/ULA/10337) .

33. Nora bergsförsamling AI:9a (1791-1800) Image 229 / page 223 (AID: v51988.b229.s223, NAD: SE/ULA/11098) . .... Nora bergsförsamling AI:8a (1775-1784) Image 254 / page 247 (AID: v51986.b254.s247, NAD: SE/ULA/11098) .

34. Nora bergsförsamling AI:9a (1791-1800) Image 229 / page 223 (AID: v51988.b229.s223, NAD: SE/ULA/11098) .

35. Grythyttan AIa:3 (1737-1743) Image 44 / page 34 (AID: v51190.b44.s34, NAD: SE/ULA/10337) . .... Grythyttan AIa:2 (1727-1740) Image 91 / page 162 (AID: v51189.b91.s162, NAD: SE/ULA/10337) . .... Grythyttan AIa:2 (1727-1740) Image 23 / page 26 (AID: v51189.b23.s26, NAD: SE/ULA/10337) . .... Grythyttan AIa:1 (1698-1721) Image 72 / page 66 (AID: v51188.b72.s66, NAD: SE/ULA/10337) . .... Hällefors DII:1 (1737-1748) Image 25 / page 44 (AID: v63664.b25.s44, NAD: SE/ULA/10427) . .... Hällefors AI:1 (1749-1753) Image 40 / page 36 (AID: v51461.b40.s36, NAD: SE/ULA/10427) . .... Grythyttan CI:2 (1718-1737) Image 21 / page 17 (AID: v53135.b21.s17, NAD: SE/ULA/10337).

Noted events in his life were:

• Moved from: 1775, Grythyttan, Örebro, Sweden.[36]

• Resided: After 1775, Grekstorp, Nora, Örebro, Sweden.[37]

• Status: gamle mannen (old gentleman), 1791, Greksdal, Nora, Örebro, Sweden.[38]

Olof married **Lisa Larsdotter** on 10 Nov 1775 in Hällefors, Örebro, Sweden.[39]

Marriage Notes: They apparently lived in Grythyttan parish, were married in Hällefors parish, and moved immediately to Nora parish.

Children from this marriage were:

3   i.   **Catharina Olsdotter**. Catharina married **Petter Jacobsson,** son of **Jacob Andersson** and **Catharina Persdotter Sundbohm,** on 11 Oct 1801 in Rockesholm, Grythyttan, Örebro, Sweden.[40]

    ii.   **Eric Olsson** was born on 17 Jan 1779 in Nora, Örebro, Sweden[36] and died in 1779.[36]

    iii. **Olof Olsson** was born on 21 May 1781 in Nora, Örebro, Sweden.[36]

7. Lisa Larsdotter was born in 1736 in Hällefors, Örebro, Sweden[41] and died on 3 Feb 1816 in Grekskog, Nora, Örebro, Sweden[42] at age 80.

Research Notes: The 1736 birth date reported in the house book does not appear in the Hällefors birth records.

Noted events in her life were:

• Moved from: 1775, Grythyttan, Örebro, Sweden.[36]

• Resided: Bef 1775, Svanvik, Sikfors Roten, Hällefors, Örebro, Sweden.[39]

• Resided: After 1775, Grekstorp, Nora, Örebro, Sweden.[37]

Lisa married **Olof Persson** on 10 Nov 1775 in Hällefors, Örebro, Sweden.[39]

---

36. *Nora bergsförsamling AI:8a (1775-1784) Image 254 / page 247 (AID: v51986.b254.s247, NAD: SE/ULA/11098)* .

37. *Nora bergsförsamling AI:9a (1791-1800) Image 229 / page 223 (AID: v51988.b229.s223, NAD: SE/ULA/11098) . .... Nora bergsförsamling AI:8a (1775-1784) Image 254 / page 247 (AID: v51986.b254.s247, NAD: SE/ULA/11098)* .

38. *Nora bergsförsamling AI:9a (1791-1800) Image 229 / page 223 (AID: v51988.b229.s223, NAD: SE/ULA/11098)* .

39. *Hällefors C:4 (1740-1774) Image 167 (AID: v53301.b167, NAD: SE/ULA/10427)* .

40. *Nora bergsförsamling AI:11a (1811-1820) Image 261 / page 253 (AID: v51992.b261.s253, NAD: SE/ULA/11098) . .... Grythyttan EI:1 (1775-1828) Image 59 / page 54 (AID: v53155.b59.s54, NAD: SE/ULA/10337)* .

41. *Nora bergsförsamling AI:10b (1801-1810) Image 241 / page 235 (AID: v51991.b241.s235, NAD: SE/ULA/11098) . .... Nora bergsförsamling AI:11a (1811-1820) Image 261 / page 253 (AID: v51992.b261.s253, NAD: SE/ULA/11098) . .... Nora bergsförsamling AI:9a (1791-1800) Image 229 / page 223 (AID: v51988.b229.s223, NAD: SE/ULA/11098) . .... Nora bergsförsamling AI:8a (1775-1784) Image 254 / page 247 (AID: v51986.b254.s247, NAD: SE/ULA/11098) . .... Nora bergsförsamling F:5 (1811-1827) Image 54 (AID: v53646.b54, NAD: SE/ULA/11098).*

42. *Nora bergsförsamling AI:11a (1811-1820) Image 261 / page 253 (AID: v51992.b261.s253, NAD: SE/ULA/11098) . .... Nora bergsförsamling F:5 (1811-1827) Image 54 (AID: v53646.b54, NAD: SE/ULA/11098)* .

Ancestor Report for Anna Helena Persdotter

Fourth Generation

8. Anders Persson[1] died on 13 Mar 1735 in Greksnäs, Grythyttan, Örebro, Sweden.[2]

Noted events in his life were:
• Resided: After 1698, Greksnäs, Grythyttan, Örebro, Sweden.[3]

Anders married **Kerstin Eriksson**[4] on 2 Oct 1720 in Grythyttan, Örebro, Sweden.[5]

Children from this marriage were:
- i. **Erik Andersson**[6] was born on 26 Nov 1721 in Greksnäs, Grythyttan, Örebro, Sweden.[7] Erik married **Lisa Hansdotter**.[8]
- ii. **Per Andersson**[6] was born on 1 Mar 1723 in Greksnäs, Grythyttan, Örebro, Sweden.[9]
- iii. **Anna Andersdotter** was born on 10 Mar 1725 in Greksnäs, Grythyttan, Örebro, Sweden.[10]
- iv. **Caisa Andersdotter**[6] was born on 12 Nov 1726 in Greksnäs, Grythyttan, Örebro, Sweden.[11]
- v. **Anders Andersson**[4] was born on 8 Jan 1729 in Greksnäs, Grythyttan, Örebro, Sweden.[12]
- 4 vi. **Jacob Andersson**.[13] Jacob married **Catharina Persdotter Sundbohm**,[14] daughter of **Petter Jakobsson Sundbohm** and **Ingrid Andersdotter,** on 9 Feb 1766 in Grythyttan, Örebro, Sweden.[15]

9. Kerstin Eriksson[4] died Est 1733.

Noted events in her life were:
• Resided: After 1720, Greksnäs, Grythyttan, Örebro, Sweden.[4]

Kerstin married **Anders Persson**[1] on 2 Oct 1720 in Grythyttan, Örebro, Sweden.[5]

10. Petter Jakobsson Sundbohm, son of **Jakob Svensson** and **Brita Persdotter Körning,** was born in 1683 in Grythyttan, Örebro, Sweden[16] and died on 31 Mar 1757 in Torrvarpsund, Grythyttan, Örebro, Sweden[17] at age 74.

---

1. Grythyttan AIa:2 (1727-1740) Image 50 / page 80 (AID: v51189.b50.s80, NAD: SE/ULA/10337) . .... Grythyttan AIa:2 (1727-1740) Image 115 / page 210 (AID: v51189.b115.s210, NAD: SE/ULA/10337).

2. Grythyttan CI:2 (1718-1737) Image 12 / page 8 (AID: v53135.b12.s8, NAD: SE/ULA/10337) .

3. Grythyttan AIa:2 (1727-1740) Image 50 / page 80 (AID: v51189.b50.s80, NAD: SE/ULA/10337) . .... Grythyttan AIa:1 (1698-1721) Image 62 / page 56 (AID: v51188.b62.s56, NAD: SE/ULA/10337) .

4. Grythyttan AIa:2 (1727-1740) Image 50 / page 80 (AID: v51189.b50.s80, NAD: SE/ULA/10337) .

5. Grythyttan CI:2 (1718-1737) Image 16 / page 12 (AID: v53135.b16.s12, NAD: SE/ULA/10337) .

6. Grythyttan AIa:2 (1727-1740) Image 115 / page 210 (AID: v51189.b115.s210, NAD: SE/ULA/10337) .

7. Grythyttan CI:2 (1718-1737) Image 23 / page 19 (AID: v53135.b23.s19, NAD: SE/ULA/10337) .

8. Grythyttan AIa:4 (1740-1767) Image 189 / page 181 (AID: v51191.b189.s181, NAD: SE/ULA/10337) .

9. Grythyttan CI:2 (1718-1737) Image 28 / page 24 (AID: v53135.b28.s24, NAD: SE/ULA/10337) .

10. Grythyttan CI:2 (1718-1737) Image 37 / page 33 (AID: v53135.b37.s33, NAD: SE/ULA/10337) .

11. Grythyttan CI:2 (1718-1737) Image 44 / page 40 (AID: v53135.b44.s40, NAD: SE/ULA/10337) .

12. Grythyttan CI:2 (1718-1737) Image 55 / page 51 (AID: v53135.b55.s51, NAD: SE/ULA/10337) .

13. Grythyttan CI:6 (1775-1796) Image 22 / page 31 (AID: v53139.b22.s31, NAD: SE/ULA/10337) .

14. Grythyttan CI:6 (1775-1796) Image 22 / page 31 (AID: v53139.b22.s31, NAD: SE/ULA/10337) . .... Grythyttan AIa:2 (1727-1740) Image 38 / page 56 (AID: v51189.b38.s56, NAD: SE/ULA/10337) . .... Grythyttan AIa:2 (1727-1740) Image 25 / page 30 (AID: v51189.b25.s30, NAD: SE/ULA/10337) .

15. Grythyttan AIa:6a (1775-1784) Image 114 / page 105 (AID: v51193.b114.s105, NAD: SE/ULA/10337) . .... Grythyttan CI:4 (1758-1769) Image 67 / page 63a (AID: v53137.b67.s63a, NAD: SE/ULA/10337) .

16. Grythyttan AIa:4 (1740-1767) Image 149 / page 141 (AID: v51191.b149.s141, NAD: SE/ULA/10337) . .... Grythyttan CI:3 (1737-1757) Image 93 / page 89 (AID: v53136.b93.s89, NAD: SE/ULA/10337) .

17. Grythyttan AIa:4 (1740-1767) Image 217 / page 209 (AID: v51191.b217.s209, NAD: SE/ULA/10337) . .... Grythyttan CI:3 (1737-1757) Image 93 / page 89 (AID: v53136.b93.s89, NAD: SE/ULA/10337) .

18. Grythyttan AIa:4 (1740-1767) Image 149 / page 141 (AID: v51191.b149.s141, NAD: SE/ULA/10337) . .... Grythyttan AIa:4 (1740-1767) Image 217 / page 209 (AID: v51191.b217.s209, NAD: SE/ULA/10337) . .... Grythyttan AIa:2 (1727-1740) Image 38 / page 56 (AID: v51189.b38.s56, NAD: SE/ULA/10337) . .... Grythyttan AIa:2 (1727-1740) Image 87 / page 154 (AID: v51189.b87.s154, NAD: SE/ULA/10337). .... Grythyttan CI:1 (1699-1715) Image 63 / page 57 (AID: v53134.b63.s57, NAD: SE/ULA/10337) . .... Grythyttan AIa:1 (1698-1721) Image 71 / page 65 (AID: v51188.b71.s65, NAD: SE/ULA/10337) .

Ancestor Report for Anna Helena Persdotter

Noted events in his life were:

- Resided: After 1698, Torrvarpsund, Grythyttan, Örebro, Sweden.[18] This homestead is also called Sundet in many documents.

- Legal action: 1726.[19] Petter's brother-in-law, Olof Olsson Slång, was the head of Sundet farm. A dispute broke out between Olof and Petter one Sunday about the use a boat to travel to church, and Olof called Petter's wife a 'slut, bloody bitch and whore'. In 1726, Petter brought a court action against Olof. "They had been arguing about who would get to use the boat to go to church. Olof lost in court and had to pay fines. But at the same court, Per Sundbom petitioned for permission to buy Slång out from the property of Torrvarpsund so that he could be sole master there, but he was unsuccessful."

- Occupation: Masmästare (master in charge of the foundry).[19] He hired and paid from his salary other workers.

- Fact: surname. Sundbom means "good gate" or "strong barrier or beam."

Petter married **Kerstin Olofsdotter**.[20]

The child from this marriage was:

    i.   **Maria Persdotter Sundbohm**[21] was born on 29 Jun 1707 in Grythyttan, Örebro, Sweden[22] and died on 11 Jul 1727 in Sundet, Grythyttan, Örebro, Sweden[23] at age 20.

Petter next married **Ingrid Andersdotter** on 25 May 1712 in Grythyttan, Örebro, Sweden.[24]

Children from this marriage were:

    i.   **Margeta Persdotter Sundbohm**[25] was born on 1 Jan 1713 in Sundet, Grythyttan, Örebro, Sweden.[26]

    ii.   **Svens Persson Sundbohm**[25] was born in 1715 in Sundet, Grythyttan, Örebro, Sweden[27] and died in 1756 in Arboga, Västmanland, Sweden[28] at age 41. Svens married **Lisa Andersdotter**.[19]

    iii.   **Brita Persdotter Sundbohm**[25] was born about 1719 in Sundet, Grythyttan, Örebro, Sweden[28] and died in 1785[28] about age 66.

    iv.   **Ingrid Persdotter Sundbohm**[25] was born on 20 Mar 1720 in Sundet, Grythyttan, Örebro, Sweden.[29] Ingrid married **Carl Jansson**[19] on 26 Dec 1743 in Grythyttan, Örebro, Sweden.[28]

    v.   **Stina Persdotter Sundbohm**[25] was born in 1726 in Sundet, Grythyttan, Örebro, Sweden.[30]

    vi.   **Cathis Persdotter Sundbolm**[31] was born on 18 Apr 1729 in Grythyttan, Örebro, Sweden.

5   vii.   **Catharina Persdotter Sundbohm**.[33] Catharina married **Jacob Andersson**,[34] son of **Anders Persson** and **Kerstin Eriksson**, on 9 Feb 1766 in Grythyttan, Örebro, Sweden.[35]

19. Cheryl Morris, Cheryl Morris's Rootweb web pages (http://freepages.genealogy.rootsweb.ancestry.com/~camorris/).
20. Grythyttan CI:1 (1699-1715) Image 38 / page 33 (AID: v53134.b38.s33, NAD: SE/ULA/10337).
21. Grythyttan AIa:2 (1727-1740) Image 25 / page 30 (AID: v51189.b25.s30, NAD: SE/ULA/10337). .... Grythyttan CI:1 (1699-1715) Image 38 / page 33 (AID: v53134.b38.s33, NAD: SE/ULA/10337).
22. Grythyttan CI:2 (1718-1737) Image 50 / page 46 (AID: v53135.b50.s46, NAD: SE/ULA/10337). .... Grythyttan CI:1 (1699-1715) Image 38 / page 33 (AID: v53134.b38.s33, NAD: SE/ULA/10337).
23. Grythyttan CI:2 (1718-1737) Image 50 / page 46 (AID: v53135.b50.s46, NAD: SE/ULA/10337).
24. Grythyttan CI:1 (1699-1715) Image 63 / page 57 (AID: v53134.b63.s57, NAD: SE/ULA/10337).
25. Grythyttan AIa:2 (1727-1740) Image 38 / page 56 (AID: v51189.b38.s56, NAD: SE/ULA/10337). .... Grythyttan AIa:2 (1727-1740) Image 25 / page 30 (AID: v51189.b25.s30, NAD: SE/ULA/10337).
26. Grythyttan CI:1 (1699-1715) Image 70 / page 64 (AID: v53134.b70.s64, NAD: SE/ULA/10337).
27. Cheryl Morris, Cheryl Morris's Rootweb web pages (http://freepages.genealogy.rootsweb.ancestry.com/~camorris/). .... Grythyttan AIa:4 (1740-1767) Image 217 / page 209 (AID: v51191.b217.s209, NAD: SE/ULA/10337). .... Kenneth Sundbom, Kenneth Sundbom Family Tree website (http://sundbom.familytreeguide.com).
28. Kenneth Sundbom, Kenneth Sundbom Family Tree website (http://sundbom.familytreeguide.com).
29. Grythyttan AIa:4 (1740-1767) Image 149 / page 141 (AID: v51191.b149.s141, NAD: SE/ULA/10337). .... Grythyttan CI:2 (1718-1737) Image 21 / page 17 (AID: v53135.b21.s17, NAD: SE/ULA/10337).
30. Grythyttan AIa:4 (1740-1767) Image 149 / page 141 (AID: v51191.b149.s141, NAD: SE/ULA/10337). .... Kenneth Sundbom, Kenneth Sundbom Family Tree website (http://sundbom.familytreeguide.com).
31. Grythyttan AIa:2 (1727-1740) Image 25 / page 30 (AID: v51189.b25.s30, NAD: SE/ULA/10337).
32. Grythyttan CI:2 (1718-1737) Image 56 / page 52 (AID: v53135.b56.s52, NAD: SE/ULA/10337).
33. Grythyttan CI:6 (1775-1796) Image 22 / page 31 (AID: v53139.b22.s31, NAD: SE/ULA/10337). .... Grythyttan AIa:2 (1727-1740) Image 38 / page 56 (AID: v51189.b38.s56, NAD: SE/ULA/10337). .... Grythyttan AIa:2 (1727-1740) Image 25 / page 30 (AID: v51189.b25.s30, NAD: SE/ULA/10337).
34. Grythyttan CI:6 (1775-1796) Image 22 / page 31 (AID: v53139.b22.s31, NAD: SE/ULA/10337).
35. Grythyttan AIa:6a (1775-1784) Image 114 / page 105 (AID: v51193.b114.s105, NAD: SE/ULA/10337). .... Grythyttan CI:4 (1758-1769) Image 67 / page 63a (AID: v53137.b67.s63a, NAD: SE/ULA/10337).

Ancestor Report for Anna Helena Persdotter

viii. **Maria Persdotter Sundbohm** was born on 7 Oct 1735 in Sundet, Grythyttan, Örebro, Sweden[36] and died on 26 Aug 1812 in Ölsboda, Nysund, Örebro, Sweden[28] at age 76. Maria married **Johan Zachrisson Berg**.

11. Ingrid Andersdotter was born about 1690 in Karlskoga, Örebro, Sweden[37] and died on 29 Mar 1754 in Torrvarpsund, Grythyttan, Örebro, Sweden[38] about age 64.

Birth Notes: The house records say her birth was 1690, but the death record says 1683.

Research Notes: She may have been born on 4 September 1892 in Fornäs, Karlskoga, possibly to Anders Errson. A less likely, but widely accepted, view is that she was born in 1689 in Grythyttan, and was the daughter Anders Ingevaldsson and Ingrid Hansdotter Skotte. Her marriage and death records clearly state she was born in Karlskoga. Another widely held view is that she first married an Olof Johansson in 1710, but the marriage record clearly states Olof's wife was Maria, not Ingrid, Andersson. Additional research is needed to determine her parents. [39]

Noted events in her life were:
- Resided: After 1712, Torrvarpsund, Grythyttan, Örebro, Sweden. [40] This homestead is also called Sundet in earlier documents.

- Occupation: barnmorska (midwife). [41]

Ingrid married **Petter Jakobsson Sundbohm** on 25 May 1712 in Grythyttan, Örebro, Sweden.[42]

---

37. Grythyttan AIa:4 (1740-1767) Image 149 / page 141 (AID: v51191.b149.s141, NAD: SE/ULA/10337) . .... Cheryl Morris, Cheryl Morris's Rootweb web pages (http://freepages.genealogy.rootsweb.ancestry.com/~camorris/). .... Grythyttan CI:3 (1737-1757) Image 82 / page 78 (AID: v53136.b82.s78, NAD: SE/ULA/10337) . .... Karlskoga C:1 (1679-1718) Image 24 / page 19 (AID: v53361.b24.s19, NAD: SE/ULA/10513).

38. Grythyttan AIa:4 (1740-1767) Image 217 / page 209 (AID: v51191.b217.s209, NAD: SE/ULA/10337) . .... Grythyttan CI:3 (1737-1757) Image 82 / page 78 (AID: v53136.b82.s78, NAD: SE/ULA/10337) .

39. Karlskoga C:1 (1679-1718) Image 37 / page 32 (AID: v53361.b37.s32, NAD: SE/ULA/10513) .

40. Grythyttan AIa:4 (1740-1767) Image 149 / page 141 (AID: v51191.b149.s141, NAD: SE/ULA/10337) . .... Grythyttan AIa:4 (1740-1767) Image 217 / page 209 (AID: v51191.b217.s209, NAD: SE/ULA/10337) . .... Grythyttan AIa:2 (1727-1740) Image 38 / page 56 (AID: v51189.b38.s56, NAD: SE/ULA/10337) . .... Grythyttan AIa:2 (1727-1740) Image 87 / page 154 (AID: v51189.b87.s154, NAD: SE/ULA/10337) . .... Grythyttan CI:1 (1699-1715) Image 63 / page 57 (AID: v53134.b63.s57, NAD: SE/ULA/10337) . .... Grythyttan AIa:1 (1698-1721) Image 71 / page 65 (AID: v51188.b71.s65, NAD: SE/ULA/10337) .

41. Cheryl Morris, Cheryl Morris's Rootweb web pages (http://freepages.genealogy.rootsweb.ancestry.com/~camorris/). .... Grythyttan AIa:4 (1740-1767) Image 217 / page 209 (AID: v51191.b217.s209, NAD: SE/ULA/10337) .

42. Grythyttan CI:1 (1699-1715) Image 63 / page 57 (AID: v53134.b63.s57, NAD: SE/ULA/10337) .

Ancestor Report for Anna Helena Persdotter

Fifth Generation

20. Jakob Svensson,[1] son of **Svens Jakobsson** and **Karin,** died before 1695.[1]

Noted events in his life were:
- Occupation: färjkarl (ferryman), 1649-1663, Torrvarpsund, Grythyttan, Örebro, Sweden. [1]

Jakob married **Brita Persdotter Körning**.[1]

Children from this marriage were:
  i. **Ingrid Jakobsdotter Sundholm**.[2] Ingrid married **Olof Olsson Slång**.[2]
  ii. **Sven Jakobsson Sundbohm**[2]
  iii. **Brita Jakobsdotter Sundbohm**[2] was born in 1686 in Sundet, Grythyttan, Örebro, Sweden[2] and died in 1773 in Grythyttan, Örebro, Sweden[2] at age 87. Brita married **Johan Fröberg**[2] on 29 Oct 1712.[2]
  iv. **Anna Jakobsdotter Sundbohm**[2] was born in 1685 in Sundet, Grythyttan, Örebro, Sweden[2] and died in 1734 in Östra Torpet, Hällefors, Örebro, Sweden[2] at age 49. Anna married **Erik Månsson**.[2]
10 v. **Petter Jakobsson Sundbohm**. Petter married **Kerstin Olofsdotter**.[3] Petter next married **Ingrid Andersdotter** on 25 May 1712 in Grythyttan, Örebro, Sweden.[4]
  vi. **Kerstin Jakobsdotter Sundbohm**.[2] Kerstin married **Erik Eriksson**.[1]
  vii. **Lars Jakobsson Sundbohm**[2] died in 1715.[1]

21. Brita Persdotter Körning,[1] daughter of **Per Larsson Körning** and **Annika Nilsdotter,** died on 26 Apr 1718 in Torrvarpsund, Grythyttan, Örebro, Sweden.[5]

Noted events in her life were:
- Resided: After 1698, Sundet, Grythyttan, Örebro, Sweden.[6]

Brita married **Jakob Svensson**.[1]

  1. Åke Norgren, Website: Människor och släkter, som levt i Bergslagen, speciellt Hällefors-Grythyttan (http://leon.amaroq.se/).
  2. Kenneth Sundbom, Kenneth Sundbom Family Tree website (http://sundbom.familytreeguide.com).
  3. Grythyttan CI:1 (1699-1715) Image 38 / page 33 (AID: v53134.b38.s33, NAD: SE/ULA/10337) .
  4. Grythyttan CI:1 (1699-1715) Image 63 / page 57 (AID: v53134.b63.s57, NAD: SE/ULA/10337) .
  5. Kenneth Sundbom, Kenneth Sundbom Family Tree website (http://sundbom.familytreeguide.com). .... Grythyttan CI:2 (1718-1737) Image 11 / page 7 (AID: v53135.b11.s7, NAD: SE/ULA/10337) .
  6. Grythyttan AIa:1 (1698-1721) Image 71 / page 65 (AID: v51188.b71.s65, NAD: SE/ULA/10337) .

Ancestor Report for Anna Helena Persdotter

Sixth Generation

40. Svens Jakobsson.[1]

Noted events in his life were:
- Occupation: färjkarl (ferryman), 1649-1663, Torrvarpsund, Grythyttan, Örebro, Sweden. [1]
- Fact: about Torrvarpsund homestead, Grythyttan, Örebro, Sweden. [2] Torrvarpsund was begun by Finns from Björkskogsnäs. Its name first appears in 1641.

Svens married **Karin.**[1]

The child from this marriage was:
> 20   i.   **Jakob Svensson.**[1] Jakob married **Brita Persdotter Körning,**[1] daughter of **Per Larsson Körning** and **Annika Nilsdotter,**.

41. Karin.[1]

Noted events in her life were:
- Legal action: 1663, Grythyttan, Örebro, Sweden.[2] "In 1663, a terrible accusation was made against the wife of the ferry man of Torrvarpsund Sven Jacobsson, Karin, that she had beaten her servant girl to death. The girl's father brought the case to court, but had to withdraw his accusation, which he had brought forward in good faith, and admit that his daughter had died of illness and give wife Karin complete restitution. That fact that she was a hot tempered woman can be seen from the court records on another occasion, when Karin had to pay fines for having torn the head cloth off a young woman on a public road and called her a thief."

Karin married **Svens Jakobsson.**[1]

42. Per Larsson Körning, son of **Lars Börjesson** and **Nilsdotter Körning,**.

Noted events in his life were:
- Occupation: bergsman (miner) and postbonde (mail farmer), Kärvingeborn, Grythyttan, Örebro, Sweden. [1] According to Sweden's 1636 mail regulations, post peasants would be appointed 2-3 miles apart along the main roads in Sweden As soon as the postbonde heard the post horn, he made himself ready to carry the mail to the next post.The postal rider would wear a badge and carry a spear and post horn. If someone interfered with the post rider, the possible sentence was death.
- Appointed: nämdeman (juryman), 1646-1684. [1]
- Fact: surname. Körning means "run" or "drive."

Per married **Annika Nilsdotter** in 1648.[3]

Children from this marriage were:
> 21   i.   **Brita Persdotter Körning.**[1] Brita married **Jakob Svensson,**[1] son of **Svens Jakobsson** and **Karin,**.
>   ii.   **Lars Persson Körning**[1]
>   iii. **Nils Persson Körning**
>   iv.   **Katarina Persdotter Körning**[1] was born in 1650 in Kärvingeborn, Grythyttan, Örebro, Sweden[3] and died on 20 May 1742 in Silvergruvan, Hällefors, Örebro, Sweden[3] at age 92. Katarina married **Kjell Persson.**[1]

---

1. Åke Norgren, Website: Människor och släkter, som levt i Bergslagen, speciellt Hällefors-Grythyttan (http://leon.amaroq.se/).

2. Cheryl Morris, Cheryl Morris's Rootweb web pages (http://freepages.genealogy.rootsweb.ancestry.com/~camorris/).

3. Åke Norgren, Website: Människor och släkter, som levt i Bergslagen, speciellt Hällefors-Grythyttan (http://leon.amaroq.se/). .... Lars Hilding, Svenska Antavlor (Swedish ancestral tablets), No. 276 .

43. Annika Nilsdotter.

Annika married **Per Larsson Körning** in 1648.[4]

---

4. *Åke Norgren, Website: Människor och släkter, som levt i Bergslagen, speciellt Hällefors-Grythyttan (http://leon.amaroq.se/). .... Lars Hilding, Svenska Antavlor (Swedish ancestral tablets), No. 276*.

Seventh Generation

84. Lars Börjesson.[1]

Noted events in his life were:
- Occupation: bergsman (miner), Kärvingeborn, Grythyttan, Örebro, Sweden.[2]
- Appointed: nämdeman (juryman), 1615-1641.[1]

Lars married **Nilsdotter Körning**.

Children from this marriage were:
- 42   i.   **Per Larsson Körning**. Per married **Annika Nilsdotter** in 1648.[2]
-       ii.   **Börje Larsson**[1] died on 1 Mar 1702 in Flosjöhyttan, Grythyttan, Örebro, Sweden.[3] Börje married **Brita**.[1]

85. Nilsdotter Körning, daughter of **Nils Eriksson Körning** and **Unknown,** died before 1656.[2]

Nilsdotter married **Lars Börjesson**.[1]

1. Åke Norgren, Website: Människor och släkter, som levt i Bergslagen, speciellt Hällefors-Grythyttan (http://leon.amaroq.se/).
2. Åke Norgren, Website: Människor och släkter, som levt i Bergslagen, speciellt Hällefors-Grythyttan (http://leon.amaroq.se/). .... Lars Hilding, Svenska Antavlor (Swedish ancestral tablets), No. 276.
3. Åke Norgren, Website: Människor och släkter, som levt i Bergslagen, speciellt Hällefors-Grythyttan (http://leon.amaroq.se/). .... Grythyttan CI:1 (1699-1715) Image 18 / page 13 (AID: v53134.b18.s13, NAD: SE/ULA/10337) .

Ancestor Report for Anna Helena Persdotter

Eighth Generation

170. Nils Eriksson Körning.[1]

Noted events in his life were:
- Occupation: bergsman (miner), Greksåsar, Nora, Örebro, Sweden.[2]

- Appointed: nämdeman (juryman), 1608-1646.[1]

Nils married someone.

Children from this marriage were:

  85   i.   **Nilsdotter Körning**. Nilsdotter married **Lars Börjesson**.[1]

          ii.   **Per Nilsson Körning**[1]

        iii.   **Erik Nilsson Körning**[1]

---

1. Åke Norgren, Website: Människor och släkter, som levt i Bergslagen, speciellt Hällefors-Grythyttan (http://leon.amaroq.se/).

2. Åke Norgren, Website: Människor och släkter, som levt i Bergslagen, speciellt Hällefors-Grythyttan (http://leon.amaroq.se/). .... Lars Hilding, Svenska Antavlor (Swedish ancestral tablets), No. 276 .

Pedigree Chart for Anna Helena Persdotter

No. 1 on this chart is the same as no. 15 on chart no. 1

8 Anders Persson
b.
p.
m. 2 Oct 1720
p. Grythyttan, Örebro, Sweden
d. 13 Mar 1735
p. Greksnäs, Grythyttan, Örebro, Sweden

4 Jacob Andersson
b. 11 Nov 1730
p. Greksnäs, Grythyttan, Örebro, Sweden
m. 9 Feb 1766
p. Grythyttan, Örebro, Sweden
d. 17 Feb 1800
p. Grekskog, Nora, Örebro, Sweden

9 Kerstin Eriksson
b.
p.
d. Est 1733
p.

2 Petter Jacobsson
b. 23 Apr 1776
p. Limåsen, Grythyttan, Örebro, Sweden
m. 11 Oct 1801
p. Rockesholm, Grythyttan, Örebro, Sweden
d. 17 Jan 1837
p. Hammarhult, Järnboås, Örebro, Sweden

10 Petter Jakobsson Sundbohm
b. 1683 cont. 43
p. Grythyttan, Örebro, Sweden
m. 25 May 1712
p. Grythyttan, Örebro, Sweden
d. 31 Mar 1757
p. Torrvarpsund, Grythyttan, Örebro, Sweden

5 Catharina Persdotter Sundbohm
b. 5 Oct 1733
p. Sundet, Grythyttan, Örebro, Sweden
d. 9 Nov 1811
p. Klingtorp, Nora, Örebro, Sweden

11 Ingrid Andersdotter
b. Abt 1690
p. Karlskoga, Örebro, Sweden
d. 29 Mar 1754
p. Torrvarpsund, Grythyttan, Örebro, Sweden

1 Anna Helena Persdotter
b. 27 Nov 1816
p. Ryttarbacken, Stadra, Nora, Örebro, Sweden
m. 30 Sep 1843
p. Grythyttan, Örebro, Sweden
d. 16 Apr 1887
p. Skärhyttan, Nora, Örebro, Sweden
sp. Anders Jansson

12
b.
p.
m.
p.
d.
p.

6 Olof Persson
b. 1721
p.
m. 10 Nov 1775
p. Hällefors, Örebro, Sweden
d. Est 1796-1800
p. Nora, Örebro, Sweden

13
b.
p.
d.
p.

3 Catharina Olsdotter
b. 19 Apr 1776
p. Grekstorp, Nora, Örebro, Sweden
d.
p.

14
b.
p.
m.
p.
d.
p.

7 Lisa Larsdotter
b. 1736
p. Hällefors, Örebro, Sweden
d. 3 Feb 1816
p. Grekskog, Nora, Örebro, Sweden

15
b.
p.
d.
p.

Pedigree Chart for Petter Jakobsson Sundbohm

No. 1 on this chart is the same as no. 10 on chart no. 42

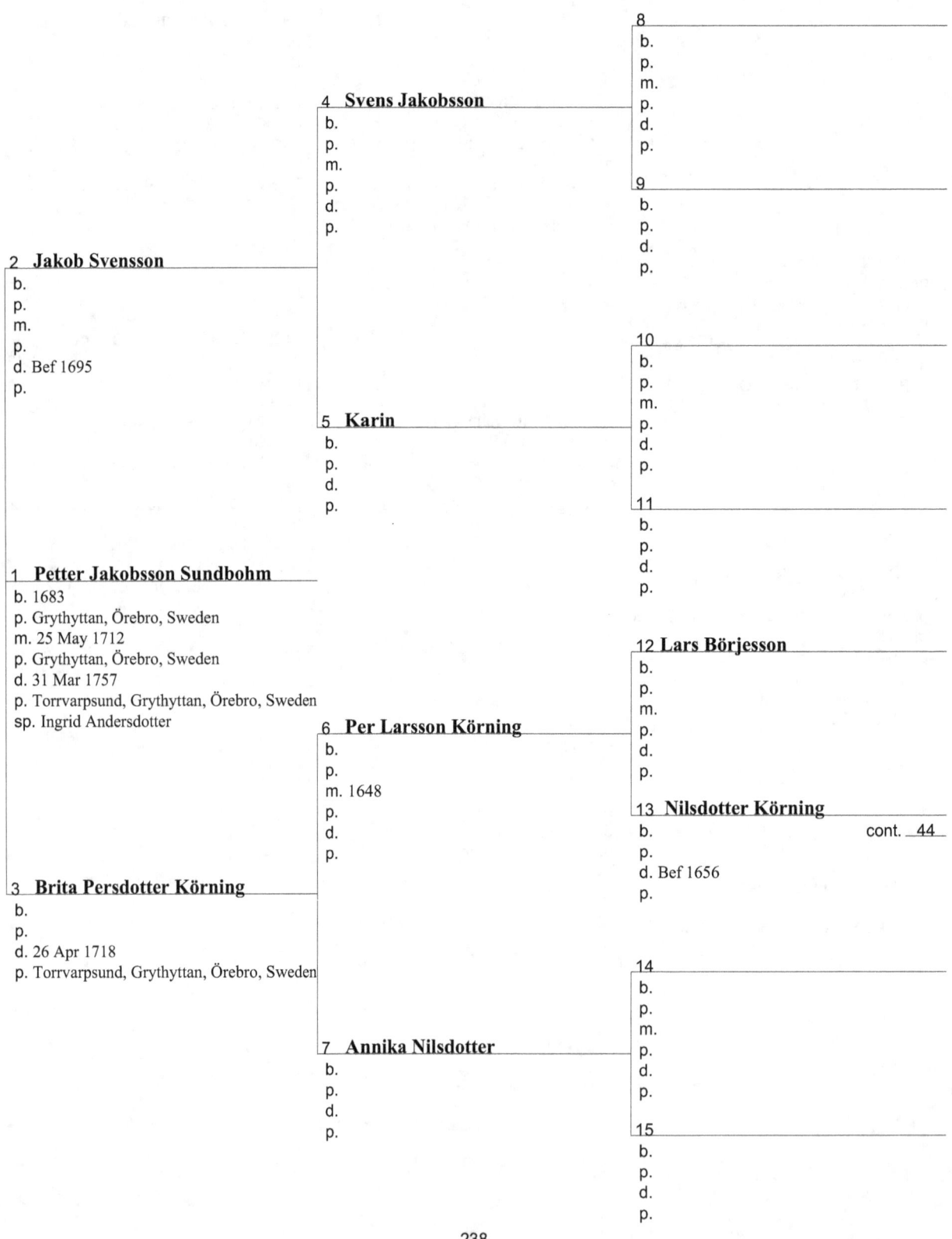

8
b.
p.
m.
p.
d.
p.

4 **Svens Jakobsson**
b.
p.
m.
p.
d.
p.

9
b.
p.
d.
p.

2 **Jakob Svensson**
b.
p.
m.
p.
d. Bef 1695
p.

10
b.
p.
m.
p.
d.
p.

5 **Karin**
b.
p.
d.
p.

11
b.
p.
d.
p.

1 **Petter Jakobsson Sundbohm**
b. 1683
p. Grythyttan, Örebro, Sweden
m. 25 May 1712
p. Grythyttan, Örebro, Sweden
d. 31 Mar 1757
p. Torrvarpsund, Grythyttan, Örebro, Sweden
sp. Ingrid Andersdotter

12 **Lars Börjesson**
b.
p.
m.
p.
d.
p.

6 **Per Larsson Körning**
b.
p.
m. 1648
p.
d.
p.

13 **Nilsdotter Körning**
b.
p.
d. Bef 1656
p.

cont. 44

3 **Brita Persdotter Körning**
b.
p.
d. 26 Apr 1718
p. Torrvarpsund, Grythyttan, Örebro, Sweden

14
b.
p.
m.
p.
d.
p.

7 **Annika Nilsdotter**
b.
p.
d.
p.

15
b.
p.
d.
p.

Pedigree Chart for Nilsdotter Körning

No. 1 on this chart is the same as no. 13 on chart no. 43

8
b.
p.
m.
p.
d.
p.

4
b.
p.
m.
p.
d.
p.

9
b.
p.
d.
p.

2 Nils Eriksson Körning
b.
p.
m.
p.
d.
p.

10
b.
p.
m.
p.
d.
p.

5
b.
p.
d.
p.

11
b.
p.
d.
p.

1   Nilsdotter Körning
b.
p.
m.
p.
d. Bef 1656
p.
sp. Lars Börjesson

12
b.
p.
m.
p.
d.
p.

6
b.
p.
m.
p.
d.
p.

13
b.
p.
d.
p.

3
b.
p.
d.
p.

14
b.
p.
m.
p.
d.
p.

7
b.
p.
d.
p.

15
b.
p.
d.
p.

Name Index

Name Index

Name Index

Name Index

Name Index

Name Index

Name Index

Name Index

Name Index

Name Index

Name Index

Name Index

Name Index

Name Index

254

Name Index

Name Index

Name Index

Name Index

Location Index

Location Index

Location Index

Location Index

www.ingramcontent.com/pod-product-compliance
Lightning Source LLC
Chambersburg PA
CBHW082130290526
45794CB00008B/2982